Schooling Reform in Hard Times

post-modern sentence

Between the catalyst
and the action the bag
lady sleeps in the
park the sign says
EXIT under the big
screen the feral
children prowl in neon
canyons lack of sound
is not the real
silence when i eat
nobody watches but
always shake the can a
few times first for
deeper satisfaction
try UTOPIA i left the
city for a better life
when PHILLIPS lights
up the night the woman
in VOGUE magazine
looks down to comb her
hair in the belly of
the whale all cats are
the same if you hold
the future in your
hands and see profit
it's red roses all the
way my door is always
open some day there'll
be enough BMWs to go
round and it'll all
grow back in a hundred
years won't it?

john knight

Schooling Reform
in Hard Times

Edited by

Bob Lingard
John Knight
and
Paige Porter

 The Falmer Press

(A member of the Taylor & Francis Group)
London • Washington, D.C.

USA   The Falmer Press, Taylor & Francis Inc., 1900 Frost Road, Suite 101, Bristol, PA 19007

UK   The Falmer Press, 4 John St, London WC1N 2ET

First published 1993

A catalogue record of this publication is available from the British Library

ISBN 0 75070 119 6 cased
ISBN 0 75070 120 X paperback

Library of Congress Cataloging-in-Publication Data are available on request

Jacket design by Caroline Archer

Typeset in 9.5/11 pt Bembo by
Graphicraft Typesetters Ltd., Hong Kong

Printed in Great Britain by Burgess Science Press, Basingstoke on paper which has a specified pH value on final paper manufacture of not less than 7.5 and is therefore 'acid free'.

Contents

Contents

Preface

This book is an exercise in policy sociology as applied to schooling policy formulation in Australia, with some comparative references to New Zealand, the United States and England and Wales. Policy sociology applies sociological analysis to the policy formulation and implementation processes and the relationship between these two processes. As such, and amongst other things, it considers the social, political and economic conditions in which policy is formulated, understood and enacted. While rejecting any simplistic formulation/implementation dichotomy, the research reported here concentrates upon the formulation of policy statements at the level of the state. Thus it is not concerned as such with curriculum development and teacher practices at the school and classroom levels. Rather, the approach is to examine the processes of policy formulation, as they are affected by broader conditions (e.g., economic and ideological) within which the state works and by debates and practices at school and classroom levels. It should be noted, however, that the structures of the state (e.g., federal, bureaucratic) mediate both sets of influences, that is, they have an impact on the content and nature of policy statements. Clearly there are different manifestations of a policy at different sites within the educational structure, but it is important to recognise that they are related in ways that are not arbitrary.

We accept that there is an almost inevitable danger in the practice of policy sociology in that policy today changes so quickly. This is certainly true of developments at the national level in Australia under the Labor governments of Hawke (1983–1991) and Keating (1991–present). It is also true of developments at the State (e.g., Western Australia, Victoria) level. It is thus pertinent in that context to speak of fast policy making, perhaps as an analogue to what some have described as the fast capitalism of the present — that section of the contemporary economy which is high tech, global and post-Fordist in nature. For the policy sociologist, with respect to the fine detail of policy, it is almost the case that what one writes today is out of date tomorrow. However, just as with the study of history, the value of pursuing policy analysis in a time of fast policy making, lies in the potential understandings it provides of the policy culture and structures of policy making and the discourses and frames of reference of contemporary policy makers. Such understandings provide some purchase on the historical character of policy development and implementation and point to future policy possibilities and probabilities.

There is some comparative work in this collection. In our view, such work is useful for it allows us to understand what is general and what is specific in the policy responses of different systems in the wake of similar economic and ideological pressures. These pressures are mediated within a given nation state by the political and cultural histories and political structures of that given nation state. In the context of fast capitalism, ideas are transported very quickly across the boundaries of nation states, while the agencies of what one might call the international state (e.g., the OECD) also have a potentially homogenising impact upon policies in education. This continues to be a neglected area in the study of schooling policy.

An important motivation for this book, however, was our dissatisfaction with those policy sociologies of Australian schooling which simply extrapolated from developments in, for example, England and Wales or in the United States. In our view, such accounts failed to acknowledge some of the mediations briefly alluded to above. More specifically, they failed to give sufficient attention to the mediation of tight economic constraints and right wing ideological pressures by Labor governments in power at the national level in Australia since 1983. Furthermore, most State governments across that time have also had Labor governments. The research out of which the book subsequently grew was concerned to ascertain what was specifically Australian and Labor about education policy during economic hard times.

What became very clear was the impact upon schooling policy formulation of the structure of the Australian state, particularly its federal formation, and the historically highly centralised provision of education at the State (i.e., not national) level where the day to day functioning of the system occurs. Indeed, since colonial times Australia has had a statist political culture. Due to historical factors and demographic features (colonialism, large sparsely populated continent), the provision of government services and administration has been centralised at the provincial level. With the federation of the colonies into States in 1901 and the establishment of a federal (national level) government, this pattern continued, although over time (particularly since World War II) the federal government has increased its own powers vis-a-vis the States. The result has been that much political activity that elsewhere happens outside the state, in Australia occurs inside the state. When the Labor Party has been in power both the Party and the trade union movement have focussed their politics around capturing and modernising the state, as it were.

Another component of Australia's statist political culture has been the bureaucratic ascendancy which has been apparent in all areas of public policy. Across the eighties, Labor has attempted to grasp tighter control of that bureaucracy through a corporate managerialist revolution. The extent of that revolution and its effect within education have been very substantial. This book explores that Labor settlement in schooling policy making.

Since the beginning of the Labor period from the early 1980s, education policy making has been a game played primarily inside the state and its peak organisations. In this corporatist context, the only players effectively allowed onto the playing field have been the government, business and employers and the trade unions. This, in a sense, has cut off the politics of policy making from civil society, and from the pluralist and democratic policy process enshrined at the national level under the earlier Whitlam Labor government (1972–1975). Here we draw attention to the way in which the Accords (a series of formal agreements) between the Australian Council of Trade Unions [ACTU], the peak council of the Australian trade union movement, and the federal Labor government have framed the role played by the teacher unions in education policy making. In a sense, their educational voice has been muted by the ACTU focus on microeconomic reform and the contributions of schooling to that process.

Each of the systems of schooling referred to has seen a changed policy emphasis from revenue inputs to educational outcomes within funding ceilings, accountability frameworks, and national guidelines. The idiosyncratic feature of the Australian development in that respect has been the fulsome and systematic embrace of competency based standards in education and training in schools, workplaces and the professions. This particular moment in schooling policy making sees an attempt to apply such a competency grid across the system nationally as a component of the ongoing reconstruction of federalism. This recent development, not dealt with at length in this collection, also reflects the statist nature of Australian political culture in that the debate is being played out primarily within the state and outside civil society. Yet the issues at stake (for example, to what ends should children be educated) are basic to civil society and liberal democracy.

To return briefly to an earlier point, such a development if it goes ahead will have a substantial impact upon what happens in schools and classrooms. However, we can be fairly certain that there will be some refraction in the move from agreed national statements to their material manifestation in school and classroom practices. Indeed, on the basis of our research, we would argue that there is some basic incommensurability between the new managerialist culture within the bureaucratic structures of policy making and teacher culture at the level of schools and classrooms. This means mediation in the processes of implementation, rather than a linearity in the processes of policy formulation and implementation.

It may be that postmodern understandings and interpretations of education policy making, in so far as they accept a dispersal of power, are less explanatory in the Australian policy situation because of the statist nature of Australian political culture. That political culture distinguishes it quite clearly from the UK and the USA which some have characterised as being almost stateless in comparison.

As suggested above, this book grew out of a research project which sought to understand the restructuring of schooling under Labor governments across the 1980s and into the 1990s in Western Australia. It was funded by a grant from the research committee at the University of Queensland. That funding is gratefully acknowledged.

A three day seminar (23–25 November, 1990) held at the Bronte Inn in Sydney at which nearly all the authors presented initial drafts of their chapters was crucial to the development of the book. This meeting was also attended by several representatives from different teachers' unions and by representatives from the Public Sector Research Centre at the University of New South Wales. That Centre, with assistance from the Australian Association for Research in Education and the Department of Education at the University of Queensland, funded the trip of Michael Apple from Wisconsin to Sydney for the seminar. Such assistance is also gratefully acknowledged. The seminar was also attended by several other persons with research and/or political commitments in related areas.

Given the importance of the Bronte seminar to the book, it seems appropriate to acknowledge those who attended and contributed. Here we include Mike

Apple, Leo Bartlett, Jill Blackmore, Sharan Burrow, Cheryl Carpenter, Adrian Carr, Bob Connell, Jane Coulter, Roger Dale, Lindsay Fitzclarence, Dave Goddard, Merrill Hammer, Miriam Henry, Michael Johnson, Ken Johnston, Jane Kenway, John McCollow, Jenny Ozga, Fazal Rizvi, Sandra Taylor and Viv White. Each made some contribution to making the book better than it might otherwise have been.

In conclusion, we would also like to thank sincerely Lynette Cowan, for her contribution to the production of sections of the manuscript, and Mervyn Partridge for his work as research assistant on the Western Australia research project. Thanks also must go to all of those who participated in interviews and so on for all of the research reported here. We would also like to thank our colleague Fazal Rizvi for his substantial contribution to the final production of the book. Finally, we thank our families for their assistance and forbearance.

Bob Lingard, John Knight and Paige Porter,
Brisbane, August, 1992.

To Carlin, Isabel and Nicholas,
the children who will judge the
restructuring

Part I: *Introduction*

Chapter 1

Restructuring Schooling towards the 1990s

John Knight, Bob Lingard, Paige Porter

Introduction

This book is about the reformation of schooling in the 1980s and the parameters which those changes have set for the provision of schooling in the 1990s. It is based on the premise that, in the context of 'hard times', most Western countries have sought to restructure public schooling, to make it more responsive to the economy. Our focus in this book is on the restructuring of Australian schooling, though the arguments we explore here have general relevance to most other English speaking countries.

We attempt to assess the comparative influence of economic circumstances and politics upon public policy formation and upon the state management structures while the Labor[1] Party is in government. Attention is given also to the mediation of educational reforms in Australia by the specificities of the federal structure of the Australian state and the constitutional and funding implications consequent on this. In short, we seek to interrogate the policies and intentions for education of the new Australian Labor Party governments of the 1980s at both federal and state levels. In so doing, though, we suggest that the analysis has a broader significance in understanding the political possibilities in educational and other state restructurings in other locations, including under non-Labour governments. Similarly, while we give particular attention to the Australian situation, much of what we say has wider implications, and we draw attention to similar developments in the US, England and Wales, and New Zealand. This book illustrates a Labor response in education policy to conditions of economic scarcity. As such, it documents one approach to such conditions which are also being experienced in other countries. How *does* one reform schooling in 'hard times'?

Reforming Public Schools

The past two decades have seen the most extensive changes to the administration and organization of public schooling in the various Australian states since the establishment of mass, compulsory schooling in the late nineteenth century. In New Zealand, England, Wales and elsewhere, including parts of the US and Canada, more or less similar changes of comparable magnitude have also been at work. There have also been substantial curricular changes, although less universally and with less constancy in form and content.

These 'reforms' have changed the nature of education bureaucracies; centre-periphery issues in public education systems are now ascendant everywhere. However, their manifestations are different in different contexts. For example, in countries such as Australia and New Zealand, which have been largely administered from a central education department, the central sectors have been substantially cut back. In New Zealand, regional and intermediate structures and support services have been reduced or eliminated. This has also been the case in Western Australia, while in Queensland and Victoria, new intermediate agencies (school support centres, etc) have been created. In countries such as England and Wales, where authority previously resided largely at the Local Education Authority [LEA] level, administrative control has moved substantially to the Boards of Governors of the individual schools, while policy direction has moved to the centre. In the United States, where power has traditionally resided in local school districts, it is the state governments which have increased their authority and responsibility. In all of these countries there have also been related and substantial changes in the relationship between the national government and the next layer in schooling policy-making.

In this restructuring of the organization and delivery of public schooling, a major focus has been the devolution of a range of responsibilities from the centre to principals/managers and school-based councils. These matters are predominantly administrative, and may include finance, staffing, salaries, equipment, maintenance of plant and so on. Whereas the form of the old, public service style bureaucracy could be likened to a pyramid, the current leaner, flatter, more corporate managerial mode is more aptly compared with a clothes-hanger (Evatt Research Centre, 1989). The stress is now upon self-governing, self-managing or self-determining schools, school-based decision-making and school-based curriculum development (but within national frameworks). In varying degrees, teachers, parents, the local community, employers and students have the opportunity to participate in school governance. The intent remains that decisions should be made 'at the appropriate level', which, with certain over-riding exceptions, is typically as near as possible to the school. There is, therefore, the intent to cut back the functions and size of the central bureaucracy, while (in theory, at any rate) deploying extra resources to the periphery. This is typically done within a constant or reducing overall budgetary allowance for the system. Similarly, as noted above, the range of external support services for schools and teachers may be downgraded or eliminated, with the consequent imposition of extra work and responsibilities upon them. In some places there is also a reduced emphasis on the need for teacher registration and formal teacher qualifications. In a sense, then, what is taking place in Australia may be described as the semi-privatisation of the public school system (Connors, 1989).

However, in addition to processes of decentralization and devolution, processes of centralization or recentralization are also at work. (See Lingard and Rizvi, 1992.) It almost seems the case that in countries which had a centralization tradition, forces of decentralization are at work, and vice versa. In different countries the details of the working out of these new structures and processes are mediated by their particular political configuration (for example, legal responsibility for education, federal versus unitary forms of government). Nevertheless, it is important to recognise that much of the restructuring of public schooling has typically been initiated from the centre, rather than the schools or the local community. (Victoria and parts of the USA may be exceptions here.) Indeed, in the name of devolution, typically, the centre asserts or retains control over the setting of broad policy objectives, the general determination of curriculum, the allocation of resources to individual schools, and the evaluation or 'auditing' of schools to ensure that central objectives are being carried out efficiently and effectively. In the Australian context, this has been described as the 'wholesaling', in contrast to earlier forms of 'retailing', of policy (Tannock, 1989). It is the application of what is now generally called 'corporate managerialism' (i.e., particular private sector forms of business management) in public sector administration in the pursuit of economic rationalism.

What this means in Australia is that the freedom which schools now have is to determine how they will implement centrally-defined policy guidelines, how they will interpret and apply the broadly defined 'common curriculum' to local circumstances and student needs and abilities, and how they can best use the resources which have been allocated to them. (The same is broadly true also for schools in England, Wales and New Zealand, although less so in the USA.) Let us be quite clear that earlier liberal-progressive views (for example, in the Whitlam era and the initial stages of the Schools Commission) of school-based decision-making and school-based curriculum development have been overlain (rather than replaced) by business-inspired conceptions of 'line management' and 'shared management' shaped by overarching concerns for efficiency and economy in the public sector. Thus, while the range of functions of the centre has been cut back and its size reduced, it still seeks to exercise an overarching control on the system. In this 'loose-tight' coupling (Weick, 1977; Peters and Waterman, 1982) the freedom which schools have is more to do with means than with ends. For this greater autonomy, however, there is increased accountability and more efficient monitoring of results, often by the use of performance indicators (Singh, 1990). Such auditing may be broadly (outcomes) or narrowly (outputs) based. It may address positive or negative changes over time within the school, comparisons with state or national standards, or comparisons with other schools. In every case, however, the stress has shifted from policy concerns with the quantity of resources provided (inputs) to schooling to a policy focus on the quantity and quality of outputs or outcomes. In the Australian policy context, this change is perhaps best exemplified by two federal education reports chaired by Peter Karmel. The first, *Schools in Australia* (Interim Committee of the Australian Schools Commission, 1973), was produced in the Whitlam Labor era (1972–1975). It was concerned to promote equality of opportunity in Australian schools, and recommended the resources needed to do this. The second, *The Quality of Education Review Committee Report* (Quality of Education Review Committee, 1985) was produced in the Hawke Labor era (1983–1991). As its title suggests, it stresses the new outputs orientation. It ought to be noted, however, that the earlier Karmel report was concerned with the equality of outcomes in an opportunity sense.

Justifications for 'Reform'

Arguably, all this implies very considerable changes not only in the structures and processes of public schooling, but also in the relationships of power and control (political, bureaucratic, professional and community) which have been constructed around them. It might be expected, therefore, that the reasons advanced to justify restructuring and devolution should be substantial and compelling. However, given the differing concerns and intentions of those whom it is now fashionable to call 'stakeholders' in the process, achieving consensus would seem problematic. What we see, then, is the attempt to create a hegemonic vision of appropriate schooling by cobbling together a number of disparate themes and issues. We briefly review some of the more significant, noting the ways in which they might be articulated in support of the current restructurings. It is useful to distinguish views whose focus is more on the level of the school from those whose concern is the system of schooling.

There are a number of positions whose focus is 'the self-managing school'. Some are based on the professional qualities and competencies of teachers and principals, which are seen as best suited to and most effectively deployed in self-managing and collegial forms of schooling. A second set of views draws more on collectivist and liberal left commitments to participatory democracy and localised decision-making. The literature on community schooling must also be taken into account. Cultural pluralism offers a further set of arguments on the rights of special or minority groups to create appropriate forms of schooling. Still other claims are grounded in arguments on parents' rights or assertions of freedom of choice. Such a view sees parents as consumers and education as a commodity that may be purchased. Just as consumers have a right to express their preferences, so should parents in their choices of educational policies and practices. While these views are conceptually distinct, they nevertheless generally support processes of devolution. At the same time, it is important to note differences in details of administrative and organizational arrangements consequent on the particular interest group involved and the type of assumptions they presume.

A second set of arguments for self-determining schools is based on the research and formulations of the US and UK 'effective schools' literature. These views merit separate attention insofar as they specify appropriate administrative structures and pedagogic relations much more clearly than the previous group of views. Their conclusions are highly detailed and prescriptive. They are, therefore, also more readily accessible for co-option by committees of inquiry, Ministries of Education, and others who seek empirically justifiable solutions to the problems of bureaucratically controlled schooling. It is in this context that Caldwell and Spinks (1988) has now become a best-seller, while its authors are in international demand as consultants on the implementation of the new frames.

In addition, we note other research studies (Rutter, Maughan, Mortimore and Ouston, 1979; Mortimore, Sammons, Stoll, Lewis and Ecob, 1988) which also address differences in school performances and outcomes and the factors which underlie them. These studies may be distinguished in some degree from the effective schools literature by their greater methodological sophistication; some at least also recognise the importance of contextual factors such as neighbourhood, class or disadvantage, gender and ethnicity.

Conceptually distinct from all of these, and addressing differences between successful and unsuccessful schools in a much more 'grounded', context-sensitive and theoretically sophisticated fashion, are more radical studies such as those of Ramsay, Sneddon, Grenfell and Ford (1983) in New Zealand. Work of this sort is more open to appropriation by socially progressive or 'left' parties who are concerned with issues of equality of opportunity, equity and social justice. It is significant that Ramsay was a member of the Picot Committee (1988) set up by a Labour government to recommend on the restructuring of New Zealand education. It is significant, also, that this committee sought to 'hardwire' the Treaty of Waitangi (signed in 1840 between the British government and the Maori Chiefs) and equity provisions into the charters of all New Zealand schools (Ramsay, 1990; this volume, Chapter 14). A thoughtful consideration of appropriate centre-periphery relations is essential if the restructured systems are to operate in social justice terms. Some thought is needed about these relations in terms of democratic rationales as well (Rizvi, 1990; Walker, 1990).

We turn now to consider justifications for change which address the systemic level of schooling. Arguments here tend to centre much more directly upon efficiency (doing things more economically) and effectiveness (getting results), and fit within the broader current debates on the reform of the public sector. It is not surprising, then, that a major set of concerns expatiates on the inefficiency, inflexibility, cost, impersonality and alienating capacity of (old-style) state bureaucracies. In Australian Labor government formulations, they have underwritten the 'leaner and meaner' restructurings on corporate managerialist lines. These claims coincide in some degree with New Right and 'economic dry' views which attack the size and extent of the state, and in particular those sectors which provide universal or extensive public services such as education and welfare. Here, claims of waste and monopolies in the public sector combine with largely unsubstantiated assertions of the much greater efficiency available from the private sector ('business') in the provision of services, and claims of the importance of competition or contestability of service provision (cf. Ramsay, 1990) in improving the speed, quality and economy of public services. In short, if educational (and other) services cannot be passed to the private sector, they should at least draw on its principles and practices. Here corporate managerial structures combine with narrowly defined economic rationalist goals in the reshaping of public schooling. We note in passing, however, a certain irony in the Australian situation, in that whereas some states' head offices were drastically reduced in numbers (to around one-third their original size, was the claim), many are now almost back to normal and costing about as much as before. (The situation appears to be similar in New Zealand.) We also note that the behaviour of some areas of the business community during the 1980s when 'greed was good' could hardly be held up as a desirable model for the public service.

The collapse of any value consensus and the related proliferation of pluralities are probably contributing factors in two things: a narrowing and focusing of goals at the centre and a displacement of other matters to the periphery. Corporate managerialism facilitates such a development (Considine, 1988). In this way, school-based decision-making may be seen as a means of managing such conflicts and as an attempt to 'sustain the legitimacy of public institutions and of the state' (Seddon, Angus and Poole, 1990, p. 49; cf. Codd, Harker and Nash, 1990). Thus, where previously in situations of inadequate services, parents and teachers would direct their complaints to the head office and politicians of the day, their attention is now diverted to the local school administration. There is, nonetheless, the possibility for some politicization of parents and communities in this circumstance. However, such an apparently loose coupling with the centre does not preclude a tighter control on more precisely defined outputs or outcomes. Here the conservative attack on alleged falling standards in contemporary schooling is in alignment with economic rationalist demands for better outcomes and managerial concerns for 'quality control' and accountability through regular audits and performance indicators.

A further set of arguments which has been particularly advanced by the federal Labor governments in Australia (1983 to present) has to do with microeconomic reform (Dawkins, 1988). (See Knight, Lingard and Porter, 1991, for a fuller analysis of this issue.) There are two aspects to this. In the first, schooling, as an industry, is in need of microeconomic reform (Bluer and Carmichael, 1991). That is, as noted above, it should become more efficient and effective in its processes and output. Workplace reform and award restructuring have become central to this agenda. This links with the second aspect, for the schooling industry is to produce people with the skills and qualities needed in the other industries to improve their performance, to adapt flexibly to changing needs and conditions, and to significantly increase the Gross National Product (GNP) and reduce the national debt (Bluer and Carmichael, 1991; Ramsey, 1990). That is, a substantial part of the microeconomic reform agenda is contingent on the reform of education. More recently, this reform has moved from a focus on structures and processes to physical facilities as well. Interestingly, the same concern for microeconomic reform is not evident in New Zealand's restructurings of education. It also appears to be a weaker concern in reforms in England and Wales, even though there has been some resurgence there of the old 'industrial trainers' view of schooling in policy (Ball, 1990; Dale, 1989).

These views nicely complement current arguments on the importance of developing Australia's human capital in the national interest (Ramsey, 1990) as well as for personal gain (the latter being a rationale for the introduction of fees in higher education). That is, education is an investment for the nation in which students are both a value-added product and the means by which the economy is to be improved. Such arguments have been behind the government commitment to increase substantially retention and participation rates in schools, technical and further education, and universities. What is being held out as a solution here is fraught with dangers for both individuals and the nation, given what we know about the flaws of such human capital theory.

The education unions are in a difficult position here for two reasons. First, they are members of the Australian Council of Trade Unions [ACTU], and thus are party to the Accord (a peak political compromise on industrial relations and incomes) between the ACTU and the national labor government. As both the ACTU and the labor government support this human capital approach, they circumscribe any oppositional voice. Second, the education unions strategically *must* support the human capital argument to ensure that education funding is not cut any further. There is a real need, however, to move beyond the antinomies of either a human capital or a cultural/educational rationale for public education provision. Furthermore, academics have been excluded from the contemporary schooling policy process in Australia in the move from a 'clientist' (Ball, 1990) to a 'corporatist' one (Lingard, 1991). With the former, academics, teachers, parents and other interest groups were included in a participatory way, while with the latter, policy has been determined by negotiation between the government, business and the unions within a human capital framework.

New Times, Hard Times?

The restructuring effected by such decision-making processes has to be understood within the context of the radical changes in the nature, functions and goals of the state in first world nations. The magnitude of these changes is now such as to merit the description, 'new times' (Hall and Jacques, 1991). They are seen in democratic capitalist countries as diverse as the United States, the United Kingdom, Australia and New Zealand where the partial shift from Fordist to Post-Fordist modes of work under the impact of new technologies has resulted in new industrial alliances.

While no single explanation for these changes is adequate, a number of points can be made. We note the shift from national to regional/multi-national and global economies, and the increasing movement of capital from country to country according to their relative attractiveness for investment or particular forms of production. We note also the range and pace of change in the social and economic relations of first world capitalist countries. Here we include the development of new technologies and the associated loss of jobs in many industries. This includes the growth of knowledge-based industries and commodities and the shift to skilled and unskilled work in the service sector.

Indeed, while generalizations of a post-industrial society or a postmodern situation may be premature and analytically inadequate (Lash and Urry, 1987), older labour-intensive industries and forms of production and social relations now coexist with service-based industries and hi-tech, Post-Fordist and information-based forms of production, niche marketing, and new forms of social relations: the new class, the service class, the under class and so on. It is this changed class structure, accompanied by the emergence of a plethora of new social movements since the 1960s, which has been characterised as 'disorganized capitalism' (Offe, 1985; Lash and Urry, 1987). Indeed, Lash and Urry argue that nation states are being simultaneously disorganized from above (pressures from the global economy) and from below (more complex class structure and a range of new social movements). They also suggest that nation states are being disorganized from within, as a result of pressures from an expanded, well educated service class, what others (for example, Alexander, 1986) have called the new middle class. In these circumstances, Lash and Urry also suggest that questions regarding the appropriate relationship between the individual and the state take on considerable political salience. It is, of course, in that way that New Right talk about smaller, less interfering government has tapped into some fairly widespread community perceptions. (See also Apple, Chapter 4, this volume.) It is also the basis of calls for more functional and participatory (as opposed to merely representative) democracy. (See Walker, 1990.)

Where labour costs are too high or workers are too militant, capital may use third-world countries for labour-intensive aspects of production and first-world countries for high-tech aspects of development. (We note, in passing, a certain arrogance in the use of postmodernism to signify the end of modernism, while most third-world countries still long for the experience of modernism.) The increasing pool of unemployed in the first world, and the subsistence level of third world wages, combine to ensure lower costs of production for capital, whilst also reducing the markets for its products. At the same time, in a depressed world economy, capital itself is experiencing substantial dislocation and instability, with corporations and industries experiencing reduced profits, substantial losses or even financial collapse.

The pressure on states, and the competition between states, to provide acceptable conditions for investment and production is evident. The changes in forms of thought (including state policies) associated with material forms of social and economic relations, is less often recognized. Cerny (1990) has argued that in some ways the state within a given nation becomes a player in the global economy, and, as such, reconstructs itself from the old welfare orientation to a new competitive orientation. Thus he speaks of a shift, from the mid-70s, from the welfare state to the competitive state.

It is in this material situation that notions of a New Right may be comprehended. This New Right is typically seen as an articulation of socially conservative, 'cultural restorationist' views with *laissez-faire* neo-liberal economic perspectives (Wexler and Grabiner, 1986) including economic rationalism. (See also Knight, Smith and Chant, 1989; Apple, Chapter 4, this volume; Dale and Ozga, Chapter 5, this volume). Cultural restorationists are concerned to restore the values and social relations of an earlier, mythical golden age. Their themes centre on the traditional family, traditional morality, social integration, the (elusive) monocultural nation. (It is interesting that the globalization of the economy has seen a resurgence of an assertive ethnicity, often regionally based.) In relation to these values, the intervention of the state is necessary to re/form the present situation and restore a more ideal society. Neo-liberals draw on the language of liberty, free choice and individualism. They comprehend a diverse range of pressures for a free market, supply-side economics, deregulating the private sector, privatizing government agencies, cutting back on social welfare and reducing the size and focus of government. Both aspects of the New Right would change our ways of thinking about the state and its functions, and about people's social and economic relationships.

That said, there are certain points which we would like to emphasize. There is no monolithic New Right. Its manifestations vary from nation to nation; the specific elements which are selected, and the particular forms in which they are stitched together, are shaped by specific political, economic, historical and social circumstances. Within nations its various impulses may be contradictory and its influences discontinuous. To conceptualise a monolithic New Right is to limit the possibilities for action against it. Nevertheless, liberal-progressive and social-democratic views are now very much on the defensive. If we cannot argue that the New Right constitutes a dominant ideology, we must at least recognise that current ideological debates are deployed upon a terrain whose features generally favour aspects of New Right views and practices (Knight *et al.*, 1989; Dale and Ozga, Chapter 5, this volume).

That given, the signal failure of the 'command' economies of Eastern Europe and the Soviet Union, the collapse of Soviet hegemony, and the fragmentation of the Soviet Union itself (disorganised socialism?) take on added significance. We are confronted with the seeming triumph of capitalism and the possible demise of socialism. Western forms of democracy now appear (on the surface, anyway) to be contingent upon New Right or neo-liberal formulations of market economics. Sadly, the human misery consequent upon a rapid transition in the east from one extreme to the other may well parallel that of the 1920s and 1930s.

It must also be acknowledged, however, that the situation of democratic western capitalism remains precarious. These are indeed new times. But they are also hard times in terms of the misery consequent on rising rates of unemployment, the increase in poverty and growth of an alienated under class, the loss of universal welfare provisions, the contraction or collapse of established industries, the replacement of permanent by casual or part-time labour, and the failure of hope. There is an irony in the growth of possessive individualism or the 'cult of selfishness' (Stretton, 1987), or what Habermas (1976) has most felicitously classified as the privatization of motivation, while the creation of a decent life for all arguably requires a more collectivist concern for the common good. The present versions of democratic Western capitalism are more bereft of relationality and collectivism than ever before. The reality of alienation remains.

In a turbulent and unsettled national and international economic scene, the democratic capitalist state now struggles to provide some minimal level of public services from a contracting fiscal base, while simultaneously having to reconstruct the conditions for capital accumulation (Offe, 1984, 1985; Lash and Urry, 1987). The very real crises of '*fin-de-siecle* socialism' (Jay, 1988) should not blind us to the increasing fragmentation and turbulence of the social formation in capitalist nations and the growing rejection of collective action and group solidarity for an individualistic and neo-social Darwinist ethos. The apparent triumph of democratic capitalism and the market as the final arbiter of social relations may not be longstanding.

The State of the Democratic Capitalist State

This is the situation in which the democratic capitalist state seeks to achieve greater efficiency and economy through restructuring the organizational forms and modes of management of its operations and the forms of delivery of services. Specifically, this has been the corporate managerialist restructuring of the state within economic rationalist (or as Walker, 1991, observes, reductionist!) parameters (Yeatman, 1990; Pusey, 1991).

In a very general sense, Offe's (1975, 1984, 1985) theory of the state informs much of the analysis provided in this volume. For our purposes, the significance of his approach is that it rejects a unitary and instrumental account of the state and instead gives emphasis to the mediating role of the structure of the state in the creation, formulation and implementation of policy. As Offe (1984, 1985) observes, the state has, in some way or the other, to balance or reconcile two apparently competing sets of demands, those of accumulation and legitimation. First, the state is involved in the provision of public services, not the production of commodities or the making of profit. In Offe's (1985) lexicon, these are decommodified practices, because they do not operate according to market relations. To enjoy the continued support of its citizens, the state must continue to provide them with a range of decommodified social and welfare services. For the necessary resources for these tasks, it is dependent, however, upon the surplus of material prosperity produced by the private sector. That is, second, it must provide suitable conditions for the accumulation of profit by capital. Offe argues convincingly that the liberal democratic state in a capitalist society can never satisfactorily solve or manage these competing legitimation and accumulation tensions. Rather, what the state does at any time, is to arrive at temporary settlements. What we have seen, since the mid-1970s, has been liberal-democratic states floundering towards a post-Keynesian settlement. In the Australian context, as discussed below, that has seen a tension between neocorporatist and New Right approaches to public policy formation. We might call the current Labor government approach the 'neo-corporate settlement'.

When the private sector is prosperous, the state is able to meet the variety of demands upon it. As Offe (1985) observes, this is a situation of 'conjunctural' policy formulation which involves a shift towards universal provision of essential services. Here the state simply responds to increased demand for services by spending more through expanded policy provision. The post-war Keynesian welfare state was the common conjunctural settlement until the mid-70s. By contrast, in periods of economic decline or contraction, when (ironically) the demand for and extent of services needed is greatest, the state lacks the resources to meet all these demands. During these times, according to Offe (1985), it moves to a 'structural' policy rationale which seeks to manage demand within tighter funding ceilings. In this condition, the state's ability to provide services is impaired; it must make hard decisions between alternative forms of need. Offe suggests further that liberal-democratic states have pursued one of two strategies to this requirement for demand-management, namely the New Right small state deregulatory approach with an associated emphasis on self-sufficiency, or a neocorporatist alternative.

Another way of conceptualising Offe's accumulation and legitimation pressures upon the state, is the 'dual state' theory advanced by Cawson and Saunders (1983). In that framework, they distinguish the politics of production (cf. economic policy directed towards accumulation) from the politics of consumption (cf. social service policy directed towards legitimation) and argue further that the former result from class politics and the latter from pluralist pressures. Such theorizing takes us well beyond class instrumentalist accounts of policy-making. In this way education is seen to be part of both the politics of production and of consumption. During times of economic constraint it appears that there will be attempts to reframe education in more overtly productive terms. In Offe's (1985) perspective, this is the attempt at recommodification of decommodified state practices. However, while governments attempt to reframe education policy as part of the politics of production, there remain pressures from a variety of sources for a continuing commitment to a social-democratic agenda within education.

The structure and operation of the state itself are also seen to have an impact on what items get onto the political agenda and what potential solutions are offered to these problems. Two significant internal features of the Australian state are its federalist political structure and the new corporate managerialist mode of public sector administration. Corporate managerialism has been the public sector response to the fiscal crisis of the state; such a mode of management has its own impact (Yeatman, 1990; Considine, 1988). The impact of Australia's federal arrangement upon Labor education policy at both state and federal levels has meant that national objectives cannot be directly implemented. Hence the mode of operation has been via the new corporate federalism (Lingard, 1991, and this volume; Bartlett, Knight and Lingard, 1991). What we mean is that the Commonwealth has sought to develop national policy in cooperation with the states (rather than coercively) through the Australian Education Council (AEC) (the intergovernmental committee of federal and state ministers for education) and the Premiers' Conferences (meetings of the state Premiers with the Prime Minister and other federal ministers). The move to national policies in schooling is just one component of the broader restructuring of Australian federalism which attempts

to create a national economic infrastructure as Australia seeks to compete effectively in the global economy.

There are some weaknesses in Offe's theory of the liberal democratic state.
These include his non-allowance for some automous action (agency) for state
workers, his neglect of gender questions, and his failure to acknowledge the impact
of the internationalization of the economy on the capacity of the nation state to
meet both accumulation and legitimation demands (Pusey, 1991, p. 210). We
would point out that there are gendered logics to both of the latter processes.
Furthermore, feminist state theories, (Franzway, Court and Connell, 1989; Connell,
1990b) in allowing for some strategic political agency for state workers, in particular femocrats, provide a useful corrective. As suggested above in the reference
to Cerny (1990), the internationalization of the economy is an important factor in
the move from a welfare to a competitive state, which sees the circumscribing of
the nation state's capacity to manage accumulation and legitimation pressures.

Is Labor Different?

Labor in Australia has pursued a modified neocorporatist (as opposed to out-
and-out privatization) approach, which has increasingly been disfigured by
the deregulatory arguments of the New Right. Labor's corporate managerialist
restructuring of the state is also clearly a response, drawing upon neo-liberal,
economic rationalist assumptions, to the structural policy condition. With the
internationalization of the economy, we note that Labor's move to abolish tariff
protection increases substantially the push towards an efficient state strategy. These
developments fly in the face of the statism endemic to Australian political culture
across its European history, where individuals have looked to the state to protect
individual rights (Rosecrance, 1964). (It is this of course which has led Pusey
(1991) to say of contemporary Australian state policy that the 'nation-building
state' has changed its mind.) However, the nature and size of the Australian
economy mean that there are real dangers in this strategy, particularly given the
move to create broader trading blocks elsewhere (for example, a united Europe)
(Castles, 1988).

Castles (1988) has documented the development and longevity (from the
1890s to the 1970s) of a specific Australian state response which he classifies as
'domestic defence'. This included a tariff-protected economy, restricted migration
program, centralized wage fixation and a residual welfare state. He argues that
since the period of the Whitlam government, Australia has tentatively groped
towards a 'new settlement' as the nation is integrated in a non-tariff protected
fashion into the global economy. Castles sees the ACTU Trade Development
Corporation study, *Australia Reconstructed* (1987), as an attempt to move towards
a new approach, 'domestic compensation'. The latter, utilized by some small economies, such as the Scandinavian countries, involves a non-tariff protected economy
backed by a highly interventionist and protective universal welfare state. His specific
point is that Labor in Australia is moving to abolish tariffs without the accoutre-
ments of domestic compensation. Domestic compensation requires a more
universalist and interventionist welfare state which seeks to protect the interests of
both business (through incentives and investment) and workers (through welfare,
training and retraining). The progressive abolition of tariffs at the same time as a
residualization of welfare (and prior to any impact of microeconomic reform) has

exacerbated internal inequalities. Until 1987, Labor in Australia attempted to handle the demands upon the state through corporate managerialism and neo-corporatist policy making, with some commitment to the social wage. The deregulation of banks and other financial institutions, the market, the commitment to budget surpluses and contracting commonwealth expenditure and the all-out economic rationalism since 1987 have reduced the policy options open to Australia, as it now lies prostrate before the piercing gaze of international financial institutions and international capital (painful!). Many of these policy options followed in the wake of both international and national business crises. In that context, the corporate state strategy has sought even greater efficiencies (Pusey, 1991).

What, then, in the present circumstances, of a party which still claims to be democratic and socialist, or at the least, social-democratic? Is Labor really different from conservative governments? The following questions, which are addressed throughout the book, seem pertinent:

- What are the policies and management structures of Labor governments in the 1980s?
- How and why does Labor restructure the public and private sectors?
- What are its intentions for industry and the economy and what are appropriate forms of intervention therein?
- How does Labor now construct and resolve issues relating to equity and social justice?
- What differences are there between the theory and practice of such conservative governments as those of Thatcher/Major and Reagan/Bush, and the socialist or social-democratic government of Hawke Keating Labor?
- To what extent can the Hawke Keating Labor government be characterized as New Right?

Anna Yeatman's (1990) recent work provides a useful and appropriate approach to Labor's efficient state strategy. She has argued that in Australia economic restructuring has achieved metapolicy status in response to economic and ideological pressures. In this situation, Labor has attempted to create a more efficient and effective public sector by appropriating private sector models of management (corporate managerialism). Labor in power has chosen this alternative over the Thatcherite model of substantial privatization. The question is whether or not this new managerialism will inhibit the achievement of equity and social justice goals. It certainly reframes those goals in both economic rationalist and managerialist terms. (See Fitzclarence and Kenway, Johnston, Rizvi, Luke *et al.*, Henry and Taylor, Carpenter, this volume.) However, such issues at least remain on the policy agenda. In Australia, as with Britain and the US, there is a ceiling on funds available for educational services. This precipitates certain policy developments, including pressure for 'more for less'. Pusey (1991) notes, however, that social-democratic residues remain at the federal level within the service departments such as education, welfare and health. In education, though, that culture has been further weakened by the 1987 abolition of the Schools Commission and the reformulation of the Commonwealth Department of Education and Youth Affairs as the Department of Employment, Education and Training, the related move towards national schooling policies through corporate federalism (Lingard, 1991) and restructurings of state systems. It is worth noting here that the Schools Commission was a strong proponent of feminist understandings of education policy, which have in many ways been swamped by the new, more masculinist, economic and training agendas. For example, the National Policy for the Education of Girls developed out of the earlier, more feminist culture, but was implemented within a more masculinist, managerialist framework (Kenway, 1990).

Hence, as the contributors to this book indicate, Labour parties have tended to appropriate elements of neo-liberal economic thought, while seeking to maintain some commitment to social justice and equity concerns, and generally excluding cultural restorationist concerns. (See Dale and Ozga, Chapter 5, this volume.) There has been a tendency under conditions of economic difficulties, however, in both New Zealand and Australian Labour, to move from the corporatization of certain public services and agencies to their privatization. The shift from corporatization to privatization is shaped by market and neo-liberal beliefs (see Davis, Weller and Lewis, 1989; cf. Wexler and Grabiner, 1986), and is of a different order to the combination of corporate managerialist structures and economic rationalist assumptions for a more efficient state. It is also significant that moves for privatization by Labour governments are a response to budgetary or current accounts deficits. This was certainly so in the New Zealand situation. In Australia, the situation is somewhat different: there has been a (thus far, successful) attempt for balanced budgets and a reduction of the commonwealth's share of foreign debt. However, the worsening economic situation from the stockmarket crash of 1987 and Australia's worsening balance of payments situation and deregulation policies, have clearly influenced the pressures for at least partial privatization of some corporate agencies (Commonwealth Bank, Qantas, Australian Airlines, Telecom . . .). A conservative government in power in Australia would most certainly take these developments further.

An important point made by Yeatman about the corporate managerialist restructuring is that it has been the Trojan horse through which Labor has sought to manage the plethora of political demands emanating from the disintegrating plurality of 1960s' social movements. In a sense, corporate managerialism can be seen as an attempt to manage and organize this feature of disorganized capitalism in a structural policy condition. As a number of chapters in this volume (Porter; Henry and Taylor; Rizvi) show, however, this move reframes and narrows equity demands to economic rather than citizenship and public-good rationales. We would emphasise that despite all of its shortcomings, the corporate managerialist/corporatist strategies are the lesser of two evils when compared with privatization ones, especially with regard to equity issues. However, with Yeatman (1990) and Pusey (1991), we would emphasize the need to democratize further the operation of corporate managerialism and the need to consider questions of democracy in schooling policy and administration.

The issue of curriculum reform merits further attention. While curriculum reform has been a major aspect of education restructuring in some countries, as Dale and Ozga stress in this volume (Chapter 5), the relationship between curriculum reform and restructuring is contingent upon local historical, political, social and economic circumstances. In the Australian context, federal Labor's push for a national curriculum (Bartlett, Chapter 15, this volume) is for microeconomic and economic infrastructural reasons, not for cultural restorationist reasons as appears to be largely the case in England and Wales under Thatcher/Major.

What Is An Appropriate Mode of Inquiry and to What Ends?: Action Critique and the Common Good

How then can we address the possibilities as well as the limitations for progressive educational policy developments and practices in the current conjuncture? What is an appropriate mode of inquiry and political practice in education? Rejecting debilitating master narratives, we need to look for resources of hope that are both practical and realistic. With Williams (1989) we do not wish to make despair convincing. There is not one resource of hope, but many, existing in creative tension.

We have already called into question 'Left' critiques which presume a monolithic New Right. Such acontextual analyses are typically cast in simple binary formulations. That given, they privilege continuity (Labor's similarities to the New Right) over discontinuity (Labor's differences from the New Right). They are therefore unable to address the practical possibilities for progressive change in the current situation. We note, for example, the irony of a situation in which critical academics in New Zealand, who had previously critiqued the very liberal-progressive *Curriculum Review* document (New Zealand Department of Education, 1987), had then to turn to its defence as a 'non-reformist reform' against the perceived New Right imperatives of the Picot Report (1988) and its subsequent implementation (Lange, 1988) and modification (Lough, 1990). Indeed, the consequent outcome in apathy, pessimism and political impotence played into the hands of those very forces to which they were opposed. However, we would stress that in many ways Labor's flirtatious Australian affair with economic rationalism appears to have set the stage for the playing out of harsher New Right approaches under a possible future Hewson-led conservative government.

We note also the inadequacies of sweeping Left critiques of public institutions such as education. Once again, this is exacerbated by an unwillingness or inability to address practicable improvements as opposed to revolutionary or utopian solutions, yet (as argued by Connell, Ashenden, Kessler and Dowsett, 1982), revolution by and large is not usually Department of Education policy. Hence we now find that market ideologues have appropriated the conclusions (not the theoretical perspectives!) of sweeping old Left critiques of public sector bureaucracies and of the continued failure of schooling to reduce or eliminate educational inequality. Indeed, some of the Left now look somewhat longingly toward the old centralized bureaucratic past. For example, as Ramsay, Chapter 14, and Dale and Ozga, Chapter 6 (this volume) point out, the New Zealand Treasury (1987) drew on these very (Left) arguments and evidence in an apparently well-researched and documented *Government Management: Brief to the Incoming Government, 1987* which advocated a New Right approach to education. The democratic socialist vocabulary became rearticulated into the services of a contradictory political agenda.

In this uncertain and difficult situation, we see the need to restate and resituate the theory and practice of social justice in and through education within the framework of a new analysis of the notion of the common good (cf. Connell, 1990a). In this book, then, we accept that a major purpose of our description, analysis and critique should be not only to understand, but to contribute towards changing existing circumstances. In thus attempting an 'action critique', we explicitly reject idealistic, utopian or final resolutions. We acknowledge that we work and manoeuvre upon a continually shifting and changing terrain, that our views must be constantly open to revision, and that any solution is temporary and proximate, creating new problems which must needs to be addressed in turn. Put another way, we assert the continuing engagement of action and knowledge, theory and praxis, in the on-going project of striving (however, imperfectly) for greater human and social good.

Hence, as against sweeping generalizations of a politically and ideologically dominant New Right, we call for a much closer examination of the specificities of situations and the inter-relatedness of text (schooling policy) and context (Hodge and Kress, 1988). We acknowledge the tensions and contradictions within policy documents and platforms (including those on equity and social justice), the cobbling and suturing of disparate themes, and the differing views which they seek to incorporate and reconcile. (Here see Knight, Smith and Sachs, 1990; Knight, Smith and Chant, 1989; Luke *et al.*, Chapter 9, this volume; Yeatman, 1990, ch. 8; Beilharz, 1987.) We note, in particular, that such texts are open to a range of meanings, including some beyond the intent of their constructors.

Here we can learn from Lather's (1991) methodology for reading texts and apply it to the question of political strategy. Lather argues for a positioning within the text which nonetheless reads ' "against" the text, against the assumptions which shape it' (p. 5). Hence, while we remain involved in the political and policy processes, we try not to be circumscribed by their epistemological blinkers. More, strategically, the 'within/against' strategy allows for a clearer apprehension of the range of possibilities in the present situation. In saying this, we acknowledge not only the need for critiques from the outside, but also the necessity to recognize material and structural inequalities outside of policy texts, a reality often neglected by poststructuralist analyses.

In this situation, the very tensions and contradictions of policy, as between, for example, equity and choice or 'freedom' and equality, create a space, a terrain which can be developed and exploited by progressive teachers, parents, academics and even bureaucrats (Laxon and Knight, forthcoming). Nor should such concepts necessarily be construed as in total opposition. Rather, we might ask in what frames they might become complementary, as in, for example, genuinely comprehensive schools or a pluralist state system of schooling. In all of this, however, we recognize that solutions remain proximate rather than absolute, and that further work always remains. Fitzclarence and Kenway (Chapter 6, this volume) argue that serious theorizing is required to come to grips with contemporary changes. Such theorizing must cater for both the heterogeneity of society and the need to work towards a common culture underpinned by a reconceptualized vision of equality (Walzer, 1983). That project involves a convergence of post-liberalism and post-marxism (Bowles and Gintis, 1987; Rizvi, forthcoming). Such theorizing must also seek to maximize the democratic possibilities in current reforms.

We would, however, note how the corporatist strategy pursued by Labor in Australia, while perhaps protecting some aspect of the social wage and union rights, has operated in an exclusionary fashion. We note also that many women, the unemployed and socially disadvantaged are also excluded by virtue of their lack of access to financial resources and representation (union and business) within the corporatist strategy.

The emergence of disorganized multinational capitalism articulates in a symbiotic fashion with a number of more recent theoretical discourses, including poststructuralism, postcolonialism, a variety of feminisms, which have both reflected and augmented the fragmentation within and between given nation states. From an array of such theoretical positions, the case is advanced that there is no longer a unitary or cohesive society or, indeed, self. There is a denial and rejection of 'master [sic] narratives', 'dominant ideologies' and 'totalizing' explanatory frameworks. Such master narratives are seen to be male and Eurocentric in character and often oppressive in their operation. The poststructuralist paradigm, by way of differentiation from structuralism, has stressed social and cultural fragmentation, 'microtechnologies of power' (Foucault, 1979), the positioning role of discourses, enabling and constraining notions of power, politics as local resistance, and so on. This paradigm also asserts the necessity for our theorizing and argumentation to go beyond simple binary characterizations of the world, (for example capitalism/ socialism, male/female, etc) and as such provides some way towards different and creative conceptualizations of the present and variegated imaginings of futures.

The more recent work of Laclau and Mouffe (1985) acknowledges the apparent failure of the master narratives of marxism to construct a democratic socialism. Within the fragmenting and pluralist situation of contemporary nation states, they address the possibilities of linking a range of progressive social groups and movements (feminists, environmentalists, some ethnic minorities, gays, workers, the unemployed . . .) using shared or similar concerns to achieve limited and short-term goals. Such alliances are certainly possible, indeed desirable, for issues of equity and social justice and participatory democracy in schooling.

However, while the non-essentialism of such theoretical developments appears attractive to some extent, we would reject any recourse to a constraining relativism which inhibited action. The problem here, as suggested earlier, is to conceptualize a common good while allowing for cultural heterogeneity and democratic participation. Sadly, what all this theorizing suggests is that at the very time when some form of the theory and practice of 'the common good' is most needed, it is difficult (though not impossible) to articulate it convincingly. It is perhaps not by accident that the decline of socialism and the primacy of market forces and practices are contiguous with the development of postmodernist and poststructuralist forms of thought (and vice versa). Yet, what is absent, indeed what appears almost impossible in poststructuralist theorizing, are those values, commitments and forms of relationship which infuse and construct social democracy, community and democratic socialism. We would want to retain notions of the rational in such considerations (Habermas, 1979) and also stress that such rationality is a capacity of all people.

That said, we remain committed to certain socially democratic practices and values — community, cooperation, equality, equity — in a word, the common good. Here, following Dow (1991, p. 1), we would define social democracy as 'an assertion that all citizens of a particular society are entitled, by reason of citizenship, to share equally in the standards of living which that society is capable of providing.' As against binary constructions of 'statist collectivism' versus 'democratic freedom', we agree with Pusey (1991) on the need for a consideration of the domains in which the state should be involved and those in which it should not. Further, the achievement of social democracy requires a maximizing of the political participation of citizens; schools have an important role to play in creating socially concerned and robust citizens. (See Porter, Chapter 3, this volume.) We would also suggest that socially democratic forms of relationship enhance, rather than diminish, personhood. These ends constitute our *telos*: a fairer, culturally richer and more human world, one that is worth imagining, and working and fighting for. For as we suggested in our discussion of 'action critique', the point of a dialectic and materialist analysis is not simply better understanding; it is for ways and means to achievable improvements within the present situation.

Our project, then, is education for the common good, which nonetheless both encourages and respects difference. This book is part of that project. In working and meeting together we have already learned something of that common good and of the possibilities of education for that end. Throughout this book, we continue our dialogue. We want to open further possibilities for progressive action, for using the present situation to advance the common good. There is perhaps some hope in the fact that while there remains only a residue of the social-democratic agenda in the structures of the education state, there appears to be a substantial residue of the same amongst teachers, within schools and classrooms.

The Book, Then ...

Specifically, in this book, there are five interrelated questions which we and our co-writers seek to address:

1 In what way do these policy developments conceptualize education: as the politics of consumption or the politics of production? That is, are they directed to the meeting of perceived needs (individual and social) as they arise, with economic considerations secondary — or are they narrowed and constrained by the need to restore profitability to the economic sector?
2 Where is their emphasis: on increasing 'human capital' 'in the national interest' — or improving the situation of those 'disadvantaged' in the social formation?
3 Which solution (if any) do they offer to economic constraints upon the provision of educational services: corporate managerialism for a more efficient and effective state — or privatization which moves provision increasingly out of the state and into the private schools?
4 What is the justification for devolution: Is it making schooling more effective and democratic through school-based decision-making and community participation — or ensuring the efficient and effective delivery of clearly defined educational services to school communities through administrative rather than political devolution?
5 What is the mediation of equity and social justice in this approach to both policy-making and policy?

In raising these points, we acknowledge that they do not constitute the totality of possible positions. Rather they construct fields of possibilities on which a range of other solutions may also be deployed.

The first section of the book addresses the broader economic, social, political and ideological context of educational reform under Labor governments in Australia, with comparative analyses of developments under a Labour government (until 1990) in New Zealand and with conservative governments in the US and the UK. Such an approach, taking account of difference as well as similarity, permits a more informed discussion of the degree to which Australian Labor has incorporated elements of New Right economic and social theory and the differences which remain between Labor and conservative regimes in the contemporary situation. It also possibly provides some purchase on political strategy.

The second section examines the reconstruction of notions of equality in Labor education policy, in particular the shift from the concept of equal opportunity to concepts of equity and social justice. (In the first section of the book, Apple considers this transformation under conservative regimes in the US.) This section begins with an analysis of Labor's restructuring of social justice in the 1980s (Fitzclarence and Kenway). Attention is then directed to shifts and developments on the terrain upon which the discourses of equal opportunity and equity have been deployed: the Disadvantaged Schools Program (Johnston), multicultural education (Rizvi), disability and mainstreaming (Carpenter), Aboriginal and Torres Strait Islander education (Luke, Nakata, Garbutcheon Singh and Smith) and gender equity (Henry and Taylor).

The third section reviews Labour's administrative and educational reforms through a series of fine-grained case studies of the Victorian (Watkins and Blackmore), Western Australian (Porter, Knight and Lingard), and New Zealand (Ramsay) situations, as well as the emerging national curriculum framework of federal Labor (Bartlett).

As William Butler Yeats wrote, when 'Things fall apart; The centre cannot hold . . .' However, economic rationalists and corporate managerialists seem to be making a pretty good attempt to hold things together. In a sense, economic reductionism has become a dominating master narrative within state policy making in Australia. Against such processes, we want to assert the valued tension between a centre which guarantees in a socially democratic way the needs of life for all citizens, while celebrating the richness, freedom and diversity of life. The demands from progressive social movements for involvement in the policy processes at all levels add a creative democratic tension to the contemporary situation. Nowhere is this tension more obvious than in debates surrounding education. Long ago, John and Evelyn Dewey (1915) noted the intimate relation between democracy and education. That realization, within the context of a concern for social justice and the common good, must be central in contemporary political projects promoting public schooling.

Notes

1 In this book, 'Labor' signifies the Australian Labor Party. 'Labour' signifies the Labour parties of the UK and New Zealand. It is also used when speaking of Labour parties generally.

References

ALEXANDER, D. (1986) 'The new class: reconstituting a neglected social construct', *Unicorn*, **12**, 1, pp. 24–9.
BALL, S. (1990) *Politics and Policy Making in Education: Explorations in Policy Sociology*, London, UK: Routledge.

BARTLETT, L., KNIGHT, J. and LINGARD, R. (1991) 'Corporate federalism and the reform of teacher education in Australia', *Journal of Education Policy*, **6**, 1, pp. 85–90.

BEILHARZ, P. (1987) 'Political theory and policy making in education', *The Australian and New Zealand Journal of Sociology*, **23**, 3, pp. 388–406.

BLUER, R. and CARMICHAEL, L. (1991) 'Award Restructuring in Teaching,' *Unicorn*, **17**, 1, pp. 24–9.

BOWLES, S. and GINTIS, H. (1987) *Democracy and Capitalism*, New York, NY: Basic Books.

CALDWELL, B. and SPINKS, J. (1988) *The Self-Managing School*, London, UK: Falmer Press.

CASTLES, F. (1988) *Australian Public Policy and Economic Vulnerability: A Comparative and Historical Perspective*, Sydney, Australia: Allen and Unwin.

CAWSON, A. and SAUNDERS, P. (1983) 'Corporatism, Competitive Politics and Class Struggle', in KING, R. (Ed.) *Capital and Politics*, London, UK: Routledge and Kegan Paul.

CERNY, P. (1990) *The Changing Architecture of Politics: Structure, Agency and the Future of the State*, London, UK: Sage.

CODD, J., HARKER, R. and NASH, R. (1990) 'Education, politics and the economic crisis', in CODD, J., HARKER, R. and NASH, R. (Eds) *Political Issues in New Zealand Education*, Palmerston North: Dunmore Press, pp. 7–22.

CONNELL, R. (1990a) 'Curriculum and social justice', *QAHET*, June, pp. 5–15.

CONNELL, R. (1990b) 'The State, Gender and Sexual Politics', *Theory and Society*, **19**, pp. 507–44.

CONNELL, R., ASHENDEN, D., KESSLER, S. and DOWSETT, G. (1982) *Making the Difference:* Sydney, Australia: Allen and Unwin.

CONNORS, L. (1989) *Futures for Schooling in Australia: Nationalization, Privatisation or Unification?* The Australian College of Education, Occasional paper no. 13, Deakin, Australia, ACT.

CONSIDINE, M. (1988) 'The corporate management framework as administrative science: A critique', *Australian Journal of Public Administration*, **47**, 1, pp. 4–19.

DALE, R. (1989) *The State and Education Policy*, Milton Keynes, UK: Open University Press.

DAVIS, G., WELLER, P. and LEWIS, C. (Eds) (1989) *Corporate Management in Australian Government*, South Melbourne, Australia: Macmillan.

DAWKINS, J. (1988) *Strengthening Australia's Schools*, Canberra, Australia: Australian Government Publishing Service [AGPS].

DEWEY, J. and DEWEY, E. (1915) *Schools of Tomorrow*, New York, NY: Dutton & Co.

DOW, G. (1991) 'What do we know about social democracy?', Paper presented to National Social Policy Conference, Social Policy Research Centre, University of New South Wales, NZ, 3–5 July.

EVATT RESEARCH CENTRE (1989) *State of Siege: Renewal or Privatisation for Australian State Public Services?* Sydney, Australia: Pluto Press.

FOUCAULT, M. (1979) *Discipline and Punish: The Birth of the Prison*, Harmondsworth, UK: Penguin.

FRANZWAY, S., COURT, D. and CONNELL, R. (1989) *Staking a Claim: Feminism, Bureaucracy and the State*, Sydney, Australia: Allen and Unwin.

HABERMAS, J. (1976) *Legitimation Crisis*, London, UK: Heinemann.

HABERMAS, J. (1979) *Communication and the Evolution of Society*, London, UK: Heinemann.

HALL, S. and JACQUES, M. (1991) *The Changing Face of Politicism in the 1990's*, New Times.

HODGE, R. and KRESS, G. (1988) *Social Semiotics*, Cambridge, UK: Polity Press.

INTERIM COMMITTEE OF THE AUSTRALIAN SCHOOLS COMMISSION (1973) *Schools in Australia*, Canberra, Australia: AGPS.

JAY, M. (1988) *Fin-de-Siecle Socialism*, New York, NY: Routledge.

KENWAY, J. (1990) *Gender and Education Policy: A Call for New Directions*, Geelong, Australia: Deakin University Press.

KNIGHT, J., LINGARD, R. and PORTER, P. (1991) 'Re-forming the education industry through award restructuring and the New Federalism', *Unicorn*, **17**, 3, pp. 133–8.

KNIGHT, J., SMITH, R. and CHANT, D. (1989) 'Reconceptualising the dominant ideology debate: an Australian case study', *Australian and New Zealand Journal of Sociology*, **25**, 3, pp. 381–409.

KNIGHT, J., SMITH, R. and SACHS, J. (1990) 'Deconstructing hegemony: multicultural policy and a populist response', in BALL, S. (Ed.) *Foucault and Education: Disciplines and Knowledge*. London, UK: Routledge, pp. 133–52.

LACLAU, E. and MOUFFE, C. (1985) *Hegemony and Socialist Strategy: Towards a Radical Democratic Politics*, London, UK: Verso.

LANGE, D. (1988) *Tomorrow's Schools: The Reform of Education Administration in New Zealand*, Wellington, NZ: Government Printer.

LASH, S. and URRY, J. (1987) *The End of Organised Capitalism*. Cambridge, UK: Polity Press.

LATHER, P. (1991) *Feminist Research in Education: Within/Against*, Geelong, UK: Deakin University Press.

LAXON, J. and KNIGHT, J. (forthcoming) 'Gender equity in Queensland education policy', *New Zealand Journal of Education Studies*.

LOUGH, N. (1990) *Today's Schools: A Review of the Education Reform Implementation Process*, Wellington, NZ: Government Printer.

LINGARD, R. (1991) 'Policy-making for Australian schooling: The new corporate federalism', *Journal of Education Policy*, **6**, 1, pp. 85–90.

LINGARD, R. and RIZVI, F. (1992) 'Theorizing the ambiguities of devolution', *Discourse*, 13, 1, (In press).

MORTIMORE, P., SAMMONS, P., STOLL, L., LEWIS, D. and ECOB, R. (1988) *School Matters: The Junior Years*, London, UK: Open Books.

NEW ZEALAND DEPARTMENT OF EDUCATION (1987) *The Curriculum Review: Report of the committee to review the curriculum for schools*, Wellington, NZ: Dept. of Education.

NEW ZEALAND TREASURY (1987) *Government Management: Brief to the Incoming government, 1987*, **II**, *Education Issues*, Wellington, NZ: The Treasury.

OFFE, C. (1975) 'The theory of the capitalist state and the problem of policy formation', in LINDBERG, L., ALFORD, R., CROUCH, C. and OFFE, C. (Eds) *Stress and Contradiction in Modern Capitalism*, Boston, MA: Lexington Books, pp. 125–44.

OFFE, C. (1984) *Contradictions of the Welfare State*, London, UK: Hutchinson.

OFFE, C. (1985) *Disorganised Capitalism*, Cambridge, UK: Polity Press.

PETERS, T. and WATERMAN, R. (1982) *In Search of Excellence*, New York, NY: Harper and Row.

PICOT, B. (1988) *Administering for Excellence: Effective Administration in Education*, Wellington, NZ: Taskforce to Review Education Administration.

PUSEY, M. (1991) *Economic Rationalism in Canberra: A Nation-building State Changes Its Mind*, Cambridge, UK: Cambridge University Press.

QUALITY OF EDUCATION REVIEW COMMITTEE (1985) *Quality of Education in Australia*, Canberra, Australia: AGPS.

RAMSAY, P. (1990) Interview with P. Porter, J. Knight, R. Lingard.

RAMSAY, P., SNEDDON, D., GRENFELL, J. and FORD, I. (1983) 'Successful and Unsuccessful Schools: A study in Southern Auckland', *Australian and New Zealand Journal of Sociology*, **19**(2), pp. 272–304.

RAMSEY, G. (1990) 'The need for national policies in education', *Unicorn*, **17**, 1, pp. 34–41.

RIZVI, F. (1990) 'Horizontal Accountability,' in CHAPMAN, J. (Ed.) *School-based Decision-making and Management*, London, UK: Falmer Press, pp. 299–324.

RIZVI, F. (forthcoming) 'Education: from liberal to postliberal', *Education Links*, **40**.

ROSECRANCE, R. (1964) 'The radical culture of Australia', in HARTZ, L. (Ed.) *The Founding of New Societies*. New York, NY: Harcourt Brace, pp. 275–318.

RUTTER, M., MAUGHAN, B., MORTIMORE, P. and OUSTON, J. (1979) *Fifteen Thousand Hours*, London, UK: Open Books.

SEDDON, T., ANGUS, L. and POOLE, M. (1990) 'Pressures on the move to school-based decision-making and management', In CHAPMAN, J. (Ed.) *School-based Decision-making and Management*, London, UK: Falmer Press, pp. 29–54.

SINGH, M. GARBUTCHEON (1990) *Performance Indicators in Education*, Geelong, Australia: Deakin University Press.

STRETTON, H. (1987) *Political Essays*, Melbourne, Australia: Georgian House.

TANNOCK, P. (1989) Interview with P. Porter, J. Knight, R. Lingard.

WALKER, J. (1990) 'Functional decentralization and democratic control' in CHAPMAN, J. (Ed.) *School-based Decision-making and Management*, London, UK: Falmer Press, pp. 83–100.

WALKER J. (1991) Presidential address to AARE Conference, Surfers Paradise, 26–30 November.

WALZER, M. (1983) *Spheres of Justice: A Defence of Pluralism and Equality*, Oxford, UK: Basil Blackwell.

WEICK, K. (1977) 'Educational organizations as loosely coupled systems', *Administrative Science Quarterly*, **21**, 1, pp. 1–21.

WEXLER, P. and GRABINER, G. (1986) 'The education question: America during the crisis', in SHARP, R. (Ed.) *Capitalist Crisis and Schooling: Comparative Studies in the Politics of Education*. Melbourne, Australia: Macmillan, pp. 1–40.

WILLIAMS, R. (1989) *Resources of Hope*, London, UK: Verso.

YEATMAN, A. (1990) *Bureaucrats, Technocrats, Femocrats: Essays on the Contemporary Australian state*, Sydney, Australia: Allen and Unwin.

Part II: *Restructuring Australian Education: Comparative Perspectives*

Chapter 2

Corporate Federalism: The Emerging Approach to Policy-Making for Australian Schools[1]

Bob Lingard

Introduction

The concept of corporate federalism has been created to indicate the way a national approach to the development of policy for Australian schooling has been utilized by the Hawke Labor government (1983–present) (Lingard, 1991). Negotiated consensus at the Australian Education Council (AEC), the intergovernmental body consisting of the federal and state education ministers, has been used to arrive at these policies and at the same time to circumvent politically the constitutional and financial realities of Australian federalism.

Corporate federalism began to emerge from the election of the Hawke Labor government in 1983, manifesting itself in the first instance in the *National Policy for the Education of Girls* in 1987. (It ought to be said, though, that the National Policy developed as a result of 'bottom-up' pressures from feminist networks and internal bureaucratic pressures; it also grew out of the feminist culture of Commonwealth involvement in schooling policy during Susan Ryan's period as Minister (1983–87).) However, the approach has developed much more fully since the 1987 Labor election victory, following which John Dawkins became the Minister for the reconstituted Commonwealth Department of Employment, Education and Training. The title of that department gives some indication of the new instrumentalist orientation, while its growth out of the corporate managerialist consolidation of the federal public service into fewer 'mega-departments' is also of significance. These two factors, notably a revitalized human capital theory and corporate managerialism, are important components of corporate federalism, along with Labor's neo-corporatist approach to policy-making.

Given the economic difficulties facing contemporary Australia and the fact that the federal government manages the economy, the Hawke/Keating governments have attempted to reconstitute education policy as part of the restructuring of the economy (Marginson, 1989, Sweet, 1989). Yeatman (1990: 102) speaks of the 'metapolicy status' granted to this restructuring. Such a desire to reframe education as a micro-economic reform tool has to take account of the politics and constitutional aspects of Australian federalism. Under the Australian constitution, education remains a residual constitutional power of the states. The federal government must also take account of the fact that schooling (unlike higher education) is a shared funding responsibility between commonwealth and state governments, with most of the funding coming from the states. But here, as with most other policy domains, the Hawke Labor government has been extremely pragmatic (Maddox, 1989), so that while the earlier Labor government of Whitlam (1972–1975) 'confronted' the federal constitution, Hawke has 'worked' it politically (Galligan, 1989: 12). In the schooling policy area, corporate federalism has been the result.

Section 51 of the constitution outlines the powers of the Commonwealth, while section 197 asserts that those policy functions not outlined in section 51 continue to reside with the states. Education is one of those residual state powers. However, section 96 allows the federal government to make financial grants to the states 'on such terms and conditions as the (federal) Parliament sees fit'. As White (1987: 10) points out: 'Education could, therefore, be supported and influenced by the Commonwealth through its money granting powers. So it has been.' The use of section 96 grants is the major way the federal government has increased its influence in education policy. Wiltshire (1986: 223) makes the point that section 96 grants have been utilized by the federal government 'for activities which are clearly the constitutional responsibility of the states'.

It is, however, section 51 (xxiiiA) which potentially at least, provides some more direct constitutional basis for federal education policy-making. The amendment to section 51, with placitum xxiiiA, resulted from what is usually called the 'social services amendment' passed by referendum in 1946 under the Chifley Labor government, as part of its move to create the welfare state. With this constitutional amendment, it is the phrase 'benefits to students' which appears to give the commonwealth concurrent power with the states in education policy-making (Tannock and Birch, 1976: 38).

Since the early 1970s, schooling has been a shared commonwealth/state financial responsibility, with the commonwealth providing about 10 per cent of all funding for government schools. It is that funding situation, along with the constitutional reality, which has necessitated the Dawkins corporate federalist strategy in schooling policy-making. That situation can be contrasted with higher education policy where the commonwealth has provided nearly all the funds since 1974, and where, as a consequence, a more coercive federalism has operated (Smart, 1991).

Corporate federalism: Theorizing its Development

Mathews (1977a,b) has provided a classification of the operation of Australian federalism from 1901 until the 1970s. In that classification, he is speaking about general federal/state relations rather than those operating in the education field. From federation until about the First World War, he speaks of 'coordinate federalism', where the Commonwealth and state governments carried out their separate tasks. From then until the Second World War, he talks of 'cooperative federalism', while the post-war period until the 1970s, following the Commonwealth's usurpation of the taxation power in 1942, he classifies as 'coercive federalism'. The latter concept is utilized to take account of the increased use of section 96 specific-purpose grants by the Commonwealth in the post-war time, which reached its apotheosis during the Whitlam Labor government (1972–75). The Mathews classification of 'coercive' contains a negative connotation which is not accepted here, for it needs to be noted that the Whitlam approach to federalism, including his extensive use of section 96 grants, was underpinned by an attempt to move towards a more universal welfare state, as part of the creation of a fairer Australia (Castles, 1988; Whitlam, 1986). The argument of this chapter is that the Hawke government has set in motion a new form of federal/state relations which is classified as 'corporate federalism'. This is still emerging, but has developed most strongly in the schooling policy domain, particularly in the Dawkins period.

Across the post-war boom period until the mid-seventies, then, the creation of the Keynesian welfare state operated in a centripetal fashion in relation to federalism. In contrast, since the end of the post-war boom from the mid-seventies, centrifugal pressures have begun to infract on the operation of federalism. Moves towards a 'new federalism' under the conservative Fraser government (1975–1983) were one indication of this; the development of 'corporate federalism' under Hawke Labor is the most recent manifestation of that tendency. Australia's declining economic circumstances and its integration in a non-tariff protected fashion into the global economy are important factors in the reworking of federalism.

How can these developments be theorized? The work on the liberal democratic state by Offe (1975, 1984, 1985) is most useful here. However, it needs to be pointed out that Offe fails to acknowledge the impact of the internationalization of the economy on how the nation state can respond to the pressures on it. For Offe, the state must attempt to balance the pressures to ensure the continuity of capital accumulation, while simultaneously ensuring its own legitimacy and that of the broader social structure by responding to democratic policy demands. There is no permanent solution to this balancing act, but simply different settlements at various historical moments (Castles, 1988). Since the end of the boom in the mid-seventies, Australia has been gesturing towards a new post-Keynesian settlement. The restructuring of federalism is part of that attempt.

Offe (1975) also stresses the important impact upon policy-making of the internal administrative and organizational arrangements of the state. These arrangements, which operate on other than class, frame both how and what gets on to the policy agenda, as well as the policy 'solutions' proffered. Federalism is one important feature of the internal structure of the Australian state.

Offe's (1975, 1984, 1985) theory of the state then moves beyond class instrumental and unitary approaches. The form of the state mediates pressures upon it, while the state to ensure its legitimacy must respond to democratic pressures in addition to those flowing from class-based politics in the economy.

For the analysis here, Offe (1985: 223–227) also makes a useful distinction between what he calls the *conjunctural* and *structural policy* conditions. The former rationale obtains in times of economic well-being, whereby governments respond to political demands for both funding and policy by simply spending more and expanding, in an ongoing incrementalist fashion, state policy coverage. By stark contrast, the structural policy condition operates in times of institutional and economic crises. Here the state, because of constraints upon its funds, seeks to manage policy demand within a given funding ceiling. The latter often sees a restructuring of the state apparatus and a renewed emphasis upon efficiency and effectiveness. Offe also suggests (1984) that corporatism or New Right small state strategy are the most likely political alternatives to the management of policy demand within the advanced capitalist economies, particularly in terms of the economic difficulties experienced since the mid-seventies. Further, Offe (1985) suggests that the conjunctural policy rationale tends to be accompanied by a Keynesian demand-side approach to economic policy formation, whereas the structural one is accompanied by a renewed supply-side emphasis upon the costs, productivity and skilling of labour.

Offe (1985) does note that while there has been a general move from the conjunctural to the structural policy condition, it is more appropriate to see different policy periods as manifesting different balances between the two rationales. This becomes clear in the chapters in this book which analyze the reframing of equity under Hawke Labor (Fitzclarence and Kenway; Henry and Taylor; Johnston; Luke *et al.*; Rizvi).

The argument of this paper is that the structural policy condition has been in operation since the latter stage of the Whitlam government (specifically the 1975 budget), while since 1983 the Hawke Labor government has sought a new policy settlement around what might be called a neo-corporatist, efficient state strategy, or more succinctly, the corporate settlement. This strategy has seen a corporate managerialist reformation of the public sector (Considine, 1988; Yeatman, 1990) underpinned by economic rationalism (Pusey, 1991) and a reformation of federal/state relations in the direction of corporate federalism (Lingard, 1991).

One clear manifestation of the move from the conjunctural to the structural policy rationale in education can be seen by contrasting the Karmel Report (Interim Schools Commission, 1973) under Whitlam with the Karmel Report under Hawke (QERC, 1985). While the former is about formulating a rational basis for expanding the federal role in schooling and providing substantially increased funds to achieve greater equality of opportunity (Whitlam, 1986), the latter is about a more efficient and effective utilization of given resources so as to achieve better results. It is the efficiency aspect of the latter which contributes towards corporate federalism.

Education under Hawke, particularly post-1987, operated under a structural policy rationale. The period of Susan Ryan (1983–1987) as federal minister saw an attempt to co-join the old Whitlam agenda (particularly with respect to gender equity) with a new instrumentalism in the face of the collapse of the full-time teenage labour market. The period since, with Dawkins as minister, has seen a new phase, marked by a corporate managerialist restructuring of the federal department and the abolition of the Whitlam-created, quasi-autonomous Schools Commission and its replacement by the advisory National Board of Employment, Education and Training (NBEET), a broadened emphasis on training, an attempted narrowing of schooling and higher education teaching and research in more instrumentalist directions, and a more interventionist federal role.

It was suggested above that Offe does not pay sufficient attention to the globalization of the economy and its impact upon the nation state's capacity to balance the accumulation and legitimation demands upon it. Cerny's (1990) work on the development of the 'competitive state' is useful in that respect. Since the mid-seventies (but particularly under Hawke Labor), the Australian state has moved away from a Keynesian welfare mode towards a competitive character. This 'competitive state' almost becomes a 'player' in the international economy, while it also attempts to assist in economic restructuring which will ensure the

Table 1   Offe's Two Types of State Policy and the Restructuring of Federalism

	Conjunctural Policy	Structural Policy
Political Strategy	Satisfy demands	Shape and channel demands to make them satisfiable (New Right and corporalist alternatives)
Economic Strategy	Manage input, order priorities (demand-side economics) Policy focus: protected national economy	Manage output, keep supply constant (supply-side economics) Policy focus: unprotected integration into international economy
System Effects	Policy 'joins on' existing system	Policy 'restructures' existing system
Societal Effects	Increased State intervention	Increased politicization
State Effects	'Compassionate' welfare state (Towards universal welfare provision)	'Efficient' competitive state (Residualizing welfare provision)
Political Effects	Population as citizens	Population as consumers
Federalism Effects	Centripetal pressures, 'coercive federalism': Commonwealth policies	Centrifugal pressures, 'corporate federalism': national policies

Note: Adapted and extended from 'Educational policy and the crisis of the New Zealand State' (p. 213) by J. Codd, 1990, in *New Zealand Education Policy Today*, by Middleton, S., Codd, J. and Jones, A., Wellington, NZ: Allen and Unwin.

competitiveness of the non-tariff-protected Australian economy in a world market.

Thus, while the post-war Keynesian welfare state precipitated centripetal pressures within the Australian nation state and Australian federalism, the Hawke strategy, under a structural policy condition, has spawned centrifugal pressures in the move to a competitive state. This is part of the attempt to create a national economic infrastructure and to break down the inefficient aspects of federalism. Here we see either a move to national policies, agreed to by the relevant inter-governmental committees, or mutual recognition of standards and regulations across state boundaries. In this new policy configuration, the Special Premiers' Conferences and the various intergovernmental committees take on a greater policy significance. In education, the AEC has become an important policy player. Corporate federalism has manifested in a variety of policy domains, including transport, schooling, the production and consumption of goods, and so on.

Table 1, developed from Codd (1990), attempts to encapsulate these developments, namely, the move from the conjunctural to structural policy rationale and the move towards a competitive, rather than welfare state. The Table indicates some of the approach problems as the state attempts to manage demands, rather than respond to them, and in so doing attempts to reconstruct citizens in the direction of consumers. The emergence of corporate federalism can be seen then as central to the restructuring of the Australia state under conditions of economic difficulties.

Discourses Underpinning Corporate Federalism

Corporate federalism is framed by a number of discourses and practices, including neo-corporatism, economic rationalism, corporate managerialism and a reconstituted human capital theory. The amalgam of these discourses constitutes a technology of power (Foucault, 1979). Some definition of these discourses will be provided below, as well as a brief analysis in relation to schooling policy.

Corporatism, or neo-corporatism, is a 'tendency for élites — capital, trade unions and the state — to determine key areas of economic policy through formalized agreements and consultations' (Head 1983: 30). Clearly, the Accord (between the trade unions and the Labor government), the economic Summit held immediately after Labor won power in 1983, the tripartite bodies such as the Economic Planning Advisory Council (EPAC), consisting of business, the unions and the government, and the industry councils, are neo-corporatist policy instruments used by the Hawke government. Neo-corporatist politics can also operate in the non-economic spheres through sophisticated systems of interest representation (Schmitter, 1974: 93). This has been another Hawke policy approach.

Neo-corporatist negotiation at the AEC has been central to the emergence of a national approach in schooling with the resulting 1989 Hobart Declaration on national goals for schooling and a national curriculum framework and a range of subsequent developments, including the creation of the Curriculum Corporation. The Dawkins-authored, May 1988 document *Strengthening Australia's Schools* with its call for a 'national effort to strengthen the capacity of our schools' was the first fully articulated expression of what this paper calls corporate federalism (Lingard and O'Brien, 1990).

The AEC development of a number of national policies (girls, goals, curriculum framework, teacher education, maths teaching) is the most overt manifestation of corporate federalism at work. *The National Policy for the Education of Girls* was the first national schooling policy to be created in Australian education history. That policy makes an important distinction between national and Commonwealth policies which is of relevance regarding the emergence of corporate federalism. That distinction was centrally important in the political negotiation of the policy. While it resulted from a different political and policy culture to the later Dawkins one, it did indicate the possibilities through negotiation at the AEC. The policy states:

> There is a necessary distinction between Commonwealth and national policies in education. Commonwealth policies relate specifically to the objectives of the Commonwealth Government, such as those addressed through the Commonwealth's general resources programs and its specific purpose programs. In contrast, a national policy in education addresses matters of concern to the nation as a whole in which a comprehensive approach to policy development and implementation is adopted by school and system authorities across the nation. A national policy, based on principles of collaboration and partnership, necessarily involves commitment and agreement from the various parties responsible for schooling, including Commonwealth, State and Territory governments and non-government school authorities (Schools Commission 1987: 11).

In a 1990 press statement (The Australian, 30 August, 1990), Dawkins pointed out that the federal government would no longer simply be a 'banker' for schools, but rather had to provide 'national leadership', which he distinguished from 'central control': a muted expression of corporate federalism.

The Australian Council of Trade Unions' (ACTU) incorporation into the economic policy advice process is also of significance here. Of particular relevance is the incorporation of the Australian Teachers' Union (ATU) and the Independent Teachers' Federation (IFT) within the ACTU strategy. At the moment, both government and non-government teachers work under state, rather than national awards. In that context, the current joint national approach of the two unions to award restructuring has been an important component in the emergence of both corporate federalism and the national approach to schooling (Foggo, 1990).

In the discourse of economic rationalism, as articulated by the Labor government, there is a stress on efficiency and effectiveness to increase the steering capacity of the state (Pusey, 1991). Such efficiency arguments are important in the emergence of corporate federalism in schooling policy-making, given that with respect to schooling policy, federalism can be seen to inhibit efficient policy formulation and delivery, as well as the utilization of schooling as a micro-economic reform tool. Gregor Ramsey (1990: 34–35), former chairperson of the National Board of Employment, Education and Training (1987–1991), has argued that the national education approach can help reduce the national debt by reducing duplication and by operating in a more efficient and effective manner.

Corporate managerialism has resulted from the dominance of economic rationalism. Under its rubric, public sector bureaucracies are restructured as a way to achieve greater outputs for given inputs. What is required is a leaner, tighter, more precisely defined management structure, and more precisely articulated policy goals, as well as the devolution to the service agencies at the work face. The new mega-department of Employment, Education and Training is structured along such lines. As Considine (1988: 9) suggests, corporate managerialism 'reduces the variety of objectives which are pursued', while lifting the level at which these objectives are set. A national approach to the formulation of broad goals for schooling flows logically from such an arrangement. Implementation is devolved to the state level. What we have as a result is corporate federalism. Kenway (1990: 67) argues that the *National Policy for the Education of Girls* 'was the first occasion upon which the principles of corporate managerialism were to be applied to education at a national level'.

The tight ministerial control over the federal department and the change agenda (a feature of the corporate managerialist style) has been important in this process (Smart, 1989). An example of this can be seen in the strict guidelines imposed on the advisory National Board of Employment, Education and Training (NBEET) and its advisory councils (NBEET Annual Report, 1988–1989: 76–83).

Human capital theory, as reconstituted in the 1980s is the final related factor in corporate federalism. Such theory presents people as objects to whom value, for both the individual and society, is added through education and training. There is here a presumption that human knowledge and skill form a kind of capital which can be invested and from which economic benefits for both the individual and the society are expected. The decline in productivity, despite increased educational expenditure during the early 1970s, led to a questioning of the veracity of human capital theory as such. However, recent and more sophisticated variants have drawn attention to the importance of a flexible and multi-skilled workforce for national economic competitiveness (Marginson, 1989; Sweet, 1989). On this point, Dawkins has been quoted as saying 'an efficient and flexible workforce was arguably the most important part of federal efforts on micro-economic reform, and could only be achieved if school and tertiary education policy were negotiated and coordinated nationally' (The Australian, 30 August, 1990).

Thus in schooling policy-making, the Hawke/Keating governments represent a new form of federalism in operation — corporate federalism. This has been more successful, influencing through negotiation and consensus, than the Whitlam approach, which used imposition. It signals a new and highly effective use of ideological and economic power by the federal government (Head, 1989). Interestingly, with the devolution, developments within the state systems and the emergence of corporate federalism nationally, the structural configuration of Australian schooling policy-making and service delivery is beginning to look like that envisaged by Whitlam. However, social democratic goals have been replaced by narrower economic ones. The aim is not greater social justice, however, which was the motivating force of Whitlam's approach, but rather the policy desire to incorporate education within micro-economic reform goals. The existence of a large number of Labor state governments over the Hawke/Keating period has facilitated this, as has the acceptance by all state governments of whatever persuasion, of the reconstruction of education as a micro-economic reform tool.

Recent Developments in Australian Federalism

Recent political developments have pushed the restructuring of Australian federalism to the fore in Australian debates (Knight, Lingard, Porter, 1991). The Special Premiers' Conference held in October, 1990 put the Prime Minister's 'new federalism' firmly on the agenda, as have subsequent conferences. It is becoming even clearer that there is a mixture of centripetal and centrifugal pressures within Australian federalism, which are seeking, on the one hand, to pull all policy domains necessary for micro-economic reform to the centre and, on the other, to devolve non-economic policies out to the States. There was a power play within the federal Labor Party around federalism connected to the Hawke/Keating leadership battle, subsequently won by Keating in late 1991. The then Prime Minister, Hawke, was prepared to grant block funds to the States, as opposed to tied grants, if the States would concede the necessary components of an effective micro-economic reform agenda to the Commonwealth. That would have been disastrous for any meaningful social justice strategy. The Commonwealth has an important role to play with respect to these matters through targeted special purpose equity programs, and as such Commonwealth intervention is necessary to ensure equality of opportunity for all. The Keating camp articulated an older style Whitlam version of federalism in the current Labor leadership stakes, in an attempt to pull 'the left' in behind his 'challenge', which was somewhat paradoxical given Keating's commitment to economic rationalism (Pusey, 1991). Since Keating's accession to the Prime Ministership, developments in the new federalism have slowed somewhat and it remains to be seen what will eventuate.

The Business Council of Australia's (1991) *Government in Australia in the 1990s: A business perspective* is the articulation of a political position *vis-a-vis* federalism which would see a much greater weakening of the Australian state and a reorientation of federalism to what could be called *business federalism*, a con-comitant of Pusey's (1991) 'business democracy'. This would see federal structures operating simply to ensure economic enterprises were competitive in the inter-national economy, with an even weaker and more residualized welfare provision. In Offe's (1984) terms, the accumulation demand upon the state would take total precedence; we would have a competitive federal state in Australia (Cerny, 1990). This would see a reversal of the common onus of burden, whereby the state is usually seen as having to intervene in or against the market so as to ensure a decent life for all. By contrast, with a new arrangement, as desired by the Business Council of Australia (1991), the market would determine what the core business of government ought to be.

The Liberal Party of Australia announced that it intends to return income tax power to the states if they win the next federal election (Sydney Morning Herald, 07/09/91). It is difficult to see them actually implementing this in government. However, such a proposal is another indication of the centrifugal pressures working within Australian federalism in the post-Keynesian and post-welfare state era.

Conclusion

As outlined above, corporate federalism began to emerge in schooling policy-making with *National Policy for the Education of Girls* (1987), which had been arrived at through AEC negotiation and consultation. However, the clearest ar-ticulation of corporate federalism appears in *Strengthening Australia's Schools* (SAS) (Dawkins, May, 1988), which, while conceding that schooling is ostensibly the constitutional prerogative of the states, stresses the need for a national effort in schooling (Lingard and O'Brien, 1990). In SAS, Dawkins calls for a common set of national goals for schooling, a national curriculum framework, a better provi-sion for maths and science teaching, a common approach to assessment, a national reporting of educational achievement, and an increase in school retention rates. The AEC subsequently in 1989 agreed to a set of national goals and curriculum framework. The AEC creation of the Curriculum Corporation to oversee national curriculum formation is important here. Other developments are under way, including the AEC's Ebbeck Report which calls for a national approach to teacher education (Bartlett *et al.*, 1991, Lingard *et al.*, 1990). The latter development fits firmly within the framework of corporate federalism, and builds upon Dawkins creation of the unified national system of higher education, which weakened the mediating role of the states in relation to the former College of Advanced Edu-cation sector. As argued elsewhere (Bartlett *et al.*, 1991), federal control of teacher education would be an important linchpin in the move to a national system of schooling.

Corporate federalism has been Dawkins' strategy in schooling policy to cre-ate a national approach. Such a strategy has been necessitated by the constitutional reality but, perhaps more significantly, by the fact that schooling is a shared funding responsibility for both Commonwealth and state/territory governments, with the Commonwealth providing about 10 per cent of overall funding for schools. It needs to be noted, however, that in tight financial circumstances for the states those funds take on greater significance. Cooperation towards a national curriculum must also be seen in that context (Bartlett, Chapter 15, this volume).

The strategy is part of the economically spawned move in Australian schooling policy-making from a conjunctural to a structural policy rationale (Offe, 1985), with the emphasis now on accountable and better outcomes within a funding ceiling. The strategy is also part of the post-1987 economic restructuring agenda which attempts to create a national economic infrastructure so that Australia can compete successfully in a non-tariff protected fashion in the global economy.

Substantial debate is required about the move to corporate federalism outlined throughout this paper. Even more debate is required about future potential developments alluded to above. The real danger within corporate federalism in schooling policy formulation is the reframing of schooling as part of the micro-economic reform agenda. Education must have goals linked to equity, individual development and the common good (Porter, Chapter 3 this volume). Education worthy of the name must, *inter alia*, develop a critical citizenry. Perhaps the power teachers have to deflect imposed central approaches provides some protection here (Crump, 1991), as does the apparent incommensurability between the cultures of managerialism/economic rationalism and those of schools and classrooms. However, a debate is required about the desirable nature of Australian federalism and where schooling ought to fit within that overview. That consideration must move beyond the simple binary alternatives of more centralization or more decentralization. The positives and negatives of a national approach to schooling policy-making need to be considered against a backdrop of related political developments and Australia's location in the international economy. Questions of equity and participatory democracy are important here and need to be returned to an agenda which has disfigured schooling policy by regarding it merely as an economic tool.

Note

1   This chapter has been developed from an earlier one, 'Policy-making for Australian schooling: The new corporate federalism', which appeared in the *Journal of Education Policy*, **6**(1), No. 1, 1991, pp. 85–90.

References

BARTLETT, L., KNIGHT, J. and LINGARD, R. (1991) 'Corporate federalism and the reform of teacher education in Australia', *Journal of Education Policy*, **6**(1), pp. 91–95.

BUSINESS COUNCIL OF AUSTRALIA (1991) *Government in Australia in the 1990s: A Business Perspective*, Melbourne, Australia: Business Council of Australia.

CASTLES, F. (1988) *Australian Public Policy and Economic Vulnerability*, Sydney, Australia: Allen and Unwin.

CERNY, P. (1990) *The Changing Architecture of Politics: Structure, Agency and the Future of the State*, London, UK: Sage.

CONSIDINE, M. (1988) 'The corporate management framework as administrative science: A critique', *Australian Journal of Public Administration*, **47**(1), pp. 4–19.

CODD, J. (1990) 'Educational policy and the crises of the New Zealand State' in MIDDLETON, S., CODD, J. and JONES, A. (Eds) *New Zealand Education Policy Today*, Wellington, New Zealand, Allen and Unwin, pp. 191–205.

CRUMP, S. (1991) 'Pragmatic policy development: Problems and solutions in educational policy making', paper presented to the Australian Association for Research in Education Conference, Surfers Paradise, Australia, November).

DAWKINS, J. (1988) *Strengthening Australia's Schools*, Canberra, Australia: AGPS.

DAWKINS, J. (1990) Report, *The Australian*, Aug. 30.

FOGGO, D. (1990) 'Benchmarks and beyond', *The Australian Teacher*, **25**, pp. 14–16.

FOUCAULT, M. (1979) 'Truth and power', in MORRIS, M. and PATTON, P. (Eds) *Michel Foucault: Power, Truth, Strategy*, Sydney, Australia: Feral Publications, pp. 29–48.

GALLIGAN, B. (1989) 'Australian federalism: perceptions and issues', in GALLIGAN, B. (Ed.) *Australian Federalism*, Melbourne, Australia: Longman Cheshire, pp. 2–14.

HEAD, B. (Ed.) (1983) *State and Economy in Australia in Australia,* Melbourne, Australia: Oxford University Press.

HEAD, B. (1989) *Policy Making in Australian Federalism: The Corporatist Dimension*, Research paper No. 9, Griffith University, Brisbane, Australia: The Centre for Australian Public Sector Management.

INTERIM COMMITTEE OF SCHOOLS COMMISSION (1973) *Schools in Australia*, Canberra, Australia: AGPS.

KENWAY, J. (1990) *Gender and Education Policy: A Call for New Directions*, Geelong, Australia: Deakin University Press.

KNIGHT, J., LINGARD, R., PORTER, P. (1991) 'Re-forming the education industry through award restructuring and the New Federalism', *Unicorn*, **17**(3), pp. 133–38.

LIBERAL PARTY OF AUSTRALIA (1991) Report, *Sydney Morning Herald*, 7 Sept.

LINGARD, R. (1991) 'Policy-making for Australian Schooling: The new corporate federalism', *Journal of Education Policy*, **6**(1), pp. 85–90.

LINGARD, R. and O'BRIEN, P. (1990) 'Strengthening Australia's schools through corporate federalism', paper presented to the Australian Sociological Association Conference, The University of Queensland, December.

LINGARD, R., BARTLETT, V.L. and KNIGHT, J. (1990) 'Teacher education: Developments and context', *Australian Teacher*, **26**, pp. 20–4.

MADDOX, G. (1989) *The Hawke Government and Labor Tradition*, Ringwood, Australia: Penguin.

MARGINSON, S. (1989) 'Labor's economic objectives in higher education: Will they be achieved?', University of Melbourne, Australia: Centre for the Study of Higher Education, Spring Lecture Series, 1.

MATHEWS, R. (1977a) 'Foreword' in WILTSHIRE, K. (Ed.) *Administrative Federalism: Documents in Australian Intergovernmental Relations*, Australia, Brisbane: The University of Queensland Press, pp. ix–x.

MATHEWS, R. (1977b) 'Revenue sharing in Australian federalism', in JAENSCH, D. (Ed.) *The Politics of New Federalism*, Adelaide, Australia: Australian Political Studies Association pp. 43–54.

NBEET (1989) *Annual Report, 1988–89*, Canberra, Australia: AGPS.

OFFE, C. (1984) *Contradictions of the Welfare State*, London, Australia: Hutchinson.

OFFE, C. (1985) *Disorganised Capitalism*, Oxford, UK: Polity Press.

OFFE, C. (1975) 'The theory of the capitalist state and the problem of policy formation', in LINDBERG, L.N., ALFORD, R., CROUCH, C. and OFFE, C. (Eds) *Stress and Contradiction in Modern Capitalism,* Massachusetts: Lexington Books.

PUSEY, M. (1991) *Economic Rationalism in Canberra: A Nation Building State Changes its Mind*, Cambridge, UK: Cambridge University Press.

QUALITY OF EDUCATION REVIEW COMMITTEE (1985) *Quality of Education in Australia*, Canberra, Australia: AGPS.

RAMSEY, G. (1990) 'The need for national policies in education', *Unicorn*, **17**(1), pp. 34–41.

SCHMITTER, P. (1974) 'Still the century of corporatism?', *Reviews of Politics*, **36**.

SCHOOLS COMMISSION (1987) *National Policy for the Education of Girls*, Canberra, Australia: AGPS.

SMART, D. (1989) 'The Dawkins "reconstruction" of higher education in Australia', paper presented to American Educational Research Association Annual Meeting, San Francisco, CA.

SMART, D. (1991) 'Higher education policy in Australia: Corporate or coercive federalism?', *Journal of Education Policy*, **6**(1) pp. 97–100.

SWEET, R. (1989) 'A new economics of education?', *Unicorn*, **15**(3), pp. 133–38.

TANNOCK, P. and BIRCH, I. (1976) 'Constitutional responsibility for education in Australia: the federal government's latent power', in HARMAN, G.S. and SELBY SMITH, C. (Eds) *Readings in Economics and Politics of Australian Education*, Melbourne, Australia: Pergamon Press, pp. 32–9.

WHITE, D. (1987) *Education and the State: Federal Involvement in Educational Policy Development*, Geelong, Australia: Deakin University Press.

WHITLAM, E.G. (1986) *The Whitlam Government*, Ringwood, Australia: Penguin.

WILTSHIRE, K. (1986) *Planning and Federalism: Australian and Canadian Experience*, Brisbane, Australia: The University of Queensland Press.

YEATMAN, A. (1990) *Bureaucrats, Technocrats, Femocrats: Essays on the Contemporary Australian State*, Sydney, Australia: Allen and Unwin.

Chapter 3

Education, The Economy and Citizenship in Australia: Critical Perspectives and Social Choices

Paige Porter

Introduction

In 1729, the English writer, Jonathan Swift, satirized the notion of a monetary value being placed on human beings in an essay entitled 'A Modest proposal for preventing the children of poor people in Ireland, from being a burden to their parents or country; and for making them beneficial to the public':

> I have been assured by a very knowing American of my acquaintance in London: that a young healthy child, well nursed, is, at a year old, a most delicious, nourishing, and wholesome food; whether stewed, roasted, baked or boiled . . . . I do therefore offer it to public consideration, . . . that the remaining hundred thousand may, at a year old, be offered in sale to the persons of quality and fortune, through the kingdom; always advising the mother to let them suck plentifully in the last month, so as to render them plump, and fat for a good table.

> Whereas the maintenance of an hundred thousand children, from two years old, and upwards, cannot be computed at less than ten shillings a piece per annum, the nation's stock will be thereby increased fifty thousand pounds per annum; besides the profit of a new dish, introduced to the tables of all gentlemen of fortune in the kingdom, who have any refinement in taste; and the money will circulate among ourselves, the goods being entirely of our own growth and manufacture. (Swift, 1729, pp. 111–2, 115, quoted in Marginson 1989a, p. 3)

While I am not aware of any present governmental attempts to put children literally *into* the fast food business in 1991, it is increasingly common for governmental policy to place a monetary value on all human beings and their activities. It is also increasingly common to attempt to administer this policy within a framework of technical and instrumental rationality. Economic rationalism and corporate managerialism in the public sector in general, and in education in particular, are pervasive and powerful — but they are not neutral. They are recognisable as a configuration of power and like all power structures, they advantage some groups and disadvantage others. They also represent the extension of the logic of the market place up the steps and into the parliament, that is, into the realm of government whose sole *raison d'être* is to service the needs of its citizens. As citizens, we are entitled, some would say obligated, to question the assumptions, values, logic and usefulness of such pervasive perspectives in the public sphere. As educators, we must recognize the way these perspectives are dominating the discussions about educational restructuring, about the quality of teaching and learning, and about the future of the teaching profession. This chapter will attempt to critique the economic framing of the current education debate and reflect on the implications for the teaching profession.

Human Capital Theory and Education

There must be more than one Australian politician who occasionally regrets one of the more significant decisions of the nineteenth century: the decision by the state to take over the responsibility for education. That century had seen a long and frequently bitter struggle between different religious groups, and between those groups and others who believed that education should be a state function. It was the latter group who won the day. Their argument was that, what was called 'free, compulsory and secular' schooling, should be the right of all citizens and the responsibility of governments.

There were many arguments as to why such a right and responsibility should exist, but essentially it was believed that such education would contribute to the development of a people who believed in and abided by peace, order and good government. It was primarily this basic notion of citizenship, limited though it may have been, which motivated those who eventually succeeded in making education a government rather than private function, and hence laid the basis for understanding the public funding of education as a public good.

The idea that education has a *direct* relationship to the economy and, in particular, that it can be manipulated so as to significantly effect the economy, is quite recent. The concepts that students can be viewed as human capital, that teachers and lecturers are trainers, that schooling and higher education should be seen primarily as an investment for a competitive future, reflect a view of the role of education — and by implication of citizenship — which must be seen historically as very narrow. More commonly education has been viewed as having very broad functions and as playing multiple roles in both personal and public domains.

The early sixties saw the first wave of human capital theory when it was frequently argued then that the provision of and access to education at all levels was directly related to national economic growth. The measurement of this was usually done on an individual level, in that it was argued that increases in education levels of individuals were related to higher incomes and to a higher gross income over life. However, it was also argued that a significant effect of this was that countries with more highly educated populations were more economically productive (Blaug, 1970). Thus, education could be conceptualized not just as consumption but also as investment, and the public was urged to consider 'investing' in education.

Human capital theory, although it has several forms, basically assumes an economic rationalistic model of human behaviour. Simon Marginson has described the basic underlying assumptions of human capital theory as including the following ideas: 1) People are seen as calculating players who act to maximize their personal economic utility. 2) The only benefits of education are economic in that all benefits can be reduced to either consumption benefits or investment benefits. 3) The benefits of education are primarily individual. 4) The social benefits of education are no more than the sum of the individual benefits (Marginson, 1989a, pp. 1–2).

In the sixties it was often assumed that the enormous post-war expansion of schooling had contributed to the post-war economic boom. However, an analysis of the relationship does not display this with clarity. For example, the post-war economic boom may, in fact, have simply coincided with the growing ideology of individualism, with the developing faith in technological progress, and with the reality of increased international competition, all of which themselves supported a growth in mass public education. In other words, the expanded education provision during this period may actually have been more the result, rather than the cause, of the economic growth and cultural development in the post war era.

Despite the enthusiasm of the early sixties, the seventies and eighties saw a disillusionment with human capital theory, and also with the possibilities of the substantial public funding of education ameliorating the various economic and social — as well as educational — problems in the hoped-for ways. Indeed, education became seen as the problem. Presumably, if more education could contribute to a strong economy and social reforms, then a weak economy and unresolved social issues must reflect a poor education system.

More recently, however, we once again hear arguments that the increasing inability of developed western countries to compete in world markets, together with their low economic productivity levels, could be improved through the preparation of a more highly trained workforce. Education is now being reconstructed as the solution once again. Within this perspective the objectives of the sixties and eighties are basically the same, i.e., to expand the investment in human capital, but the emphasis is different. The sixties were inclined to stress more the value of the social investment in education at the public expense. The eighties has a more laissez-faire perspective with a much stronger emphasis on education as a private investment (Marginson, 1989a). One of the dangers of course is that if the theory is not accurate and does not reflect reality it will only be a matter of time until education is seen as the problem again.

Marginson has argued that the popularity of the theory amongst educational policy makers may actually be related to the way in which, rather than reflecting reality, the theory creates reality. He has pointed out that the investment concept of human capital theory has not been successful in international economic circles, such as national income accounting, where education is still viewed primarily as consumption, but it has been influential in national educational policy-making. Its success may be related to the way in which policies based on this view actually create the behaviours they assume. In other words producing this model in real life may be one of the objectives of the policy. For example, the Higher Education Contribution Scheme (HECS) may cause tertiary students to think more vocationally, and hence make choices more based on their perceptions of the eventual economic return of the particular courses, rather than on either their own particular interests or on the desire to acquire a broad general education (Marginson, 1989a, p. 22).

However, the reality is that there is actually very little research evidence to support the usefulness of a strong human capital theory in education. Indeed what research exists suggests that any effects may be very narrow and selective rather than broad and universal (Maglen, 1988; Marginson, 1989b). The problem is that politically the perception may be that there is simply no other game in town. Mr John Dawkins, Federal Minister for Education, in an OECD speech in 1988, commented that the renewed interest in human capital theory was due to the 'heightened recognition of the limits of *macro*economic policies to deal with the economic problems' and hence the greater attention being given again to *micro*economic theories (Dawkins, 1988, p. 1). Within this perspective education and training are seen as microeconomic tools for governments to refine. It is essential to understand that the education debate in Australia is overwhelmingly dominated by this perspective of education as a microeconomic tool. This direct relationship between education and the economy is the basic assumption underlying most federal policy and much state policy under both Labor and Liberal governments.

An important additional point about human capital theory which needs to be stressed is its gender bias. Like most other economic theories, it focuses almost entirely on the world of paid work, thereby ignoring both the gendered division of labour, and the multiple ways in which the unpaid labour of women supports the economy. As economic theories in general revolve around the notions of the production, distribution, and use of income, wealth and commodities, any activities in a society for which workers are not paid, nor goods exchanged, are difficult to deal with and typically ignored. Consequently, economic theories have little to do with the world of work in the home, in the volunteer area, in the servicing of men, children, the handicapped, and the aged, and thus the work of many women and its role in the economy.

There are numerous examples of this, such as the way that economists have described the so-called postwar 'working womans' revolution', in which women have been portrayed as entering the world of work for the first time *en masse*. As Matthews has pointed out, the reality is, that in the nineteenth century, women produced jams, breads, shirts, cared for children and did the family accounts out of sight. The main difference now is that in the twentieth century, women produce jams, breads, shirts, care for children and do the accounts, visibly and for money (Matthews, 1984). The gendered division of labor remains. Matthews has described this as a trick of perspective, not a radical change in womens' experiences.

> The trick lay in the definition of work, its nature and its place. By and large, masculine economists have classified as work only that which is clearly performed within the masculine capitalist market place — the commanding heights; that which is directly organised by the traditional processes of that marketplace — as in large corporate or state enterprises; and that which is defended by the traditional institutions of the male working class — the trade unions. But the commanding heights have never comprised the whole economy, the processes of large enterprises have never monopolised the ways of making a livelihood, and the trade unions have both inadvertently and deliberately excluded many workers from their protection. (Matthews, 1984, p. 55)

In the case of human capital theory in education, insofar as this perspective has tried to relate education levels to either individual or social income, or to national economic goals, it must be noted that it has never ever been conceptualised in relation to women in unpaid work. Nor has it ever attempted to account for the 'investment' in the education of girls who eventually marry and withdraw either permanently or sporadically from the paid workforce. Theoretically, they are unproductive while working in the domestic economy. Its explanatory power has been very debatable with regard to the work of many, particularly men, in the paid workforce, and it has entirely omitted the work of women in unpaid labour. Indeed, the concept of either a public or a private investment in education, when the differences in men and women's lives are taken into account, becomes unclear and its usefulness must be seriously questioned.

However, even though there is little research evidence of a direct relationship between education and the economy, and even though human capital theory would seem to exclude half of the human race, there may still be an indirect relationship which is worth exploring. David Tyack, an American historian, described what he termed the 'turning points' in American educational history which seemed to follow major changes in the economy. For example, in the early 20th century, industrialization and the development of large factories corresponded with the development of large urban education bureaucracies, and a movement in both towards standardization of production and control by bureaucratic managers. Developing corporate forms of the organization of work stressed greater division of labor, specialization, hierarchy, and supervision. American schooling followed corporate form and, combined with the need to coordinate mass immigration, educational reforms introduced more educational specialization, testing and measurement and streaming (Tyack, 1974).

Economic Trends and Their Implications for Education

One economist who tried to tease out the actual as opposed to theoretical relationship between the economy and education is Henry Levin of Stanford University. Levin has recently elaborated on the kinds of economic trends he sees as dominating our present era, and the future, and their implications for education and teacher education in all their forms. He describes these economic trends as: 1) the continuing development of internationalism; 2) the extension of new technologies; 3) the reorganization and restructuring of the workplace; and 4) the rise in 'at-risk' children or those who, due to a lack of resources in their homes and communities, are unlikely to succeed in schools (Levin, 1988). This is a potentially useful approach and I would like to explore Levin's analysis and extend it to Australia.

The first economic trend Levin identified is internationalism, or the extent to which the interconnections between national economies and the rest of the world have increased substantially (Levin, 1988, pp. 3–8). This can be observed in Australia in its balance of payments deficit, which basically reflects the situation that we purchase more from other countries than they purchase from us. It can also be observed in the Australian government's proportion of foreign debt, which means that we must borrow internationally to pay for the operation of our national (and state) programs. All of this means that we are increasingly dependent upon many other nations particularly nations other than those which dominated colonial and the immediate post-colonial Australia (i.e., the UK and USA). Australia's economic need for new international markets will arguably be acquired in direct relation to the international knowledge and skills of our own business people. On top of this is the increasing immigration from non-English speaking countries, especially Asia, with which Australia must clearly develop new relations.

All of this increases the need for Australian schooling to prepare youth for *both* operating in an increasingly multicultural society, and for becoming knowledgeable about other areas of the world with which we would do business. It also implies that teachers and students will need proficiency in foreign languages especially Asian languages; that both will need an adequate exposure to the history and culture of other countries; and that both will need a knowledge of world geography in terms of physical political, economic, and social features.

The second economic feature highlighted by Levin is the dramatic increase in the use of new technologies (such as computers, micro-processors, robots, electronics, biotechnology, materials science), both in the home and the workplace (Levin, 1988, pp. 8–12). These technologies — and the groups they empower or neglect — have both obvious and hidden characteristics, and are changing the way goods and services are produced and consumed in all aspects of our everyday life. One example of the covert operation of the new technologies has been identified by Connell (1990). He has drawn attention to the computer industry, and described the way in which, in its interaction with schools, the concept of private intellectual property may be strengthened at the expense of public knowledge. The logical extension of Connell's argument at the higher education level could mean that the traditional central function of the university as a producer of free public knowledge to be shared by all would disappear into the private marketplace. These covert messages embedded in the availability of technology which itself is embedded in the ideology of the marketplace need to be monitored.

However, it is apparent that such information-processing technology affects all areas of all of our lives and that future workers and citizens need to be technologically literate. The implications of these changes for education are clearly that all teachers and students will need to have a general understanding of the technology, and of its social, political and economic consequences, that they need to be familiar at least with the main common applications such as micro-computers and that they should also have some familiarity and experience with different types of instructional technologies.

The third economic trend lies at the heart of the present education debate; it is the restructuring and reorganization of the workplace (Levin, 1988, pp. 12–20). This is a term in common usage which applies to the education workplace for teachers as well as other workplaces. Levin's definition is most useful:

> Restructuring refers to changes in the workplace which alter the roles and skill requirements of workers. Largely in response to the challenges of economic competitiveness, firms are altering their organization and occupational roles in two ways. First, they are moving away from long production runs of standardized goods and services to flexible production of customised goods and services designed to meet the changing needs of particular clientele. Second, they are increasing the degree of worker participation in all major decisions of the firms, but especially in those that pertain to production. (Levin, 1988, p. 12)

This is the late twentieth century development which some economists have called 'post-fordism' after the image of Henry Ford's early twentieth century automobile assembly line. In other words we have moved past the assembly-line stage of economic development and are entering a new phase.

Customized production, where products are specifically made for discerning customers, is seen as a way for advanced industrial countries to exploit their own talents, thus leaving standardized production to the newly industrialized countries which can produce such goods much more cheaply. Customized production is facilitated by a highly educated, initiative-oriented and flexible workforce. It will require worker participation, or the reorganization of workers into teams or semi-autonomous work-groups with considerable delegated responsibilities. In this situation less supervision is required and the ability of workers to work both on their own and in groups, to coordinate, and to communicate is emphasized. Productivity has been shown to be increased through such organization in many areas. Another element of workplace restructuring involves the deregulation of a number of industries such as the banking, communications and the transportation industries. This involves a considerable loosening up of previously narrow occupational roles and encourages new flexibility in many associated jobs in these major industries with large workforces. These elements of workplace restructuring lie at the heart of the Hawke Labor governments' microeconomic reform agenda.

Restructuring the workplace requires proactive not reactive workers. The competencies that such workers will need, that teachers will need to be educated to encourage in students, that teachers will need to be able to exemplify as workers themselves in restructured schools, and that principals will need to foster, include the following: initiative; cooperation; the ability to work in groups; the ability to be involved in peer training; the ability to evaluate their own work; communication skills; reasoning; problem-solving abilities; decision-making abilities; the ability to obtain and use information; planning skills; and the ability to know how to learn (Levin, 1988, pp. 17–19).

The increase in children 'at-risk', or 'those who by virtue of a lack of resources in their homes and communities are unlikely to succeed in schools as they are currently constituted', is the fourth development Levin has identified which has serious economic consequences and, of course, important social consequences as well (Levin, 1988, pp. 21–3). Such students are on the increase, due to dwindling resources, and the current high levels of unemployment in Australia are accelerating this trend. It is apparent that many children do not participate adequately now in either education or the workplace. In addition to the obvious social and humane considerations, such children will increasingly have a negative impact on economic productivity and on training and education costs, not to mention the potential costs of the social welfare and the justice systems. The implications of these developments for teacher education are particularly important as the need grows to prepare teachers who can develop strategies at the school level, which will enable them to work closely with such students, their parents, and with other staff in flexible and intensive ways. The nation cannot afford, in any sense of the word, to allow an increasingly large section of the population to grow up as non-participants, alienated within their own society.

The purpose of spending so much time on this kind of detailed analysis of the relationship between the economy and education is to stress that, insofar as we understand the connections, they would seem to be more indirect than direct. Furthermore, they reflect the need for education to develop aspects of our culture at least as much as our economic activities. This analysis indicates the need for education to pursue the following objectives: a concentration on cultural learning in our own and other countries; the development of the ability to think, take initiative, solve problems and operate in groups; the acquisition of the knowledge, use and social consequences of new technologies; and an understanding of how to cater for groups who do not ordinarily participate fully in either education or the workforce. The picture of the ideal worker which comes through this notion of a restructured workplace is one with high levels of general education in a range of cultural and scientific areas, who can operate in the local, national and the international world with confidence, and who has the imagination to develop new markets, create new ideas and new products, and not simply fit into traditional or existing patterns.

These are not the implications of economic thinking that many educational policy makers in Australia have drawn. This picture is not always the image of the ideal worker, the ideal learner, nor the ideal teacher, nor of the relationship between the economy and education which is being promoted at this time in many Australian educational policies, particularly those emanating from the federal government. Yet a clever society that is trained but not educated, that cannot create knowledge but relies on importing it, that does not value learning and teaching but rather bureaucratizes them, and that does not see cultural development as closely connected to economic development is a contradiction in terms.

Economic Rationalism and the Corporate Management of Public Sector Schools

Hand in hand with the increasing use of a narrow human capital perspective on the relationship between education and the economy, has been the development of what is sometimes called economic rationalism and corporate managerialism in the public service including State departments and ministries of education. It is essential to understand the links between present schooling reforms, education restructuring across Australia, and public sector restructuring in general. Educators ignore these influences at their peril. What is happening in education is also happening in other government departments. Borrowed from sections of the corporate world, the new dominant managerialism developed partially as a response to economic hard times and to problems in the old style large centralized public service departments, and in particular to their ability — or inability — to solve problems. It also developed in conjunction with the increasing control of the executive arm over the legislative arm in Westminster systems.

The new direction involves a strategic approach based more on outputs rather than inputs, on results rather than processes, and can be recognized in the development of such things as corporate plans, mission statements, devolution, program budgeting, program evaluation, performance indicators, and performance appraisal. The concept of generic managerial skills is part of this approach as well, for example, the idea that managers can manage without substantial knowledge of the content area they are managing. The intention is to tighten up government performance in the interests of efficiency and effectiveness. Financial hard times are taken for granted. Getting more for less is a common theme. The 'efficient corporate state', rather than privatization policies, is seen as the best way for the state to attempt to balance the facilitation of the capital accumulation process and increasing demands for social and welfare services.

There is no doubt that reforms in the old style public service were long overdue, and that many of the innovations have resulted in useful changes, including the focus on achieving results rather than just operating programs, getting rid of unnecessary rules and over-heavy central offices, and greater efficiency. However, there are also dangers, most obviously in the potential for mechanistic, instrumental, undemocratic administration which has hidden rather than debated values, which ignores any ends which cannot be measured, which assumes that managers can manage independently of the knowledge and values they hold, and which neglects social justice and equity issues. Peter Wilenski, the former head of the Commonwealth Public Service Board, has argued recently that the approach, as embraced in some parts of the public service, in fact ignores the more recent developments in private sector management which actually stress leadership and caring rather than simply mechanistic management:

> The message of the business management texts is clear: hard times demand a complex and subtle blend of qualities — of self-knowledge and determination, of creativity, flexibility, intuitive decision-making and a nurturing disposition — rather than the ruthless simplicity of a Rambo or a Gordon Gekko. (Wilenski, 1988, p. 211)

Mark Considine (1988), in a thoughtful analysis of the corporate managerialist framework in the public sector, describes it as seriously flawed, primarily because it attributes the efficiency problem to one of control. He characterizes the framework as focusing on four features: a product format, instrumentalism, integration, and purposive action. The basic issues include the following:

1 The product format is inappropriate for many public services as it over values quantifiable outputs, and includes questionable attitudes about citizenship which reify citizens solely as economic agents (taxpayers and consumers).
2 Instrumentalism, by focusing on control as the issue, ignores important other political dimensions and denies other kinds of democratic input.
3 Integration tightens control primarily to politicians and senior managers, actually denies the stated value of decentralization, and contradicts private practice, especially in innovative areas, when duplication and fragmentation can be beneficial.
4 Purposive action reflects unwarranted optimism about technical rationality under central direction, and is first and foremost a governmental response to the economic crisis.

However, it also reflects a naive, simplistic, and even old-fashioned view of democracy which is potentially a threat to that very system, not the least because it has great appeal to a small number of key ministers in central portfolios (i.e., treasury and finance) who are able to use the premises to exercise their own control (Considine, 1988).

Equity, Citizenship, The Common Good and Education

There are substantial implications within both economic rationalism and corporate managerialism in the public sector for equity, for citizenship, and for conceptions of the common good, all areas of central concern in public education. In relation to equity, it is important to question the extent to which the values underlying the new managerialism are compatible with the goals of equity. Marian Sawer (1989) has documented the difficulties encountered federally in the Equal Employment Opportunity area and with the Sex Discrimination Act with the adoption of managerialism in the Commonwealth government. For example, the preference for performance indicators and for competencies in relation to government activities may be useful, but are not seen as sufficient to ensure social justice. This is because 'there is little room in the new managerialism for the concept of empowering the groups who are the targets of social justice strategies and enabling them to participate more effectively in the policy process and in evaluation' (Sawer, 1989, p. 148). Instead value-free managers, with portable management skills, seeking short term visible individualistic runs on the board are empowered. Sawer points out that 'Managerialism and collectivism do not seem to mix any more than managerialism and multiculturalism' (Sawer, 1989, p. 149).

In relation to citizenship and the common good, I would argue that the ultimate logical end of economic rationalistic conceptions of human behaviour is the dissolution of these notions. Citizenship implies reciprocal responsibilities between members of a group, especially with regard to care and protection. Democratic governments are structured so that citizens will have a voice in determining *both* the interests of the group in the first instance, *and* the outcomes of the group acting as a collectivity as the government. It is in this sense that consensual government must have a notion of the common good (even when neo-pluralistic perspectives and postmodern theories pull against it). Corporate managerialism in the public sector, together with economic rationalism, portrays itself as concerned simply with more cost-efficient means to democratically determined ends, but often actually determines the ends not just the means. To the extent that it does this, democracy is marginalized in the interests of a narrow definition of efficiency.

More particularly, education itself can easily be recognized as a common good and not just a private resource. As Connell has pointed out:

> My education is of course a resource for me. To that extent the 'human capital' folk have it right. But my education is also a resource for other people. My education affects the quality of life of the people I interact with in my life and work. That is a feature of education which cannot be commodified unless I charge a fee every time I open my mouth . . .

> That is to say in another way that education is a common good. We could go back to Plato, the first person who spelt out a theory of social justice and its connection with education, for the roots of that idea. Given that education is a common good as well as an individual good, its value depends not only on how it is distributed but also on what it qualitatively is.

... Because of what we know about the way the educational service is taken up by different social groups, and because of the character of education as a public good, I would argue that the content of education must be central to social justice issues. (Connell, 1990, p. 7)

The danger at the moment, of course, is that much of the current economic rationalist rhetoric would prefer to treat education not as a citizen right but as a commodity. Free market ideology commodifies all aspects of life, thereby preempting notions of citizen rights. The pragmatic veneer of free market ideology ('It's only about getting bread on tables in the most efficient and effective way . . .') masks its ideological base, thus side-stepping public debate about rights versus commodities.

In reality the increased complexity of the modern state is pushing democracy to its ultimate test. Simplistic notions, for example that democracy is ensured by elected governments, and that public bureaucracies neutrally implement the wishes of those governments, are no longer believed even by primary school students. The importance of finding new ways to democratize the modern state is one of the most important contemporary tasks of all citizens. Anna Yeatman, in her analysis of the modern administrative state, focuses on the vigorous advocacy of democratic values which will be required. She sees this as including 'open government, due process, natural justice, client-oriented public services, the participation of relevant publics in the development and delivery of services, equitable access to public services and to public employment . . .' (Yeatman, 1990, p. 48). She describes the ideal model as 'a partnership in democratic governance . . . which involves, along with the elected government of the day, the positive participation in the business of this governance of both the citizenry and public servants . . .' (Yeatman, 1990, p. 57).

Conclusion

The situation now in education is that narrow economic thinking in the form of the economic rationalism and corporate managerialism has the potential to stifle creative change in all levels of education. It also has the potential to stifle the ability of schools, colleges and universities to facilitate creative change in society. Unless we come to terms with this, it is not unlikely that a decade from now the so-called 'education industry' will once again be blamed for its supposed failures.

The realities are, in fact, that education is not the only player in the economic game, that it has an indirect and not direct relation to the economy, and that it has an equally crucial relationship to the development of culture. Cultural development also has a close relationship with economic development and both the cultural and the economic roles of schooling need to be recognised in the present education debate.

Furthermore, the exploration of new ways to democratize the complex late-twentieth century state is something that will not only affect the delivery of educational services to children and youth, but a task in which students can be actively involved. The role of the schools in facilitating the understanding of the importance and value of democratic processes is a project in which it is time to re-engage. 'Reflective morality' is the term used by John Dewey to indicate an intellectual process by which people in a democratic society might deal with and resolve political and social problems (Dewey, 1962). Reflective morality needs to be taught in schools as well as vocational skills for employment. The crucial feature of a public education system is, in fact, its contribution to the construction of citizenship and the common good in broad terms rather than the economy in narrow terms.

It is in the interaction of cultural, economic and democratic development that the future directions for education and education policy lie. It is likely that the only way society can benefit from more highly educated workers, and from the advance of new technologies, is to both increase worker initiative and discretion in the workplace and to facilitate citizen involvement in the administrative state. New technology does have the potential to further routinize work tasks, but it could also expand the decision-making role of workers so as to take advantage of their increased education and skill levels. This is because 'the organization of the modern workplace is based upon social and economic choices rather than being technologically determined. In this sense, a workplace with greater human challenges, worker discretion, and allocative efficiency is also one that is consistent with technological advance' (Levin, 1987, p. 210).

Similarly, the organization of the modern state is, in reality, based on social choices and is not determined solely by the present economic situation of scarce resources. Scarce resources may indicate competition, but situation does not dictate how that competition will be acted out. Nor are economic perspectives the only appropriate world view for the modern state. Concerns for equity, for social justice, for democratic processes and for the common good are at least as important. A government that is willing to grapple with greater human challenges, that has greater citizen involvement, and more distributive justice, is also one that is consistent with technological advance and economic productivity.

These are the choices that are presently facing us. The changes that eventually emerge in education from present initiatives will be remembered in the future as either reflecting a period when education contributed to the development of a routinized, non-participative workplace, as well as to a government in retreat from democracy — or a period when education contributed to the development of a workplace with greater opportunities for human initiative, discretion and participation, as well as to a government in which democracy was reconstructed, reflective morality rediscovered, and a new commitment made to the pursuit of a newly defined common good.

References

BLAUG, M. (1970) *Economics of Education*, Middlesex, UK: Penguin.

CONNELL, R.W. (1990) 'Curriculum and social justice', keynote address, presented to the 1990 Queensland Curriculum Conference, Brisbane, Australia: Griffith University.

CONSIDINE, M. (1988) 'The corporate management framework as administrative science: A critique', *Australian Journal of Public Administration*, **47**, 1, pp. 4–18.

DAWKINS, J.G. (1988) Opening Statement by the Chairman to OECD Intergovernmental Conference on Education and the Economy in a Changing Society, Canberra, Australia, 16 March.

DEWEY, J. (1962) *Reconstruction in Philosophy*, Boston, MA: Beacon Press.

LEVIN, H.M. (1987) 'Improving productivity through education and technology', in BURKE, G. and RUMBURGER, R. (Eds), *The Future Impact of Technology on Work and Education*. London, UK: Falmer Press.

LEVIN, H.M. (1988) *Economic Trends Shaping the Future of Teacher Education*. Stanford, CA: Center for Educational Research, Stanford University.

MAGLEN, L.R. (1988) *Challenging the Human Capital Orthodoxy: The Education-Productivity Link Re-examined*, Melbourne, Australia: Economics Department, Monash University.

MARGINSON, S. (1989a) 'Human capital theory and education policy', unpublished paper based on a lecture to the Social Policy course, University of New South Wales, Sydney, Oct.

MARGINSON, S. (1989b) 'Labor's economic objectives in higher education: Will they be achieved?', Study of Higher Education Spring Lecture Series, Melbourne, Australia: University of Melbourne.

MATTHEWS, J.J. (1984) *Good and Mad Women: The Historical Construction of Femininity in Twentieth Century Australia*, Sydney, Australia: Allen and Unwin.

SAWER, M. (1989) 'Efficiency, effectiveness and equity', in DAVIS, G., WELLER, P. and LEWIS, C. (Eds), *Corporate Management in Australia*, Melbourne, Australia: Macmillan, pp. 138–53.

TYACK, D.B. (1974) *The One Best System. A History of American Urban Education*, Cambridge, MA: Harvard University Press.

WILENSKI, P. (1988) 'Social change as a source of competing values in public administration,' Australian Journal of Public Administration, **XLVII**, 3, pp. 213–22.

Yeatman, A. (1990) *Bureaucrats, Technocrats, Femocrats: Essays on the Contemporary Australian State*. Sydney, Australia: Allen and Unwin.

Chapter 4

Thinking 'Right' in the USA:
Ideological Transformations
in an Age of Conservatism[1]

Michael W. Apple

Reconstructing Education

In many nations, a coalition of conservative forces is now resurgent in education. Yet, many discussions of this tendency have remained either overly abstract or have not situated it within the larger ideological conflicts that have occurred over the past decade. In this chapter, I shall provide a suggestive account of how and why this movement has been so successful. I shall take as my point of departure the Right's transformation of some of the major concepts we use to form and evaluate educational policy and practice.

Concepts do not remain still very long. They have wings, so to speak and can be induced to fly from place to place. It is this context that defines their meaning. As Wittgenstein (1973) so nicely reminded us, one should look for the meaning of language in its specific contextual use. This is especially important in understanding political and educational concepts, since they are part of a larger social context, a context that is constantly shifting and is subject to severe ideological conflicts. Education itself is an arena in which these ideological conflicts work themselves out. It is one of the major sites in which different groups with distinct political, economic, and cultural visions attempt to define what the socially legitimate means and ends of a society are to be.

In this chapter, I want to situate the concern with equality in education within these larger conflicts. I shall place its shifting meanings both within the breakdown of the largely liberal consensus that guided much educational and social policy since World War II and within the growth of the New Right and conservative movements over the past two decades that have had a good deal of success in redefining what education is for and in shifting the ideological texture of the society profoundly to the right. (See Apple, 1988b; Giroux, 1984.) In the process, I want to document how new social movements gain the ability to redefine (often, though not always, in retrogressive ways) the terms of debate in education, social welfare, and other areas of the common good. At root, my claim will be that it is impossible to fully comprehend the shifting fortunes of the assemblage of concepts surrounding equality (equality of opportunity, equity, etc.) unless we have a much clearer picture of the society's already unequal cultural, economic, and political dynamics that provide the centre of gravity around which education functions.

As I have argued at considerably greater length elsewhere, what we are witnessing today is nothing less than the recurrent conflict between 'property rights' and 'person rights' that has been a central tension in our economy (Apple, 1985, 1988a,b). Gintis (1980, p. 194) defines the differences between property rights and person rights in the following way:

> A 'property right' vests in individuals the power to enter into social relationships on the basis and extent of their property. This may include economic rights of unrestricted use, free contract, and voluntary exchange; political rights of participation and influence, and cultural rights of access to the social means for the transmission of knowledge and the reproduction and transformation of consciousness. A 'person right' vests in individuals the power to enter into these social relationships on the basis of simple membership in the social collectivity.

It is not surprising that in our society dominant groups 'have fairly consistently defended the prerogatives of property,' while subordinate groups on the whole have sought to advance 'the prerogatives of persons' (Gintis, 1980). (See also Bowles and Gintis, 1986.) In times of severe upheaval, these conflicts become even more intense and, given the current balance of power in society, advocates of property rights have once again been able to advance their claims for the restoration and expansion of their prerogatives, not only in education but in all of our social institutions.

The United States' economy is in the midst of one of the most powerful structural crises it has experienced since the depression. In order to solve it on terms acceptable to dominant interests, as many aspects of the society as possible need to be pressured into conforming with the requirements of international competition, reindustrialization, and (in the words of the National Commission on Excellence in Education) 'rearmament'. The gains made by women and men in employment, health and safety, welfare programs, affirmative action, legal rights, and education must be rescinded since 'they are too expensive' both economically and ideologically.

Both of these latter words are important. Not only are fiscal resources scarce (in part because current policies transfer them to the military), but people must be convinced that their belief that person rights come first is simply wrong or outmoded given current 'realities'. Thus, intense pressure must be brought to bear through legislation, persuasion, administrative rules, and ideological manoeuvring to create the conditions right wing groups believe are necessary to meet these requirements (Apple, 1988b).

In the process, not just in the United States, but in Britain, Australia and New Zealand as well, the emphasis of public policy has materially changed from issues of employing the state to overcome disadvantage. Equality, no matter how limited or broadly conceived, has become redefined. No longer is it seen as linked to past *group* oppression and disadvantagement. It is simply now a case of guaranteeing *individual choice* under the conditions of a free market (Anderson, 1985, pp. 6–8). Thus, the current emphasis on excellence (a word with multiple meanings and social uses) has shifted educational discourse so that underachievement is once again increasingly seen as largely the fault of the student. Student failure, which was at least partly interpreted as the fault of severely deficient educational policies and practices, is now being seen as the result of what might be called the biological and economic marketplace. This is evidenced in the growth of forms of Social Darwinist thinking in education and in public policy in general (Bastian, Fruchter, Gittell, Greer and Haskins, 1986, p. 14). In a similar way, behind a good deal of the rhetorical artifice of concern about the achievement levels in, say, inner city schools, notions of choice have begun to evolve in which deep-seated school problems will be solved by establishing free competition over students. These assume that by expanding the capitalist marketplace to schools, we will somehow compensate for the decades of economic and educational neglect experienced by the communities in which these schools are found. (I wish to thank my colleague Walter Secada for his comments on this point.) Finally, there are concerted attacks on teachers (and curricula) based on a profound mistrust of their quality and commitments.

All of this has led to an array of educational conflicts that have been instrumental in shifting the debates over education profoundly to the right. The effects of this shift can be seen in a number of educational policies and proposals now gaining momentum throughout the US: 1) proposals for voucher plans and tax credits to make schools more like the idealized free market economy; 2) the movement in state legislatures and state departments of education to raise standards and mandate both teacher and student competencies and basic curricular goals and knowledge, thereby centralizing even more at a state level the control of teaching and curricula; 3) the increasingly effective assaults on the school curriculum for its supposedly anti-family and anti-free enterprise bias, its secular humanism, its lack of patriotism, and its neglect of the character traits, dispositions and culture of the western tradition; and 4) the growing pressure to make the needs of business and industry into the primary goals of the educational system (Apple, 1986, pp. 171–90). These are major alterations, ones that have taken years to show their effects. Though I shall paint in rather broad strokes here, an outline of the social and ideological dynamics of how this has occurred should be visible.

The Restoration Politics of Authoritarian Populism

The first thing to ask about an ideology is not what is false about it, but what is true. What are its connections to lived experience? Ideologies, properly conceived, do not dupe people. To be effective they must connect to real problems, real experiences (Apple, 1990; Larrain, 1983). As I shall document, the movement away from social democratic principles to an acceptance of more right-wing positions in social and educational policy occurs precisely because conservative groups have been able to work on popular sentiments, to reorganize genuine feelings, and in the process to win adherents.

Important ideological shifts take place not only by powerful groups 'substituting one, whole, new conception of the world for another'. Often, those shifts occur through the presentation of novel combinations of old and new elements (Hall, 1985, p. 122). Let us take the positions of the Reagan administration as a case in point, for as Clark and Astuto (1986) have demonstrated in education, and Piven and Cloward (1982) and Raskin (1986) have shown in the larger areas of social policy, significant and enduring alterations have occurred in the ways policies are carried out and in the content of those policies. Clark and Astuto point out that during the Reagan term, the following initiatives have characterized its educational policies: reducing the federal role in education; stimulating competition among schools with the aim of 'breaking the monopoly of the public school'; fostering individual competition so that 'excellence' is gained; increasing the reliance on performance standards for students and teachers; an emphasis on the 'basics' in content; increasing parental choice 'over what, where, and how their children learn'; strengthening the teaching of 'traditional values' in schools; and expanding the policy of transferring educational authority to the state and local levels (p. 8).

The success of the policies of the Reagan administration and those of Bush, who has largely continued them, like that of Thatcherism in Britain, should not simply be evaluated in electoral terms. They need to be judged by their success as well in disorganizing other more progressive groups, in shifting the terms of political, economic and cultural debate onto the terrain favoured by capital and the right (Hall and Jacques, 1983, p. 13). In these terms, there can be no doubt that the current right wing resurgence has accomplished no small amount in its attempt to construct the conditions that will put it in a hegemonic position.

The right in the United States and Britain has thoroughly renovated and reformed itself. It has developed strategies based upon what might best be called an 'authoritarian populism' (Hall, 1980, pp. 160–1). (I realise there is a debate about the adequacy of this term. See Hall, 1985; and Jessop, Bonnett, Bromley and Ling, 1984.) As Hall has defined this, such a policy is based on an increasingly close relationship between government and the capitalist economy, a radical decline in the institutions and power of political democracy, and attempts at curtailing liberties that have been gained in the past. This is coupled with attempts to build a consensus, one that is widespread, in support of these actions (Hall, 1980, p. 161). The New Right's authoritarian populism has exceptionally long roots in the history of the United States. The political culture here has always been influenced by the values of the dissenting Protestantism of the seventeenth century. Such roots become even more evident in periods of intense social change and crisis (Omi and Winant, 1986, p. 214).

The New Right works on these roots in creative ways, modernizing them and creating a new synthesis of their varied elements by linking them to current fears. In so doing, the Right has been able to rearticulate traditional political and cultural themes and because of this has effectively mobilized a large amount of mass support.

As I noted, part of the strategy has been the attempted dismantling of the welfare state and of the benefits that working people, people of color, and women (these categories are obviously not mutually exclusive) have won over decades of hard work. This has been done under the guise of anti-statism, of keeping government off the backs of the people, and of free enterprise. Yet, at the same time, in many valuative, political, and economic areas, the current government is extremely state-centrist both in its outlook, and very importantly in its day to day operations (Hall, 1985, p. 117).

One of the major aims of a Rightist restoration politics is to struggle in not one but many different arenas at the same time, not only in the economic sphere but in education and elsewhere as well. This aim is grounded in the realization that economic dominance must be coupled to 'political, moral, and intellectual leadership' if a group is to be truly dominant and if it wants to genuinely restructure a social formation. Thus, as both Reaganism and Thatcherism recognized so clearly, to win in the state you must also win in civil society (Hall, 1984, p. 117). As the noted Italian political theorist, Antonio Gramsci, would put it, what we are seeing is a war of position. 'It takes place where the whole relation of the state to civil society, to "the people" and to popular struggles, to the individual and to the economic life of society has been thoroughly reorganised, where "all the elements change" ' (Hall, 1980, p. 166).

The Right then has set itself an immense task, to create a truly 'organic ideology', one that seeks to spread throughout society and to create a new form of national popular will. It seeks to intervene 'on the terrain of ordinary, contradictory common-sense', to 'interrupt, renovate and transform in a more systematic direction' people's practical consciousness. It is this restructuring of common-sense, which is itself the already complex and contradictory result of previous struggles and accords, which becomes the object of the cultural battles now being waged (Hall, 1988, p. 55).

In this restructuring, Reaganism and Thatcherism did not create some sort of false consciousness, creating ways of seeing that had little connection with reality. Rather, they 'operated directly on the real and manifestly contradictory experiences' of a large portion of the population. They did connect with the perceived needs, fears, and hopes of groups of people who felt threatened by the range of problems associated with the crises in authority relations, in the economy, and in politics (Hall and Jacques, 1983, p. 19–39; see Hunter, 1984).

What has been accomplished has been a successful translation of an economic doctrine into the language of experience, moral imperative, and common sense. The free market ethic has been combined with a populist politics. This has meant the blending together of a rich mix of themes that have had a long history (nation, family, duty, authority, standards and traditionalism) with other thematic elements that have also struck a resonant chord during a time of crisis. These latter themes include self interest, competitive individualism (what I have elsewhere (Apple, 1985) called the possessive individual), and anti-statism. In this way, a reactionary common sense is partly created (Hall, 1983, pp. 29–30).

The sphere of education has been one of the most successful areas in which the Right has been ascendant. The social democratic goal of expanding equality of opportunity (itself a rather limited reform) has lost much of its political potency and its ability to mobilize people. The panic over falling standards and illiteracy, the fears of violence in schools, the concern with the destruction of family values and religiosity, all have had an effect. These fears are exacerbated, and used, by dominant groups within politics and the economy who have been able to move the debate on education (and all things social) onto their own terrain, the terrain of standardization, productivity and industrial needs (Hall, 1983, pp. 36–7). Since so many parents are justifiably concerned about the economic futures of their children, in an economy that is increasingly conditioned by lowered wages, unemployment, capital flight, and insecurity (Apple, 1988b), rightist discourse connects with the experiences of many working-class and lower-middle-class people.

However, while this conservative conceptual and ideological apparatus does appear to be rapidly gaining ground, one of the most critical issues remains to be answered. How *is* such an ideological vision legitimated and accepted? How was this done (Jessop *et al.*, 1984, p. 49)?

Understanding the Crisis

The right-wing resurgence is not simply a reflection of the current crisis. Rather, it is itself a response to that crisis (Hall, 1983, p. 21). Beginning in the immediate post-World War II years, the political culture of the United States was increasingly characterized by American imperial might, economic affluence, and cultural optimism. This period lasted for more than two decades. Socially and politically, it was a time of what has been called the 'social democratic accord', in which government increasingly became an arena for a focus on the conditions required for equality of opportunity. Commodity-driven prosperity, the extension of rights and liberties to new groups, and the expansion of welfare provisions provided the conditions for this compromise between capital and labor, and with historically more dispossessed groups such as blacks and women. This accord has become mired in crisis since the late 1960s and early 1970s (Hunter, 1987).

At the very centre of this hegemonic accord was a compromise reached between capital and labor in which labor accepted what might be called 'the logic of profitability and markets as the guiding principles of resource allocation'. In return they received 'an assurance that minimal living standards, trade union rights and liberal democratic rights would be protected' (Bowles, 1982, p. 51). These democratic rights were further extended to the poor, women, and people of color as these groups expanded their own struggles to overcome racially and sexually discriminatory practices (Hunter, 1987, p. 12). Yet, this extension of (limited) rights could not last, given the economic and ideological crises that soon beset American society, a set of crises that challenged the very core of the social democratic accord.

The dislocations of the 1960s and 1970s — the struggle for racial and sexual equality, military adventures such as Vietnam, Watergate, the resilience of the economic crisis — produced both shock and fear. Mainstream culture was shaken to its very roots in many ways. Widely shared notions of family, community, and nation were dramatically altered. Just as importantly, no new principle of cohesion emerged that was sufficiently compelling to recreate a cultural center. As economic, political, and valuative stability (and military supremacy) seemed to disappear, the polity was itself 'balkanised'. Social movements based on difference (regional, racial, sexual, religious) became more visible (Omi and Winant, 1986, pp. 214–5). The sense of what Marcus Raskin (1986) has called 'the common good' was fractured.

Traditional-social democratic 'statist' solutions, which in education, welfare, health and other similar areas took the form of large scale attempts at federal intervention to increase opportunities or to provide a minimal level of support, were seen as being part of the problem not as part of the solution. Traditional conservative positions were more easily dismissed as well. After all, the society on which they were based was clearly being altered. The cultural center could be built (and it had to be built by well-funded and well-organized political and cultural action) around the principles of the New Right. The New Right confronts the 'moral, existential, [and economic] chaos of the preceding decades' with a network of exceedingly well organized and financially secure organizations incorporating 'an aggressive political style, on outspoken religious and cultural traditionalism and a clear populist commitment' (Omi and Winant, 1986, pp. 215–6).

In different words, the project was aimed at constructing a 'new majority' that would 'dismantle the welfare state, legislate a return to traditional morality, and stem the tide of political and cultural dislocation which the 1960s and 1970s represented'. Using a populist political strategy (now in combination with an aggressive executive branch of the government), it marshalled an assault on 'liberalism and secular humanism' and linked that assault to what some observers have argued was 'an obsession with individual guilt and responsibility where social questions are concerned (crime, sex, education, poverty)' together with strong beliefs against government intervention (Omi and Winnant, 1986, p. 220).

The class, racial, and sexual specificities here are significant. The movement to create a conservative cultural consensus in part builds on the hostilities of the working and lower-middle classes toward those above and below them and is fuelled as well by a very real sense of antagonism against the new middle class. State bureaucrats and administrators, educators, academics, journalists, planners, and so on, all share part of the blame for the social dislocations these groups have experienced (Omi and Winant, 1986, p. 220). Race, gender, and class themes abound here, a point to which I shall return in the next section of my analysis.

This movement is of course enhanced within academic and government circles by a group of policy-oriented neo-conservatives who have become the organic intellectuals for much of the rightist resurgence. Currents running deep in their work include a society based on individualism, market-based opportunities, and the drastic reduction of both state intervention and state support (Omi and Winant, 1986, p. 227). They provide a counterpart to the New Right and are themselves part of the inherently unstable alliance that has been formed.

Building the New Accord

Almost all of the reform-minded social movements (including the feminist, gay and lesbian, student and other movements of the 1960s) drew upon the struggle by blacks 'as a central organizational fact or as a defining political metaphor and inspiration' (Omi and Winant, 1986, p. 164). These social movements infused new social meanings into politics, economics, and culture. These are not separate spheres. All three of these levels exist simultaneously. New social meanings about the importance of person rights infused individual identity, family, and community, and penetrated state institutions and market relationships. These emerging social movements expanded the concerns of politics to all aspects of the 'terrain of everyday life'. Person rights took on ever more importance in nearly all of our institutions, as evidenced in aggressive affirmative action programs, widespread welfare and educational activist programs, and so on (Omi and Winant, 1986, p. 164). (See Bowles and Gintis, 1986, on the 'transportability' of struggle over 'person rights' from politics to the economy for example; see also Apple, 1988.) In education this was very clear in the growth of bilingual programs and in the development of women's, black, Hispanic, and Native American studies in high schools and colleges.

There are a number of reasons the state was the chief target of these earlier social movements for gaining person rights. First, the state was the 'factor of cohesion in society' and had historically maintained and organized practices and policies that embodied the tension between property rights and person rights (Apple, 1985, 1988). As such a factor of cohesion, it was natural to focus on it.

Second, 'the state was traversed by the same antagonisms which penetrated the larger society, antagonisms that were themselves the results of past cycles of [social] struggle.' Openings in the state could be gained because of this. Footholds in state institutions dealing with education and social services could be deepened (Omi and Winant, 1986, pp. 177–8).

Yet even with these gains, the earlier coalitions began to disintegrate. In the minority communities, class polarization deepened. The majority of barrio and ghetto residents 'remained locked in poverty', while a relatively small portion of the black and brown population were able to take advantage of educational opportunities and new jobs (the latter being largely within the state itself) (Omi and Winant, 1986, pp. 177–8). With the emerging crisis in the economy, something of a zero-sum game developed in which progressive social movements had to fight over a limited share of resources and power. Antagonistic rather than complementary relationships developed among groups. Minority groups, for example, and the largely white and middle-class women's movement had difficulty integrating their programs, goals and strategies.

This was exacerbated by the fact that, unfortunately, given the construction of a zero-sum game by dominant groups, the gains made by women sometimes came at the expense of blacks and browns. Furthermore, leaders of many of these movements had been absorbed into state sponsored programs which (while the adoption of such programs was in part a victory) had the latent effect of cutting off leaders from their grass roots constituency and lessened the militancy at this level. This often resulted in what has been called the 'ghettoization' of movements within state institutions as movement demands were partly adopted in their most moderate forms into programs sponsored by the state. Militancy is transformed into constituency (Omi and Winant, 1986, p. 180).

The splits in these movements occurred as well because of strategic divisions, divisions that were paradoxically the results of the movements' own successes. Thus, for example, those women who aimed their work within existing political/economic channels could point to gains in employment with the state and in the economic sphere. Other, more radical, members saw such progress as too little, too late.

Nowhere is this more apparent than in the black movement in the United States. Even though there were major gains, much of the movement became a 'mere constituency', 'locked into a bear-hug with state institutions' (Omi and Winant, 1986, p. 190; Apple, 1989). Yet, the movement's integration into the state latently created conditions that were disastrous in the fight for equality. A mass-based militant grass-roots movement was defused into a constituency, dependent on the state itself. And very importantly, when the neoconservative and Right-Wing movements evolved with their decidedly anti-statist themes, the gains that were made in the state come increasingly under attack and the ability to recreate a large scale grass roots movement to defend these gains was weakened considerably (Omi and Winant, 1986, p. 190). Thus, when there are right-wing attacks on the more progressive national and local educational policies and practices that have benefited people of color, it becomes increasingly difficult to develop broad-based coalitions to counter these offensives.

In their failure to consolidate a new radical democratic politics, one with majoritarian aspirations, the new social movements of the 1960s and 1970s 'provided the political space in which right-wing reaction could incubate and develop its political agenda (Omi and Winant, 1986, p. 252). Thus, state reforms won by minority movements in the 1960s in the United States, and the new definitions of 'person rights' embodied in these reforms, 'provided a formidable range of targets for the "counter-reformers" of the 1970s'. Neoconservatives and the New Right carried on their own political project. They were able to rearticulate particular ideological themes and to restructure them around a political movement once again (Omi and Winant, 1986, p. 155). These themes were linked to the dreams, hopes and fears of many individuals.

Let us examine this in somewhat more detail. Behind the conservative restoration is a clear sense of loss: of control, of economic and personal security, of the knowledge and values that should be passed on to children, of visions of what counts as sacred texts and authority. The binary opposition of we/they becomes very important here. *We* are law abiding, 'hard working, decent, virtuous, and homogeneous'. The *theys* are very different. They are 'lazy, immoral, permissive, heterogenous' (Hunter, 1987, p. 23). These binary oppositions distance most people of color, women, gays, and others from the community of worthy individuals. The subjects of discrimination are now no longer those groups who have been historically oppressed, but are instead the 'real Americans' who embody the idealized virtues of a romanticized past. The *theys* are undeserving. They are getting something for nothing. Policies supporting them are 'sapping our way of life', most of our economic resources, and creating government control of our lives (Hunter, 1987, p. 30).

These processes of ideological distancing make it possible for anti-black and anti-feminist sentiments to seem no longer racist and sexist because they link so closely with other issues (Hunter, 1987, p. 33). All of these elements can be integrated through the formation of ideological coalitions that enable many Americans who themselves feel under threat to turn against groups of people who are even less powerful than themselves. At the very same time, it enables them to 'attack domination by liberal, statist elites' (Hunter, 1987, p. 34).

This ability to identify a range of 'others' as enemies, as the source of the problems, is very significant. One of the major elements in this ideological formation has indeed been a belief that liberal elites within the state 'were intruding themselves into home life, trying to impose their values'. This was having serious negative effects on moral values and on traditional families. Much of the conservative criticism of textbooks and curricula rests on these feelings, for example. While this position certainly exaggerated the impact of the liberal elite, and while it certainly misrecognized the power of capital and of other dominant classes (Hunter, 1987, p. 21), there was enough of an element of truth in it for the Right to use it in its attempts to dismantle the previous accord and build its own.

A new hegemonic accord is reached, then. It combines dominant economic and political elites intent on modernizing the economy, white working-class and middle-class groups concerned with security, the family, and traditional knowledge and values, and economic conservatives (Hunter, 1987, p. 37). It also includes a fraction of the new middle class whose own advancement depends on the expanded use of accountability, efficiency, and management procedures which are their own cultural capital (Apple, 1986, 1988b). This coalition has partly succeeded in altering the very meaning of what it means to have a social goal of equality. The citizen as free consumer has replaced the previously emerging citizen as situated in structurally generated relations of domination. Thus, the common good is now to be regulated exclusively by the laws of the market, free competition, private ownership, and profitability. In essence, the definitions of freedom and equality are no longer democratic, but *commercial* (Hall, 1986, pp. 35–6). This is particularly evident in the proposals for voucher plans as solutions to massive and historically rooted relations of economic and cultural inequality.

This ideological reconstruction is not imposed on unthinking subjects. It is not done through the use of some right-wing attempt at what Paulo Freire has called 'banking', where knowledge and ideologies become common sense simply by pouring them into the heads of people. The ruling or dominant conceptions of the world and of everyday life 'do not directly prescribe the mental content of the illusions that supposedly fill the heads of the dominated classes (Hall, 1988, p. 45). However, the meanings, interests, and languages we construct are bound up in the unequal relations of power that do exist. To speak theoretically, the sphere of symbolic production is a contested terrain just as other spheres of social life are. 'The circle of dominant ideas does accumulate the symbolic power to map or classify the world for others', to set limits on what appears rational and reasonable, indeed on what appears sayable and thinkable (Hall, 1988, p. 45). This occurs *not* through imposition, but through creatively working on existing themes, desires, and fears and reworking them. Since the beliefs of people are contradictory and have tensions because they are what some have called polyvocal (Mouffe, 1988, p. 96), it is then possible to move people in directions that one would least expect given their position in society.

Thus, popular consciousness can be articulated to the right precisely because the feelings of hope and despair and the logic and language used to express these are 'polysemic' and can be attached to a variety of discourses. Hence, a male worker who has lost his job can be antagonistic to the corporations who engaged in capital flight or can blame unions, people of color, or women 'who are taking men's jobs'. The response is constructed, not preordained, by the play of ideological forces in the larger society (Mouffe, 1988, p. 96). And, though this construction occurs on a contradictory and contested terrain, it is the right that seems to have been more than a little successful in providing the discourse that organizes that terrain.

Will the Right Succeed?

So far I have broadly traced out many of the political, economic, and ideological reasons that the social democratic consensus that led to the limited extension of 'person rights' in education, politics, and the economy being slowly disintegrated. At the same time, I have documented how a new 'hegemonic bloc' is being formed, coalescing around New Right tactics and principles. The question remains: Will this accord be long lasting? Will it be able to inscribe its principles into the very heart of the American polity?

There are very real obstacles to the total consolidation within the state of the New Right political agenda. First, there has been something of a 'great transformation' in racial identities (Omi and Winant, 1986, p. 165). Thus, even when social movements and political coalitions are fractured, when their leaders are co-opted, repressed, and sometimes killed, the racial subjectivity and self-awareness that were developed by these movements has taken permanent hold. 'No amount of repression or cooptation [can] change that.' In Omi and Winant's (1986, p. 166) words, the genie is out of the bottle. This is the case because, in essence, a new kind of person has been created within minority communities. (I say *new* here, but the continuity of racial struggles for freedom and equality also needs to be stressed. See Harding, 1981.) A new, and much more self-conscious, *collective* identity has been forged. Thus, for instance, in the struggles over the past three decades by people of color to have more control of education and to have it respond more directly to their own culture and collective histories, these people themselves were transformed in major ways. (See Hogan, 1982, pp. 32–78 for a discussion in relation to class dynamics.) These transformations will make it exceedingly difficult for the Right to incorporate the perspectives of people of color under its ideological umbrella and will continually create oppositional tendencies within the black and brown communities. The slow, but steady, growth in the power of people of colour at a local level in these communities will serve as a countervailing force to the solidification of the new conservative accord.

Added to this is the fact that, even within the new hegemonic bloc, even within the conservative restoration coalition, there are ideological strains that may have serious repercussions on its ability to be dominant for an extended period. These tensions are partly generated because of the class dynamics within the coalition. Fragile compromises may come apart because of the sometimes directly contradictory beliefs held by many of the partners in the new accord.

This can be seen in the example of two of the groups now involved in supporting the accord. There are both what can be called *residual* and *emergent* ideological systems or codes at work here. The residual culture and ideologies of the old middle class and of an upwardly mobile portion of the working class and lower middle-class (stressing control, individual achievement, 'morality', etc.) has been merged with the emergent code of a portion of the new middle class (getting ahead, technique, efficiency, bureaucratic advancement) (Apple, 1986).

These codes are in an inherently unstable relationship. The stress on new right morality does not necessarily sit well with an amoral emphasis on careerism and economic norms. The merging of these codes can last only as long as paths to mobility are not blocked. The economy must pay-off in jobs and mobility for the new middle class or the coalition is threatened. There is no guarantee, given the unstable nature of the economy and the kinds of jobs being created, that this pay off will occur (Apple, 1988b; Carnoy, Shearer & Rumberger, 1984).

This tension can be seen in another way which shows again that, in the long run, the prospects of such a lasting ideological coalition are not necessarily good. Under the new, more conservative accord, the conditions for capital accumulation and profit must be enhanced by state activity as much as possible. Thus, the free market must be set loose. As many areas of public and private life as possible need to be brought into line with such privatized market principles, including the schools, health-care, welfare, housing, and so on. Yet, in order to create profit, capitalism by and large also requires that traditional values are subverted. Commodity purchasing and market relations become the norm and older values of community; 'sacred knowledge', and morality will need to be cast aside. This dynamic sets in motion the seeds of possible conflicts in the future between the economic modernizers and the New Right cultural traditionalists who make up a significant part of the coalition that has been built (Apple, 1986). (See also Levine, 1984.) Furthermore, the competitive individualism now being so heavily promoted in educational reform movements in the United States may not respond well to traditional working-class and poor groups' somewhat more collective senses.

Finally, there are counter-hegemonic movements now being built within education itself. The older, social democratic accord included many educators, union leaders, minority group members, and others. There are signs that the fracturing of this coalition may be only temporary. Take teachers, for instance: even though salaries have been on the rise throughout the country, this has been countered by a rapid increase in the external control of teachers' work, the rationalization and deskilling of their jobs, and the growing blame of teachers and education in general for most of the major social ills that beset the economy (Apple, 1985, 1988b). Many teachers have organized around these issues, in a manner reminiscent of the earlier work of the Boston Women's Teachers' Group. (See Freedman, Jackson, and Boles, 1982.) Furthermore, there are signs throughout the country of multiracial coalitions being built among elementary and secondary school teachers, university-based educators, and community members to collectively act on the conditions under which teachers work and to support the democratization of curriculum and teaching and a rededication to the equalization of access and outcomes in schooling. The Rethinking Schools group based in Milwaukee provides one example. (See Apple, 1988; Bastian, *et al.*, 1986; Livingstone, 1987.)

Even given these emerging tensions within the conservative restoration and the development once again of alliances to counter the attempted reconstruction of the politics and ethics of the common good, this does not mean we should be at all sanguine. It is possible that, because of these tensions and counter movements, the Right's economic program will fail. Yet its ultimate success may be in shifting the balance of class forces considerably to the right and in changing the very ways we consider the common good (Hall, 1983, p. 120). Privatization, profit, and greed may still substitute for any serious collective commitment.

We are, in fact, in danger of forgetting both the decades of hard work it took to put even a limited vision of equality on the social and educational agenda and of the reality of the oppressive conditions that exist for so many Americans. The task of keeping alive in people's minds the collective memory of the struggle for equality and the 'person rights' in all of the institutions of our society, is one of the most significant tasks educators can perform. In a time of conservative restoration, we cannot afford to ignore this task. This requires renewed attention to important curricular questions. Whose knowledge is taught? Why is it taught in this particular way to this particular group? How do we enable the histories and cultures of the majority of working people, of women, of people of color (these groups again are obviously not mutually exclusive) to be taught in responsible and responsive ways in schools? Given the fact that the collective memory that is preserved in our educational institutions is more heavily influenced by dominant groups in society (Apple and Christian-Smith, 1991), the continuing efforts to promote more democratic curricula and teaching are more important *now* than ever. For it should be clear that the movement toward an authoritarian populism will become even more legitimate only if the values embodied in the conservative restoration are made available in our public institutions. The widespread recognition that there were, are, and can be more equal modes of economic, political, and cultural life can only be accomplished by organized efforts to teach and expand this sense of difference. Clearly, there is educational work to be done.

Note

1 More extended discussion of the arguments made in this chapter appear in Walter Secada (1989) (Ed.) *Equity in Education*, London, UK: Falmer Press and Henry Giroux and Peter McLaren (1989) (Eds) *Critical Pedagogy, The State and Cultural Struggle*, (Albany, NY: University of New York Press).

References

ANDERSON, M. (1985) 'Teachers unions and industrial politics', unpublished doctoral thesis, School of Behavioural Sciences, Macquarie University, Sydney, Australia.

APPLE, M. (1985) *Education and Power*, New York, NY: Routledge.

APPLE, M. (1986) 'National reports and the construction of inequality', *British Journal of Sociology of Education*, 7, 2, pp. 171–90.

APPLE, M. (1988a) 'Facing the complexities of power: For a parallelist position in critical educational studies,' in COLE, M. (Ed.) *Rethinking Bowles and Gintis*, London, UK: Falmer Press.

APPLE, M. (1988b) *Teachers and Texts*, New York, NY: Routledge.

APPLE, M. (1989) 'The politics of common-sense,' in GIROUX, H. and McLAREN, P. (Eds) *Critical Pedagogy, the State and Cultural Struggle*, Albany, NY: State University of New York Press.

APPLE, M. (1990) *Ideology and Curriculum* (2nd ed.), New York, NY: Routledge.

APPLE, M. and CHRISTIAN-SMITH, L. (Eds) (1991) *The Politics of the Textbook*, New York, NY: Routledge.

BASTIAN, A., FRUCHTER, N., GITTELL, M., GREER, C. and HASKINS, K. (1986) *Choosing Equality: The Case for Democratic Schooling*, Philadelphia, PA: Temple University Press.

BOWLES, S. (1982) 'The post-Keynesian capital-labor stalemate', *Socialist Review*, 12, 5, pp. 44–72.

BOWLES, S. AND GINTIS, H. (1986) *Democracy and Capitalism*, New York, NY: Basic Books.

CARNOY M., SHEARER, D. and RUMBERGER, R. (1984) *A New Social Contract*, New York, NY: Harper and Row.

CLARK, D. and ASTUTO, T. (1986) 'The significance and permanence of changes in federal education policy', *Educational Researcher*, 15, pp. 4–13.

FREEDMAN, S., JACKSON, J. and BOLES, K. (1982) *The Effects of the Institutional Structure of Schools on Teachers*, Somerville, MA: Boston Women's Teachers' Group.

GINTIS, H. (1980) 'Communication and politics', *Socialist Review*, 10, pp. 189–232.

GIROUX, H. (1984) 'Public philosophy and the crisis in education', *Harvard Educational Review*, 54, pp. 186–94.

GIROUX, H. and McLAREN, P. (Eds) (1989) *Critical Pedagogy, The State and Cultural Struggle*, Albany, NY: State University of New York Press.

HALL, S. (1980) 'Popular democratic vs. authoritarian populism: Two ways of taking democracy seriously', in HUNT, A. (Ed.) *Marxism and Democracy*, London, UK: Lawrence and Wishart, pp. 157–85.

HALL, S. (1985) 'Authoritarian populism: A reply', *New Left Review*, 151, pp. 115–124.

HALL, S. (1986) 'Popular culture and the state', in BENNETT, T., MERCER, C. and WOOLLACOTT, J. (Eds) *Popular Culture and Social Relations*, Milton Keynes, UK: Open University Press, pp. 22–49.

HALL, S. (1988) 'The Toad in the Garden Thatcherism among the theorists', in NELSON, C. and GROSSBERG, L. (Eds) *Marxism and the Interpretation of Culture*, Urbana: University of Illinois Press, pp. 35–73.

Michael W. Apple

HALL, S. and JACQUES, M. (1983) 'Introduction,' in HALL, S. and JACQUES, M. (Eds) *The Politics of Thatcherism*, London, UK: Lawrence and Wishart, pp. 9–18.

HARDING, V. (1981) *There Is a River: The Black Struggle for Freedom in the United States*, New York, NY: Vintage Books.

HOGAN, D. (1982) 'Education and class formation', in APPLE, M. (Ed.) *Cultural and Economic Reproduction in Education*, Boston, MA: Routledge and Kegan Paul, pp. 32–78.

HUNTER, A. (1984) 'Virtue with a vengeance: The pro-family politics of the New Right', unpublished doctoral thesis, Waltham, MA: Department of Sociology, Brandeis Univesity.

HUNTER, A. (1987) 'The politics of resentment and the construction of middle America', unpublished paper, American Institutions Program, University of Wisconsin, Madison.

JESSOP, B., BONNET, K., BROMLEY, S. and LING, T. (1984) 'Authoritarian populism, two nations and Thatcherism', *New Left Review*, **147**, pp. 32–60.

LARRAIN, J. (1983) *Marxism and Ideology*, Atlantic Highland, NJ: Humanities Press.

LEVINE, A. (1984) *Arguing for Socialism*, Boston, MA: Routledge and Kegan Paul.

LIVINGSTONE, D. (Ed.) (1987) *Critical Pedagogy and Cultural Power*, South Hadley, MA: Bergin and Garvey.

MOUFFE, C. (1988) 'Hegemony and new political subjects: Towards a new conception of democracy', in NELSON, C. and GROSSBERG, L. (Eds) *Marxism and the Interpretation of Culture*. Urbana: University of Illinois Press, pp. 35–73.

OMI, M. and WINANT, H. (1986) *Racial Formation in the United States*, New York, NY: Routledge and Kegan Paul.

PIVEN, F. and CLOWARD, R. (1982) *The New Class War*, New York, NY: Pantheon Books.

RASKIN, M. (1986) *The Common Good*, New York, NY: Routledge and Kegan Paul.

SECADA, W. (Ed.) (1989) *Equity in Education*, London, UK: Falmer Press.

WITTGENSTEIN, L. (1973) *Philosophical Investigations*, translated by E. ANSCOMBE, Oxford, UK: Basil Blackwell.

Chapter 5

Two Hemispheres — Both 'New Right'?: 1980s Education Reform in New Zealand and England and Wales

Roger Dale and Jenny Ozga

Introduction

There are many apparent similarities between the *Tomorrow's Schools* (Lange, 1988) reforms in New Zealand and the Education Reform Act (ERA, 1988) in England and Wales. These apparent similarities are not confined to the superficial. They are often seen as responses to the breakdown of the Keynesian Welfare State (KWS), in particular, they are seen as having been generated by a common set of educational ideas, usually known as New Right. What makes these apparent similarities so intriguing, and at another level so important, is that they seem to point to the possibility of a particular set of ideas about education, held in common across two societies which, though they draw to a greater or lesser degree on a common heritage, nevertheless display major differences economically and politically, as well as in the organization of their education systems. This comparison is made all the more piquant by the fact that the English reforms were introduced by a Conservative government and the New Zealand reforms by a Labour government. Of course, looking beyond New Zealand and England, many commentators have argued that New Right ideas now dominate the education system of all advanced English speaking countries.

This raises important questions at a number of levels, especially about the role of ideas in forming education and other social policy. It sometimes seems that the proposal is an ideological version of the convergence thesis. A comparison of the New Zealand and English educational reforms is thus of interest not only in itself but also as a useful, albeit simple and limited, test of 'ideological convergence'/'universal triumph of the New Right' arguments. While the former is a central purpose of this chapter, that purpose can, in any case, only be fulfilled effectively by an approach that simultaneously allows the broader question to be asked. For *ad hoc* comparisons, however superficially striking and appealing they may be, only rarely, and then inadvertently, improve our understanding of the issues on either side of the comparison. It is not that such comparisons are necessarily misleading, but that they are unenlightening, because they stay at the level of appearances. An excellent recent example of work that reinforces this view is Hall's (1989) very interesting collection of essays on the different ways that broadly

Keynesian ideas were interpreted and taken up in different countries, and how and why their influence varied. Understanding what Keynesianism meant in a particular country means understanding the country as well as Keynesianism. The parallels with New Right influences on education need not be laboured, though we should note that in any case, the best comparative studies of education — for instance Margaret Archer's comparison of centralized and decentralized education systems (Archer, 1979), or, more recently, Andy Green's fine study of the links between education and state formation (Green, 1990) — go behind and beyond surface similarities and seek more fundamental comparisons between the systems under review.

With this in mind, we shall address two major planks of the 'ideological triumph' argument. We will first of all consider the appropriateness of the term 'New Right' to describe the philosophy of the two sets of reforms, and then examine those reforms with a view to comparing how and why different parts of the New Right doctrine were taken up within them.

The New Right

Since the beginning of the 1980s Western countries have witnessed an extremely rapid growth in the prominence, sophistication and influence of what have come to be called New Right theories. The translation of such theories into policy is often taken to have gone furthest in Britain and the United States, but the extent and the speed of their implementation in New Zealand since 1984 surpasses that found in any other country. (See Hood, 1990; Boston, Martin, Pallot and Walsh, 1991.)

It is essential to recognize that the term New Right not only covers a range of views, but it also contains sets of ideas (for example, neo-liberalism and conservatism) in some ways mutually contradictory. One major component of New Right ideas is that of liberalism or neo-liberalism, that is, economic ideas about the importance of free markets allied to political ideas stressing the importance of individual freedom and the need to curtail state interference/intervention in individual lives.

Neo-liberalism is by no means monolithic, but one of its key strands is its critique of the welfare state. This critique has a number of linked aspects. At the basis of the critique are the views that individuals know better than the state what is good for them, that the market is a more efficient and more just institution for the distribution of all goods and services (including those formerly and currently distributed through the welfare state) and that inequality between individuals and groups is a natural feature of society that cannot be overcome by socially remedial action.

In this view, the role of the state agencies is nearly always likely to be malign and to make things worse rather than better. The role of the state should be minimized and confined to the maintenance of a stable social order for the operation of the market and the rectification of the very worst excesses of the market. The analyses of the short-comings of intervention and of the virtues and strengths of the market complement each other.

Thus the view that individuals know their own business and welfare best, and that this can be maximized through the market, is complemented by the view that government is ineffective, inefficient, unaccountable and overbearing. State bureaucracies are inevitably restricted in the range of services they can provide and needs they can meet. They must provide a single set of services to meet a huge range of needs. The market, on the other hand, is much more flexible and able to adjust easily and quickly to meet even minority needs. In any case, where government has intervened (the argument goes), it tends to make things worse rather than better. This is because state bureaucracies are inherently inefficient, owing to the need to maintain their own structures and to the cost of collecting the taxes that finance them.

The point about malign inefficiency is crucial in the New Right case. It is centred on the view that all welfare state bureaucracies, including (especially) education systems, come to serve their own interests rather than those of their clients, that is, they are captured by the producers of the service rather than serving the consumers. This is possible because the careers of those in the public service do not flourish on the basis of market demand for services; public servants are guaranteed jobs for life, with progress and promotion only loosely related to performance. Thus welfare state professionals perform in the ways most convenient and appealing to them and are quite able to ignore clients' needs.

The other side of the argument about individuals knowing what is best for them is that this may mean declining standards of life for some, because they will make the wrong decisions, and may consequently increase social inequality. It can also be argued that it is likely to make individuals more responsible because they will recognize that their prosperity and survival above a very basic level are entirely in their own hands, and they cannot expect to be bailed out by the state.

Finally, the market itself can be used as a very effective tool for social shaping or engineering. Through adjustments in the costs and benefits of any behaviour, individuals can be persuaded to choose what is in the national interest. The differential pricing of human capital, for instance, can theoretically ensure qualified personnel in every segment of the labour market, based entirely on individuals' rational calculation of the costs and benefits to them of extra years in education and the benefit of beginning to earn a salary. Thus encouraged, all individuals will maximize their potential and abolish all traces of structural social inequality.

Education policy is seen as having been guided by the self-interest of the bureaucrats and the 'producers'. The neo-liberal view is that the best policy is to do nothing but to make it possible for the individuals concerned to make their own choices of welfare services just as they make their own choices of groceries, cars and hairdressers. Even better, the only good social policy is one that removes an area from the scope of social policy.

The other main strand of the New Right is conservatism, which stresses the importance of order, traditional values and social hierarchy. Conservatives are not opposed to any or all state intervention, but to the effects of welfare policies that weaken individual incentives, family responsibility and self-reliance, while encouraging permissiveness and dependency, and threatening the traditional values, authority and social order, whose maintenance is their highest priority. While conservatives abhor the effects of the welfare state, they see the state as the only bulwark against permissiveness and the erosion of traditional moral and social values.

Our argument is that while the English reforms contain clear traces of both these strands of New Right thought, the New Zealand reforms derive from one particular aspect of its neo-liberal strand. Furthermore, the differences are due not to different shades of meaning attached to ideologies, but to how those ideologies are interpreted in translating the problems the world economy presents to the particular nation-state into a set of political problems to which the ideology might also suggest a set of solutions. These translations are never carried out on the basis of ideology alone, but in the context of the existing historical specificities of the particular nation-state and its political processes, even when it is seen as essential to change these. (See Dale, 1990a.) Consequently, the blanket use of the term New Right to describe both sets of reforms may conceal as much as it reveals. We shall attempt to put forward alternative means of analysis.

There are some important similarities between the ERA in England and Wales and associated legislation and the *Tomorrow's Schools* reforms in New Zealand. Both, for instance, are associated with a shift from demand-led to supply-led economic policy, and more broadly with what Offe calls a shift from a conjunctural to a structural mode of political rationality, where the essence of a good policy moves from meeting the maximum number of demands to reducing and channelling those demands so as to fit the available resources. (See Offe, 1985; for applications to education policy, see Dale, 1989; Codd, 1990 and Lingard, Chapter 2, this volume.) The main aim of the structural mode/supply-side approach is to reduce legitimate demands on the state with their inevitable pressures on public spending. Both have weakened, or removed bodies intervening between central government and individual schools, and both have sought to reduce as far as possible the power of the education professionals. However, these apparent similarities conceal some, but do not exhaust the full range, of the differences between the two sets of reforms. We will consider briefly five important differences between the two reforms.

The Historical Background of the Reforms

In England and Wales, the Education Reform Act of 1988 was the culmination (possibly) of more than a decade of intense debate and struggle over education. The debates encompassed a wide variety of topics (some of which will be touched on below) and they spawned a great deal of educational legislation during the 1980s. Some of that legislation paved the way for the ERA, and the decade of debate certainly prepared the ground ideologically for the major changes it signalled. That legislation, and in particular attacks on teachers' salaries and conditions of service and their negotiating rights, had also generated internal hostility, bitterness, disillusionment and demoralization in the teaching force. (See Dale, 1989; Ball, 1990.)

Thus, in England the ERA represented a key stage in a process which had begun at least a decade earlier, and which continues, unchecked by Thatcher's abrupt departure. Although the years with which we are chiefly concerned form the period of Thatcher's Prime Ministership, and though her involvement in education reform was close, personal and significant, she is, neither in her personal capacity nor in her embodiment as 'Thatcherism', a sufficient explanation of reform. The process of change began with the Great Debate of 1976, instituted by the Labour Government of James Callaghan, which signalled the identification of education as a problem, though that problem was primarily construed in terms of economic failure. Education's inadequate contribution to wealth creation was identified in the context of economic crisis and public expenditure cuts. Efficiency and economy were major policy aims, and the pursuit of economy eroded local government autonomy and wore down the professionals.

There then followed a significant shift from the straightforward reduction of resource to the more complex agenda of 'revising the ideology' (Dale, 1989). Policy documents became preoccupied with standards; there was official endorsement of the view that they are falling. Progressive educational methods became held responsible more than ever for this decline. Progressivism was said to predominate in the English primary classroom, while secondary schooling standards had been eroded by cross-curricular initiatives which damaged academic subjects and by teachers and teacher educators in pursuit of illegitimate political aims.

The background to the New Zealand education reforms was very different. Though there had been educational debate in the 1980s, it had been of a relatively conventional kind. The report of the Organization for Economic Cooperation and Development (OECD) examiners of the New Zealand education system, published in 1983, mentions 'substantial client satisfaction', 'highly professional administration' and 'high standards but not extravagant provision' — all of which were to be ignored if not contradicted in the education debates only three or four years later. There was, though, no compelling evidence of 'crisis' in New Zealand education.

However, it is essential to note the dramatic shift that took place between the first and second terms of the fourth Labour government. From the time of Peter Fraser's famous 1939 dictum that,

> The Government's objective, broadly expressed, is that every person, whatever his [sic] level of academic ability whether he be rich or poor, whether he live in town or country, has a right, as a citizen, to a free education of the kind for which he is best fitted, and to the fullest extent of his powers. So far is this from being a mere pious platitude that the full acceptance of the principle will involve the reorientation of the education system . . . . (Cited in New Zealand Dept. of Education, 1962, p. 11)

a concern with the social effects and individual outcomes of education has been central in New Zealand. In the early 1980s the OECD report on New Zealand education had pointed to the emphasis on social and cultural goals in the system, a view which was confirmed by the then National Party Minister of Education, Merv Wellington. However, Wellington's perceived reactionary views led to considerable conflict with the teachers' organizations, and teachers became major supporters behind the Labour Party's 1984 election victory. There followed what MacPherson (1989), who contributed to the State Services Commission's work on the *Picot Report* (NZ Department of Education, 1988), calls 'a period of naive euphoria . . . due to the settling of campaign promises and to the portfolio being largely insulated from the effects of a steadily worsening economy'.

The Compass of the Reforms

There were major differences here. They are signalled most clearly in the titles of the two sets of reforms. The New Zealand reforms were based on the report of the Taskforce to Review Educational Administration. The English reforms were ensconced in the Education Reform Act, which had been known colloquially in its passage through Parliament as the GERBIL, the Great Education Reform Bill. Though, as we have just pointed out, the ERA was able to build on a decade of educational reform, its framers nevertheless sought to be comprehensive and detailed in their prescriptions for the education system. They included reforms of curriculum, assessment, the structure and administration of education and teacher appraisal, for instance. The New Zealand reforms were more limited in their compass. They did not touch on the curriculum or assessment, or indeed the processes and content of education, at all, but concentrated on how it was to be administered (though it was assumed by some that administrative changes would lead to curricular and other changes). The differences are symbolized by their respective cornerstones. The cornerstone of the English reforms was the National Curriculum and the testing regime associated with it, and that of the New Zealand reforms was the School Charter, which set out the responsibilities of the school Board of Trustees to the Ministry of Education. It is significant that there would be far more argument about Secretary Baker's (1989) characterization of the ERA, because there were so many other competing candidates for central importance, such as the assessment measures, LMS (Local Management of Schools), GMS (Grant Maintained Schools), etc., than there would be for New Zealand, where the reforms were unidimensionally administrative, and where the Charter was clearly the key feature of the reform.

The Sources of the Reforms

The fact that the two sets of reforms were opposed by similar groups of forces in both countries (essentially those associated with the broadly social democratic thrust of education that had characterized the education systems of both countries for the previous forty years or so, and especially by organized teachers), should not allow us to overlook the fact that they had rather different sources. The New Zealand reforms were initiated as part of a very wide-ranging reform of public administration and radical review of the proper balance of roles between and state and the market. In 1984–7 this policy (known broadly as Rogernomics, after Roger Douglas, the Minister of Finance, in the 1984–7 Labour government, and its major architect and animator) carried all before it in its campaign to set free the forces of the market. (See Jesson, 1989; Easton, 1989.) However, when the radical reforming gaze was directed towards the social and welfare services after the 1987 New Zealand election victory, fundamental divisions, which were to culminate in the removal of Douglas from the Cabinet and David Lange's resignation from the Prime Ministership, began to appear, and education reform was one of the sites on which they were played out. The Rogernomics line on education is set out very clearly in Volume 2 of *Government Management*, the Treasury's advice to the incoming government in 1987. This document has been subjected to a great deal of scrutiny and criticism (for example, Grace, 1988, 1990; Lauder and Wylie, 1990; Middleton, Codd and Jones, 1990), but it is wrong to suppose that the education reforms that followed it were a direct reflection and implementation of those Treasury proposals; Picot was not a case of *post* Rogernomics, ergo *propter* Rogernomics. (For an elaboration of this view see Peter Ramsay's chapter 14 in this volume; see also Gianotti, 1989.) A major reason for this is that David Lange himself took on the Education portfolio after the 1987 election and seems to have used it as a means of forestalling or mitigating the effects of a full-scale application of a Rogernomics/Treasury/State Services Commission (SSC) policy of cut, slash, burn and/or privatize to education.

What was clear, however, was that there was a single dominant agenda for the education reforms and the issue was how far it would be installed. Picot represented a setback, rather than a conclusive defeat for the Treasury/SSC approach. As Wilson (1991) has made very clear, each of the modifications that the Picot proposals underwent — their translation into the *Tomorrow's Schools* (Lange, 1988) legislation, and the revisions proposed (only six months after the introduction of *Tomorrow's Schools*) in *Today's Schools* (Lough, *et al.* 1990), the report of a working party set up by the SSC — represented a clawing back of ground by the Treasury and SSC. The New Zealand reforms were informed by one source, then; the opposition to them was based, not on a coherent alternative, or even a divergent policy, but on a 'brute' opposition to the principles on which they were based.

The sources of the English reforms were much more complex. As we have already pointed out, they contained conservative as well as neo-liberal elements, and it is possible to identify a modernizing vocationalist tendency too. (See Dale, 1989; Ball, 1990.) These elements, which included reactions to the moral panics and riots of the 1980s, the issue of parental choice, and the need to direct education to the promotion of economic ends, were not merely conflicting but sometimes contradictory. What is especially important about them, however, is that the differences between the various strands were not confined to, and settled during, the policy formulation period, but that all elements were successful in sponsoring strands of the reforms that were set in place during the 1980s. The ERA itself, then, was marked by contrasting strands, with various of its features representing victories for one or other ideological element over its competitors. As in New Zealand, the legislated reforms underwent some modification in the process of implementation.

There were, however, two important differences between the modification processes in the two countries. As we pointed out above, in New Zealand the modification was initiated outside the education system and represented an attempt on the part of those outside the education system, who had sponsored and initiated the major reform of public administration of which the education reforms were a front, to draw back the ground that they had lost in the policy-making period. In England, as Stephen Ball (1990) has shown so effectively, modification took place through the institutions set up on the legislation, and was initiated by those within the system whose earlier submissions had been rejected or marginalized in the policy-making process.

The Direction of the Reforms

This follows rather directly from the previous difference. The New Zealand reforms might be seen as intending a radical departure from any previous form of educational administration the country had known. The English reforms can be seen, by contrast, as an attempt to re-establish the key structural and ideological elements of earlier education systems, that had been undone or undermined by decades of social democratic 'interference'. In essence, it might be said that the direction of the English reforms was backwards, and of the New Zealand reforms forward. The shared assumptions about producer-capture and malign-inefficiency may have led to broadly similar policy responses in both countries, but the solid content of the English educational reform program is more a reassertion of previous patterns and assumptions than a radically new departure. It represents a rupture with the immediate past, but it is also a restoration of the *status quo ante bellum*. In particular, it marks a return to the informing principles of English education policy, those of differentiation and stratification, which had been challenged and partially obscured by limited moves towards equality of opportunity, particularly in the 1960s.

The essential point being made here is that much of the content of English educational reform policies, including the 1988 Act, may be best understood as reasserting a principle that had characterized provision throughout the 19th century, and that was enshrined in curricular provision and structures of schooling. The preservation of patterns of differentiation is, in Johnson's (1989) words, 'the hallmark of English education'. He elaborates:

> The public system has always been shadowed by sizeable private and voluntary provision, often socially exclusive and without the presence of academic selection. Higher education has been persistently divided, according to fine distinctions, more social than intellectual in character (e.g., university versus polytechnic; Oxbridge versus 'the rest'). Within state schooling the elementary-secondary division has been recuperated, first in the grammar-secondary-modern split, then in the distinction between direct grant and other former grammar schools and the comprehensives, and even with the system itself . . . .
>
> A similar pattern of differentiation can be found in curriculum categories. The most persistent division has been between the academic (or 'pure') and the vocational/technical (or 'applied'). 'Vocational', despite its clerical connotations, has often been a metaphor for 'working-class'. It implies the technical, the manual, and in recent years has been strongly associated with 'training'. Any area of the curriculum with both 'pure' and 'applied' sides is liable to bifurcation on these lines . . . . In these disastrous dichotomies, elite status has lain via the 'academic' routes . . . . The overwhelming value to the nation of vocational or technical knowledges has periodically been urged, but this inversion has rarely been sustained or institutionalized. It has been rarer still to challenge the divisions altogether . . . .
>
> The science-humanities division is active in relation to gendered social identities . . . . I believe that these associations are especially strong in English culture as a consequence of the long-term educational features. I am thinking of the identification of working-classness with the practical and manual; the association of femininity with evaluation activities and humanities disciplines, but not with hard knowledge, not with science; or the association of blackness with physical culture and the creative arts; or, on the reverse sides of these relations, the association of the power of

white, middle-class men with the academic, the 'objective', and with personal investment in the mental as relatively abstracted from practical concerns. These associations are part of a larger pattern, perhaps, by which social differences are particularly strongly marked, culturally, in English society, in ways that seem bizarre to outsiders. (Johnson, 1989, pp. 98–9)

There is a strong historical resonance. The nineteenth century pattern of English education was diverse and differentiated; it operated to reinforce inequality and to maintain class divisions. The 1988 Act's combination of state regulation and market forces recreates the divided pre-war system. In Johnson's words:

Some thoroughly nineteenth-century features re-emerge: charitable trusts, limited, proprietorial conceptions of 'the public', appeals (often unavailing) to pin-striped-trousered philanthropists.

So how can these shifts of power be explained? They conform to the classic dynamic of *laissez faire*. State interventions are rendered essential, first to establish market conditions, and then to deal with the consequences. The government must crush local authorities, the major source of resistance to its plans. It must then introduce some guarantees into the market situation in the shape of the National Curriculum. This allows control of freedom. It does not 'trust the people' as parents any more than it trusts the teachers; it regulates both. Indeed further interventions will follow to counter resistances and other consequences. This state-enhancing dynamic need not surprise, unless we continue to think of the market, ideologically, as freedom or spontaneous provision. Free markets are really systems of social relationships that must be sustained by coercion or consent. They need appropriate superstructures.

Far from being a modernization, it seems a massive reversion: back to the combination of tight curriculum control and dispersed localism of the pre-1870 voluntary system. (Johnson, 1989, p. 115)

In contrast, the New Zealand reforms were self-consciously radical and innovatory. It was not merely in the immediate past that the education system had been misdirected and misled. The problem was a chronic one and could not be solved by tinkering. Nor, most importantly for our argument here, could it be solved by harking back to and reintroducing the models of an earlier Golden Age, for there was no previous age that appeared golden from the perspective of the radical neo-liberal reformers driving the reforms of which the Tomorrow's Schools legislation was part.

The New Zealand reforms represented little continuity with any of the major discourses of education in New Zealand in the 1980s. (For an elaboration of these points, see Dale, 1990b.) It did not follow the 'education in the service of modernization' line of the OECD examination of the New Zealand education system in 1983. Nor did it continue the discourse of the *Curriculum Review*, a quintessentially liberal professional document to which the teaching profession contributed heavily, and by which they set great store. The most direct response to the economic-social policy relationship of the 1984–7 government, the Royal Commission on Social Policy (RCSP) (published a very short time before Picot) had equally little impact. Though it did pay attention to the economic context to which Rogernomics was the 1984–7 government's response, it was premised on the continuing importance of fundamental Welfare State principles and even their extension, especially in the areas of gender and ethnic equality.

Significantly, the report on educational provision that the RCSP commissioned was entitled 'How Fair is New Zealand Education?' The only New Zealand educational discourse of the 1980s that might be seen to have even remotely influenced the educational reforms set in turn by the 1987–90 Labour government, was what might be called the discourse of teacher accountability. Its major source was a Parliamentary Select Committee chaired by Noel Scott, Associate Minister of Education, who was a former Inspector of Schools. The report of this committee pointed to problems of structure and accountability (especially of teachers) within the education system. However, it received little attention at the time of its publication (1986) and only came to public notice when it was employed by the (National Party) opposition Education spokesperson, Ruth Richardson, during the 1987 election campaign.

The View of Teachers

The Scott Report brings to light one other difference between the two sets of reforms, that of their view of, and assumptions about, the teaching profession and its (actual and rightful) place in the education system. Both sets of reforms attack what is called (significantly in New Zealand more than in England) 'producer capture'. (For an excellent investigation and analysis of 'producer capture' see Bertram, 1988.) Both see teachers as part of the problem, rather than as part of the solution. However, the reasons for this problem, and the solutions proposed for it, differ between the two countries.

In New Zealand, the problem is seen as stemming largely from the very close, even symbiotic relationship between teachers' professional organizations, and their officials, and the Ministry of Education. (See MacPherson, 1989.) This relationship, which was rooted in the frequency of movement from senior elective positions in the teachers' professional organizations to senior positions in the Ministry of Education, was one of the issues that troubled the Scott committee.

However, though both sets of reforms were directed at reducing the power of organized teachers, the reasons were rather different. In New Zealand, as we have indicated, the reasons were essentially formal, even as matters of accountability. In a sense, the problem was not as much what teachers did (which was left very largely unmolested in the education reform), as that it was teachers who determined that it should be done, unaccountably and seemingly as a right, as a matter of course. The reforms focused on the role of teachers in the administration of education (which they took to be excessive); they address the processes and content of education that were the outcomes of such egregious influence. Whether this was because these processes and contents were regarded as acceptable, or because it was assumed that they would automatically change as a result of the devolution of formal power over what went on in schools' Boards of Trustees, is not clear.

In England, on the other hand, *what teachers did* with the influence they had managed to capture was very much an issue. The attack on teachers took a particular form; it suggested that teachers were using the education service as a way of propagating left-wing views, views which were not supportive of existing social structures and which did not support capitalist values. The following quotation from Sir Arnold Weinstock, a prominent and influential industrialist, is a good example of the genre. It suggested that teachers were using the education service as a way of propagating left-wing views, views which were not supportive of existing social structures and which did not support industrial, capitalist values:

— the United Kingdom is a democracy in which all the six political parties with significant voting support (Labour, Conservative, Liberal, Scottish National Party, Plaid Cymru, Ulster Unionist) are committed to a certain view about the organization of industry — that we should have a mixed economy in which free enterprise plays a major wealth-creating role. It is, therefore, particularly disturbing that many practitioners in our educational system perpetuate attitudes which are unhelpful, to say the least, to industry in general and more especially to free enterprise industry.

Teachers fulfil an essential function in the community, but having themselves chosen not to be into industry, they often deliberately or more usually unconsciously instil in their pupils a similar bias. In so doing they are not serving the democratic will. And this is quite apart from the strong though unquantifiable impression an outsider receives that the teaching profession has more than its fair share of people who are actively politically committed to the overthrow of liberal institutions, democratic will or no democratic will . . . . (Weinstock, 1976, pp. 5–6)

It is important to understand the centrality of the New Right attack on teachers to the reform program in England. Teachers were, of course, scapegoats elsewhere, perhaps most conspicuously in the USA, where *A Nation at Risk* (Commission on Excellence in Education, 1988) found teachers guilty of the equivalent of an act of war against the state.

In England, as in New Zealand, teachers were held responsible for most, if not all educational ills, but unlike New Zealand they were held responsible for many other ills as well. Scapegoating of teachers was a continuous process, from the appearance of the first *Black Papers* (Cox and Dyson, 1969). Teachers have been held responsible for economic failure, the breakdown of law and order, the destruction of family life, the erosion of traditional values. Such scapegoating is not a process confined to the tabloid (and 'quality') press, it is part of the language of policy-makers. Seifert (1987) has pointed to the Secretary of State's provocative handling of the negotiations leading up to and during the 1985–7 teachers' pay dispute. The settlement of that dispute saw the loss of teachers' negotiating rights and the establishment, through the Teachers' Pay and Conditions Act, 1987, of contractual duties. As Seifert comments:

The Act gives unprecedented powers to a Secretary of State to impose pay and conditions on a group of public employees with passing reference only to their employers and unions. It coincides with general policy over the abolition of national pay bargaining, and the development of regional and merit payment systems aimed at achieving labour market flexibility while dividing employees against each other. This process has already begun in mining, the civil service and the national health service. Its main purposes are to circumvent powerful national union organisations, prepare for private systems, and to force down wages through the competition of worker against worker in regional labour markets. (Seifert, 1987, p. 251)

The importance of the attack on teachers is that it marked a return to a constant pre-occupation of education policy makers in England, that of control of the teaching workforce. It marked a departure from the post-war mode of partnership, which attempted control through the appearance of consensus.

Control of the teaching force is always problematic, given the contradictory demands made on teachers which follow from the inherent contradictions of educational practice. There are only a limited number of strategies available for the management of these tensions. These are reducible at their extremes to either tight central control and prescriptive central management of a deskilled labour force, or the licensing of responsible autonomy, in return for professional behaviour. The period we are reviewing marked a reassertion of tight control after a prolonged post-war period where partnership operated as the form of control. That mode depended on management of the tension between selection and expansion of opportunity. Again, this is a deep-seated tension in English education, which resurfaced in increasingly unmanageable form in the disputes over comprehensivization in the 1960s and 70s.

This has been a selective comparison of the English and New Zealand reforms, but it does make it possible to isolate some important differences. First, in England and Wales education was made a scapegoat for a wide range of social, and especially economic, shortcomings. A major and explicit thrust of the reform was making education more responsive to economic needs. In New Zealand, on the other hand, the OECD reviewers' suggestion that the education system might do more to address the issue of rising youth unemployment was shrugged off by a reference to proposed transition education programmes which were seen as an adequate response to what was perceived as a short term problem. Though increasing attention was paid to the economic contribution of education towards the end of the decade, such concerns did not play any significant and separate part in the Labour Government's educational reforms. (There is a significant difference here also to the Australian Labor press for education as a major instrument for micro-economic reform.)

Second, in England and Wales the restratification of the education system appears to have been a major objective in its own right. It was both enabled and 'encouraged' by the legislation (Dale, 1991). In New Zealand, by contrast, though the legislation made the stratification of schools more possible, it was not similarly encouraged; the stratification of the education system, as such, appears not to have been a major objective of the reforms. Rather it was a possible, and certainly not unwelcome, outcome of the enhanced inter-school competition that could result from the apparent devolution of greater control over their own affairs to individual schools.

Third, though 'doing something about the teachers' was very clearly a central aim of both sets of reforms, there were significant differences in the way the problem was addressed. In England and Wales the teachers were tackled both more directly and more specifically; the approach is characterised by legislation depriving teachers, specifically, of their right to negotiate their salaries and conditions of service. In New Zealand, teachers were not so directly attacked. They were subject to policies, strategies and mechanisms directed at the public service as a whole, not themselves as a specific group. They did not lose negotiating rights (and when union-threatening industrial legislation was introduced by the 1990 National government, its target was all unions, not just teachers).

In summary, these differences underpin three fundamental distinctions. First, they demonstrate what we suggested at the beginning of this chapter, that the English reforms embraced both conservative and liberal wings of the New Right (albeit somewhat contradictorily), while the New Zealand reforms concentrated on one particular strand of neo-liberalism in the reform of the relationship of the state and market and especially of public administration. This is linked to the second fundamental distinction, that the English reforms have as their purpose dismantling an education system that is as ill-directed as it is ineffective and the return to a system that underpinned a different kind of society, that is, a re-stratified education system. In New Zealand the intention was to create something new and radical, with no suggestion that any earlier solutions or form of society were possible or desirable outcomes.

In essence, the New Zealand reforms are part of an attempt to curtail the state's area of responsibility for the provision of services and consequently its accountability for that provision. Thus, while, as we noted above, the New Zealand legislation contained the potential for expanded parental choice of schools (the kernel of neo-liberal education policy), that was never highlighted. A much more important priority was getting the state off the legitimation hook (with its costly and inefficient consequences) by effectively taking education out of the arena of national public debate. When matters are in the political arena, public choice theory suggests, well-organized interests are encouraged to pursue their own benefit; electors are envisaged to seek and politicians to provide (from public money) ever increasing services. The creation of school charters and the allocation of funding to schools on a strict formula basis addressed that issue by seeking to lay down comprehensively and conclusively (and thus putting beyond argument) what each individual school intended and was able to do, and above all what it was accountable for doing. And this, rather than any other part of neo-liberal, or conservative ideology, was the aspect of the New Right that most directly informed the New Zealand reforms.

The third fundamental distinction is that in the English reforms the reform of education was absolutely central; it was what they were about. Educational issues were far the most prominent, effectively the only issues addressed, the only issues it was intended to change, at least directly. By contrast, the New Zealand reforms are better seen as one strand of the major reform of public administration. The reform of administration is central, explicit and more or less exclusive. Changes to the areas of educational practice that were at the heart of the English reforms — curriculum, assessment, the purpose of schooling — are addressed only indirectly or incidentally in the New Zealand reforms. And while accountability and control were key issues in both reforms, in England it was the accountability and control of the education system specifically that was in question, in New Zealand the accountability and control of the whole public service.

There is, however, one final difference between the two sets of reforms that we have not yet discussed, the fact that one was produced by a Conservative, and one by a Labour government. In this final section of the chapter we wish to offer some rather brief explanations of that difference and in doing so, to examine some of the assumptions and possible consequences of the two sets of reforms. A significant obstacle to carrying out such an analysis is the current ubiquity of the concept of the New Right. We have already set out our broad reservations about its use and in this section of the chapter we shall try to set out an alternative means of examining current differences in education policy.

We will attempt to do this by focusing on the intentions, strategies and consequences of the two sets of policies, rather than reading these off from a more or less prior assumption about their ideological provenance. The two pairs of concepts are Hirschman's 'voice'–'exit' distinction (Hirschman, 1970, 1980, 1986), and Dahrendorf's (1988) distinction between 'entitlement to' and 'provision of' goods and services. Very briefly, exit and voice represent alternative forms of responses to dissatisfaction or discontent with organizations of which people are members or which exercise some influence or control over their lives. Exit, as its label suggests, is a response that takes the form of withdrawal from the organization. A voice response attempts to reduce the dissatisfaction by complaint, criticism or suggestion. Exit is an individualistic, economic response, while voice is a participatory, political response. Exit (leaving one organization for another competing one) provides little information to the abandoned organization about the nature of its deficiencies. Voice, on the other hand, is what Hirschman calls information-rich; in order to have a chance of being effective it must at least indicate the organization's shortcomings, and, preferably, indicate better and feasible alternatives.

Dahrendorf's concepts of provision and entitlement arose from what he calls the 'Mendoza paradox'. When Dahrendorf visited Nicaragua, Mendoza was the foreign Minister. Dahrendorf asked him about the scarcity of goods on the shelves of shops, and Mendoza replied that before the revolution the shelves had been as well stocked as those in Miami, but no one had been able to afford to buy anything. Now the shelves may be only sparsely lined, but everyone could afford to buy what was there. The first case represents what Dahrendorf calls 'provision', the second, 'entitlement'. Entitlement is essentially concerned with the *distribution* of goods and services and which individuals or groups are entitled to them. Provision is concerned with the *availability* of goods and services. So, the Nicaraguan example saw a shift from a high level of provision and low level of entitlement, pre-revolution, to a high level of entitlement and a low level of provision, post-revolution.

It should immediately be clear that there are affinities between exit and provision, and between voice and entitlement. Indeed, they might be used to distinguish, in a very basic way, major strands of political thought. Certainly, superiority of exit over voice, and the greater importance of increasing provision than increasing entitlement are fundamental assumptions of liberal politics, and liberal policies can be read as attempting to enable and encourage conditions (such as the availability of choice and unfettered markets) in which they can flourish. Socialist policies adopt the opposing positions, prioritizing collective over individualistic principles. They seek to create conditions that enable and encourage the implementation of those principles, such as shared control and shared benefits.

These are clearly polar types, and there are few, if any, pure examples of either, though as a set of aspirations they have clearly had substance historically. However, the Keynesian welfare state, (KWS) which dominated to a greater or lesser extent the policies of most Western countries for three decades and more after World War II, did not represent at all a pure type of Exit/Voice and Entitlement/Provision combination. KWS policies were marked by the drive to expand entitlement as a condition of increasing provision; significantly, neither exit nor voice mechanisms were much in evidence.

It should be noted, too, that the category of entitlees in the KWS was varied across, and within, what Esping-Andersen (1989) calls the three worlds of welfare capitalism, and by no means straightforward. Certainly in those countries where the KWS became dominant in the train of social democratic-trade union coalitions, entitlement tended to be 'worker-associated'; it was not universal but was based on the needs of full-time (almost always male) workers and their dependants. There was extremely limited opportunity to develop provision outside the welfare state, and the consequent absence of the conditions (choice, competition) necessary to its existence made the exit alternative not only completely ineffectual, but a self-denying, and occasionally illegal, response. There were formal opportunities to exercise voice, but those rarely attained substance in what was often in effect a producer monopoly.

These features of the KWS became especially important as the fiscal consequences of sustaining it became more and more difficult for governments to bear. For if it was external fiscal crises that fundamentally undermined the KWS, they did not create the crisis alone, nor could responses to the crisis of the KWS address its fiscal aspects only. The lack of democracy, accountability and efficiency that came to be associated with the KWS, if they did not directly bring about its downfall, became of central importance in framing attempts both to save the welfare state, albeit in a reduced form, and to redirect and restructure welfare provision in a wholesale manner.

It is here, it seems to us, that the beginnings of an explanation of the differences in the English and New Zealand education reforms lies, and where we may find some enlightenment on the paradox of a neo-liberal Labour government. Seeing these changes as representing different contributions of voice and exit, provision and entitlement, seems to enable a more nuanced explanation than the blanket use of New Right terminology. This the case even when the main direction of the changes in the two countries is, on the surface, broadly similar: an increase in provision and encouragement of exit, a revision of the conditions and scope of voice, and curtailment of entitlement. The differences in the outcomes of such broadly similar sets of assumptions and intentions arise in particular from the nature and intensity of the fiscal crisis facing the country, its place in the world economy and existing provision. These jointly set a framework for the operation of politics at a national level. (For an elaboration of this argument, see Dale, 1990a.)

How, then, are we to understand the two sets of reforms and the differences between them? In England and Wales, as we have argued above, the reforms were focused on education, were *status quo* restoring, and included both liberal and conservative elements. These features, it seems to us, are made possible by a view of the fiscal crisis/economic decline as soluble/arrestable by a return to traditional ideological roots. The solution lay there because the problem lay in what had supplanted those ideological traditions for 40 years — egalitarianism (entitlement), which both reduced motivation and self-responsibility, and was distinctly unnatural. The extension of voice, too, had had malign effects, both generally, in the more effective enfranchising of previously subordinate groups (and consequent threats to the natural hierarchy essential to a healthy society), and particularly in the monopolization of voice in key areas by self-interested groups, such as trade unions. Together these factors had both destroyed key institutions (education was an important example) and sapped the country's ability to respond effectively to the crisis it faced. As the neo-liberal stalwarts, Harris and Seldon (1987), put it, 'The essential requirement of reform is not the creation of "voice" on "representative" governing or political bodies but the creation of "exits" by which parents or patients can escape from unsatisfying schools or hospitals.'

It is here that we see the two strands of the New Right coalescing, in the emphasis on maximizing individual personal responsibility. This was seen as essential both economically and socially, though it did not so much form the basis of compromises between the different strands as provide a cohering umbrella for the various components of the educational reforms. The key to the reforms, then, might be seen as the extension of individual choice within a nationally responsible framework. The possibility of exit would both enhance individuals' ability to take responsibility for their own lives, and constitute a threat that would make all schools 'pull their socks up'.

In the ERA, this was achieved by both enabling and encouraging consumer choice in education, and by increasing voice locally but stilling it nationally. The former objective was to be achieved through requiring schools to publish information about themselves in such a way as to facilitate consumer comparison between them (see Sallis, 1988), by removing restrictions on their entry, and by funding them on a per pupil basis, which meant that in effect each potential pupil brought with her/him a quasi-voucher to the school. Together these procedures laid the basis for the inter-school competition, based largely on schools' records of academic achievement.

The voice-related objective was met in three main ways. First, a National Curriculum was introduced. The means of its introduction was imposition not negotiation. The prescribed areas of the curriculum that would occupy the great majority of pupils' time in school were laid down, and changed, by the Secretary of State. The content of the curriculum areas was determined by subject committees appointed by and answerable to the Secretary for Education; if he did not like their proposals he could, and did, send them back for reconsideration. This National Curriculum was to be backed up by a program of compulsory testing of all pupils in all subjects at the ages of 7, 11, 14 and 16. There was little, if any, opportunity to exercise voice under these circumstances. When the Secretary of State did look outside his own department for advice, it was to people appointed by, responsible to, and removable by him. In spite of this, as Stephen Ball (1990) has shown, voice was not entirely stilled in the implementation of the National Curriculum, though this was distinctly in the face of what was intended.

Second, it was not only in their enforced absence from the National Curriculum discussions that, as we have noted, the teacher unions effectively had their voice removed. They were excluded from all consultation on national education policy, including the negotiation of their own salaries and conditions of service. One effect of this was to persuade the largest and most 'education voice'-oriented of the teacher unions, the National Union of Teachers, to organize itself much more on a regional than a national basis.

Third, greater power to decide school policy was devolved to Boards of Governors, elected by and answerable to, parents of children at the school. They were given control of their own school budgets, including teacher salaries, giving them the potential to go with the motivation the exit provisions created, to shape and market their school in a competitive way.

The broad outlines of this pattern of increasing voice locally and stilling it nationally are found in New Zealand too, *mutatis mutandis*. It raises the interesting and important point that at a national level voice has tended to be exercised in the interest of expanded entitlement and at a local level in the interest of increased provision. The reasons for this are clear. It is in the essence of provision that what is provided is not available to everyone, while the opposite is the case with entitlement. Governments, being elected by universal suffrage, are naturally loath to increase and diversify provision to the extent to which it would benefit some voters at the expense of others, and keen to introduce policies with a broad, if not universal, appeal. Of course, interest groups have a powerful influence on governments, but their campaigns are necessarily broadly rather than narrowly based, and aimed at increasing provision generally, frequently in order to redress inequalities of entitlement. It is this kind of use of voice, and its associated demand-led political rationality (see Offe, 1985), that governments in both countries (indeed across the western world in general) have been determined to frustrate, because of the constantly rising spiral of demands and costs they associate with it. Interest groups now have very much less influence on either provision or entitlement at a national level.

Voice has been displaced to the local level, where the obverse of the above arguments holds. If there is little point in seeking specific provision at a national level, there is equally little point in seeking to expand entitlement at the level of an individual school. In England and Wales the procedures introduced to maximize parental choice militate strongly against the possibility of increasing entitlement, and in favour of increasing provision across a limited range of pupils and activities. As Joan Sallis points out, the kind of information schools are required to make available to parents suggests 'a strong implication that parents need to know more about schools in order to *compare* them, not so that they may through their own understanding play a more supportive role in their own' (1988, p. 30; emphasis in original). The simultaneous encouragement of an exit relation and discouragement of a voice relation to the school could hardly be better demonstrated.

What this does also is to make parents even less of a natural homogeneous constituency than ever. It means that, more than ever, parents' collective interests in the welfare of the whole school are subordinated to their individual interests in the welfare of their own children in competition with other children. One frequently observed reflection of this is found in the differences in the number of parents attending teacher consultation evenings (about their child(ren), very high attendance) and those attending meetings to do with school-wide issues (very low, frequently not quorate, in governors' report-back sessions in England and Wales). This could also have the effect of fostering what Hirschman (1981, p. 242) calls a 'treacherous voice':

[When] different consumer-members have different ideas about what improvements are needed, and the ideas and tastes of the activists differ systematically from those of the non-activists, to the extent that it is successful, the voice of the activity group will cause the quality of the product or policy to vary in such a fashion that benefits are bestowed primarily or exclusively on them.

This raises echoes of another important concept that we discussed earlier, 'capture'. If capture is defined as using not just insider voice to gain inordinate group interest as provision, rather than extending entitlement (i.e., provider capture), but as using representative voice to do the same thing, we can see that one possible consequence of the ERA is to enable, even encourage, further middle-class capture (as opposed to provider capture) of the education system.

The background to the changes in New Zealand differed considerably from that in England and Wales. The problems facing the New Zealand economy were much greater and more intense than those facing the United Kingdom economy. Both the country's traditional solutions and the early 1980s recent attempts to use neo-Keynesian routes out of the problem had failed badly (see Shirley, 1990) and the ground was prepared for radical departures that explicitly rejected previous solutions and sought to introduce neo-liberal reforms across both private and public sectors. (See Easton, 1989; Jesson, 1989; Hood, 1990.) The state was seen as both playing too great a role in the economy, stifling the operations of the market, and taking far too great a share of the country's income. The solution was both to reduce the role of the state and to reform the public administration. These reforms were to address the problem of government overload that was placing such a burden on the country. Government overload was the result of politicians' propensity to buy votes by making extravagant promises to expand state provision, and of bureaucrats pursuing their own interests, seeking to extend their empires and operating unaccountably, not subject to the rigours of the market or to the consequences of failure or overspending. It was this set of problems that the extension of the economic reforms to the social sector was intended to tackle. The general reform of public administration preceded and made possible the reform of the Welfare State. Consequently, as we have stated above, education administration as part of public administration, and not educational practice, was the focus of the reforms.

This does not mean, however, that education was treated identically to health, or transport, or whatever. While one aim of the reform of educational administration was clearly to address the government overload arguments (to de-politicize it, and to nullify teacher capture), this was not done by handing it over wholesale to the market. If education was too important to be left to the professionals, it was also too important to be left to this market. *The Tomorrow's Schools* reforms can be seen as an attempt to set education outside both politics and the market.

The substance and consequence of this claim can be clarified by utilizing a typology of possible means by which public bodies can improve efficiency developed by Dennis Young (quoted in Hirschman, 1981, p. 234). These means are systematic performance evaluation, decentralization, and competition. While the ERA in England and Wales contained elements of all three methods, the New Zealand reforms utilized only the first two. Significantly the competition-exit option, which would see increased market competition between schools and reduced government involvement, though it might have been formally enabled by the legislation, received no encouragement from it. There was no requirement to provide the kind of consumer guide information that would enable parents to choose between schools. The policy of schools recruiting from specified zones was not significantly modified. While Boards of Trustees did take on a considerable range of new responsibilities, these did not include teachers' salaries. Their potential for action was also restricted by the requirement to carry out the requirements of the School Charter. Though the Charters were written by individual Boards of Trustees, 80 per cent of their content was prescribed by national government and was common to all schools. There is, indeed, a good deal of substance in the claims that what was devolved to schools was not political power, but administrative obligations. The legislation certainly made it exceptionally difficult for efficiency to be improved by exit.

The Charter was the key mechanism by which accountability was to be ensured. Together with the funding formula, which allocated schools extra resources for various categories of special needs, such as large numbers of poor children and ethnic minority children, it was distinctly a mechanism with the potential to enhance entitlement rather than provision. Among its compulsory sections were provisions relating to gender and ethnic equity. The scope of the charters was greater than the scope of the English National Curriculum, even though it should be noted that New Zealand had a form of national curriculum in place before the reforms were introduced, and that curriculum did not fall within the ambit of the Charter. Both set limits to what could happen in schools, but the limits in England and Wales applied to the curriculum only, and in New Zealand to the greater part of all the schools' activities. The National Curriculum in England was to be monitored by continuing extended assessment. In New Zealand the Charters were the major means of ensuring school accountability and were to be monitored by the Education Review Office.

In its original form, the Charter, too, had the potential to be a very important voice mechanism. However, this possibility disappeared in the fine-tuning of the legislation (or clawing back of ground lost by the neo-liberal Treasury and State Services Commission), while the monitoring mechanism itself was to be weakened by action from the same bodies.

If the school charter was the cornerstone of the education reform in New Zealand, its precise meaning was never unambiguous and it changed considerably (and rapidly) in the course of the transformation of the Picot Report into the Education Act and beyond. These changes have been meticulously detailed and insightfully interpreted by Codd and Gordon (1991). They start from the use of the Charter concept in the Picot Report, whose charters 'would contain a mission statement, a set of specific objectives, details concerning how the school is to be organised and managed, details on the program of learning and teaching, and specific statements covering respect of diversity, student care and staff development'. However, Picot also states that the 'charter of each institution will be approved nationally by the Minister, on the recommendation of the Ministry. It then becomes a contract between the state and the institution, and between the institution and its community' (NZ Department of Education, 1988, p. 46).

This ambiguity was perpetuated in the *Tomorrow's Schools* document, but the modified draft produced in May 1989 by the charter framework implementation group, and intended as the definitive basis on which charters would be written, contained some significant changes. Two are of particular importance. First, on the recommendation of the four evaluators (all distinguished educators) who had been appointed to oversee the reforms, a 'paramount principle' was introduced which states that the *needs of children and their learning shall be paramount*. Most significantly, the charter itself no longer had the status of a contract but was to be an agreement with two signatories, the chairperson of the Board of Trustees and the Minister of Education. The third party, namely the community, was effectively excluded from the legal partnership. Moreover, only one of the signatories, the Minister, had the power to withdraw the charter at anytime. However, the May 1989 framework also contained the following clause, 'The Minister of Education upon approving this charter undertakes to provide services and funding to a formula to be determined by the Minister from time to time, to enable the board of trustees to meet the requirements of the charter'.

There was a further modification in the Education Act of August 1989, from the charter as an agreement between the boards and the Minister, to an 'undertaking by the Board to the Minister', reversing the direction of the undertaking set out in the draft of three months before. However, in January 1990, when the charter development process was almost complete (and when the legislation had been in position for more than three months), an amended charter framework was issued to all schools that redefined the relationship between state and school board as an undertaking rather than an agreement and removed the ministerial commitment to fund schools. In a further change, the paramount principle was deleted so that it could not be used in litigation 'to negate or modify other aims in the charter'.

These two major changes had extremely significant implications for education in New Zealand. First, as Codd and Gordon pointed out, the 1989 Charter framework had opened up possible avenues for a transfer of real power as well as a devolution of responsibility, and these in January 1990 they sought to close off. Charters 'had effect as an undertaking by the Board to the Minister'. This removed the possibility of Boards of Trustees making demands for funding that could be legitimated by an agreement to enable charter requirements to be met, and, in confirming the May 1989 charter framework's exclusion of the community as a legitimate voice, ensured that all Boards of Trustees were the only body with any legal relationship within the Ministry. These two factors not only legitimated a single voice in schooling, but simultaneously moved it further towards the administrative and away from the political sphere.

Second, the removal of the 'paramount principle' simultaneously undermines teachers' professional influence and reinforces the equity principles contained in the 80 per cent of the charter laid down by the Ministry of Education. Giving priority to 'the needs of children and their learning' would expand the area of discretion for the professional group whose expertise inheres precisely in the identification of those needs; it would by the same token, make the paramount principle of the charter a technical matter rather than, as the EEO of the Picot Taskforce has represented its view of the charter, 'a mechanism . . . in which schools and communities will be required to get into dialogue about what the school is there for and how it can be achieved' (Gianotti 1989, p. 193). Removing the paramount principle also reduced the possibility of its being used as a means of schools' relegating the other major features of the charters, especially those requiring commitment to principles of equity (which have, since the election of the National Government in 1990, in any case been made voluntary rather than compulsory parts of school charters).

The shift from the Picot proposals on the charter to the January 1990 revisions entailed an abandonment of the radical devolution recommended by Picot (which Geoffrey Palmer (1988, p. 5) approvingly referred to as 'empowering government and community at the expense of bureaucrats') in what was intended as locating decision-making ability at the appropriate point and not as a cost cutting exercise. (Picot had refused to take on the leadership of the committee without the assurance that if their deliberations pointed in the direction of extra spending they would be able to commend that.) Instead, the January 1990 version of the charter effectively devolved day-to-day administration (and transaction costs) to Boards of Trustees and left central control in the hands of the Minister, with the community, for the time being disempowered, with no direct access to the Minister and dependent on the Board of Trustees to channel their responses.

The entitlement-voice possibilities (see p. 107) of the Charter were reduced further as a result of the report of the Lough Committee, *Today's Schools*. This committee, set up by the State Services Commission, recommended the halving of the personnel of the Education Review Office and an increased emphasis on techniques of management. This shifts the onus of accountability from a national and comprehensive (via the Charter) monitoring to school-based management. This has a number of consequences. First, as is the intrinsic purpose of administration and management, if it does not still voice, it seeks to limit, channel, control and instrumentalize it. It seeks technical solutions and this includes not only depoliticizing (removing voice) but also a tendency to freeze a particular entitlement-provisions balance. It seeks to do this as a means of confining and controlling the central problem in managing schools, which is that their goals are multiple, ill-defined and contradictory, characteristics that are imbued with and, in part underpinned by, the entitlement-provision balance.

That leaves the strategy of decentralization which, as Hirschman (1981) notes, can be considered a form of intensifying voice, as the remaining one of Young's three means of improving efficiency. Increasing or maintaining efficiency at the local level, of course, depends to a considerable extent on a stable entitlement-provision balance being struck and maintained at a national level, which it is in the essence of efficiency to stabilize locally. (Efficiency differs in this respect from effectiveness, which may be improved by altering that balance.) Certainly, the Charter-funding formula arrangement at national level did incorporate such a stable balance between entitlement and provision. This very stability, of course, meant that national balance was beyond local voice. However, the original Charter proposals did contain the possibility of making voice effective at a local level by challenging that balance. This was to be achieved through the notion of community accountability. As we have seen, the Charter, as first conceived, was a three-way contract between government, Board of Trustees [BOT] and the community. The community disappeared finally in one of the earlier versions of the Charter, largely, we may assume, because of the Treasury's attachment to principal-agent theory, which lays down that any agent, here the BOT, must only work to one principal, here, the government. The principal-agent language, incidentally, also confirms the nature of efficiency within context: the principal provides the agent with a stable set of requirements. (On principal-agent theory in the New Zealand context, see Bushnell and Scott, 1988, who also emphasize the need for clarity of goal-setting by principals.)

Though the community's formal status in the administration of education may have disappeared, it is still constantly referred to in discussions of the administration, control and accountability of schooling. (The only parallel to this in the English reforms is the right of community representatives such as the Chief Constable to sit on Boards of Governors.) In whatever form, though, it should be clear that the community is a means for deploying voice to increase the effectiveness rather than merely the efficiency of schooling. One major reason for this is that it is much more difficult to confine something as amorphous and multifaceted as the community within a supply-led mode of political rationality, where policy demands have to be accommodated within given levels of resource; the community is always more likely to respond like the electorate as a whole, to expand demand and entitlement, than it is to respond like a defined body with statutory powers and responsibilities. It is also important to note that a community role as originally envisaged would inhibit, if not prevent, 'voice treachery', by both rejecting the 'cake-sharing' rather than 'cake-expanding' assumptions of BOT control, and by making the BOT responsible to it as well as to the government.

It is, however, doubtful how far the community could have been an effective voice even if it had retained the formal status recommended in its early drafts of the Charter legislation. This is because it is, in O'Donnell's terms (developed in Hirschman 1986, pp. 82–3), an example of horizontal rather than vertical voice, that is 'the utterance and exchange of voices *among* citizens' rather than 'actual communication addressed to the authorities by a citizen or . . . an organization representing a group of citizens'. Further, '[h]orizontal voice is a precondition for vertical voice; for the latter to emerge from the former it is frequently necessary for members to forge a tie aiming themselves and to create an organization that will agitate for their demands'. The irony is that one of the reasons that the community was so frequently invoked was that it had precisely the qualities that would prevent it developing vertical voice: it was not the kind of single-issue interest group that would press demands, but a much more amorphous entity. Not only this, but it would replace and delegitimate those interested bodies.

In all these circumstances, then, voice brought into being by decentralization is effectively confined to monitoring efficiency. The only alternative (but one that is employed through a rate of 600 letters a day sent to the Ministry of Education) is pleading to the centre for an alteration of the entitlements-provision balance struck in the Charter-funding formula arrangement.

If the consequences of the reforms in England seem likely to make 'middle-class capture' more likely (which would not be wholly inimical to the initiators of the reforms), in New Zealand the likeliest consequence appears to be strengthening the voice, both locally and nationally, of the teacher unions, which, of course, would be wholly inimical to the initiators of the reform. The reason that this outcome appears likely is that with few opportunities for exit, the reduction of external monitoring, the consequent emphasis on the efficiency role of the BOTs and the impossibility of converting community into a vertical voice (but its stifling effect on the development of other vertical voices within the community), the teacher unions represent the only authoritative vertical voice able to address both national and local educational issues. The only alternative might be seen as the School Trustees Association [STA], the official body representing BOT members nationally. However, the STA is not an authentic vertical voice, being based on local vertical voices rather than a genuine horizontal voice. In addition, it is limited both by its own statutory position and that of its members, which effectively confine it to commenting on how they can collectively improve the efficiency of this system rather than being a voice to change it.

Conclusion

In this chapter we have focused on the educational reforms that were introduced in the 1980s in England and Wales and in New Zealand. In doing so, we have had two major questions in mind: do the reforms demonstrate that the New Right dominates educational policy in Anglophone countries in rather similar ways; and is seeing them as rooted in New Right ideology a useful way of analyzing the two sets of reforms? The English and New Zealand reforms provided a useful basis for addressing these questions, since their apparent ideological similarity, in spite of their countries' very different economic conditions and the fact that one was ruled by a Conservative government and the other by a Labour government, have often been remarked on.

The basic thrust of our argument, which linked both the questions we were interested in, was that an unreflective and uncritical use of the New Right as an explanation of what had taken place concealed rather more than it revealed. We sought to show this in the case of the first question (about New Right dominance of Anglophone educational policy) by demonstrating that the two sets of reforms drew on distinct strands of New Right ideology. In the ERA in England and Wales, neo-liberal and conservative strands of New Right thought were both employed, in somewhat uneasy combination. In New Zealand, conservatism played little, if any, part in the reforms and what is often taken as almost the defining characteristic of neo-liberal thought in education, the encouragement of privatization, was also absent. The emphasis was on the reform of the role of the state and of public administration, informed by particular strands of neo-liberal thought.

We proceeded to try to explain these differences. One explanation lay in the different contributions of educational reform in the two countries, responses to the economic, political and social problems they faced. We argued that the English case represented a movement back to a previous educational regime which it was supposed would constitute a more effective response to those problems. In New Zealand, by contrast, we suggested that the reforms had less to do with education *per se* and more to do with a radical reform of state-market relations and public administration in general, and represented a clear departure from anything the country had attempted before.

In addressing the second question, the value of New Right as an analytic tool, we argued that a more useful analysis of the assumptions and consequences of the two sets of reforms might be derived from linking together two powerful pairs of concepts: Hirschman's exit and voice, and Dahrendorf's entitlement and provision. This enabled a powerful, suggestive and detailed analysis of the reforms that did not rest on any a prioristic assumptions of New Right influence.

Our overall conclusion is that in order to understand adequately any set of reforms to educational policy, they have to be placed in both a world economic context and a national historical context. Beyond this, we need to employ analyzes that enable us to understand more clearly the assumptions and outcomes of specific policies. We have criticized the blanket use of the New Right for this purpose, attempted to give substance to these criticisms, and to suggest an alternative framework for analysis that seems highly promising.

References

ARCHER, M. (1979) *Social Origins of Education Systems*, London, UK: Sage.
BAKER, K. (1989) 'Reform in education', *Institute for Policy Studies Newsletter*, August, pp. 4–6.
BALL, S.J. (1990) *Politics and Policy Making in Education*, London, UK: Routledge.
BERTRAM, G. (1988) 'Middle class capture: A brief survey', in *Report of the Royal Commission on Social Policy*, **3**(2), Wellington NZ: Government Printer, pp. 109–170.
BOSTON, J. MARTIN, J. PALLOT, J. and WALSH, P. (Eds) (1991) *Reshaping the State: New Zealand's Bureaucratic Revolution*, Auckland, NZ: Oxford University Press.
BUSHNELL, P. and SCOTT, G. (1988) 'An economic perspective', in MARTIN, J. and HARPER, J. (Eds) *Devolution and Accountability: Studies in Public Administration, no. 4.* Wellington: Government Printer, pp. 19–36.
CODD, J. (1989) 'Education policy and the crisis of the New Zealand state', in MIDDLETON, S., CODD, J. and JONES, A. (Eds) *New Zealand Education Policy Today*, Wellington, NZ: Allen and Unwin, pp. 195–205.
CODD, J. and GORDON, L. (1991) 'School charters: the contractualist state and education policy', *New Zealand Journal of Education Studies*, **26**, 1, pp. 21–34.
COMMISSION ON EXCELLENCE IN EDUCATION (1988) *A National Risk*, Washington, DC: U.S. Department of Education.
COX, S. and DYSON, A. (1969) (Eds) *Fight for Education: A Black Paper*, London: Critical Quarterly Society.
DAHRENDORF, R. (1988) *The Modern Social Conflict.* London, UK: Weidenfeld and Nicolson.
DALE, R. (1989) *The State and Education Policy*, Milton Keynes, UK: Open University Press.
DALE R. (1990a) 'Regulation theory, settlements and education policy', paper presented to NZARE Conference on Education Policy, Massey University, Palmerston North, NZ.
DALE, R. (1990b) 'Recent changes in New Zealand education policy: Education Reform or Administrative Reform?', unpublished paper, University of Auckland, NZ.
DALE, R. (1991) 'Strategy and mechanism in the implementation of education policy: Enabling, encouraging, effective, empowering?', unpublished paper, University of Auckland, NZ.
EASTON, B. (Ed.) (1989) *The Making of Rogernomics*, Auckland, NZ: University of Auckland Press.
ESPING-ANDERSON, G. (1989) *Three Worlds of Welfare Capitalism*, Berkeley, CA: University of California Press.
GIANOTTI, M. (1989) 'Educational administration: Reflections on the Picot Report,' in PHILLIPS, D., LEALAND, G. and MACDONALD, G. (Eds) *The Impact of American Ideas on New Zealand's Education Policy, Practice and Thinking*, Wellington, NZ: NZ-US Education Foundation and NZCER, pp. 190–8.
GRACE, (1988) 'Education: Commodity or public good?' Inaugural lecture, Victoria, NZ: University of Wellington.
GRACE, G. (1990) 'Labour and education: Crisis and settlements of education policy', in HOLLAND, M. and BOSTON, J. (Eds) *The Fourth Labour Government: Politics and Policy in New Zealand*, Auckland: Oxford University Press, pp. 165–91.
GREEN, A. (1990) *Education and State Formation*, London, UK: Macmillan.

HALL, P. (1989) *The Political Effect of Economic Ideas: Keynesianism Across Nations,* Princeton, NJ: Princeton University Press.

HARRIS, R. and SELDON, A. (1987) *Welfare without the State,* London, UK: Institute of Economic Affairs.

HIRSCHAM, A.O. (1970) *Exit, Voice and Loyalty: Responses to Decline in Firms, Organisations and States,* Cambridge, MA: Harvard University Press.

HIRSCHAM, A.O. (1981) *Essays in Trespassing,* Cambridge, UK: Cambridge University Press.

HIRSCHAM, A.O. (1986) *Rival views of Market Society,* New York, NY: Viking.

HOOD, C. (1990) 'De-Sir Humphreyfying the Westminister model of bureaucracy', *Governance,* **3,** 2, pp. 205–14.

JESSON, B. (1989) *Fragments of Labour,* Auckland, NZ: Penguin.

JOHNSON, R. (1989) 'Thatcherism and English education: Breaking the mould or confirming the pattern?', *History of Education,* **18,** 2, pp. 96–121.

LANGE, D. (1988) *Tomorrow's Schools: The Reform of Education Administration in New Zealand,* Wellington, New Zealand: Government Printer.

LAUDER, H. and WYLIE, C. (Eds) (1990) *Towards Successful Schooling,* London, UK: Falmer Press.

LOUGH, N., COWIE, D., CARPINTER, P., GRIEG, D. and O'ROURKE, M. (1990) *Today's Schools: A Review of the Education Reform Implementation Process,* Wellington, NZ: Government Printer.

MACPHERSON, R.J.S. (1989) 'Why politicians intervened in the administration of New Zealand education', *Unicorn,* **15,** 2, pp. 107–12.

MIDDLETON, S., CODD, J. and JONES, A. (Eds) (1990) *New Zealand Education Policy Today.* Wellington: Allen and Unwin.

NEW ZEALAND DEPARTMENT OF EDUCATION (1962) *Report of the Commission on Education in New Zealand* (The Currie Report) Wellington, NZ: Government Printer.

NEW ZEALAND DEPARTMENT OF EDUCATION (1988) *Administering for Excellence: Effective Administration in Education* (The Picot Report), Wellington, NZ: Government Printer.

OFFE, C. (1985) *Disorganized Capitalism,* Cambridge, UK: Polity.

ORGANIZATION FOR ECONOMIC COOPERATION AND DEVELOPMENT (1983) *Report on New Zealand Education,* Paris, France: OECD.

PALMER, G. (1988) 'Political perspectives', in MARTIN, J. and HARPER, J. (Eds) *Devolution and Accountability: Studies in Administration, no.34.* Wellington, NZ: Government Printer, pp. 1–7.

SALLIS, J. (1988) *Schools, Parents and Governors: A New Approach to Accountability,* London, UK: Routledge.

SEIFERT, R. (1987) *Teacher Militancy: A History of Teacher Strikes 1896–1987,* Lewes, UK: Falmer Press.

SHIRLEY, I. (1990) 'New Zealand: The advance of the New Right', in TAYLOR, I. (Ed.) *The Social Effects of Free Market Policies: An International Text,* Brighton, UK: Wheatsheaf.

THE TREASURY (1987) *Government Management: Brief to the Incoming Government, Vol. II, Education Issues,* Wellington, New Zealand: The Treasury.

WEINSTOCK, A. (1976) 'I blame the teachers', *Times Educational Supplement,* 23 January.

WILSON, K. (1991) 'The Picot Report and the legitimation of "Education Policy".' Unpublished MEd. thesis, Massey University, Palmerston North, NZ.

Part III: *Restructuring Educational Discourse: Equality and Social Justice*

Chapter 6

Education and Social Justice in the Postmodern Age

Lindsay Fitzclarence and Jane Kenway

Introduction

The concept 'social justice', as it has been applied to education, has become an integral part of the Federal Labor government's strategy of social integration which, in turn, is part of its more comprehensive political program associated with the establishment and renovation of the Prices and Incomes Accord. In our view, social justice policies are thus called upon to serve purposes which include and go beyond the legitimation of state actions and the amelioration of social disadvantage. They are to play a role in unifying the nation behind the cause of economic mobilization. In making this case, we will begin with a critical examination of current approaches to social justice. We will then explore the wider contexts which have contributed to Labor's reconstruction of social justice policies for education. Our suggestion is that Labor's political strategy has been designed to cope with the contingencies of what has been labelled the postmodern age and that despite its best intentions, its approach is too restricted to be able to address the social justice issues which the current conjuncture sustains and generates. This leaves us with the question: Does the postmodern age require that we rethink the means by which social justice in and through education may be achieved?

The Labor Government and Social Justice

Social Justice and Education

In 1988 the Federal Labor government published *Towards a Fairer Australia: Social Justice Under Labor* (1988) which, basically, reviews its achievements and outlines its policies in the following areas: employment, education and training, social security, taxation, health, housing, community services, working conditions, legal rights, Aborigines and Torres Strait Islanders, women, multiculturalism and veterans. The government's policy statement includes the following:

> This government's fundamental objective is to develop a fairer, more prosperous and more just society: A society in which every Australian

receives a fair share of the nation's growing wealth. The four key elements of a just society are: equity in the distribution of economic resources; equality of civil, legal and industrial rights; fair and equal access to essential services such as housing, health and education; and the opportunity for participation by all in personal development, community life and decision-making.

The Government . . . is committed to taking the broad strategic action required to achieve social justice. It is committed to making social justice both a primary goal of economic policy and an indispensable element in achieving economic policy objectives. (pp. vi–vii)

Towards a Fairer Australia indicates that the government seeks to develop a social justice 'package' in which pertinent policy areas may be considered together and coordinated and, most importantly, which will operate in tandem with economic policy.

Since 1988, the government has published a number of documents and publicity brochures on social justice generally and on particular areas of concern. In all of these, the above definition of social justice, centring on notions of equity, equality, access and participation, is restated. Amongst the documents with a general focus is *Towards a Fairer Australia: Social Justice Strategy Statement 1990–91* (1990). Like its predecessor, this statement outlines achievements ('an impressive record of income security and welfare reform in the 1980s') and signals future directions. An achievement of pertinence here is what is described as 'a major change in emphasis', that is the 'transformation' from a 'passive system providing income support to an active system that is integrated with the education, employment, training, child care and rehabilitation systems . . . ' (p. 5). Elsewhere in the document this 'active' system is identified as a policy designed 'to reduce dependency on social security' (p. 6). It is clear that education and training programmes are vital to this transformation. Overall, the emphasis is on 'more effective integration of economic and social policy' (p. 2). Included amongst those documents aimed at particular areas of need and activity is a number which target Australian youth. The key document here is *The Federal Government's Strategy for Young Australians: The Youth Book, 1989–90* (1989). Also included in this category is *Towards a Fairer Australia : Social Justice and Program Management: A Guide* (1989), which seeks to assist all government departments to identify their social justice objectives and assess their impact and effectiveness.

As we indicated, education and training are a central part of the government's approach to social justice. Equally, they are central to its approach to restructuring and revamping the economy. These three discourses come together in all the social justice policy documents since 1988 when this trend began in *Towards a Fairer Australia*. For instance, in the *Social Justice Strategy Statement: 1990–91* (1990) the government's key objectives for education and training are stated thus: 'to enhance equity and increase skill levels across the work force' (p. 3). Education and training are seen as 'the key to avoiding the intergenerational transfer of disadvantage and hardship', and as 'essential to providing the vocational skills necessary to ensure that people are able to obtain meaningful and productive jobs throughout their working lives' (p. 3). Clearly then, under the current Labor government, there is a very strong articulation between education, the economy and social justice. Amongst its priority areas are vocational and trade training, labour market preparation, employment experience programs, and industry training.

Within the school and tertiary sector, the broad social justice emphasis is on access, increasing school retention rates and expanding access to higher education. As the government points out, in 1990 over 60 per cent of young people stayed on at school in the post compulsory years, in contrast with 30 per cent in 1983. The target for 1992 is 65 per cent. Between 1983 and 1990 an increase in student numbers of almost 60 per cent has occurred in the tertiary sector (*Social Justice Strategy Statement, 1990–91*, 1990, p. 3). A range of income and other support schemes designed to encourage young people to continue their education or to pursue various forms of training have been developed. Students 'at risk' of leaving secondary school early, have been defined as a special category to be addressed. Within the access discourse, more education is equated with enhanced employment prospects.

In addition to these broad approaches is a set of apparently discrete policy initiatives relating to the needs of special groups, some of which were initiated by the previous Labor government between 1973 and 1975. Such programs have been designed for disadvantaged schools, country areas, students with intellectual and physical disabilities and Aboriginal education. Also in existence are the *National Policy for the Education of Girls in Australian Schools* (Schools Commission, 1987), *National Aboriginal and Torres Strait Islanders Education Policy* (1989), the *Federal Government Strategy for Rural Education and Training: A Fair Go* (1988), and a *National Agenda for Multicultural Australia* (1989). While most of these programs, policies and strategies are only concerned with the school sector, some refer to tertiary and other forms of education. In *Higher Education: A Policy Statement* (Dawkins, 1988), equity is identified as a national priority alongside the government's economic objectives. In 1990 the government published *A Fair Chance For All: Higher Education That's Within Everyone's Reach*. Equity objectives and targets are set for disadvantaged groups and strategies are suggested to assist institutional planning. Currently, no such overall social justice statement exists for Australian schools.

The government's approach to social justice in and through education has a number of significant features. Access to education as vocational preparation is without doubt the master discourse. Policies directed towards greatly enhanced retention, those designed to steer students into maths, science and technology subjects and those designed to tighten the connection between school, employment and the work place demonstrate very clearly the manner in which social justice has become married to economic policy. The disadvantaged are seen to benefit because their career prospects are enhanced and the nation is seen to benefit because the skills base of the population is improved. However, the extent to which either is true remains very much open to question. Certainly, as Smith, Burke, Smith and Wheelwright (1988) observe, the connection between increased credentials and economic growth has not been established. Further, as many labour market analysts point out, there is little unequivocal evidence about future trends in employment demand. Rapid technological, cultural and economic changes are making medium and long term predictions hazardous to say the least. Nonetheless, the strongest indications in Australia seem to be that expansion in high technology industries will result in fewer skilled jobs and more jobs demanding low skill, offering low wages and, overall, they will not be the areas of greatest employment growth anyway. If Australia is to follow the pattern of the US, the growth areas are in low-skilled clerical, and retail trade service occupations. (See further Watkins, 1986.)

Retention policies reflect the shift from passive to active social justice policy. Many young people who may historically have received unemployment benefits now stay on at school, and again we see the logic of multiple pay-offs. Government funds are saved through a reduction in dole payments and such students allegedly increase their employment prospects. Again, the extent to which the disadvantaged remain disadvantaged despite their extra education remains an open question. Affirmative action takes the very restricted form of financial support for those in most financial hardship. Beyond that, retention is seen to provide equal opportunities to all individual students. Failure is thus individualized and structural discrimination in both education and society is downplayed. Nonetheless, the government is able to legitimate its behaviour by proclaiming that the dramatic increases in retention are a sign of its commitment to enhanced life chances for the disadvantaged. However, retention and participation, alone, do not adequately address the issue of educational discrimination and disadvantage. Even though the nature of the post-compulsory curriculum has been a 'hot' educational issue for some time at the Commonwealth and State level, beyond the Participation and Equity Program (1984–86) and the Blackburn Report in Victoria, its implications for social justice in most mainstream state education department documents have not been of particular concern. One wonders if State and Commonwealth governments are not just shifting the zone of educational privilege upwards, from the upper-secondary school to the tertiary sector and within the tertiary sector to certain areas of knowledge.

The access dimension of the government's social justice policies is reflected very strongly in the concept of targeting percentage increases for certain groups by certain dates. For instance what we see in *A Fair Chance For All* is a proportional representation approach to equity. The ideal is that eventually disadvantaged groups are to be represented according to their proportions in the general population. While this may seem fair, it is a rather restrained approach to social and educational injustice. In a certain sense this is a managerialist view of equity which is tailored well to the corporate management cloth which is now draped over the entire public sector enterprise. While targeting has some obvious benefits (for instance its focus on groups rather than individuals), it has a number of inherent dangers, not the least being that it oversimplifies the problems and may well become an end in itself. An input, throughput and output mentality often accompanies the notion of targeting and the injustices which are inherent in the knowledges that people gain access to are only considered worth addressing to the extent that they inhibit throughput and output. The possibility that knowledge itself may significantly shape an unjust society or has the potential to reshape society more justly seems to be outside of consideration. However, targets, once reached, provide evidence that justice has been achieved. They thus legitimate policy and conceal their own limitations.

The emphasis on access has also meant that postcompulsory schooling and higher education have become the zone *par excellence* for social justice effort. Within the limits of the government's vocational access approach, this may well make sense, but there is much persuasive research evidence to suggest that the seeds of educational inequality are often sown in the earlier years and are inherent in the structures and content of the system itself. Of course this point is not neglected in a number of the policies and programs designed to help students with special needs, but as these seem to be subsidiary to the master discourse, and as they increasingly bow to the will of the master, such insights are in danger of being lost. With the economy as the 'master discourse', those aspects of injustice which are not connected to matters economic slip off the policy agenda. This leads us to a further point. The integrated social justice approach has led to a shift of focus away from the student to youth whose needs are to be addressed via youth policy packages. This has meant that education and training, although central, have become only two of many areas for policy development for young people. Although, again, there are benefits in this approach, what this seems to have meant for education is a loss of depth and quality in overall policy. Nowhere is this more evident than in the shopping list approach to educational disadvantage. Social justice has become a catch-all term, pluralist in the extreme. In its use of the term, the Government seems more concerned to satisfy interest group politics than to carefully develop a concept of injustice which is able to comprehend the structural connections between apparently diverse phenomena. Consequently, policies which address special needs are little connected to each other and fail to recognize the compounding effects of aspects of disadvantage. That aside, visible policies for special interests have the capacity to help repress dissent and allow the government to sustain an image of concern.

The overarching point is that the government has based its approach to social justice and education on the fundamental premise that it can tie social justice to its economic imperatives in general and both can be tied to a dramatically restructured education system. But is this the case? In order that we may attend to this question we will now progressively widen the focus of our analysis. Let us begin by considering the government's current approach to education in Australia.

A succinct way to highlight the main features of its approach is to identify the key words in the current education policy lexicon. These are: restructuring, efficiency, effectiveness, accountability, rationalization, performance indicators, corporate management, education markets, investment, national goals, national curriculum, retention, training, schooling for work, user pays, productivity, standards, equity, social justice. The ideas which these key words represent have informed wide-ranging decisions on matters of educational policy, administration and curriculum at the level of the school, the states and federal government. They also have implications for the relationship between schools and different sections of the wider community. They also imply certain priorities and foci for the curriculum and suggest modes of evaluating the performance of students, teachers and schools. Considered together, these key words also imply particular ways of addressing the issue of educational inequality.

The most obvious feature of the current period is that employment, education and training now belong to one department and have become so closely integrated they are almost inseparable. It is not at all hyperbolic to suggest that as economic priorities are driving educational priorities, so education is being reconceptualized as training and both are primarily to solve the economic needs of the nation and the employment needs of the individual. Mr Dawkins, as Minister for Employment, Education and Training, provided the blueprint for education in the late twentieth century in *Strengthening Australia's Schools: A*

Consideration of the Focus and Content of Schooling (1988), which included the following statement:

> Schools are the starting point of an integrated education and training structure in the economy. They provide the foundation on which a well-informed, compassionate and cohesive society is built. They also form the basis of a more highly skilled, adaptive and productive workforce. (p. 2)

Generally, despite some internal differences and priorities, the Labor government's primary concern is with foreign debt and trade performance, with managing the economy in ways which will make Australian industries efficient and internationally competitive, thus creating greater wealth in Australia. It is concerned to generate structural adjustments which will bring about such a result and is looking at taxation, financial markets, transport and communication, the public sector and reduced protection for industry. Education and training are important components of this policy. Indeed, education systems are to be closely tied to industry and to economic growth. This intention is made clear in the Dawkins and Holding document, *Skills Formation in Australia* (1987). The national need for greater productivity and prosperity, and changing circumstances in the economy, are seen to demand a 'highly trained and flexible labour force' (p. 4) and the formal education system is to produce the appropriately skilled population. Vocational education and such school subjects as mathematics, science and technology, in particular, are to play a major part. Economic rationalism has significant curriculum implications.

Broadly, as the above key words indicate, whatever technologies of control the government has at its disposal are currently being deployed in the interests of restructuring education so that it will cost the state less and serve the economy more. This is not the place to support this contention with a detailed account of the federal government's key policy decisions for education. (See however, Junor, 1991; Marginson, 1990.) Suffice it to say that although the weight of its effort has mostly been felt in the tertiary sector, it has sought to influence all sectors except preschool. In very broad terms its efforts have had a number of characteristic features which, in our view, have particular implications for social justice. Underlying policy are two central strategies: privatization and intervention. The privatization strand includes the following dimensions: the transfer of the costs of education from the state to the consumer, via various user-pay schemes; the encouragement of industry to invest in education and training both personally and in order to shape educational programmes, emphases and directions; and the commodification of knowledge. Knowledge is to be regarded as an investment which pays off for individuals in a job, for industry in a better trained labour force and for the nation in economic growth. Education is to be thought of in market terms and the market is to guide educational priorities and funding. Education is to be decentralized, power is to be dispersed to the local institutional level.

Alongside these privatization policies are those which intervene in order to ensure that privatization accords with national goals. Hence the government has set priorities and parameters to guide local decision-making. These have been offered via policy documents but they have also been delivered via the media. By these means the government has ensured that meaning has been mobilized in the ways it prefers. As a consequence it becomes clear, for example, that only certain knowledge is really worthy of personal and national investment leading to marketable credentials and national growth. Via such meaning-making practices, it has also ensured that institutions recognize that the government's approach to social justice is the one best way, indeed, the only way. The government has intervened further in order to tighten up spending and management structures, and to reorganize education along business lines. It has also revitalised its disciplinary mechanisms by encouraging such things as performance indicators and standards testing. In order to facilitate such adjustments, the Labor government has restructured the relationship between federal and State education authorities and, despite state rivalries and differences, education is becoming national. (See Lingard, Chapter 2, this volume.) The mechanisms which will allow the Commonwealth to more effectively steer school education are currently being put into place. Since 1988, the Minister has worked with the Australian Education Council (consisting of all Directors General and Ministers of Education from the States and Chief Executive Officers from the Territories) in the attempt to develop national goals for schooling, common curriculum frameworks and national reporting on performance. Of course it should be noted here that the goals and frameworks do express a concern for equity issues, although again, the extent to which equity is an overriding concern remains open to question.

The government has stated that social justice is a national priority. And, as we indicated earlier, its interventions have included a number of social justice initiatives, some with more ameliorative potential than others, some operating largely symbolically and playing a legitimating role. As noted, there are some internal contradictions to the government's approach. However, these pale in comparison with those which are manifest between its social justice and its privatization imperatives. Metaphors associated with markets dominate the government's attempts to privatize education and, given that markets operate according to the logic of profit, they cannot, in our view, be brought into a satisfactory union with social justice policies and must inevitably subvert them. For a more complete understanding of the developments outlined above it is necessary to widen the lens a little further and consider the wider political context.

Social Justice in the Context of Labor Party Policy

During the period following the Whitlam Labor government's term in office (1972–5) when the Australian Labor Party (ALP) was in opposition, it set about establishing a political platform which could be sold to the public. It was agreed that this platform must be substantially different both from the policies of the Fraser Liberal government (1975–1983) and from the approach employed by the Whitlam government. What was required was a fresh approach to the problem of stagflation (the inflation/unemployment connection). The task involved forging increasingly closer links between the upper echelons of the ALP and the union movement. Eventually there developed a comprehensive approach with the potential to reach across different social strata, offer consensus in place of confrontation and, of significance for our analysis, make the concept of social justice very visible. With the support of key union officials, the ALP prepared a draft of the Economic Accord in 1982. In February 1983 the first 'official' version of the document was complete. This document, in its original version, ' . . . is taken to constitute a set of economic policies designed to achieve a lower rate of inflation and a lower rate of unemployment' (Stilwell, 1986, p. 25). It integrated the ideal of social justice into its overall logic in a very visible way, and made a notable link between social justice and macroeconomic management. The underlying purpose was to develop a mechanism for tightening control over the national dimensions of economic reform in order to produce a more flexible and adaptive relationship between the Australian and the international economy. Along with the language of social justice was an associated stress on factors associated with international competition.

A range of policies was developed to support the Accord, including one on education. The general objective noted in the education policy reads that the 'ALP and ACTU agree that the prices and incomes accord should embrace the area of educational opportunities. The agreed objective in this area is that educational opportunities and the real level of funding will be maintained and where possible expanded' (Statement of Accord, 1983). The National Economic Summit, conducted immediately after the ALP won office in 1983, stated this educational objective in more specific terms. Point number 45 in the Communique reads:

> The Summit believes that education, training and retraining are of fundamental importance to the nation's present and future well-being and require a commitment of community resources to ensure a capacity to adapt and expand, with particular attention to disadvantaged groups. There is an urgent need to develop programs which raise education retention rates for the young and participation rates at tertiary institutions, increase our capacity to adapt to technological change, increase our educational research effort, and improve our management techniques. (National Economic Summit Communique, 1983)

These proclamations contain the seeds of the associations we have already noted, between the ideal of social justice in general and specific reforms to the education system. However, as we have also noted, behind these policy developments and their associated rhetorical claims, there is evidence of a more powerful set of concerns. At the very heart of this political program is an attempt to convert the Australian economy from one which is largely dependent on primary industry to one which can compete in the high-tech international market place. The macro- and micro-economic reform programs designed to bring this about are held together in a theoretical position which can be called laborist social democracy. And, at the centre of this position is the idea that wage restraint provides a means of holding inflation in check and stimulating overseas investment.

Having developed its wide-ranging economic program, the next task for the government was to effect its legitimacy. It had to develop a discourse which would persuade people to put the national interest above self and sectional interest. The politics of consensus has been one mechanism by which public support has been sought and maintained. Selling this position has also meant that a number of other key ideas have been kept to the fore in all policy areas. Consequently, social reform, the social wage and indeed social welfare have been reconceptualized within the boundaries of macro- and micro-economic reform strategies. As we implied earlier, closure has been achieved about what is to be seen as reasonable and possible in these areas. Concepts such as social justice, equity, participation and conciliation have been central here, partly because a Labor government runs the risk of demonstrating bad faith if its policies do not express a concern for social inequality and democracy. Clearly then, people had to be encouraged to support the cause but they also had to be persuaded to play their part in bringing about economic change. In this regard, a new lexicon of key terms and ideas has come into prominence over the last few years. The Government has sought to represent the Australian culture, the economy, the work place and industrial relations in ways which will both describe their ambitions and fulfil them. The language involved in new representations of the culture and the economy includes: restructuring the economy, enterprise culture, productive culture, clever country, financial deregulation, world competitive, markets and marketing, the current account problem, investment initiative, consensus and negotiation, efficiency, productivity and technology. New images of the workplace and industrial relations include the following terms: microeconomic reform, local initiative, centralized wage-fixing, workplace reform, flexibility, multiskilling, career path, award restructuring, enterprise bargaining. And finally, the language of social justice is meant to imply the preferred political direction. These key terms have become the basis for developing a comprehensive representation of the new political and economic order; an order which is portrayed as clearly different from either that which existed under the previous Labor government or that which is associated with the Liberal opposition.

For this discourse to become hegemonic, it has been important for its key proponents to harness the support of those who will refine, replay and amplify its message to the nation. In short, it has needed a set of organic intellectuals (see Gramsci, 1971), who will make respectable and popularize its ambitions. Accordingly, the Labor government has been skilled in persuading the popular media to adopt its language and promote its preferred images of itself and the nation. It has also found it helpful to have some more robust theoretical support. Pusey (1991) offers an extensive account of the work of the economic rationalists. Let us then offer two examples of the work of Labor's organic intellectuals.

John Mathews is one such person. He has brought theoretical respectability to the idea of consensus politics which has dominated Australian politics since 1983, when the ALP came to office. According to Mathews (1989), Australia has developed a progressive system which he calls 'associative democracy'. This idea encapsulates the process at stake with the Economic Accord with its bi- (or tri-) partisan arrangement worked out between employers, unions and government. Mathews argues that this arrangement has been demonstrated to be theoretically and empirically superior to other approaches using more centralized bureaucratic methods of government. He argues that,

> The outcome in terms of employment, inflation, unemployment and investment is widely recognised as being superior to the outcomes achieved in other countries by more neo-liberal-inspired strategies. The long run economics of this process have been analysed . . . as constituting a distinctive 'associational' model of social coordination, operating in addition to the coordination achieved by markets, governments and local communities . . . .

At a time when 'neo-liberal productivism' has provided a dominant model of restructuring in the 1980s, particularly in the UK and USA, involving the rapid introduction of new technologies and enterprise reorganisation, bypassing unions and consultative processes, and resulting in extreme polarisation of skills and incomes, Australia has been able to hold to an alternative course, instituting structural change which is both dynamically efficient and maintains commitment to social solidarity and equity. (pp. 1–2)

Mathews' proclamations represent a more sophisticated rendering of the rhetoric which has come to dominate political discussions in recent years. The 'mateship' ethic gets reworked and we are reminded of the virtues of collective social struggle. Solidarity, equity, progress and output are held together in the logic of this discourse and from within it the ideas of macro- and micro-economic reform have emerged. For instance, the strategy of award restructuring has developed as a means of making concrete the virtues of consensus politics.

A recent account of changes within the Illawarra region of New South Wales helps to clarify how this discourse is being developed by other social commentators. Julianne Schultz is typical of those who provide the makers of the Accord with a service different from that provided by intellectuals such as Mathews. She translates these ideas into stories for the more popular press. In an article in *Australian Society*, titled 'Wollongong Revisited', Schultz (1990) re-examines the city she critically commented on five years before (Schultz, 1985). She tells of the problems of old style industry (the rust bucket industries of coal and steel production of the past) and of old style politics. The intransigence of Malcolm Fraser, the former Liberal party Prime Minister, is the iconic representation of this outmoded political style, consistent with the description offered in the comment by John Mathews above. The new Wollongong which Schultz describes is represented in terms of a renovated local economy which has been able to attract new forms of investment and produce new relationships between industry and community. For example we are informed that 'after decades of standing aloof from the Wollongong community, BHP decided five years ago to become involved and committed itself to spending at least $800,000 on supporting local sporting, welfare and youth activities' (p. 16). At a more fundamental level, Schultz's account is a representation of localized restructuring of industry and the formation of workplace reform in which multiskilling is linked to industrial efficiency and competitiveness. It is also an account of the increasingly important role of education within this process, as noted in the comment that the University of Wollongong ' . . . is one of the most significant businesses in the city — it's almost a case of Wollongong having changed from a steel town to a university city in less than ten years. There is a very real possibility that the next step towards becoming a high-tech city could be in the next decade' (p. 17).

Schultz's comments contain the ambiguous qualities of many uncritical descriptions of contemporary social life. Complex changes with their multiple origins are described as if they have arisen directly from past events. The reality that various external factors are playing themselves out in this setting is thus screened from view. Further, a reading of the new is offered which operates both as description and as a mechanism of bringing the new into effect. This approach to constituting reality is similar to that used by the current Labor government.

One tactic within this political strategy is to set up arbitrary historical markers. The historical marker which has been established in current debates about social justice is the year 1983, when the Labor government with Bob Hawke as Prime Minister came to power. The way this marker is used strategically is clearly demonstrated in the preceding quotations from Schultz. Policy moves since 1983 are projected in a positive sense, while policy developments of the previous government are negatively positioned. The link between this strategy and the idea of social justice is clearly demonstrated in the government documents reviewed earlier in this chapter. These documents make constant claims about social justice advancements when compared with the preceding conservative government's term in office (1975–1983). In the most general sense the tenor of this strategy is noted in the comment that:

> These achievements have been built on a unique approach to managing the economy; an approach which has put jobs first. Despite the economic difficulties which faced Australia in 1983, the Government has created more than one million jobs and significantly reduced unemployment. Under the terms of the innovative Prices and Incomes Accord, the Government, the ACTU and ordinary workers have joined in partnership which has delivered jobs and wages moderation matched by massive improvements in the social wage; improvements which have been achieved even as total Government has been restrained. (*Towards A Fairer Australia*, 1988, p. i)

Rhetoric and description are pitched at the surface level, where image is most important. Indeed, rhetoric and description become fused.

A Different Perspective and Some Perplexing Questions

It is our contention that, if we are to critically interpret the government's social justice policies, we cannot accept as the whole story what is presented to us in government publications or those written by proponents and supporters of the Accord and associated policies. Neither can we equate the image with the real. An alternative possibility is to see the political processes being noted here as an ultimate attempt to cope with complex pressures associated with securing a place in the rapidly changing global economy and culture. Indeed they are best recognized as a response to, and part of, the emergence of a new international economic and cultural order. Let us elaborate.

Some writers claim that in the late twentieth century we live in social and cultural conditions which differ markedly from those of the early twentieth and late nineteenth century. (See further, Sharp, 1985.) Others go so far as to argue that these changes are so fundamental that the current condition must be named in order that it may be distinguished from earlier periods, hence the nomenclature, the postmodern age or condition. (See Baudrillard, 1981; Jameson, 1984; Lyotard, 1984.) While recognizing the controversy that surrounds such claims, we believe that the government's recent political strategy is best understood if we can identify some of the key features of the postmodern age.

One such key feature is that the pace of change is 'white hot', as the sociologist

Anthony Giddens says. Another is what has been described as the communications revolution which has arisen from what has been called the techno-scientific revolution. (See Baudrillard, 1981; Hinkson, 1987.) New technologies of information and communication have significant implications for culture, society and the economy, and thus for social interaction and human subjectivity. Such technologies have helped to facilitate the cultural dominance of the commodity. They have done so by revolutionizing processes of production and reducing the need for manual work but also by invading people's lives with both a flood of commodities and seductive images which generate desire. As a result, people now define themselves less as workers and more as consumers, and non-market relationships are redefined according to the logic of the market. Commodification and consumption tend to produce a selfish individualistic culture where the main moral imperative is gratification (Edgar, 1989). Further, new technologies have altered the relationships between space and time, and thus have dramatically changed our patterns of communication and integration. The face-to-face has become increasingly replaced by more abstract and global ways of relating. (See further, Hinkson, 1987.) Developments in science have brought about the communications revolution; scientific rationality has been its legitimating ideology, and both have clearly had a pervasive influence over many aspects of our life form.

While all such changes are pertinent to our argument, of particular pertinence are the implications of the techno-scientific and communications revolution for the state. New technologies interact with economic matters to help facilitate transnational enterprises, the operations of which challenge the capacity of nation states to control their own economies and cultural and natural environments. Indeed, new technologies of communication are demonstrating an increasing potential to bypass state boundaries. The state thus attempts to steer, but is also steered by the cultural and economic logic of the new technologies of communication. Broadly, from this point of view the power of the nation state, its capacity for better or worse to control its subjects and their form of life, is significantly reduced. As states struggle to transform their national economies and as they direct their resources accordingly, what we see is a shedding of welfare responsibilities. What also becomes evident is that information and communications and scientific discourses are deployed to legitimate such adjustments and to reassert control over populations which are increasingly dispersed across international information culture. Policy-making becomes increasingly caught up in the marketing and policing of images and the difference between the image and 'the real' becomes difficult to determine as the state variously uses and abuses media outlets and is used and abused by them. As we demonstrated in the first part of this chapter, such trends are evident in the government's handling of the economy and social justice.

The techno-scientific revolution has, as noted above, facilitated a shift in the nature of production itself. The move is from industrial towards postindustrial; from 'rust bucket' (old technology) towards 'sunrise' (new technology) industries and from primary towards service industries. Both accompanying and facilitating this shift has been the development of a new form of social labour. Indeed, at the very heart of this transformation is the work of the 'intellectually trained', those who apply established intellectual and scientific skills in work geared to the ends laid down by the owners or controllers of large scale industrial and administrative complexes (Sharp and White, 1968, p. 15).

The intellectual techniques which such people deploy are abstract and portable. They have many applications and are thus, in many senses, universal. (See Sharp, 1985.) Mental labour both replaces and displaces manual labour. Nonetheless, it is clear that the Labor government believes that this segment of the workforce must be expanded considerably in order that Australia may move competitively into the international economy. This is the logic which lies beneath its efforts to retain more students at school and to expand and make more comprehensive the tertiary sector. Workers must not only be highly trained and flexible, they must be prepared to put their knowledge to work for the nation. Educators, industry, unions and the state must unite behind the cause of the 'clever country' (the concept used by the Australian Prime Minister to denote a desired knowledge-based economy). 'Really useful knowledge', that worth national and personal investment, has increasingly been defined as either technical and scientific, or that which services and expands the market economy. Hence students are steered towards maths, science, technology, commerce, business studies and Asian languages. Education institutions are to gear themselves accordingly and put the weight of their efforts and their funds in these directions.

Of course restructuring education has not simply been about rearranging our values with regard to knowledge. It has also been about expansion and improvement at the same time as containing costs. The postmodern challenges to the welfare state have led governments to rethink the social wage. When the government is able to transfer costs to consumers it does so. Education is therefore to become an investment enterprise for industry and students alike. However, renegotiating its relationship to the welfare state is a process which is fraught with political danger for a Labor government, and so the postmodern condition poses particular problems of legitimacy and conscience. It calls for a new political strategy. Clearly the government believes that the various imperatives associated with the Accord answer this call. The Accord not only blurs the traditional boundaries between the personal and the general, micro and macro, the national and international, it encourages a new nationalism; it calls for collective and collaborative effort behind a cause which is both workable in all interests and just. Because it challenges the cult of selfishness mentioned earlier, social justice can be achieved, it is argued, through the principles of the Accord. This point is clearly demonstrated in the following comment in a newspaper article designed to link the Accord and social justice:

> The Government has provided new jobs, boosted industry, improved industrial health and safety and has success in other areas. Most of those successes have been achieved through the Accord and co-operation with the unions.

> That is still the best way for the Government to proceed. In the interests of all Australians there should be further co-operation to obtain those things still outstanding from the Accord. (Trades Hall Talk, 1989)

According to this view, the best way to help the educationally and socially disempowered is to provide them with the support and encouragement which enables them to join the swelling ranks of the intellectually trained. The needs of the state and the individual in the postmodern age can thus be addressed. Indeed a cult of educational selfishness can be encouraged to work in the national interest.

New information technologies have provided the means by which this message has been transferred to all parts of the country. Indeed, images and meaning have been generated and circulated which not only attract and attach people to this discourse, but which also persuade them that it is working in the interests of all. This discourse has become so pervasive that it has virtually colonized both the meaning of the term social justice and perceptions of the way to achieve it. The Accord has thus constructed a bridge between traditional political opponents, the Right and the Left. What is becoming increasingly apparent is that despite surface differences, there is a deep cultural agreement which unites previous political foes. This agreement is the empirical reality of the open market, which is seen and portrayed as the only game in town. The Left, with its history of collaborative struggle around ideas of collective ownership and equality, has increasingly come to accept the conditions of the game. Struggle no longer centres on issues related to the fundamental core of social organization. It now tends to centre on issues of individual opportunity and mobility within the terms of the Accord.

However, another feature of the postmodern age is that social injustice continues as an awesome reality. (See Dilnot, 1990; Raskall, 1987.) The social inequalities which characterized the modern era have not gone away (see The Social Justice Collective, 1991) although it seems that some may have been reshaped by the new social frame. For instance, the changed nature of work has lead to the redundancy of many workers, and structural unemployment has become a feature of social life. Alongside this trend we now recognize that the decreasing need for workers in material production has resulted in a dramatic increase in fractional employment. An examination of the facts and figures on wealth distribution, employment patterns and expenditure on welfare demonstrates not only some of the unfortunate and distressing consequences of the conditions described above, but also allows us to see what lies behind the images of amelioration, which are presented in the government's social justice pamphlets and media representations. As Australia sinks into recession and as the unemployment figures rise, it is clear that the Accord has not, at least in the short term, produced the desired results. Clearly, those who are concerned about social inequality need to continue the task of exploring the increasingly complex nature of the many forms of injustice which remain with us. Equally, the exploration and production of ideas and strategies designed to effect social justice must continue. The need for such work has not gone away, it has become more difficult but more pressing.

Not so clear are the new forms of injustice and exploitation that the postmodern condition both generates and obscures. When we talk of the postmodern condition we are using a term which invokes us to start to consider complex new issues. For example, we now recognize new concerns related to access to the complex information technologies, about the damage being done to people's bodies in the name of the scientific progress of medicine and to the life chances of subsequent generations as a result of environmental destruction which is now increasingly evident. Even less evident are the means by which these can be uncovered and addressed. While we have some understanding of the role that certain forms of education play in constituting the postmodern condition, we are not at all sure of the sorts of education which may constitute it more justly. Thus, we acknowledge the need for new research efforts where some of the complex issues noted here can be placed on the arena of debate. Currently, in the field of education there is an urgent need for a comprehensive and critical understanding of the central

Lindsay Fitzclarence and Jane Kenway

characteristics of the postmodern setting. We need to know much more about the reciprocal and other relationships between this setting and education. And, on the basis of this knowledge, we must answer the mega-question: What is the most appropriate curriculum for this complex and perplexing period, particularly for those who bear most of the personal costs of these hard times?

References

A Fair Chance For All: Higher Education That's Within Everyone's Reach, (1990) Canberra, Australia: Australian Government Publishing Service.
AUSTRALIAN LABOR PARTY and the AUSTRALIAN COUNCIL OF TRADE UNIONS (1983) *Statement of Accord Regarding Economic Policy.*
BAUDRILLARD, J. (1981) *For a Critique of the Political Economy of the Sign*, St Louis, MO: Telos Press.
COMMONWEALTH GOVERNMENT (1989) *Federal Government's Strategy for Young Australians: The Youth Book, 1989–90,* Canberra, Australia: Australian Government Publishing Service. [AGPS]
COMMONWEALTH GOVERNMENT (1990) *Soual Justice Strategy Statement: 1990–91*, Canberra, Australia: AGPS.
DAWKINS, J. (1988) *Higher Education: A Policy Statement*, Canberra, Australia: Australian Government Publishing Service.
DAWKINS, J. (1988) *Strengthening Australia's Schools: A Consideration of the Focus and Content of Schooling*, Canberra, Australia: AGPS.
DAWKINS, J.S. and HOLDING, A.C. (1987) *Skills Formation in Australia*, Canberra, Australia: AGPS.
DILNOT, A.W. (1990) 'The distribution and composition of personal sector wealth in Australia', *The Australian Economic Review*, 1st Quarter, pp. 33–40.
DEPARTMENT OF EMPLOYMENT, EDUCATION AND TRAINING (1989) *National Aboriginal and Torres Strait Islands Education Policy: Joint Policy Statement*, Canberra, Australia: Commonwealth of Australia.
EDGAR, D. (1989) 'Time we ended the cult of the self', *The Age*, March 3, p. 13.
Federal Government Strategy for Rural Education and Training, A Fair Go, (1988) Canberra, Australia: AGPS.
GRAMSCI, A. (1971) *Selections from Prison Notebooks*, ed. and trans. HOARE, Q. and SMITH, G., New York, NY: International Publishers.
HINKSON, J. (1987) 'Post-Lyotard: A critique of the information society', *Arena*, **80**, pp. 123–54.
JAMESON, F. (1984) 'Postmodernism, or the cultural logic of late capitalism', *New Left Review*, **146**, pp. 53–93.
JUNOR, A. (1991) 'Education: Producing or challenging inequality?' in The Social Justice Collective (Ed.), *Inequality in Australia: Slicing the Cake*, Melbourne, Australia: Heinemann, pp. 163–192.
LYOTARD, J. (1984) *The Postmodern Condition*, Manchester, UK: Manchester University Press.
MARGINSON, S. (1990) *Labor's Economic Policies in Higher Education*, Melbourne, Australia: Federated Australian University Staff Association.
MATHEWS, J. (1989) 'Towards an "Australian model" of restructuring', paper delivered to TASA Sociology Conference, LaTrobe University, Melbourne, Australia December, 1989.
National Agenda for a Multicultural Australia: Sharing Our Future (1989) Canberra, Australia: AGPS.

NATIONAL ECONOMIC SUMMIT COMMUNIQUE, April, 1983, Canberra, Australia.

PUSEY, M. (1991) *Economic Rationalism in Canberra: A Nation-Building State Changes its Mind*, Cambridge, UK: Cambridge University Press.

RASKALL, P. (1987) 'Wealth, who's got it? Who needs it?', *Australian Society*, May, pp. 21–4.

SCHOOLS COMMISSION (1987) *National Policy for the Education of Girls in Australian Schools*, Canberra, Australia: AGPS.

SCHULTZ, J. (1985) *Steel City Blues: the Human Costs of an Industrial Crisis*, Ringwood, Australia: Penguin Books.

SCHULTZ, J. (1990) 'Wollongong revisited', *Australian Society*, September, pp. 15–17.

SHARP, G. (1985) 'Constitutive abstraction and social practice', *Arena*, **70**, pp. 48–82.

SHARP, G. and WHITE, D. (1968) 'Features of the intellectually trained', *Arena*, **15**, pp. 30–3.

SMITH, B., BURKE, G., SMITH, S. and WHEELWRIGHT, T. (1988) 'Proposals for change in Australian education: A radical critique', *Discourse*, **9**, 1, pp. 1–38.

THE SOCIAL JUSTICE COLLECTIVE, (Eds) (1991) *Inequality in Australia*, Melbourne, Australia: Heinemann.

STILWELL, F. (1986) *The Accord . . . And Beyond*, Sydney, Australia: Pluto Press.

Towards a Fairer Australia: Social Justice And Program Management: A Guide (1988) Canberra, Australia: Australian Government Publishers Service.

TRADES HALL TALK (1989) 'The accord: Still the best road toward social justice', *The Geelong Advertiser*, April 12, p. 15.

WATKINS, P. (1989) 'Flexible manufacturing, flexible technology and flexible education: Visions of the postfordist economic solution', in SACHS, J. (Ed.) *Technology Education in Australia*, Australia Curriculum Development Centre, Canberra.

WATKINS, P. (1986) *High Tech, Low Tech and Education*, Geelong, Australia: Deakin University Press.

Chapter 7

Inequality and Educational Reform: Lessons from the Disadvantaged School Project[1]

Ken Johnston

Introduction

The most concrete manifestation of the Commonwealth government's commitment to equality in Australia is the Disadvantaged Schools Program (DSP). Based on the concept of positive discrimination, the Program allocates each year about $50 million to around 1400 disadvantaged schools. Around 16 per cent of the students in both government and non-government schools benefit from the extra resources. In order to receive the additional funds, teachers and parents in the selected schools must work together to develop school level projects to improve the learning outcomes of the students. The proposals are considered by Program committees, containing both parents and teachers, and if approved are funded on an annual basis. In general, the projects are required to advance the overall objectives of the DSP — improved learning; more meaningful and enjoyable schooling; and closer relationships between the school and the community.

The DSP is not a recent phenomenon. In fact, it is one of the few special purpose Commonwealth educational programs that spans two Labor administrations. Born in 1975, in the heady atmosphere of educational reform under the Whitlam government, it survived, relatively unscathed, the recessions and drastic cuts to public conservative Coalition government and now lives on under a second Labor administration with a very different reform agenda. With such a history, the Program provides an interesting case-study of the politics of educational change over the last sixteen years. Does the DSP continue to exhibit the values of equality and educational reform of the 1970s? Does the Hawke Labor government espouse the same vision of social justice in education that motivated the founders of the Program? To what extent has the Program adapted its structures, practices and philosophy to reflect the profound economic and social changes that have occurred since 1973 and the very different reform program of Labor in the 1980s?

The concept of reform is a normative one; progress for one person is decline for another. This implies that at each moment of reform there is a political and ideological contest between competing parties and interests to structure the social relations of schooling in a particular way. In the remainder of this chapter I will look at the DSP in the context of two such contests. The first, which gave rise to the educational reform movement of the 1970s, had a particularly formative influence on the character of the DSP. It was a moment in post-war history of relative affluence and optimism. Education was regarded as a powerful motor to create a more just and equal society. The second moment of reform, which began in the 1980s, and which is still setting the terms of educational debate, coincided with a time of economic scarcity and managerial reform. The egalitarian impulse has waned. If education is still regarded as a force for social change, it is as a motor of microeconomic reform, producing efficient skilled workers to suit a competitive, restructured economy.

Working Within a Bottom-up Model of School Reform

The period of reform that gave rise to the DSP was characterized by a ground-swell of popular movements, all seeking in various ways to redefine social and cultural boundaries. Conventional gender boundaries came under the critical scrutiny of the women's movement and gay organizations. Aborigines and migrants in their different ways questioned Anglo stereotypes of Australian nationalism and pointed to economic and social boundaries that excluded them from economic and political power. In the cultural sphere, musicians, writers and artists redefined the taken-for-granted boundaries between their work and the audience and art and politics. It was a period of considerable cultural criticism, and schooling was by no means immune from this struggle to rethink traditional boundaries.

Three particular boundary shifts in education had a significant impact on the subsequent structure and operation of the DSP. The first was a shift in the mode of power and control within education (Pusey, 1980). A few of the key mechanisms of hierarchical control in the highly centralized and bureaucratized public education systems that had evolved since the nineteenth century were relaxed in the 1970s to allow decision-making to devolve lower down in the system. Teachers were no longer automatically inspected every few years, and inspectors adopted a more consultative role. Centralized, external exams were modified and in some states, such as Queensland, disappeared altogether. Centrally devised and imposed syllabus statements gave way to curriculum guidelines that stressed principles and procedures but little mandatory subject matter. School-based curriculum development became the norm, especially in the primary schools.

The management of schooling in Australia is a state rather than a Commonwealth responsibility and the changes outlined above worked their way at varying speeds through the Education Departments in the different states. But coinciding with these developments was an important shift in the State/Commonwealth boundary itself. The period leading up to the election of the Labor government in 1973 was marked by a vigorous public campaign to highlight the inadequate funding of schooling in Australia. The campaign created a popular mandate for the incoming government to increase its role in schooling and redefine the State and Commonwealth relationship (Birch and Smart, 1977). Drawing on this mandate, the government established the Commonwealth Schools Commission with representatives from the teachers' unions, the parent organizations, and the government and non-government systems of education. The Commission was responsible for advising the government on the needs of schooling throughout

Australia and administering special purpose Commonwealth school programs such as the DSP.

A second, important set of boundary changes influenced the nature of learning and teaching itself. The DSP took shape in the midst of a revival of child-centred progressivism. This movement, which contested the traditional authoritarian approach to schooling, gave rise to an increase in the number of private parent-controlled alternative schools, the formation of annexes run on child-centred informal lines and attached to conventional public schools, the introduction of informal open classrooms, an emphasis upon discovery-learning and activity methods, and an increased emphasis upon collaborative learning and team-teaching (Schoenheimer, 1973; Hill, 1977; Otto, 1982).

Although short-lived, the progressive movement of the 1970s questioned a whole set of boundary relationships that lay at the heart of conventional schooling. Through its critique of streaming and testing (Knight, 1974; Taylor, 1980), it questioned the way in which children came to be labelled and treated as bright or slow. By stressing informality, and negotiated learning (Hannan, 1985), the progressive movement redefined the traditional boundaries between teachers and learners. In terms of knowledge, the progressivists emphasized the importance of experience, choice and relevance as a means to close the divide between abstract academic knowledge and practical everyday knowledge (Middleton, 1982). They also sought to narrow the gap between the school and the community and develop closer relationships between teachers and parents (Pettit, 1980).

Finally, a set of developments occurred that influenced the very definition of education and social justice. The traditional response to problems of educational inequality in Australia has been to distribute educational resources throughout the community on as equal a basis as possible. This application of *distributive justice* created large centralized public education bureaucracies that allocated resources between schools on a per capita basis. In principle, teachers were assigned to schools on the basis that students, whether they lived in the city or the bush, a working-class suburb or a more genteel area, would have a more or less equal chance of encountering well qualified staff. Behind this policy of distributive justice lay the hope that a uniformly resourced system would ensure that socially disadvantaged children would use their abilities to climb by means of schooling into the upper echelons of society.

By the late 1960s, this hope began to wear very thin. A range of statistical studies proved beyond doubt that the kind of formal equality of opportunity embodied in the policies of distributive justice had not diminished the severe inequalities of opportunity that characterized the school system (Ancich, Connell, Fisher and Koff, 1969; Fitzgerald, 1976). There began a massive research effort both in Australia and overseas to discover the social and psychological reasons as to why particular groups of children failed to take up and use the opportunities provided by an equally resourced system. (Refer to Connell, 1977, and Goodman, 1979, for a review of this research.) As a result of that work there developed a more radical, interventionist social justice strategy.

The new strategy was based upon a notion of *compensatory justice*. Research had shown conclusively that individual ability was not something that existed fully formed, waiting only for the removal of impediments to access and participation before it could attain its potential. (Refer to Henry, Knight, Lingard and Taylor, 1988, pp. 190–204 for a review of the studies that led to this conclusion.)

Studies of child-rearing, socialization and language acquisition confirmed in their different ways that ability was, in fact, socially constructed in day-to-day relationships and interactions. If your ability and future life-chances were influenced by the parents you chose to have, this was not because they passed on to you a set of genes that steered you in a certain direction, but because you acquired from them a social inheritance, a set of dispositions, a cultural capital on which you could draw to negotiate your way through the competitive world of school and work.

As far as social justice was concerned, the environmentalist logic in this line of argument pointed clearly in the direction of compensation and positive discrimination. If ability was socially constructed, and if it was possible to identify the social and cultural factors that led to success at school, then surely it was incumbent upon a socially just society to make those qualities available to all children regardless of their social circumstances.

The changes outlined above contributed to the character of what in retrospect was a very distinctive movement for educational reform. Behind this movement was a political alliance that included a modernizing Labor Party, a parent movement that had developed new organizational skills in the campaigns around increased funding for public education, teacher activists who were extending the boundaries of teacher unionism beyond the traditional industrial model, and an emerging strand of sociological and educational studies that provided an intellectual rationale for a more radical, interventionist program of reform. It was this movement which had a formative influence upon the nature and operation of the DSP.

I will use three metaphors to trace this influence. Firstly, the DSP became a beach-head for the Commonwealth into the government and non-government systems of education in the states. The Commonwealth was faced with the problem of bringing about egalitarian reform in school systems over which it had very limited powers of governance. Blackburn, a member of the Interim Committee which recommended the establishment of the DSP, recalled (1989) that the Committee worked on the assumption that the increased powers of the Commonwealth should be restricted to providing additional resources. The strategic question, therefore, was how to work within that limit to bring about the extensive changes in organizational and teaching practices that were required to achieve more equal educational outcomes.

The solution was to develop the DSP as a special purpose program in which resources and decision-making power could be placed in the hands of those close to the chalk-face in the classroom. In effect, the Commonwealth strategy was to side-step the cumbersome state education bureaucracies and empower those at the grass roots of the systems who it believed possessed the energy and motivation to bring about change. The rationale was explained in retrospect by Blackburn (1990, p. 3):

> It (the Interim Committee) wanted the extra funds to go directly into the schools rather then be under the control of system authorities. This desire arose from its observation that the high degree of centralised control over schools then operating in public systems imposed rigidities which prevented teachers from exercising professional initiative in a search for methods more effective in promoting learning in the schools concerned

. . . . The committee therefore wanted to set up the program in a way which developed and used professional initiative and expertise of teachers and gave them major responsibility for designing and implementing improvements.

The central mechanism for achieving this end was the requirement that there should be collective input into the planning and implementation of projects at the school level. In order to obtain funds, schools were expected to analyse the needs of the school community, critically look at their own activities, and demonstrate that the proposed projects would lead to more effective and enjoyable outcomes for students. The final decision about funding rested with a regional or systemic DSP committee on which teacher and parent representatives had a major voice. What this meant in effect was that schools and systems were expected to establish democratic procedures that would give classroom teachers and parents a major voice in how the Program was to be implemented on the ground.

At this point we can introduce our second metaphor. The organizational model that characterised the DSP formed a conduit from the broader movement of popular educational dissent into the rigid, centralized state bureaucracies for a range of new ideas and practices. There were a number of strands to this movement: parent and teacher alliances formed to fight for increased funding for public education; young teachers excited about radical critiques of education they had encountered in their training; catholic nuns who saw in the DSP a way to renew their mission to the poor; and students and teachers critical of the authoritarian nature of schooling. The DSP provided a small space within the systems for teachers and parents who were active in this movement of popular dissent to try out ideas and work for change at the level of the school (Johnston and White, 1989).

In this context, the broad aims of the Program and the school-based nature of educational reform take on a special significance. Unlike experimentally-based compensatory programs, such as Title I in the USA, the DSP is not a single-focus program designed from above to test out whether a targeted group of disadvantaged students benefit from a particular intervention. Instead of a single, uniform response to educational disadvantage, the design of the Program ensures a plurality of school-level responses to the problem of educational inequality. The strength of the Program has always depended upon a strong, self-generating network of teacher and parent activists who are primarily concerned with making schools more responsive to the needs of disadvantaged students, rather than upon a group of external specialists who compensate for the deficiencies of individuals with specific learning problems. Indeed, the important task of theorizing about disadvantage and how it might be redressed rests on the shoulders of those who have experienced educational inequality in their own working and personal lives, rather than on outside educational experts.

The focus on organizational reform allows us to introduce a third metaphor; in its operation the DSP has been akin to a virus within the system. With its built-in requirement for democratic decision-making and whole school planning, the Program became a democratic implant in a hierarchical body. The impulse for administrators and teachers who were content with the prevailing patterns of power and decision-making was to reject it, fearful that it would eventually spread throughout the system. Outright rejection was not easy, however, because of the resources involved. For the more autocratically minded, it was a catch-22 position: reject it and have fewer resources, accept it and have less power.

Resistance to the democratic, participatory nature of the Program was not only a defensive reaction towards a wider sharing of power within the schools and on regional and state committees. It was also a reaction to a change in the social relations of authority. When teachers and parents acted on the basis that they had a right to express their views and participate in decisions, they were sometimes seen as undermining the deference and respect which accompanied the traditional pattern of authority. For those who were used to the male world of executive power, the threat, as the following teacher recollected (Johnston and White, 1989, p. 25), also involved a shift in gender relations as well:

> Some teachers saw the period as one in which they were going to change the system and have all sorts of exciting innovations, whereas others like the principal saw authority being undermined, especially by women. The executive as a whole, the people who had reached status positions, suddenly felt that there was a new wave that didn't give them quite the respect and courtesy that they expected.

Disempowerment for some became empowerment for others. Teachers and parents experienced an extension of their roles in the school. First, it gave them an opportunity to ask some fundamental questions about whose school it was, and the purposes it should serve. These questions were normally seen as being part of an executive prerogative, outside the classroom teachers' and parents' domains. Second, it provided for teachers and parents the basis for a strong sense of 'ownership' of the Program. Through collaboration and joint decision-making, they worked through the issues and in the process became committed to the projects they constructed. Third, as the following comment from a DSP coordinator indicates, it reduced the isolation of the classroom teacher and allowed the sharing of experience and resources:

> The DSP has given some hope to these teachers. There is a strong sharing element in the program and when people come together, they find out that what they are experiencing is happening in other schools as well. And they share ways of addressing those concerns. When teachers are given more responsibility in the total planning of the school, they realise they are not powerless (Johnston and White, 1989, p. 14).

Accommodating to a 'Top-down' Model of School Reform

The philosophy, structure and operation of the DSP reflected the diverse strands that made up a broader educational reform movement in the early 1970s. In the context of those times, the Program was a powerful agent for school-level egalitarian reform. The times, however, have fundamentally changed, forcing the Program to adapt to a very different educational reform movement. In contrast to the earlier one which challenged important taken-for-granted educational boundaries from below, the more recent attempt to restructure educational relationships has adopted a 'top-down' strategy of managerial reform. But despite the change in the locus of power, the current reform movement is no less radical in its consequences than the earlier one; it too attempts to replace a prevailing educational discourse with a new orthodoxy and redefine the boundary relations of education.

Two aspects of the current educational reform movement have a particular bearing on social justice and the DSP. The first is the way in which educational inequality has been displaced as a central concern of policy. It may seem strange at a time when social and economic inequalities in Australia have assumed greater prominence, that educational inequality has become increasingly marginalized in policy debates. The dramatic nature of this displacement is nowhere more sharply revealed than in two educational reports to the Commonwealth government from committees chaired by Professor Peter Karmel. Equality was the dominant theme in *Schools in Australia*, the first of the reports (Interim Committee of the Australian Schools Commission, 1973), which recommended a massive increase in Commonwealth funding for Australian schools and a range of special purpose programs including the DSP. Twelve years later, in a second major review, Karmel shifted the focus from education's role in the reproduction of poverty to its contribution to the production of wealth. *Quality of Education in Australia* argued that with the national economy under siege and the need for a more skilled, productive and competitive workforce, educational inequality must be placed on the backburner until such time as the economy once more produced a surplus to redistribute to the poor (Quality of Education Review Committee, 1985).

The second aspect is the way in which the central bureaucracy has tightened administrative control over the flow of information and ideas. At the Commonwealth level, it is an attempt to make education serve national economic goals. There is a stress on vocationalism, education and training, closer connections between schooling and industry, the need for a trained flexible workforce, mathematics and science as priority areas, and a focus on skills-formation for a more competitive, knowledge-based economy. At the state level, the objective is to contain public expenditure on education by means of managerial reform. Hence the emphasis on measurable outcomes, efficiency, effectiveness, and accountability. Both strands embrace the notion that education is a marketable commodity and that market forces result in a more efficient, productive use of resources in education.

In order for this new reform agenda to gain ideological ascendancy, it was necessary to delegitimize or dismantle the institutional basis of its predecessor. The abolition of the Schools Commission marked an important step in this process. Through its various reports, conferences and personnel, the Commission provided an important source of legitimation for teacher activists who were struggling to bring about change in DSP schools. In the early period of the Program, as the following teacher recalled, the Commission documents took on the aura of revealed truth itself:

> The people I knew studied Chapter 9 of Karmel and wanted to use it as God's own Bible. Someone would do something, only to hear someone else say, 'Oh, you can't do that. If you look on page 21, you'll see that it's wrong.' There was this amazing clinging to the document. I can remember having a copy of Karmel and the first Triennium Report which were annotated and cross-referenced and indexed so that you could flick to the right pages (Johnston and White, 1989, p. 16).

The Commission was abolished in 1987 and its administrative powers, including responsibility for the DSP, transferred to the Commonwealth Department of Education, Employment and Training (DEET). Under the new arrangement, the Minister and senior bureaucrats in DEET, many of whom had acquired an economic rationalist position in areas such as trade, industry and treasury, regained the important ideological influence that had previously been exercised by the semi-autonomous Schools Commission. The representative body which replaced the Commission, the Schools Council, was smaller and politically weaker; it had little infrastructural support of its own to develop independent policy advice and no direct administrative control over Commonwealth school programs like the DSP. When staff from the disbanded Commission joined the DEET bureaucracy, they encountered economic rationalism as the dominant policy discourse. A new knowledge had become privileged and their own, based on the discourse of egalitarian reform of the earlier reform period, was delegitimated in the process. In the process, they were linguistically disenfranchised.

These changes at the remote and rarefied levels of the Canberra bureaucracy have had consequences for the very legitimacy of the DSP itself. With the replacement of the Commission by the weaker Schools Council there is no longer an effective institutional buffer between the Program and the dominant policy discourse of economic rationalism within DEET. The Program, therefore, is in an increasingly vulnerable position. Its legitimacy, as I have argued above, was primarily founded upon the discourse of egalitarian and progressive reform of the earlier reform movement. Should it continue to reiterate the old agenda of reform, knowing that it has little legitimacy in the upper reaches of power? Should it learn to speak the new language? Is it possible indeed for an equity program to adopt the language of economic rationalism and still speak on behalf of the disadvantaged? It is little wonder that workers in the Program at various levels experience tension and a degree of confusion in this contradictory situation. I will examine two particularly important aspects of this tension.

Outcomes and Indicators

At first sight, it would seem that the form of the DSP is admirably suited to input-output type evaluation: it had a separate and easily identifiable source of funds and an explicit set of documented goals. In other contexts (for example, Title I in the USA), these same features give to compensatory programs a very evaluation-driven character: a pre-test to select the disadvantage, a treatment to overcome the disadvantage and a post-test to see whether it had worked. But for a number of reasons the DSP never assumed that character:

- The goals of the Program were deliberately broad and diffuse to encourage variability of response at the local level.
- The funds were targeted at the heterogeneous school body rather than at a sub-set of disadvantaged students withdrawn for special treatment.
- The definition of need and school-level response rested with grassroots teachers and parents who, on the whole, were more concerned with the practicality and process of program delivery than with measuring output measures.

- Within the Program there was a deep and widespread distrust of conventional forms of standardized testing and objective measurements, especially in regard to their effects on the disadvantaged.

As the following DSP coordinator commented, the process of initiating change tended to overshadow the measurement of its effects:

> The Program was interpreted very much as a delivery of school programs. When you look at it, that's what schools are doing, they are running programs — literacy, numeracy, camp excursion programs, living skills, technology and computer awareness programs. They're delivering programs. If you focus the school's attention and say, 'Okay, what programs are you going to run?', you don't always get at the issue of assessment . . . . At some stage we should be building upon the fact that we can't just talk about delivering programs. You have got to think about what course you are going to offer, and what you are going to assess in the course. How is it going to be assessed? How do you know it's made a change? What outcomes have you seen from this? (Connell, Johnston and White, 1990, p. 36)

Evaluation has, in fact, been a constant feature of the Program over the years, but of a very different sort to the cost-benefit analysis that tries to quantify inputs and outputs. The beginning of the Program coincided with the popularity of action research. In the early days, teachers adopted this method to draw up profiles of their school and neighbourhood as a preliminary step to setting priorities for funding. Post-project evaluation has also been a consistent and frequently required part of the Program, although it has been rarely used to quantify outcomes in a statistical manner.

But a strength in the context of the earlier period seems a weakness in the changed circumstances of the present. Input-output measures assumed political significance when administrators were required to demonstrate that particular programs were cost-effective. This became the situation in the early 1980s:

> The overall growth of the public sector slowed, and with it public spending on education — which began to decline as a proportion of GDP in the 1980s. Education authorities now had to manage slowly growing, static or even contracting budgets. Deciding where cuts would be made, choosing between conflicting purposes, establishing priorities in a zero-sum situation, suddenly became the key to educational administration. (Connell, *et al.*, 1990, p. 20)

According to economic rationalist thinking, cost-effective schooling requires the icy winds of market competition and deregulation. In the effort to heighten competition between public schools, and between the public schools and private schools, the various state systems have introduced such measures as dezoning, financial devolution, and an increase in the number of selective and specialist schools. Conditions have been created for entrepreneurial principals to promote their wares in order to increase their market share. Output measures assume an added significance in this more market-oriented world of education: for the school

character of their client groups. It would be ironical if, as a result of these pressures, the DSP comes to experience a new lease of life providing bandaids for schools unable to compete in the cut and thrust of the educational marketplace.

But there is another side to corporate managerial-style devolution as far as the Program is concerned. Although the language differs from state to state and system to system — global budgeting, program budgeting, corporate goals, mission statements or five-year plans — the outcome in terms of practice is similar; schools are increasingly required to specify their goals, their action plans and strategies, and arrange their budget accordingly. While most practitioners are happy with the idea that they should explicitly state their goals, they are often less than happy to spend time responding to external demands for such things as elaborate mission statements. A high school principal in a recent study illustrates the mixed reactions to such demands:

> My missionary is out looking for the mission statement and I think the cannibal has put him in the pot. I shouldn't be flippant but I mean there has been so much garbage written in my life about mission statements. I mean I could sit down here and now and write a mission statement and it would be really tremendous. Whether anyone agrees with it, who cares? We (the staff) sat and agonised over a mission statement and we actually have it half written. The staff and students have taken twelve months to write it so we could see it as a working document not just a piece of paper. I don't know who asked us to write it! How about that? (At the time) I thought it was important to do, to summarise where we're going. Long-term plans are being developed here too, the direction (to do so) comes from above. In this state everything is being put back on principals and the school community. That's fine as long as we have the power to go with it. What the problems are at present is a devolution of responsibility but not authority . . . . I don't mind doing this if it is useful to the school but if it isn't, I tell them to bugger off you are wasting my time. (Connell, *et al.*, 1990, p. 77)

The DSP has an ambiguous relationship to these demands for corporate planning at the school level. To some degree, DSP schools have prepared their staff and parent communities for this role. Through its requirement that the school community look critically at the needs of the students and its own organizational practices, the Program has pioneered whole-school planning and shared decision-making. From this point of view, DSP schools have less trouble than other schools in accommodating to the new corporate planning model. But from a different perspective, accommodation implies a loss of distinctiveness and a dilution in the focus of the Program. This trend, noted in a recent report is already apparent:

> But the more DSP-funded activity is integrated into the life of the school, the less easy it is to 'evaluate' as a separate activity . . . . In a system where program budgeting is now applied to all activities of a school, the school's planning cycle lists the various activities for a given year and monies are committed as they become available. In this region there is a *de facto*, per capita DSP funding, so the school knows (more or less) what its DSP grant will be in advance, and can insert that figure into its planning process. Which of a range of activities happens to be funded by the DSP

is essentially arbitrary. We asked the chair of the DSP committee which of the line items were funded by the DSP and she confirmed that within the school only she and Principal would be able to tell. (Connell, *et al.*, 1990, p. 78)

I have been examining the fortunes of a major equity program as it has lived its days through one educational reform period to another. There is no simple conclusion to this story. One reading might point to the fact that the basic organizational structure of the Program has remained virtually intact for sixteen years and conclude that the DSP has largely been insulated from fluctuations in the political and educational climate. Another reading might conclude that the Program, reflecting the values and conditions of an earlier reform movement, has outlived its day. Neither of these readings is satisfactory, for each fails to give due weight to the historical complexity of the DSP.

One of the remarkable features of the DSP over its sixteen years of existence has been its capacity to renovate its philosophy and practice in response to limits and pressures. Some of these constraints were generated from within its own organizational practice, whereas others derived from outside the Program. In responding to these limits and pressures, the DSP has become a social institution in its own right, with its own culture and sense of history. Nor has it been a static institution. The Program is sustained and developed by a network of activists (teachers, parents and administrators) who have struggled over the years to understand and combat educational disadvantage.

That activity is at the heart of the DSP and it continues, in good times and bad. In good times, when educational equality occupies a central place in the educational agenda, the Program enjoys a legitimacy, and workers in the field are enlivened through contact with a wider movement of egalitarian reform. When times are bad and educational equality is displaced to the margins, the DSP moves into a more defensive mode. It is in this light that we must assess the accommodations made by the Program to the demands of the movement for economic rationalist and corporate managerial reform. They are rearguard actions to shore up the legitimacy of the Program. Such actions, although time-consuming, are necessary to allow the really important work of school-level egalitarian reform to continue.

Note

1. While I take responsibility for the ideas and argument in this chapter, I would like to acknowledge that they have developed out of an ongoing discussion with Vivian White and Bob Connell, fellow workers on the Poverty, Education and the Disadvantaged Schools Project at Macquarie University.

References

ANCICH, M., CONNELL, R.W., FISHER, J.A. and KOLFF, M. (1969) 'A descriptive bibliography of published research and writing on social stratification in Australia, 1946–1967', *Australia and New Zealand Journal of Sociology*, **5**, 1, pp. 69–73.
BARTLETT, L., KNIGHT, J. and LINGARD, R. (1991) 'Corporate federalism and the reform of teacher education in Australia', *Journal of Education Policy*, **6**, 1, pp. 91–5.

BIRCH, I. and SMART, D. (Eds) (1977) *The Commonwealth Government and Education 1964–1976: Policy Initiatives and Developments*, Richmond, Victoria, Australia: Drummond.

BLACKBURN, J. (1989) *Policy Ideas in the Disadvantaged Schools Program*, an unpublished paper prepared for the Commonwealth Department of Employment Education and Training, April, 1989.

COMMONWEATH SCHOOLS COMMISSION (1985) *Quality and Equality: Commonwealth Specific Purpose Programs for Australian Schools*, Canberra, Australia: Commonwealth Schools Commission.

CONNELL, R.W. (1977) 'Class and personal socialisation', in *Ruling Class, Ruling Culture*, Cambridge, UK: Cambridge University Press.

CONNELL, R.W., JONHSTON, K.M. and WHITE, V.M. (1990) *Measuring Up: Assessment of Student Outcomes and Program Effectiveness and the Educational Implications for Child Poverty in the Disadvantaged Schools Program*, a report to the Schools Council of the National Board of Employment, Education and Training, Canberra, Australia.

DAWKINS, J. (1988) *Strengthening Australia's Schools*, Canberra, Australia: Australian Government Publishing Service [AGPS].

DEPARTMENT OF EMPOLYMENT, EDUCATION AND TRAINING (1989) *Program Guidelines, 1989–90*, Canberra, Australia: AGPS.

FITZGERALD, R. (1976) *Poverty and Education in Australia*, fifth main report of the Poverty Commission, Canberra, Australia: AGPS.

GOODMAN, D.M. (1979) *Educational Disadvantage: a Bibliography*, Canberra, Australia: Schools Commission.

HANNAN, B. (1985) *The Democratic Curriculum*, Sydney, Australia: Allen and Unwin.

HENRY, M., KNIGHT, J., LINGARD, R. and TAYLOR, S. (1988) *Understanding Schooling: An Introductory Sociology of Australian Education*, London, UK: Routledge.

HILL, B. (1977) *The Schools*, Melbourne, Australia: Penguin.

INTERIM COMMITTEE OF THE AUSTRALIAN SCHOOLS COMMISSION (1973) *Schools in Australia*, Canberra, Australia: AGPS.

JOHNSTON, K.M. (1981) 'Ambiguities in the school and community debate: An analysis of the past, A new hope for the future', *New Directions in School and Community*, **2**, pp. 45–73.

JOHNSTON, K.M. and WHITE, V.A. (1989) *A Program in Action: Changing Practice in the Disadvantaged Schools Program*, Report 6 of the Poverty, Education and the DSP Research Project, Sydney, Australia: Macquarie University.

KNIGHT, T. (1974) 'Powerlessness and the student role: structural determinants of school status', *The Australian and New Zealand Journal of Sociology*, **10**, 2, pp. 112–7.

MIDDLETON, M. (1982) *Marking Time*, Sydney, Australia: Methuen.

OTTO, R. (1982) 'A View of alternative education as a contribution to social change', *La Trobe Working Papers in Sociology*, **62**.

PETTIT, D. (1980) *Opening Up Schools: Schools and Community in Australia*, Ringwood, Victoria, Australia: Penguin Books Australia.

PUSEY, M. (1980) 'The legitimation of state education systems', *Australia and New Zealand Journal of Sociology*, **16**, 2, pp. 45–52.

QUALITY OF EDUCATION REVIEW COMMITTEE (1985) *Quality of Education in Australia*, Canberra, Australia: AGPS.

SCHOENHEIMER, H. (1973) *Good Australian Schools and Their Communities*, Melbourne, Australia: Technical Teachers Association of Victoria.

SCOTT, B. (1989) *Schools Renewal: A Strategy to Revitalise Schools Within the New South Wales State Education System*, Sydney, Australia: Management Review, NSW Educational Portfolio.

TAYLOR, S. (1980) 'School experience and student perspectives: A study of some effects of secondary school organization', *Educational Review*, **26**, 2, pp. 37–52.

Chapter 8

Multiculturalism, Social Justice and the Restructuring of the Australian State

Fazal Rizvi

Introduction

Under the Labor Government in Australia, the public policy of multiculturalism has had a rocky ride. Throughout the 1980s, it has been subjected to much criticism from both the political Right and the Left, and while it has continued to enjoy the support of the state, the form that this support has taken has undergone several changes. The pluralist emphasis of the Liberal view of multiculturalism has been replaced by a rhetoric of social justice that highlights issues of access, equity and fairness. And, in symbolic terms at least, multiculturalism under Labor appears to have been transformed into a more radical policy. However, when we look at the material resources that have been available to implement multiculturalism, a very different picture emerges. We find that most of the services and programs that are funded under the general label of multiculturalism do not any longer enjoy the same level of support. Under Labor, many programs, such as the Multicultural Education Program, have been abandoned, while the funding for other programs, such as the Ethnic Schools Program, has been drastically reduced. More significantly, the structure of many welfare services available to migrant and minority groups has changed, with a greater reliance on 'user-pays' principles. There would appear to be a fundamental mismatch between Labor's commitment to the idea of a multiculturalism powered by the principles of social justice and its preparedness to support these principles with appropriate levels of funding and forms of service delivery.

It might be tempting to explain this mismatch by pointing simply to the economic difficulties that the Government faces. It could be suggested, for example, that in hard times resources are just not available to fund adequately the welfare programs of a Government committed to social justice. While this argument is certainly plausible, it does not, in my view, provide an adequate explanation for the mismatch. To understand adequately the contradictory nature of Labor's reformulation and support for multiculturalism, we need to consider the nature of its attempts to restructure the state, and, in particular, to examine the consequences of its program of administrative reforms on the practices of multiculturalism.

In this chapter, I argue that Labor's restructuring of the Australian state has not been a neutral exercise, and that it has had major implications for the way the public policy of multiculturalism has been practised. While it is true that Labor has attempted to deal with many of the contradictions contained in the Liberal view of multiculturalism, and reorient it towards a more comprehensive agenda of social justice, this reorientation has become trapped within Labor's wider concern with the restructuring of the Australian state towards a more market-driven political economy and an administrative structure that is more responsive to the forces of the market. Indeed, as I shall endeavour to demonstrate, even the principle of social justice has been re-articulated in such a way as to link it essentially to market considerations. Thus, multiculturalism has become a policy which, while rhetorically endorsed, is no longer supported in any specific interventionist way. Working with a distinction between 'policy formulation' and 'policy realization', the Government seems to have assumed that its basic task is to put the policy framework of multiculturalism into place, increasingly leaving the task of policy realization to market forces. I shall argue that such an instrumentalist assumption is fundamentally flawed, and that it is based on a logic that is incompatible with the principles of a caring social democratic society.

The Role of the State in the Construction of Multiculturalism

As a social and educational policy, multiculturalism did not emerge in Australia until the mid-1970s, but by the time Labor assumed power in 1983, it was well-entrenched on the political landscape of the country. It is important to note, however, that the emergence and rapid rise of multiculturalism cannot be explained in terms of the organic growth of a social movement. Multiculturalism has never been a social movement in the way that the concept has been described by sociologists writing in the tradition of Touraine (1977). For one such sociologist, Gilroy (1987), social movements mark out new interpretive and participative communities in which political action and organization occur outside the mainstream frameworks prescribed by the state. Social movements do not only challenge the current mode of production, of the way in which a society appropriates its scarce resources, but also seek 'collective control over socio-economic development as a whole' (Gilroy, 1987, p. 224). They represent an oppositional discourse, challenging the state to work towards 'universalizing the issue of emancipation beyond the particularistic interests of industrial workers employed full time in work that produces surplus value'. Gilroy suggests that the distinctive feature of social movements is that they are 'located in their common struggle for the social control of historicity' (pp. 224–5).

Far from being an oppositional discourse which emerged organically as a result of some collective social action, multiculturalism in Australia is best viewed as a construction of the state. As a policy it resides very much within the mainstream political framework, and it certainly does not challenge the current mode of production. It was formulated by the state in response to what the state saw as a growing crisis in ethnic relations. For in the early 1970s, there was a widespread recognition among most sections of the Australian community that migrant groups were systematically disadvantaged in Australia, and that the policy of assimilation had served only to reproduce the existing patterns of inequalities. Assimilation was increasingly rejected as a policy instrument capable either of fulfilling the needs of migrants or of containing migrant unrest.

In an influential paper, Jakubowicz (1981) has argued that the policy of multiculturalism represented an attempt by the state to contain the growing political and economic demands of minority groups, and to restore their acquiescence to the existing structure of Australian capitalism. There is ample evidence to support this argument, as can be seen by an examination of the successive reports produced by various government agencies in the 1970s, which warned of the 'unacceptable alternatives' Australia would confront if the increasingly volatile ethnic communities were not controlled (Australian Ethnic Affairs Council, 1977, p. 7). Contrary to current right-wing rhetoric, multiculturalism was never some socialist conspiracy but a policy tool developed to defuse social conflict and maintain existing social order.

Jakubowicz's argument also serves to explain the logic behind the Galbally Report (1978), a major reference point of the liberal view of multiculturalism. For in reviewing 'the effectiveness of the Government programs and services for migrants', as he was asked to do, Galbally was also responding to another state imperative — namely, to produce a set of recommendations and programs that would contain ethnic militancy, and thus ensure the social conditions necessary for the accumulation of capital. The Galbally Report thus spoke repeatedly of Australia being at 'a critical stage' and of facing the dangers of further heightened social tensions. It regarded ethnic discontent as a major problem that required urgent state mediation, since it had the potential of undermining existing political economic institutions.

However, there was nothing new about Galbally's solution to the migrant problems. The view of multiculturalism he proposed was in fact a version of cultural pluralism, a doctrine promoted from time to time in the United States for almost a century (Olneck, 1990). It was an idea that had also been promoted in Australia, initially by the Whitlam Labor Government's first Minister of Immigration, Al Grassby (1973), and later in the various reports of the Australian Ethnic Affairs Council. Essentially, Galbally's multiculturalism represented a liberal welfare philosophy which demanded recognition of the contribution of the immigrants of non-English speaking backgrounds to the development of the Australian nation. It made the notion of 'the Australian' problematic, and suggested that all migrant cultures should be encouraged to flourish in Australia around a shared core of basic democratic norms and values that are uniquely Australian. The Galbally Report listed social cohesion, cultural identity, and equality of opportunity and access as the key principles essential for a multicultural society.

Within the framework of these principles, the Galbally Report (1978) made a number of policy recommendations. Around the principle of equality, it suggested that 'all members of our society must have equal opportunity to realise their full potential and must have equal access to programs and services', while around the principle of cultural identity, it maintained that 'every person should be able to maintain his or her culture without prejudice or disadvantage and should be encouraged to understand and embrace other cultures'. The Galbally Report was remarkably brief on the principle of social cohesion, but insisted that the state should establish wide-ranging welfare and advisory services to facilitate the full participation of migrants in the mainstream institutions. Exactly what these mainstream institutions were was less clear in the Report.

This concern with equity was consistent with developments in the area of Education. The establishment of a National Advisory and Consultative Committee on Multicultural Education (NACCME) led to the publication of a series of Research and Discussion Papers that attempted to reconstruct multicultural education away from the liberal pluralist concerns to the social-democratic objectives of social justice for various disadvantaged ethnic groups. A national policy on languages (Lo Bianco, 1987) no longer viewed the teaching of community languages largely as a way of ensuring the maintenance of diverse cultural traditions, but as a way of reconciling a range of demographic, economic, and political interests. In it, the issues of access to mainstream institutions played an overriding role. These developments responded to the issues of the persistence of educational inequalities, and raised questions about the structural features of multi-ethnic schools in which such inequalities are reproduced.

The chairperson of NACCME, Laksiri Jayasuriya (1987), highlighted the importance of the idea of social justice in any reconstruction of the policy of multiculturalism. Jayasuriya believed that the experiences of minority ethnic groups could no longer focus exclusively on the needs of the first generation migrants. Disadvantage, he argued, functions and is distributed in different ways for second and third generation ethnic minorities. The issues articulated by migrant women and the needs of the migrant aged, moreover, imply that ethnic affairs in Australia cannot be adequately explored in terms of the maintenance of cultural identity, because that identity has a very diffuse and changing form.

Jayasuriya's remarks highlighted the changing nature of the social, cultural and economic conditions in which Labor had to reconstruct its policy of multiculturalism. In Australian society, for example, racism now functioned in a different way, and had more recently become aligned to debates over the nature and scope of migrant intake. The increasing visibility of Asian immigrants in the cities had been an important factor in Australians re-examining the issues of the nation's ethnic composition. Since the so-called Blainey debate on migration and Australian identity began in 1984, various pressure groups approached ethnic issues in a more cavalier fashion, using economic, and sometimes environmental, arguments to obscure what had effectively been racist sentiments.

In a very useful paper, Castles (1987) attempted to summarize the new conditions present in Australia that any new agenda in multiculturalism had to take into account. Castles argued that new models for ethnic affairs must now respond to the 'maturing of the migratory process', that is, the existence of the second and third generation Australians of non-English speaking background; the changes in economic, social and political conditions in Australia, that is, Australia's growing financial deficit problem, making any expansion of migrant services difficult to justify; the commitment of both Labor and Liberal parties to principles of economic rationalism; the changes in the character of current immigration, and with it an emergence of new forms of racism.

It is within this context that Labor's attempts at redefining multiculturalism must be viewed. But the notion of context is not a simple one; it denotes a variety of circumstances. It does not describe a set of static functional conditions, but is something that is dynamically linked to the constantly changing conditions. The context is composed of a whole variety of objects, only some of which are highlighted to serve particular political purposes. What is regarded as the context, and the constraints it places on various policy options, is a matter for considerable political debate. Any assessment of the context reflects a particular set of political interests. This is true for both the analyst and the state. The state thus articulates its policies against the background of a particular interpretation of the social and economic conditions facing the nation; just as the conditions might change, so do the interpretations.

Thus, in its early period, Labor's multicultural policy was guided by the assumptions of traditional welfare reformism — the concern for the disadvantaged and a belief in the capacity of the state to promote social justice through judicious interventionist programs. However, by the time the Jupp Report was published, these assumptions were already under attack, as the Government increasingly accepted certain aspects of the analysis of the 'economic context' that the New Right thinkers such as John Stone had been putting forward for some time. It accepted many of the ideas of the economic rationalists, with their emphasis on unrestrained capital growth, the free market, economic individualism, the minimalist state, and private property as the basis of individual freedom (see Pusey, 1991). Labor also championed the idea of the need for a reduction in the levels of personal tax by cutting back on public spending, and particularly the so-called 'unproductive' welfare spending, including spending on migrant welfare programs. In 1985, the Government's deregulation of the money market marked a decisive moment at which the processes of the restructuring of the Australian state towards a market economy operating on so-called 'dry' principles commenced in earnest. At the same time, however, Labor insisted that it had not abandoned its traditional commitment to social justice and wished to see multiculturalism redefined in terms of its social democratic ideals. But as Castles (1987) observed, an agenda for multiculturalism governed by such ideals could not easily be justified on the neo-classical economic postulates, since Labor's call for social justice seemed to 'run counter to the tide of pragmatism in a crisis-ridden Australia' of the late '80s.

In *The National Agenda for a Multicultural Australia* (Office of Multicultural Affairs, 1989), released by the Prime Minister in July 1989, the Labor Government attempted to deal with this contradiction. The Agenda's main argument was formulated in a discussion paper a year earlier. The rearticulated policy of multiculturalism emphasized the following principles:

> The current policy of the Commonwealth government emphasises three aspects of multiculturalism: respect for cultural differences, social justice and economic efficiency.

> The cultural dimension means that all Australians should be free to develop, adapt and express elements of their individual cultural heritage, within the unifying framework of a commitment to Australia, its laws and institutions . . . .

> The social dimension means that the structures and purposes of Australian society should acknowledge and be responsive to the diversity of its population . . . conformity to a particular cultural stereotype should

not be the price demanded in return for equal treatment or the right fully to participate in society.

The economic dimension of multiculturalism means that Australia should be able to make effective use of all the nation's human resources (Advisory Council on Multicultural Affairs 1988, pp. 5–6).

In the Agenda itself, the Government insisted that it saw no major contradiction between the three dimensions of its policy on multiculturalism. Indeed, as the Prime Minister (Office of Multicultural Affairs, 1989, p. v) indicated, 'The Agenda has been developed within the context of economic restraint that is the hallmark of my Government . . . It addresses not only issues of equity but also of economic efficiency.' Further, the Agenda states that the Government's multicultural initiatives are set within 'fiscal responsibility, fully conscious of the need for budgetary constraints imposed by national economic imperatives' (p. 1).

Note here the reification of the economic context which is said to imply certain imperatives! The Agenda continues: 'Increasingly governments and the community are seeking better value for their resources. This requires changes to organisations and structures which will result in a lasting capacity to respond to cultural diversity without the need for on-going external or additional support' (p. 51). Here the cultural objective of diversity has been subjugated to the over-riding principle of fiscal responsibility. Further indication of the Agenda's basic priority with the economic is revealed in its assertion that: 'People, as much as machines, are a critical input to economic performance and growth. Effective and efficient development and utilization of our resources is essential if Australia's economic potential is to be realised fully' (p. 26). Here, cultural policy is once again shown to be a servant of economic policy, with migrants seen as a human resource which is not being fully utilized to facilitate Australia's economic objectives.

The Government's social and cultural concerns, including its social justice strategy, are thus expressed within the frameworks of its economic objectives. And while there is a great deal of sentiment in the Agenda about the need to ensure social and economic justice, to ensure that all Australians enjoy equal life chances and have an equitable share of nation's resources, that all Australians are able to maintain and develop their cultural heritage, and that all Australians have an opportunity to participate fully in society and the decisions which directly affect them, these cultural objectives are overshadowed by the main thrust of the Agenda, to ensure that all Australians are able 'to develop and use their potential for Australia's economic and social development' (p. 1). It is to this latter objective that the Government's Action Plan, arising out of the Agenda, is targeted. Thus, improved migrant access to education and training provisions, measures to extend the teaching of English as a Second Language, especially in the workplace, and review of ways to improve the linkage between post-school English as a Second Language and the rest of the education and training system are the main initiatives to be funded directly as a result of the recommendations of the Agenda. Missing from the Action Plan are the community programs that were supported by Galbally, including a community languages and bilingualism program, programs that might confront racism in Australian society or indeed programs that might help those who are not, or are unlikely to be, in the workforce.

Social Justice and the Restructuring of the State

Labor's *Agenda for a Multicultural Australia* cannot in my view be adequately understood without a reference to the conceptual and political links it has to the Government's attempts to restructure the Australian state. The discourse of restructuring has been a constant theme of the Labor Government. It emerged out of its view that the Australian economy it inherited in 1983 was crisis-ridden and needed to be restructured to make it more competitive internationally, believing this to be possible only if Australia developed its manufacturing base, its high tech capacity and its image as a more reliable industrial player within the international economic community. In order for this restructuring to be successful, the Government insisted further that many of the country's major institutions would have to undergo substantial changes. For example, the processes of restructuring require major changes in the areas of training, education and skill formation in order to provide new industries with a more flexible, multi-skilled workforce. The emphasis has thus been on greater productivity; and whatever changes might contribute to it, however indirectly, are assumed to be good. Accordingly, the Government's policies on both immigration and ethnic affairs have become rearticulated within the framework of human capital theory, which the logic of restructuring clearly assumes. Migrants are hence regarded as human resources whose distinctive inputs are to be valued, and whose skill levels need to be developed. Evidence for this shift in policy may be found in the Fitzgerald Report (1988) which stresses that the skill demands of Australian industry should now be the central feature of migration policy.

As Anna Yeatman (1990, p. 101) has pointed out, 'the overwhelming tenor of debates about public policy response to the challenges of restructuring is economistic.' Non-economistic, cultural or political concerns are either relegated as secondary or rearticulated in economic terms, as issues of motivation, about the conditions necessary to promote productive investment or about the kind of investment that should be made in human capital to facilitate increased economic growth and productivity. How the polity can be made economically active, creative and entrepreneurial becomes the key issue. In this respect, Yeatman (1990, p. 101) argues, 'the moral components of economic activity have been neglected.' Yeatman's argument is especially relevant to an analysis of *The National Agenda for a Multicultural Australia* and the Fitzgerald Report (1988) on immigration, for, as she (1990, p. 103) suggests:

> Both these reports accord the agenda of economic restructuring a central place in their recommendations, so that both a specific immigration policy and multiculturalism are strategically aligned with an effective national economic response to the challenges of restructuring. The mixing of the discourse of economic restructuring with the discourses of immigration on the one hand and multiculturalism on the other is especially interesting for its introduction of a cultural dimension into the business of restructuring.

The mixing of discourses Yeatman speaks of can also be found in the Government's social justice strategy. It is this ideological move that serves to explain the way Labor has attempted to deal with the apparent contradiction we have already noted between its view of a multiculturalism guided by the principles of social justice and its commitment to basic tenets of economic rationalism.

The idea of social justice is a highly contested one. It does not represent a timeless or static category. It has been interpreted in a variety of ways in accordance with the changing forms of injustice and the way they have been perceived. Indeed, the Australian Labor Party (ALP) does not have, and never has had, a uniform understanding of the idea of social justice. It is however possible to identify, within the ALP, two major traditions of thinking about its meaning and significance, which have, throughout its one hundred years of history, struggled for supremacy. Indeed, it may plausibly be argued that it is this differing understanding of the notion of social justice that is the basis of the formation of the various factions within the ALP (MacIntyre, 1985). The current policy debates simply represent the triumph of one particular understanding over the other, for it is only within the framework of that understanding that it is possible to reconcile the competing discourses of social justice and economic rationalism.

The two traditions of thinking about social justice can be identified as liberal-individualist and socialist. The liberal-individualist view conceptualizes social justice variously in terms of either 'desert' or 'fairness'. Perhaps the most outstanding contemporary advocate of the view of social justice that emphasizes justice as fairness is Rawls (1972). To derive his principles of justice, Rawls constructs a hypothetical state of ignorance in which people do not know of the social position they might occupy in the future — with regards, for instance, to their income, status and power, and also to their natural abilities, intelligence, strength, etc. In such a state, Rawls argues, people, acting in their own self-interest, would inevitably select principles that are likely to do them least harm and maximize their chances of happiness. This philosophical projection leads Rawls to suggest two principles — the most extensive basic liberty compatible with similar liberty for others; and equal distribution of primary social goods . . . unless unequal distribution is to the advantage of the least favoured.

In opposition to Rawls' view, Nozick (1974) has presented a view of social justice that emphasizes 'desert'. Writing in the tradition of Locke and Sidgwick, Nozick argues that Rawls' theory ignores the issue of people's entitlements. Most theories of social justice, he points out, focus only on the end distribution of holdings; they pay little attention to the processes by which holdings were acquired. Nozick suggests that it is the justice of the competition, that is, the way competition is carried on, not its result, that counts. Now while the differences between Rawls and Nozick are considerable, they both assume that people always act in their own self-interest. They both assume individualistic liberty as a value prior to any consideration of social justice. And they both assume community to be simply a sum of the individuals who reside in it.

The other tradition of thinking about social justice within the ALP is based on a very different set of assumptions. That tradition is derived from Marx, and stresses the idea of needs. As Beilharz (1989, p. 94) has pointed out, 'it is qualitatively different to the preceding understandings, in that need is viewed as a primary rather than a residual category, and it is this which sets this view off from the charity-based arguments about the "needy" which are compatible with either the "desert" or the "fairness" principles'. This needs tradition highlights a more collectivist and co-operative image of society.

For the purposes of this paper, it is important to note that liberal-individualist and socialist traditions rest on very different understandings about the nature of the relationship between social justice and the market. The liberal-individualist assumes the logic of the market, regarding it as the basic provider of social justice, of employment, services and welfare. The state is seen as a vehicle for promoting the activities of the market, and it is assumed that the market, if left to operate freely, will be able to deliver the distributive fairness on its accord. For the socialist, on the other hand, as Agnes Heller (1976) has pointed out, the idea of social justice may not necessarily be incompatible with markets, but it is unlikely to be achieved when the market is not controlled in sufficiently rigorous ways. State activity is thus seen as market replacing, correcting its excesses, and minimizing the costs of its arbitrary exercise.

During the time Labor been has been in power throughout Australia, it has been the liberal-individualist view of social justice, and more particularly the view of social justice as 'desert', that has been dominant. Thus, as Beilharz (1989, pp. 92–3) has argued of the Victorian Government's social justice strategy:

> (its) hope is that the economy itself can be steered in the direction of 'social justice' — a non-sequiter outside the logic of markets, necessarily introducing residual welfare mechanisms in order to buoy up the human flotsam which cannot negotiate justice for itself through the market. To argue in this way is necessarily to introduce the logic of charity, and the language of the 'needy', for there are citizens, and there are those outside the city gates, who are deserving compassion.

A deficit view of social justice is necessarily introduced, with women, migrants, the disabled and the poor, and especially the unemployed, regarded as the disadvantaged to whom the market, through its agency, the state, has a special compensatory responsibility. Beilharz suggests further that social justice understood in this way is not so much a universal principle as an administrative principle, the practical symbol of which is targeting of funds. It is important to note, moreover, that the structure of this kind of thinking allows for social justice to be postponed until a market-led recovery has been achieved, which may be never!

The Federal Labor Government's social justice policy rests on similar assumptions. It suggests that freedoms, prosperity and equity can only be delivered by the market. With such reliance on the market, the Government's major responsibility becomes that of good management of the social and cultural conditions necessary for capital accumulation. Labor's restructuring program may be seen in this light. Among the assumptions that lie behind the restructuring is the belief that the less the state is involved in market operations the better. Thus, tariffs have been cut, controls on the conduct of the market have been reduced, controls over banking and finance have been removed, tax breaks have been given to speculators to borrow abroad, new concentrations of wealth and media have been permitted, and a program of the sale of public enterprises has been commenced. All this has often been justified on the grounds that free association of buyers and sellers in an open market will bring a fair and equitable exchange. The Nozickian notion of 'desert' has thus become well-established as the basis of social justice.

Throughout the 1980s, Labor's proud boast was its achievement in the area of job creation. It was argued that the best thing the Government could do was to create jobs. This reflected the Government's 'labourism' (Maddox, 1989), a view that implicitly confirmed, through the instrument of the Accord between the Government and the Australian Council of Trade Union, those in paid employment a privileged place in the structures of decision-making. It implies that labour alone is somehow more deserving. But the problem with this view is that it confuses social justice with employment, thus in a society like Australia confirming the reliance on the market as the fundamental provider of welfare. In this labourist discourse, the position of the unemployed (now 10 per cent of the population) and unpaid women workers becomes an untenable one. They are left, so to speak, outside the city gates!

This labourist perspective has had major implications for multiculturalism, since most migrants do not constitute the mainstream citizen who has been given a voice in the corporatist decision-making structures that the Government has developed. As a social policy, moreover, as we have already noted, multiculturalism is now valued only to the extent that it contributes in some fashion to meeting economic objectives. Within the framework of this instrumentalism, the idea of administrative efficiency has played a major part. This concern for efficiency is linked to Labor's program of administrative reforms. But such reforms have also served to undermine any progressive potential that a view of multiculturalism governed by the principles of social justice might have had.

Multiculturalism and Labor's Program of Administrative Reform

A program of administrative reform was part of an agenda Labor had outlined before it was elected to government in 1983. In government, a White Paper, *Reforming the Australian Public Service*, released in December 1983, gave substance to this agenda. The opening paragraph of the Paper set the tone: 'The responsiveness, efficiency and accountability of Commonwealth institutions have a major impact on the quality of Australian democracy.' One of the Paper's architects, Wilenski (1986), was to write later that efficiency, democracy and equity were the key dimensions of Labor's program of administrative reforms. Such a program was clearly going to be supportive of the interests of migrant communities, since it promised to provide 'a representative and diverse bureaucracy whose decisions are more open to public influence, to public scrutiny and appeal'. It also projected an administration which is just and fair 'in dealing with individual citizens and groups relying on the services it provides' (Wilenski 1986, p. 185).

However, just as the implementation of the program had begun, the Government shifted the terms in which it was couched. In 1986, in response to its fears about the 'balance of payments crisis', it altered the priority it gave to the principles of equity and democracy, leaving efficiency as the supreme measure against which to judge performance. The reforms became more reactive than reforming. The Prime Minister 'exhorted managers to be tough and hard-nosed in the essential drive to restructure Australia's economy and enjoined the Service to facilitate industries to achieve national objectives and reduce demands on the taxpayer' (McInnes 1990, p. 110). With this turn-around, the Government reforming agenda, both of public administration and of multiculturalism, became subjugated to its new-found commitment to managerialism.

Managerialism is now the dominant discourse of public policy. According to Considine (1988), it represents an economistic culture, which views the business of public administration in corporatist terms, as more or less effective and efficient instrument of producing goods and services. The economistic criterion of cost-efficiency becomes paramount, regardless of the political character of these good and services. But as Yeatman (1990, p. 2) points out:

> Since there is often no market principle to sanction the economic performance of public agencies it becomes meaningful in this context to view cutbacks to their budgets as enforcing more efficient performance. Where it is possible to introduce something that looks like the market principle, effort is made to do so. Accordingly, agencies are permitted, if not encouraged, to cross-charge each other for their services, and to commercialise their services in the open market.

Managerialism also has the consequence of redefining citizens as consumers of publicly provided goods. Public administrators are thus encouraged to place emphasis on the consumer's right to choose from the range of services provided. But as Yeatman (1990, p. 2) argues:

> The effect of this reasoning is that 'consumers' of public goods and services are atomised in relation to each other, and the assumption is made that they can understand and express their preferences independent of any collectively oriented and/or political dialogue about how best to explore, express, and meet their needs in relation to publicly provided goods and services. They are no longer members of a public community of citizens, but become instead private self-interested actors.

Such a view has major implications for the discourse of multiculturalism. To begin with, it has the effect of 'privatizing' ethnicity. It implies the view that ethnicity is somehow irrelevant to public policy. Since autonomous actors are thought to be both the primary category of social analysis, and the object of the provision of public good and services, ethnicity is rendered an aspect of the individual's identity related to ancestry, origins of home background (see Olneck, 1988). Such a logic suggests that ethnic traditions are a matter of individual choice. It leads to the *reductio ad absurdum* that just as an individual might, for example, support a particular football team, so he or she might have a preference for maintaining a cultural tradition. Just as the state has no right to dictate which team an individual supports, nor should it tell them how to organize their private lives around a particular ethnic identification.

Such a suggestion, however, ignores the fact that ethnicity has a relational, public and collective character. It is not an object of individual preference, but is socially formed and is constantly developing. Ethnicity is collectively organized, and is related to other social structures in ways that are not arbitrary. The social experience of ethnic groups is not confined to matters of life-style. Various ethnic groups occupy particular positions within the class structure of Australian society and play an important role in the production of social and economic relations. The social significance of ethnicity is constantly being formed and struggled over, and the state is crucially implicated in this process because it defines the legitimacy of certain cultural and political practices over others. Ethnicity then provides an important focus both for the understanding of the dynamics of Australian life and for organizing political activity. An administration that ignores these facts overlooks the distinction between the private and the public dimensions of social life. The needs for services of many migrants has a public character. The need for an interpreter service, for example, is not a private need of a self-interested actor, but something that is relationally linked to migrant participation in public institutions.

And yet it has been precisely this kind of service that has been severely cut and/or privatized. In maintaining its commitment to develop a system of administration that is fiscally efficient and responsible, Labor's successive budgets have restrained public sector activity through staff cuts, program rationalization, increasingly tight welfare targeting and privatized services. Many of these managerialist reforms have been implemented in the name of efficiency and strategic necessity, but whether it is possible to make public administration more efficient and productive simply by reducing outlays and staff numbers is a question that has seldom been asked.

The Government's deregulation and privatization strategy has clearly rested within a business rather than a service framework, with the assumption that there is no place in the public sector for independent agencies that do not have the potential to raise revenue. It is not surprising then that given their inability to pay, the poor, many migrants amongst them, have had to carry the greatest burden of the Government's program of managerial reforms. Thus, many migrants have been hard hit by the commercialization of such public service as legal advice, travel, interpreter services, and even the programs in community languages and the teaching of English as a Second Language (ESL).

In the public services that remain, the Government has sought to achieve efficiency by two other initiatives: the introduction of Program Management and Budgeting (PMB) and the rationalization of functions through the strategy of mainstreaming. The basic aim of PMB is to develop a regularized system of accountability and control. Program objectives, outputs and outcomes are closely monitored in an effort to provide clear indication of what agencies do and how much it costs. The efficiency and effectiveness indicators reveal the extent to which programs satisfy the purpose for which they were established. While PMB may be an appropriate instrument in a factory where inputs and outputs can be neatly controlled, in human service terms, statements of objectives and cost allocation are never easy to produce, nor do they provide a reliable guide to the performance of agencies. Thus, educators working in an ESL class, for example, may perform a variety of useful social and cultural tasks, in addition to teaching English, with little possibility of a technological tool such as PMB ever being able to capture the significance and importance of the functions educators perform.

Mainstreaming has been the other strategy through which the Government has been able to abolish many of the welfare programs for ethnic minorities. It has argued that the mainstream bureaucratic agencies could provide such services as language and interpreter programs, legal aid and counselling, more efficiently. This approach to the funding and the organization of services involves the previously ethnic-specific services to be incorporated into a delivery system which is directed at the whole community.

The arguments put forward for mainstreaming have invoked narrowly defined egalitarian principles which suggest that the needs of all Australians should be catered for through the same general services, available to the entire community. It is efficient, since it is cheaper for the country, and it provides minorities with the opportunities to become familiar with the distinctive nature of Australian institutional practices and customs. The earlier approach, it is argued, always involved the danger that ethnic-specific services were becoming marginal. While this code-language for rationalization and cut-backs might seem attractive, it overlooks the distinctive historical character of both the needs of the ethnic minorities and the ability of the mainstream bureaucracy to meet them.

Jakubowicz (1987) has suggested that, in accepting the notion of mainstreaming, the Labor Government has avoided addressing issues concerning racism within the framework of which the relationship between bureaucracies and ethnic minorities is historically defined. The argument for mainstreaming overlooks the fact that the institutions into which previously ethnic-specific services are to be mainstreamed remain insensitive to the needs of most ethnic minorities. Nor has the Government developed a credible strategy to bring about changes to the way existing administrative structures deal with ethnic issues. Jakubowicz (1987, p. 31) has argued that the Government 'accepts the mainstream in communication as elsewhere as inherently valued, whilst in fact that mainstream serves the interests in the "main" of the most of the power male Anglo-Saxons'. This argument reveals the strategy of mainstreaming to rest on the assumptions of assimilation, since the cultural practices of the Australian administrative system clearly favour the dominant group, for these practices are arranged around a set of values that assume a distinctive Anglo-Australian way of organizing relationships between the public and the public service.

Ultimately, however, it is the agenda of economic rationalism that has guided the Government towards mainstreaming, rather than either the assumptions of assimilation or some deeper concern for social justice. Mainstreaming as a policy concept has been used to cut ethnic-specific services, with the assumption, perhaps more of a hope, that mainstream institutions will assume a multicultural stance towards their activities; that is, their processes of policy development and modes of service delivery will incorporate a concern for cultural diversity and the special needs of migrants. A degree of goodwill is expected from bureaucracies, but this objective cannot be sustained by any evidence; nor has it been accompanied by any concrete programs that might seek to educate mainstream service providers.

Conclusion

In this paper I have sought to explain the fundamental contradiction between Labor's commitment to a view of multiculturalism governed by the principles of social justice and its attempts to restructure the Australian state using the instruments of economic rationalism and managerialism that have led to the abolition or rationalization of many of the welfare programs developed under the rubric of a liberal discourse on multiculturalism. I have suggested that in 1983, Labor had a good grasp of the ambiguities and tensions inherent in the liberal view, and upon election it had moved quickly to develop a policy of multiculturalism more consistent with its traditional commitment to social democracy. However, many of its initiatives in this area have more recently become overwhelmed by and subjugated to its economic and administrative agendas.

The Government has argued that its attempts at restructuring the Australian economy by a series of deregulatory moves would ultimately benefit all Australians. But, even if this market logic were sound, and many doubt that it is, I have argued that its social costs have been considerable. Not only has Australia surrendered many of its policy options to the vagaries of the markets, but its social justice objectives have also become overshadowed by the rampant managerialism that these moves towards economic restructuring have ushered in. The notion of social justice has been redefined to now mean merely a matter of respecting an individual's unconstrained choices by giving them equal access in the market place. It has been assumed that the task of justice is to facilitate and support the market rather than to constrain it. These developments have had most regressive consequences for the policy of multiculturalism which, in the *National Agenda for a Multicultural Australia* (1989), has been rearticulated in instrumentalist terms, as a social policy to facilitate the processes of economic revival and restructuring. Cultural concerns that multiculturalism once highlighted have been overridden by a Government more interested in the contribution migrants might make to economic recovery. With such a fundamental reorientation, the policy has lost any progressive social democratic potential that it might have had.

References

ADVISORY COUNCIL ON MULTICULTURAL AFFAIRS (1988) *Towards a National Agenda for a Multicultural Australia*, Canberra: Australian Government Publishing Service [AGPS].

AUSTRALIAN ETHNIC AFFAIRS COUNCIL (1977) *Australia as a Multicultural Society*, Canberra, Australia: Australian Government Publishing Service. [AGPS]

BEILHARZ, P. (1987) 'Reading politics: Social theory and social politics', in *Australian and New Zealand Journal of Sociology*, **23**, No. 3, pp. 388–406.

BEILHARZ, P. (1989) 'Social democracy and social justice', in *Australian and New Zealand Journal of Sociology*, **25**, No. 1, pp. 85–99.

BULLIVANT, B. (1981) *The Pluralist Dilemma in Education: Six Case Studies*, Sydney, Australia: George Allen and Unwin.

CASTLES, S. (1987) 'A new agenda for multiculturalism', paper presented at the conference, *Whither Multiculturalism?*, La Trobe University, Melbourne, Australia, April.

CASTLES, S., KALANTZIS, M., COPE, B. and MORRISEY, M. (1988) *Mistaken Identity: Multiculturalism and the Demise of Nationalism in Australia*, Sydney, Australia: Pluto Press.

CHIPMAN, L. (1980) 'The menace of multiculturalism', in *Quadrant*, **24**, No. 10, pp. 3–6.

CONSIDINE, M. (1988) 'The corporate management framework as administrative science; a critique', *Australian Journal of Public Administration*, **47**, 1, pp. 4–19.

DE LEPERVANCHE, M. (1984) 'Immigrants and ethnic groups', in ENCEL, S. and BRYSON, L. (Eds), *Australian Society*, 4th edition, Melbourne, Australia: Longman-Cheshire. pp. 170–228.

FITZGERALD, S. (1988) *Immigration: A Commitment to Australia*, Canberra, Australia: AGPS.

FOSTER, L.E. (1981) *Australian Education: A Sociological Perspective*, Sydney, Australia: Prentice-Hall.

FOSTER, L.E. and STOCKLEY, D. (1984) *Multiculturalism: The Changing Australian Paradigm*, Avon, UK: Multilingual Matters.

Fazal Rizvi

GALBALLY REPORT (1978) *Report of the Review of Post-Arrival Program and Services for Migrants, Migrant Services and Programs*, **1**, Canberra, Australia: AGPS.
GILROY, P. (1987) *There Ain't No Black in the Union Jack*, London, UK: Hutchinson.
GRASSBY, A.J. (1973) *A Multicultural Society for the Future*, Canberra, Australia: AGPS.
HELLER, A. (1976) *A Theory of Needs in Marx*, London, UK: Allison and Busby.
JAKUBOWICZ, A. (1981) 'State and ethnicity: Multiculturalism as ideology', in *Australian and New Zealand Journal of Sociology*, **17**, No. 3, pp. 4–13.
JAKUBOWICZ, A. (1987) 'Days of our lives: Multiculturalism, mainstreaming and "special" broadcasting', in *Media Information Australia*, **45**, August, pp. 18–32.
JAYASURIYA, L. (1987) 'Ethnic minorities and social justice in Australian society', *Australian Journal of Social Issues*, **22**, No. 3, pp. 481–97.
JUPP, J. (1986) *Don't Settle for Less*, Canberra, Australia: AGPS.
LINGARD, R. (1982) 'Multicultural education in Queensland: The assimilation of an ideal', in YOUNG, R., PUSEY, M. and BATES, R. (Eds), *Australian Policy Issues and Critique*, Geelong, Australia: Deakin University, pp. 60–83.
LO BIANCO, J. (1987) *National Policy on Languages*, Canberra, Australia: Australian Government Printing Service.
MCINNES, M. (1990) 'Public service reform under Hawke: Reconstruction or deconstruction?', *The Australian Quarterly*, **62**, No. 2, pp. 108–124.
MACINTYRE, S. (1985) *Winners and Losers*, Sydney, Australia: Allen and Unwin.
MADDOX, G. (1989) *The Hawke Government and the Labor Tradition*, Melbourne, Australia: Penguin Press.
NOZICK, R. (1974) *Anarchy, State and Utopia*, Oxford, UK: Blackwell.
OFFICE OF MULTICULTURAL AFFAIRS (1989) *The National Agenda for a Multicultural Australia*, Canberra, Australia: AGPS.
OLNECK, M. (1990) 'The Recurring Dream: Symbolism and ideology in inter-cultural and multicultural education', *American Journal of Education*, 98, pp. 147–74.
PUSEY, M. (1991) *Economic Rationalism in Canberra: A Nation-Building State Changes its Mind*, Cambridge, UK: Cambridge University Press.
RAWLS, J. (1972) *A Theory of Justice*, Oxford, UK: Clarendon Press.
TOURAINE, A. (1977) *The Self-Production of Society*, London, UK: University of Chicago Press.
WILENSKI, P. (1986) *Public power and Public Administration*, Sydney, Australia: Hale and Iremonger.
YEATMAN, A. (1990) *Bureaucrats, Technocrats, Femocrats*, Sydney, Australia: Allen and Unwin.

Chapter 9

Policy and the Politics of Representation: Torres Strait Islanders and Aborigines at the Margins

Allan Luke, Martin Nakata, M. Garbutcheon Singh, Richard Smith

Introduction

Many of the chapters in this book argue that Australian governmental policy over the last decade has neglected a systematic analysis of the intersections of class, gender, race and state power in the reconfiguration of education systems. A key aspect of such an analysis is an understanding of the strategic role of policy discourse in the playing out of such power. This chapter is about the discourses of current policy on Torres Strait Islander and Aboriginal education. It is a study in the politics of representation, of how discourses and institutional practices construct and position groups and communities within the polity, and it is an exploration of the significant material, economic and cultural effects of such policies.

At the onset of Labor's tenure in federal government in 1983, Torres Strait Islanders and Aborigines had heightened expectations of Labor's social welfare policies. Despite a decade of policy studies and formation, the fundamental questions of Aboriginal affairs remain unresolved. In a comprehensive overview of Labor policy, Jennett (1990, p. 246) documents what she considers the historical emergence of 'unavoidable difficulties' in social, economic and educational initiatives for Aboriginal affairs. She argues that redistributive social policy and programs are subject to resurgences in scepticism towards the welfare state. Relatedly, Jennett holds, such programs elicit and make visible conflict over fundamental societal, racial and economic divisions and interests.

A further set of difficulties lies with questions of identity, subjectivity and solidarity which have arisen among Islanders and Aborigines themselves. According to Jennett, Aborigines and Islanders view themselves as a wronged people with inalienable claims to ancestors, land and resources. This position increasingly is juxtaposed to the critique that the state and its non-Aboriginal representatives do not have legitimate stakes in Aboriginal affairs, but that the adjudication of such matters is the proper domain of self-determining and self-identifying indigenous groups. Nonetheless, the mainstream belief persists that Aborigines and Islanders are yet another disadvantaged group (Jennett, 1990: p. 247). Jennett goes on to point out that the interdependence of welfare services provision and political goals of land rights have led to an increasing public and governmental perception that the problems are intractable.

This complex situation only strengthens widespread perception among Islanders and Aborigines that while Ministers and chief executives of Aboriginal affairs should advocate indigenous peoples' goals and aspirations, ultimately they are unable to speak and act on behalf of those interests. Further, there is considerable conflict within the ranks of Islander and Aboriginal groups over the prioritization of political, economic and social goals. This conflict becomes increasingly visible as the level of site and clientele-specificity of policy is increased, even when broad or overall goals are agreed upon.

In this context, we can view emergent Labor policy of the 1990s as characterized by the 'material [textual] practice whereby attempts are made to remedy threats to . . . [governmental and state] legitimacy' (Burton and Carlen, 1977, p. 377). Recent and current analyses of educational crises are framed by the shared perception that Labor policy has been marked progressively by the development and implementation of a technocratic rationality and corporate culture, textually represented in the series of inquiry, tribunal and policy documents which have taken centre-stage in the reconfiguration of such areas as higher education, the production of scientific expertize, migrant and English as a Second Language education, workplace education and literacy, and Islander and Aboriginal policies. Such rationality is, the argument goes, forwarded in terms of notions of consensus that ignore and silence the 'distributional implications of policy choice' (Stewart and Jennett, 1990, p. 2), and articulated in the syntax of the human capital rationale: social equality via increased economic productivity (see Knight, Lingard and Porter, Chapter 1; and Porter, Chapter 3, this volume). As the articles in the present volume indicate, the 'New Corporatism' of Labor is considered by many to have done little to alter patterns of inequality in Australian society. Within such a scenario, the position for Islanders and Aborigines is, *prima facie*, more desperate than that of any other group.

But even if the historical bases and contemporary consequences of Aboriginal educational policy are empirically identified, these do not fully explain the sites and logic of state corporatism, particularly in terms of how that power entails the configuration and reconfiguration of the populaces and peoples in question. What policy texts represent, simulate and do is never self-evident, literal or fully transparent. Particularly in dealing with policy ostensibly sympathetic to the plights of marginal groups, we cannot construe it as a simple set of truths or distortions and misrepresentations that reveal or hide unambiguous structural realities about social relations, relations to means of production, and cultural domination.

This chapter does not aim to rewrite Aboriginal and Torres Strait Islander educational policy and practice from a materialist or foundationalist perspective. That task is rightly for members of those communities. Instead, the four of us — two Australians of colour, a Torres Strait Islander and a White Australian — focus on the discursive strategies of recent policy which, we argue, frame Islander and Aboriginal concerns in terms of the New Corporatism and preclude and silence a fuller materialist analysis and strategy. The text in question here is the recent *National Aboriginal and Torres Strait Islander Education Policy* (Department of Employment, Education and Training, (DEET), 1989; hereafter NATSIEP). Because discourse analysis has become a rubric for virtually any kind of textual study, we begin with a brief statement of the parameters and assumptions of our analysis.

Following a thematic reading of key constructions in the NATSIEP text, we take on the material implications of this particular policy for Islander and Aboriginal education.

Policy as Discourse

Differing textual genres historically develop conventions for reading and constructing the social. Commonwealth policy documents are material, social and institutional practices which together constitute a textual corpus, intertextually referring to and 'quoting' each other. Entailed is a politics of representation:

> Participants in contests over meaning attempt to capture or dominate modes of representation. They do so in a variety of ways, including inviting and persuading others to join their side, coopting the oppositions' discourse, silencing opponents by attacking them or, in extreme cases, imprisoning them. When the attempt to dominate is successful, a hierarchy of meanings is formed, in which one of the many possible ways of representing the world gains primacy over others. (Mehan, Nathanson and Skelly, 1990, p. 137; cf. Mehan, 1989)

This is, of course, not to assume that such documents are monoglossic entities, that they collude in the provision of a singular, non-contradictory position or hierarchy of meanings. If such texts represent in contradictory ways diversities of interests (Bahktin, 1986), then of crucial importance are the discourse strategies and moves used to suture over, to hide, to appropriate difference, and those strategies which are deliberately polysemous, which can be read differently as referring to and operating in the interests of competing audiences.

But all textual representations and readings are not equal in their material or institutional force. The power of modern bureaucratic discourse lies in its capacity both for the maintenance of moral and political legitimacy, and for the moral and economic regulation of the subject. Policy texts are not just referential descriptions of extant conditions and clienteles, but are public speech acts used to represent and to simulate the bureaucratic and ostensibly collective 'doing' of something of substance. This is achieved through texts which 'systematically form the objects of which they speak' (Foucault, 1972, p. 49). Such a claim should not lead to the spurious conclusion that if everything is circumscribed by discourse, than all there is is discourse. For indeed subject construction ultimately leads back to consequential effects: how the subjects, clients and problems of policy are constituted and positioned in the discourse of policy becomes an actual act of power and regulation over those very subjects in the world.

Our strategy, then, is not to analyze policy by reference to its ideological distortion of the 'real', as Marxist textual theory from Voloshinov onwards has undertaken (Luke, in press). Nor does it centre on a political economy of the 'writing' of the text, tracing who was involved, where, according to which ascribed interests, as much policy analysis attempts. While we do not discount these as productive ways of untying and critiquing policy, we here undertake a thematic 'interruption' of the text (Silverman and Torode, 1980) which disrupts and makes visible its namings and syntax for constructing and representing an apparently coherent, nature-like message and agenda. Further, we take policy texts — their actual implementation and deployment notwithstanding — as public evidence of hegemonic claims open for scrutiny and contestation (Laclau and Mouffe, 1985).

The Document

Aboriginal and Torres Strait Islander education policy has been the site of various forms of recognition and reconstruction of Aboriginal identity, community and problems. In an historical move characteristic of postcolonial discourse (cf. Franco, 1988; King and McHoul, 1986), texts that alternately spoke for and about aboriginal peoples have been superseded by texts which ostensibly speak on behalf of them and are (increasingly, at least in part) authored by them. In other words, since the demise of the White Australia policy, discourses of discrimination and exclusion have been progressively supplanted by those of inclusion. Thus, the texts of policy have shifted from deliberate dismissal and omission to strategies for incorporation via representation.

In the latter half of the 1980s, Labor moved progressively to increase consultation and involvement of Aboriginal and Islander communities in the development of educational policy. At the least, all policy documents call for increased consultations and 'appropriate mechanisms for negotiation' (for example, Department of Employment, Education and Training/National Board of Employment, Education and Training, 1989); accordingly, NATSIEP itself sets as key goals 'increased participation' in educational decision-making with the ultimate goal of community 'self-management'. Recent policies and analyses like the *Report of the Aboriginal Education Policy Task Force* (Aboriginal Education Policy Task Force, 1988) have been jointly authored by Aboriginal representatives, consultants and civil servants. That Task Force was commissioned by the Commonwealth in April, 1988 to 'advise on all aspects of Aboriginal education in Australia, assess the findings of recent research and policy reports, and prepare priorities for the funding of existing programs and new initiatives' (Aboriginal Education Policy Task Force, 1988, p. 3). In its terms of reference, the Task Force was 'to make recommendations as a matter of urgency on Aboriginal education policy for inclusion in the 1988–89 Budget' (p. 4). These policy developments have culminated in NATSIEP (DEET, 1989), which has been accompanied with estimated rises in Commonwealth funding of Aboriginal and Islander education from $112.5 million in 1989 to $143.5 million in 1990. Most recently, Labor has foreshadowed the articulation of a connected policy on Aboriginal and Torres Strait Islander language and literacy (Department of Employment, Education and Training, 1991).

As the foreword to the document indicates, NATSIEP 'represents a cooperative effort to develop more effective processes for the education of Aboriginal People' (DEET, 1989, p. 5). The policy document is divided into four sections: 1) an introduction which argues the need for such a policy and explains its development; 2) a statement of purposes; 3) a statement of educational goals; and 4) 'agreed arrangements for policy implementation' which stress Commonwealth/State cooperation, financial arrangements and evaluation.

We take up the politics of representation of that document in terms of four constitutive themes: 1) the construction of Torres Strait Islanders, Aborigines and their Others; 2) the construction of their universal 'rights'; 3) the construction of preferred educational goals and practices; and 4) the construction of what will count as 'successful' achievement of the policy. In other words, we ask: Who are the subjects constructed by the policy? How are their rights framed? What kinds of educational provisions are said to be capable of meeting these? How are we to assess the efficacy of the various practices forwarded by the policy?

Theme 1: Islanders, Aborigines, and their Others

Across the document the term 'Aboriginal people' is used to represent all Aborigines and Torres Strait Islanders. As such, it assumes a universality of 'Aboriginality' which represents diverse groups and interests. Like most Commonwealth documents and academic papers, it includes Torres Strait Islanders under the general rubric of 'Aborigines'. Such nominalizations, like acronyms, do indeed serve purposes of textual economy, avoiding the repetition of a more complex naming of client group(s). However, this generic term has become idiomatic in policy, academic literature, and popular press reports alike, commatizing and relegating Torres Strait Islanders into an 'included' but indistinct status as subjects (Nakata, 1990). In effect, it acts as a marker of status identity and relationship, and relative domination/subordination: the same is achieved in the patriarchal nominalization of someone and his or her partner as 'The John Does'. Further, we note the historical and continuing absence of other groups, for instance, Kanakas and South Pacific Islanders from the grids of policy that categorize Aborigines and Migrants.

These definitions of the clientele — however literally accurate or inaccurate they might be — point to the larger issue of the construction of 'Aborigines' as a homogeneous populace. Qualifiers are introduced (e.g., '*many* Aboriginal people seek "two-ways" education of a bi-lingual and bi-cultural nature' (DEET, 1989, emphasis added, p. 9); 'Aboriginal people *generally* seek education'), and there is recognition of the 'diversity of Aboriginal circumstances and needs' (emphasis added, p. 9). Nonetheless, the policy proceeds from the assumption of existence of such inclusive entities as 'Aboriginal culture and identity' (p. 8), framed as a 'living . . . part of the nation's heritage' (p. 5).

There is ongoing debate among Aborigines about 'Aboriginality' as an essential, identifiable characteristic of culture and ethnicity — a debate paralleled in other sites by analyses of ethnic essentialism by aboriginal and minority groups, and feminist debates over gendered 'essence' (e.g., Collins, 1990). Even among Torres Strait Islanders, as Nakata (in press) has recently argued, socioeconomic, linguistic, ethnic and demographic variation makes the nominalizations common in educational literature, however worthy their intentions, problematic. The policy nonetheless proceeds under the assumption of a *homogeneous group unmarked by gender and class*.

The use of the umbrella term Aboriginal further implies that the life, experiences, issues and needs of individuals, communities and cultures are more or less shared, identifiable and thus can be met through a set of generalizable policy moves (Nakata, 1990). In spite of qualifiers, the educational needs and aspirations of this singular identity are by inference presented as representing those of all communities. Aboriginal thus stands as a universal term for a homogeneous group which represents no one specific group. The effect of this naming is to express and gain consensus from specific groups through what appears to be a textual representation of their interests. However, such phrasing effectively marginalizes and silences the specific demands, issues and circumstances of localities.

The textual construction of 'Aborigine' and 'Aboriginality' is further defined in terms of absence and omission. What is ostensibly missing in educational provision becomes the goal of the policy: namely, 'equity between Aboriginal people and other Australians in access, participation and outcomes in all forms of education by the turn of the century' (DEET, 1989, p. 7). In terms of actual educational 'outcomes', this translates into 'attainment of skills', 'successful completion of Year 12', '*same* graduate rates from award courses in technical and further education', 'to the *same* standard as other Australian students' (emphasis added, p. 15). Here the end point of effective policy is seen as the addressing of a series of socioeconomic and educational 'lacks'; which in turn call out for equity with mainstream White Australians, the latter presented as a singular entity with *intra*group equity. The yardstick for equity, further, is indexed against a statistical grid of norms achieved in Year 12 retention, Colleges of Technical and Further Education graduate rates and so forth.

The intertextual connotations here are curious, because according to other Commonwealth policy documents on education, social class and gender, the non-Aboriginal population continues to experience diverse kinds and levels of educational inequality, where achievement, tertiary entry and technical 'skilling' fell along historical fault lines of urban/rural location, gender and class (cf. Johnston, Chapter 7; Rizvi, Chapter 8; Henry and Taylor, Chapter 10, in this volume; Henry, Knight, Lingard and Taylor, 1988). Accordingly, then, the absences and aims of this marginalized group are defined by reference to an imaginary centre, a mainstream Australian population whose educational, social justice and economic rights are presented as non-problematic, guaranteed and achieved. This discursive move amounts to a defining of Islander and Aboriginal exclusion by reference to an imaginary gender and class-free space which, according to a range of sources, is a fiction (for example, Kenway, 1990; Jennett, 1990; Kalantzis, Cope and Slade, 1989).

The NATSIEP, then, names Islanders and Aborigines as a 'diverse' group. That diversity — of communities, cultures, genders, classes, colours — is explicated in terms of its alterity, in terms of a homogeneous Other: 'mainstream' Australians. The terms of educational policy, then, posit the imaginary norms of the Other as the goals and benchmarks for Islanders and Aborigines. The NATSIEP text thus turns on a double move: at once it detaches Islanders' and Aborigines' educational exigencies from related identities, issues and policies regarding gender and colour and class. At the same time, it measures and gauges 'lack' and achievement of peoples at the socioeconomic margins by reference to a textually constructed, fictive centre.

Theme 2: The Discourses on Needs and Rights

These educational goals are posed within the text as natural and logical extensions of Aborigines' and Islanders' needs for universal human rights, also ostensibly achieved by non-Aboriginal groups. The Foreword to the policy states that:

The Australian Government is a signatory to several international covenants recognising international standards for the protection of universal
human rights and fundamental freedoms. These include the International
Convention on the Elimination of All Forms of Racial Discrimination
and Universal Declaration of Human Rights and the International
Covenants on Economic, Social and Cultural Rights and Civil and Political Rights. (DEET, 1989, p. 5)

Here the construction of rights is contingent on two significant intertextual
references, first to the existence of multiple international documents by the Australian government.

However this construction also signals a series of textual absences. First, there
is no indication whether there are similar covenants without Australian signatories
among or regarding aboriginal, fourth world peoples. Second, and more significantly, the inclusion is evidence of the inability of the Labor Government to
institute legislative conventions for protecting human rights despite repeated
electoral promises, hence the necessity for the NATSIEP document to appeal to
the Government's external affairs commitments. This statement thus signals the
non-existence of Federal legislation, constitution or treaty to ensure as a right
assigned to people by law, protection from racial discrimination and legal guarantees for specific human, economic, social, cultural, civic and political rights.
Without textual bases that have the power to guarantee them, Islander and
Aboriginal peoples cannot force legal decisions on whether such (absent) laws are
being upheld or not. While such cases could, in theory, be presented to the World
Court or United Nations, Australian citizens do not have recourse to internal
institutions where the Government's failure to abide by international conventions
can be adjudicated with any binding force.

As for the actual textual construction of such rights, the NATSIEP refers to
universal and fundamental rights. Reference to the United Nations' declarations
on human rights names rights as 'natural' rather than social constructs. This appeal
to the problematic notions of 'basic' or 'moral' rights is carried forward in
the text, where it is asserted that 'other Australians' are able to take for granted
certain 'inalienable' or 'fundamental rights' (p. 7). Again the text establishes
a lack, of rights in this instance, on the basis of their existence among the
Other. If, as has been noted there, such constructions mark the absence of domes-
tically enshrined rights, then indeed the assertion that mainstream Australians
themselves have recourse to fundamental human rights is erroneous, if not
mischievous.

However, the NATSIEP document also can be read as directly asserting that
a basic level of security of rights is essential for all Australians, particularly for
Islanders and Aborigines, whose security in their country has been most tenuous
since invasion/colonization (cf. Norman, 1987, pp. 136–54). As such, the NATSIEP
may be read as a muted, if virtually submerged, critique of the Hawke government's failure to guarantee in writing the security of Islander and Aboriginal
people, at least in the terms set out in international conventions. However, this
critique is muted indeed. The document sutures over the omission by neglecting
to spell out the most obvious proposal which might flow on from this absence:
the declaration of a Bill of Rights, and the finalization of treaty guarantees. Given
the subsequent enumeration of educational problems experienced by Islander and

Aboriginal peoples, these would be required to put some legal, perlocutionary force behind and beyond the ameliorative educational strategies which NATSIEP and other policy texts forward. Such documents would be required to attend to the negative and positive dimensions of human security, including freedom from racial violence and discrimination, as well as determination of the basis for the just acquisition of their lands and fair educational opportunities (Norman, 1987). If, as the NATSIEP document claims, the government is committed to redistributive justice, then the desired pattern of distribution requires a more explicit textual and institutional statement than that document itself provides.

Theme 3: The Cultural Goals and Consequences of Schooling

How these rights are to be achieved via educational provision pivots on the construction of educational goals and outcomes. These in turn are embedded in Theme 1, the construction of the Islander/Aboriginal subject-in-culture: Islander and Aboriginal 'distinctive cultures' are viewed as 'a rich and important part of the nation's living heritage' (DEET, 1989, p. 5). Accordingly, educational lacks emerge as the result of, *inter alia*, 'the historically-developed education processes of Aboriginal culture [that] have been eroded in many communities for a variety of reasons'.

'Erosion' here is presented as agentless passive (cf. Kress, 1989). Nobody is party to the 'erosion' (a metaphor about an inevitable natural process) which is said to occur for 'various [unspecified] reasons'. The purpose of educational policy, then, is to halt or reverse or redress that process via schooling, with no consideration of the well-documented historical and contemporary structures and functions of these same education systems for colonization and enculturation. Central, then, are educational/anthropological goals of 'maintenance', 'recognition' and 'reinforcement', 'respect for' the 'status' of 'distinctive cultures'. In effect, the historical role of state power in the education, control and subordination of Islander and Aboriginal peoples is silenced; education is then readily lodged within an agenda of cultural maintenance and the transmission of useful skills.

At least part of the responsibility for this erosion is laid squarely at the doors of schooling: 'education arrangements and procedures established from non-Aboriginal traditions have not adequately recognised and accommodated the particular needs and circumstances of Aboriginal people' (p. 5). Hence, the NATSIEP generated priorities for Islander and Aboriginal education are premised on the notion that distinctive cultures are threatened by educational arrangements and practices from non-Aboriginal traditions. However, such an argument directs responsibility at cultural mis-'appreciation' and mis-'understanding', rather than at the systemic workings of power in state institutions like schools.

This situation, NATSIEP claims, can be dealt with through generalizable educational principles and goals:

> Aboriginal people have consistently called for . . . sensitivity and effectiveness of educational services. Aboriginal people generally seek education that is more responsive to the diversity of Aboriginal circumstances and needs, and which recognises and values the cultural backgrounds of students . . . . Many Aboriginal people seek 'two way' education of a

bilingual and bi-cultural nature, in order for them to maintain or restore their cultural identity and acquire useful skills for their participation in Australian social and economic life. (DEET, 1989, p. 9)

The Aborigine and Islander are constituted as of cultural significance to the nation's living heritage, as in danger of losing that culture. The goals are said to be 'sensitive' and 'effective' education, which will 'accommodate cultural difference'. What is omitted here is a reconnection of these educational goals with something more than maintenance and function.

Because so little explicit attention is devoted to the parameters of power in educational and state systems, the educational provisions appear to be those of accommodation and amelioration. Do powerful knowledges and competencies for a late-capitalist, information economy simply flow on logically from the increased retention rates and skills levels to be achieved through culturally appropriate education? (Walton, in press). While such provisions are arguably necessary for such power, are they sufficient?

Theme 4: Corporatism and Performance Indicators

Answers to the foregoing questions pivot on the issue of how success in the achievement of the policy's goals will be gauged. NATSIEP states at its outset that it is 'predicated upon the principles of social justice, equity, economic efficiency and cost-effective service delivery' (p. 6). It further asserts that the success of its implementation will be measured using 'performance indicators . . . [to] include changes in Aboriginal participation in different sectors of education' (p. 17). These indicators are to be ascertained and implemented jointly by State and Commonwealth jurisdictions.

This emphasis complements Themes 1 and 3 above: for if lack and needs are to be marked by reference to normative statistical benchmarks of mainstream Australian society, then indeed the amelioration of lack can be likewise measured. NATSIEP's success thus is contingent on what it intertextually indexes in broader Commonwealth education policy: the discourses of corporatism and human capital.

Statements of rights, diversity, and maintenance notwithstanding, in this way NATSIEP is sutured into corporate managerialist strategy. Within the policy itself this gives rise to a number of problems. The means — 'bottom-up' consultative policy making and implementation — stand in contrast with the ends, which stress the reductive measurement of 'cost-efficient delivery'. The range of educational provisions for equity (for example, 'two-way education', and increased 'involvement of Aboriginal people in educational decision-making' (p. 14)) here are juxtaposed against corporate criteria, which by their very operation militate against diversity, local flexibility and communication (Singh, 1990). So whatever power over educational decision-making and practice is granted to Islanders and Aborigines, the criteria for what will count as 'economic efficiency' at the provision of education for 'social justice' remain lodged within centralized State and Commonwealth grids of specification.

As noted, NATSIEP recognizes the need for responsiveness 'to the diversity of Aboriginal circumstances and needs' (p. 9). This point is reiterated in boldface:

'It is no less a task to improve the responsiveness of provided educational services to the differing needs and circumstances of Aboriginal communities' (p. 11). Yet, none of the statistics provided in the NATSIEP begin to account for this play of diversity. In terms of its own discourse of both needs and output stated in terms of performance indicators, the reiteration of 'national aggregate' data (p. 10) further complicates matters. We here consider two of these issues briefly, particularly as they connect with the previously discussed construction of Islander and Aboriginal identity and educational goals.

First, a significant limitation of performance indicators is that broad aggregate data on 'Aboriginal people' and the 'national equivalent', conceal the conflict and play of difference within each putatively homogeneous group. As noted, it provides no statistical sensitivity to the diversity recognized in the prose text. The use of 'national equivalent rates' also cancels the socioeconomic and cultural diversity of needs and circumstances among 'other Australians' (p. 10), statistically constructing an imaginary norm against which human subjects and collectivities can be graded for 'normalisation' (Hacking, 1981).

Second, if this statistical data on educational retention levels, achievement and other outcomes were to be disaggregated, the categories for identifying locality and difference would themselves be problematic. None of the statistical data relating to attendance, attrition, truancy, retention, transition or graduate rates are broken down even in terms of the most rudimentary urban/rural categories, much less to differentiate Aborigines from Torres Strait Islanders. Congruent with the overall construction of the Islander/Aborigine subject noted in Theme 1, class, gender or cultural differences do not figure in this statistical reportage.

There is an additional broad family of intertextual relations which are marked off by the invocation of performance indicators. According to Kenneth Baker (1989), then British Secretary of State for Education and Science, the 'new consumer-oriented approach' to education in the UK was promoted by switching the terms of the debate from inputs to 'outputs', verifiable in terms of 'a new system to measure educational performance'. Across English-speaking countries, this kind of economic rationalism and educational commodification has operated as an extension of New Right ideology. (See Apple, Chapter 4; Dale and Ozga, Chapter 5; this volume.) The shift in focus from redistributive processes to product outcomes effectively deflects questions about the character and quality of teaching and learning, and the adequacy and appropriateness of curriculum, pedagogy and policy.

There is wide debate over serious inadequacies and limitations in the purposes and practices of existing Islander and Aboriginal education programs, whether in schools or tertiary institutions (Folds, 1987; Human Rights and Equal Opportunity Commission, 1988). Yet the nuances and positions of these critiques are not taken up intertextually in the NATSIEP. Throughout, the discourses on the complex causes and consequences of Aboriginal educational programs are subordinated to a linear model of cost-efficient delivery. Yet an emphasis on performance indicators here has the force of deferring and glossing questions about the structures, experiences, and conditions of schooling. In and of themselves, performance indicators are incapable of explicating for Islanders and Aborigines the benefits of schooling, or the relationship of increased participation to extant knowledge/power effects of schooling. To put it simply, they may just signal increased participation in a systematically disempowering education.

Narratives of Incorporation?

All texts are heteroglossic, offering and eliciting a range of voices, reading and writing positions and practices. Policy texts (like other forms of political discourse) effectively aim at inclusion, to speak and be read differently by a variety of constituencies (Bahktin, 1986). We have here developed but one possible reading of this central text of Islander and Aboriginal education, a text which marks Labor's public attempt to index definitive progress in the face of increasingly widespread scepticism that sufficient action has been taken, or alternatively, that further action needs to be taken.

We have not set out to refute the policy on empirical or foundational grounds, but rather to foreground its themes and logic. This analysis leads to several (preliminary) conclusions. First, the NATSIEP policy imperatives are more problematic and less real than they first appear. Relatedly, the explanatory constructions and logic that drive the policy cannot be reduced to a set of 'truths and untruths'; they are themselves readings and rewritings of the subjects, conditions, and sites in question. In addition, we have argued that the particular approach to outcomes taken in the policy is situated in a wider discourse of control in corporate educational politics (cf. Wexler, 1987).

Whether or not the NATSIEP represents, furthers, expresses or forms Islander and Aboriginal interests is thus a moot point. But like all policy discourse, its hierarchy of meanings opens for public scrutiny nodal points for political and institutional action. There can be little doubt that this policy tables issues for debate, contestation, and the development of institutional practice which hitherto were hidden or omitted. In this sense, the power of its very presence as a citation and reference point for Islanders and Aborigines in local sites (for example, local councils, consultative and funding bodies, education authorities, health and welfare units, schools, colleges and universities) should not be underestimated. Already, as spaces for political/educational action have appeared in regional and local communities and organizations, its corporate logic no doubt has been turned upside down and inside out (cf. Laclau, 1991, p. 33). Thus, regardless of its viability and coherence as a political program for increasing the power of Islanders and Aborigines over their own lives, communities, and larger political institutions — the policy as text is unfinished. Rather than setting the agenda for a realizable future, as per its stated intentions, it establishes a field of possibilities for sites where power will be redistributed.

Nonetheless, as a policy text it also serves to define and position both the subjects about which and to whom it ostensibly speaks. As we have shown here, each of the central constructs in the text can be analyzed in terms of its inter- and intratextual references, inclusions and omissions. Further, each already has been debated and contested by Aborigines, Islanders and those working in Aboriginal education on the basis of its truth and validity claims. However, such constructions do not operate in isolation: the positioning of subjects and readers gains its efficacy by embedding these constructions within a syntactic chain. Taken together, the various themes we have looked at constitute the following narrative:

Aborigines & Islanders [Other] (protagonist) -----> Erosion of rights, culture, education (problem) ---> Need for cultural maintenance/useful skills (goal) -----> culturally appropriate schooling (attempt/try) ----->

increased performance indicators (outcome) -----> cultural maintenance, self-management and economic development (resolution).

Like sentence-level syntax, narrative structure naturalizes particular forms of agency and efficacy. Particular means-ends, cause-effect, process-product relations become the taken-for-granted assumptions driving NATSIEP.

We can interrogate this story in terms of how and according to what premises it operates. It begins from a binary opposition between two homogeneous groups: Aboriginal and mainstream Australian, each class-free, gender-free and colour-free. Defining the protagonist in terms of its Other enables the 'problem' to be scripted in terms of the need for both cultural preservation and normalization. In so doing, it defines the protagonist, its goal, and problem in such a way that paradigmatically rules out a materialist critique of institutionalized disempowerment and marginalization. In effect, questions of the institutional basis of differential power/knowledge are deferred to a norm: the equality, rights and educational provision allegedly extant for mainstream Australians, as indicated by their aggregated performance data. As the result of this framing, the attempt to solve the problem and the outcome both appear as foregone conclusions: that appropriate schooling will lead to increased performance indicators, which in turn are conducive to resolving the (socioeconomic) problem posed at its onset. So staged, the story further confirms the value of a particular narrative template — the new corporatism — for 'reading' and solving social problems.

Of this closed textual narrative, we have here asked:

1) What are the particular needs of diversity in local sites? What are the intersections between class, urban/rural location, and gender and Aboriginality? Do women of colour, the urban, the isolated have special cases to be made in terms of redistributive rights?

2) Are the proposed educational interventions, including a diversity of two-way education, culturally responsive pedagogy, and bilingual and bicultural education, necessary and sufficient to achieve sociocultural power/knowledge?

3) What will a change in profile on the grid of performance indicators achieve for Islander and Aboriginal groups? What will be achieved if indicator rates improve, but if miseducation continues to reconcile many Islander and Aboriginal people to their socioeconomic and political marginalization?

4) What will be the extent and power of Islander and Aboriginal control over and input in educational decision-making given that outcomes will be judged according to performance indicators?

That Islander and Aboriginal women and girls are distinct groups, that urban Aboriginal youth have distinct subjectivities and politics from community youth which may or may not entail 'cultural maintenance' (Dawes, 1990): these are just some of the diversities silent in the document. Equally silent is the diversity that proposed educational provisions may engender. If indeed schools have had complicity in the marginalization of Islander and Aboriginal peoples, what kinds of complicity will culture-sensitive agendas, judged in terms of performance indicators, generate? Power at the margins? And with the failure of performance indicators to fix structural inequality, who will be held responsible? Islander and Aboriginal educators and decision-makers involved in 'bottom-up' consultative participation? The communities themselves? These are questions of the material effects of the discourse which bear close inspection.

We have not here taken on the reconstruction of the NATSIEP — nor signalled concrete directions for that reconstruction. That, as we said at the onset of this chapter, is the responsibility of those peoples who are presently engaged in readings and rewritings of the document in their interests. We have marked out a key point for consideration in that process. Our analysis asks whether the proposed narrative is one of incorporation: an incorporation of Islander and Aboriginal needs, aspirations, diversity and expertize into Labor's corporate rationality, and, as importantly, an incorporation into a fictional norm of the 'clever' society with a Knowledge-based economy as desired by the Labor government.

Acknowledgment

The authors wish to thank Hugh Mehan for his comments on the possibilities of 'politics of representation' as a framework for policy analysis.

References

ABORIGINAL EDUCATION POLICY TASK FORCE (1988) *Report of the Aboriginal Education Policy Task Force*, Canberra, Australia: Department of Employment, Education and Training.

BAKER, K. (1989) 'Educational reform: An international issue', Sydney, Australia: presentation to the Institute of Public Affairs.

BAKHTIN, M.M. (1986) *Speech Genres and Other Late Essays*, trans. MCGEE., V.W., EMERSON, C. and HOLQUIST, M. (Eds) Austin, TX: University of Texas Press.

BURTON, F. and CARLEN, P. (1977) 'Official discourse', *Economy and Society* 6, pp. 377–407.

COLLINS, P.H. (1990) *Black Feminist Thought*. Bloomington, IN: Indiana University Press.

DAWES, G. (1990) 'Physical graffiti: The pursuit of pleasure for an Aboriginal and Islander subculture', Sydney, Australia: paper presented to the Annual Conference, Australian Association for Research in Education.

DEPARTMENT OF EMPLOYMENT, EDUCATION AND TRAINING (DEET) (1989) *National Aboriginal and Torres Strait Islander Education Policy: Joint Policy Statement*, Canberra, Australia: Commonwealth of Australia.

DEPARTMENT OF EMPLOYMENT, EDUCATION AND TRAINING (1991) 'Australian language and literacy policy', Canberra, Australia: Draft discussion paper.

DEPARTMENT OF EMPLOYMENT, EDUCATION AND TRAINING/NATIONAL BOARD OF EMPLOYMENT, EDUCATION AND TRAINING (1989) 'A fair chance for all: National and institutional planning for equality in higher education', Canberra, Australia: Draft Discussion Paper.

FOLDS, R. (1987) *Whitefella School: Education and Aboriginal Resistance*, Sydney, Australia: Allen & Unwin.

FOUCAULT, M. (1972) *The Archeology of Knowledge*, trans, Sheridan Smith, A.M. New York, NY: Harper and Row.

FRANCO, J. (1988) 'Beyond ethnocentrism: Power and the third-world intelligentsia', in NELSON, C. and GROSSBERG, L. (Eds) *Marxism and the Interpretation of Culture*, Urbana, IL: University of Illinois Press, pp. 503–18.

HACKING, I. (1981) 'How should we do the history of statistics?' *Ideology and Consciousness*, **8**, pp. 15–26.

HENRY, M., KNIGHT, J., LINGARD, R. and TAYLOR, S. (1988) *Understanding Schooling: An Introductory Sociology of Australian Education*, London, UK: Routledge.

HUMAN RIGHTS AND EQUAL OPPORTUNITY COMMISSION (1988) *Toomelah Report: Report on the Problems and Needs of Aborigines Living on the New South Wales-Queenland Border*, Sydney, Australia: Human Rights and Equal Opportunity Commission.

JENNETT, C. (1990) 'Aboriginal Affairs Policy', in JENNETT, C. and STEWART, R.G. (Eds) *Hawke and Australian Government Policy*, Sydney, Australia: Macmillan, pp. 245–83.

KALANTZIS, M., COPE, B., and SLADE, D. (1989) *Dominant Culture and Minority Languages*, London, UK: Falmer Press.

KENWAY, J. (1990) 'Gender justice? Feminism, state theory and educational change', *Discourse*, **11**, 2, pp. 55–76.

KING, D.A. and MCHOUL, A.W. (1986) 'The discursive production of the Queensland Aborigine as subject: Meston's Proposal, 1895', *Social Analysis*, **19**, pp. 22–39.

KRESS, G. (1989) 'History and language: Towards a social analysis of linguistic change', *Journal of Pragmatics*, **13**, pp. 445–560.

LACLAU, E. (1991) *New Reflections on the Revolution of Our Time*, London, UK: Verso.

LACLAU, E. and MOUFFE, C. (1985) *Hegemony and Socialist Strategy*, London, UK: Verso.

LUKE, A. (in press) 'Ideology', in SIMPSON, J.M. MEY, J.L. *et al*, (Eds) *The Encyclopedia of Language and Linguistics*, London, UK and Aberdeen, Scotland: Pergamon Press & Aberdeen University Press.

MEHAN, H. (1989) 'Beneath the skin and between the ears: A case study in the policics of representation', unpublished Manuscript, San Diego, CA: University of California.

MEHAN, H., NATHANSON, C.E. and SKELLY, J.M. (1990) 'Nuclear discourse in the 1980s: The unravelling conventions of the Cold War', *Discourse and Society* **1**, pp. 133–66.

NAKATA, M. (1990) *Constituting the Island Subject: A Discourse Analysis of Policy and Research*, paper presented to the Annual Conference, Australian Association for Research in Education, Sydney, Austral.

NAKATA, M. (in press) 'The Islander subject on the oral-literate continuum: A reply to Watson', *The Aboriginal Child at School*.

NORMAN, R. (1987) *Free and Equal: A Philosophical Examination of Political Values*, Oxford, UK: Oxford University Press.

SILVERMAN, M. and TORODE, B. (1980) *The Material Word: Some Theories of Language and Its Limits*, London, UK: Routledge and Kegan Paul.

SINGH, M.G. (1990) *Performance Indicators in Education*, Geelong, Australia: Deakin University Press.

STEWART, R.G. and JENNETT, C. (Eds) (1990) *Hawke and Australian Government Policy*, Sydney, Australia: Macmillan.

WALTON, C. 1991 (in press) 'Aboriginal education in Northern Australia: A case study of literacy policies and practices', in FREEBODY, P. and WELCH, A. (Eds) *Knowledge, Culture and Power: International Perspectives on Literacy as Policy and Practice*, London, UK: Falmer Press.

WEXLER, P. (1987) *Social Analysis of Education*, London, UK: Routledge and Kegan Paul.

Chapter 10

Gender Equity and Economic Rationalism: An Uneasy Alliance

Miriam Henry and Sandra Taylor

Introduction

Within the somewhat uneven history of gender equity policy development over the past two decades, initiatives in girls' schooling have developed steadfastly to the point that Australia now has a national policy on girls' education — an education policy landmark in the rocky arena of Australian federalism. This chapter traces some of the influences which helped to shape — and modify — the *National Policy for the Education of Girls in Australia* (hereafter the National Policy) and speculates on the significance of this policy and its predecessors in effecting progressive changes in girls' lives. In so doing, it examines the broader and contradictory policy context within which girls' schooling policies have evolved and are being implemented. Our discussion traverses complex terrain, bearing in mind Kenway's point that:

> policies on gender and education do not exist or have their effects in isolation from other matters of policy, or from other social or administrative issues and processes . . . they should not be studied in isolation (1990, p. 7).

Implicit in these introductory comments is our view of policy as an essentially political process which 'cannot be discussed or even conceptualised in a social vacuum' (Titmuss, 1974, p. 16). We would agree with Graycar that:

> social policy is primarily a socio-political process. One cannot talk about benefits and their distribution without becoming deeply enmeshed in the politics of allocations — in striving for an understanding of the political values that underpin allocation and of the operational techniques that bring them to fruition or frustration (1978, p. 1).

Additionally, and as part of the process of examining the 'politics of allocations' in relation to gender equity and girls' schooling reform, our discussion draws on feminist concerns about the omission of women in social policy analysis — bearing in mind that feminist analyses themselves are politically and theoretically diverse (see Eisenstein, 1984; Pascal, 1986; Franzway, Court and Connell, 1989; Kenway, 1990).

Finally, our discussion involves central questions about the role of the state in effecting social change. Disentangling the threads of state power in order to examine how 'competing needs and demands are refracted, mediated and trans-lated into actual policies' (Sharp and Broomhill 1988, p. 29) requires a considera-tion of such vexed issues as the internal dynamics of the state (Franzway, *et al.*, 1989; Yeatman, 1990) including the complexities of Australia's political federal structure (Lingard, 1991), and the interconnections and contradictions between state processes, capitalism and patriarchy (Eisenstein, 1985; Sharp and Broomhill, 1988; Franzway, *et al.*, 1989; Kenway, 1990). We have drawn on feminist accounts of the state which, dovetailing with the policy orientation above, emphasize the state as a set of dynamic, historically located and complex processes rather than, simply, a set of institutions:

> The state is not a thing; it does not exist as a single, monolithic entity. It is a complex of relationships, embodying a certain form of power operating through various institutional arrangements . . . . The state is a social-political process, the result at any given moment of struggles and demands. (Burton, 1985, pp. 104–5)

The National Policy in Context

Before moving to a consideration of the National Policy itself, it is useful to briefly review the background which led to its development. In particular, the economic and political factors shaping the government's policy approach are relevant to our discussion. Over the years, various approaches to address gender inequalities in education have been taken by governments, based on differing political ideologies, and also influenced by different versions of feminism which generate different strategies for change. Thus, the political and ideological context has been especially significant in relation to policies concerning gender equity because value positions underlying policies in this area are often more overt than in other policy areas.

Additionally, the complexities for education policy of Australia's federal structure are relevant to a discussion of the National Policy. For while policies relating to schools and Technical and Further Education (TAFE) have been largely the responsibility of the states, and those relating to the tertiary sector have been largely the responsibility of the Commonwealth, this division has by no means remained static (Lingard, 1991). Hence, through the establishment of the Schools Commission and the Curriculum Development Centre, the Whitlam government intervened significantly in school policy matters, especially in areas of reform and innovation such as the education of girls. At the same time, the states have be-come increasingly involved in tertiary education policy — with implications for the education of women and girls. More recently, the Labor government's aboli-tion of the Schools Commission and establishment of a Schools Council reporting to the National Board of Employment Education and Training, has strengthened the Commonwealth's control over schooling, while, some would argue, weakening its reformative edge.

The Commonwealth government first began to respond to pressures from the women's movement during the Whitlam years of the early 1970s and allocated funds for initiatives such as women's refuges, women's health centres and family planning clinics. However, the optimism of these years was short lived, and during the Fraser Liberal government years women's affairs were given a lower priority. With the election of the Hawke government in 1983, and also the growing awareness of the importance of the women's vote, policies to improve the status of women achieved higher priority again. The Sex Discrimination Act (1984) and Affirmative Action legislation (1986), directed towards improving the status of women, particularly in the workplace, were passed; and in 1988 the government set out its National Agenda for women.

Developments in the area of policy relating to the education of girls have reflected these broader changes in social policy. The Schools Commission, set up by the Whitlam Labor government late in 1973 to advise the Commonwealth government on policy issues, took up equality as a major theme. Girls were defined as a disadvantaged group needing special attention, and a comprehensive report on the education of girls in Australia, *Girls, School and Society*, was produced (Schools Commission, 1975). This was belatedly acted upon in 1982 with the establishment of the Schools Commission Working Party on the Education of Girls. Their report, *Girls and Tomorrow*, reviewed progress since the publication of *Girls, Schools and Society*, and suggested priorities for action — one being the development of a national policy in the area of girls' schooling (Schools Commission, 1984a). The Schools Commission played a significant role as a catalyst for reform by raising awareness about gender inequalities in education through the publication and dissemination of reports and resource materials. It also allocated funding to the states through various programs for projects relating to the education of girls. In 1987, the Commonwealth government, through the Schools Commission, drew up the *National Policy for the Education of Girls in Australian Schools* after extensive consultation with state education departments (Schools Commission, 1987). It is significant that this was the first attempt to develop a national policy in any area of schooling which, as has been mentioned earlier, has traditionally and constitutionally been the responsibility of the states.

The main educational focus in the first term of the Hawke government was the Participation and Equity Program (PEP) which had a major emphasis on the education of girls (Schools Commission, 1984b). This was no doubt largely due to the efforts of Senator Susan Ryan who was Minister of Education from 1984–7, and who came from a background in teaching as well as an involvement in the Women's Movement. Senator Ryan also had a major responsibility for the successful passing of the previously mentioned Sex Discrimination Act and the Affirmative Action legislation — probably the most significant reforms affecting women in the 1980s. The Participation and Equity Program (and the Schools Commission philosophy in general) was underpinned by an 'equality of outcomes' thrust, and in relation to gender issues, the PEP Discussion Paper drew attention to sex differences in subjects studied at school, in career choices and also in the post-compulsory phase of education. The school experiences of girls were related to their limited options in the labour market and the associated implications for women's economic dependency and future life chances were indicated. Significantly, under the PEP guidelines, submissions for funding had to take account of equity issues if they were to be successful. Such pressures proved to be effective in states such as Queensland where there had been a reluctance to address gender issues in education. Many useful initiatives were taken under this program at the school level, though it suffered severe funding cuts in its third and final year of implementation.

Development of policies relating to the education of girls at the state level had varied considerably from state to state. In most cases developments resulted from active lobbying on the part of various teachers' unions and womens' groups in the late 1970s, but federal policy pressures and the availability of funds were significant in others. In some state education systems, for example Victoria, New South Wales and South Australia, special Equal Opportunity Units were set up, and provisions were made for specialist staff and for the development of much needed resource materials. In other politically more conservative states the education of girls was placed on the agenda after a long struggle. For example, in Queensland there was a deliberate refusal throughout the years of the Bjelke-Petersen National Party government to recognize the education of girls as an issue (Lingard, Henry and Taylor, 1987). Despite a policy statement in 1981 entitled 'Equal Opportunity for Girls and Boys' (Queensland Department of Education, 1981, p. 15), the government provided no financial commitment for staff or resource materials in the area, and consistently opposed any initiatives which specifically focused on improving the situation for girls. It was not until 1986 that the Queensland Education Department appointed a full time Equal Opportunity Officer, for the first time signalling an explicit commitment to the issues, even though there was a two-year delay before Queensland formally endorsed the National Policy for the Education of Girls in Australia.

The National Policy was developed through extensive consultation with education authorities and interest groups in all states and, as has been indicated, was the first national policy in any area of schooling. It attempted to build on initiatives already taken by state governments and outlined a comprehensive policy framework with objectives, and priority areas for meeting those objectives, for the period 1988–1992. Connors and McMorrow (1988) argue that the presence of Susan Ryan as Minister of Education was crucial to the education of girls being treated as a priority by the government and that the policy developments legitimized and encouraged those who were working for change in schools and systems. With reference to 'the dedicated cadre of professionals', working particularly within state schools and systems, they comment:

> These women understood the stage reached in Commonwealth-State relations: they recognised the need to secure a more practical commitment from the States; they were aware of the limitations of continued reliance on Commonwealth intervention through special purpose programs; and they saw national cooperation as one way to preserve and expand the limited resources available for research and development to improve the education of girls. (Connors and McMorrow, 1988, p. 258)

The Schools Commission favoured the consultative approach which drew on existing state programs as likely to achieve long term benefits, though Connors and McMorrow (1988) report the disappointment felt by those on the Commission when neither the Commonwealth or State governments were willing to tie themselves to a formal program of implementation strategies. In the Interim Report of the National Policy (Schools Commission, 1986), school authorities were asked to consider the range of strategies they would be prepared to implement within the National Policy. However, formal commitment was resisted, resulting in 'the proposed national plan of action being replaced by a set of illustrative strategies' (Connors and McMorrow, 1988, p. 259). The states agreed to draw on these illustrative strategies in the implementation of the policy and also agreed on the proposed reporting and review procedures. However, this was a much weaker form of agreement than the hoped for commitment to an agreed plan of action with direct funding implications. Connors and McMorrow report that 'the agreed reporting procedures were intended as a safeguard against endorsement of the National Policy becoming a substitute for action, as well as a means of providing information useful to educators and policy makers' (1988, p. 265). With the demise of the Schools Commission, however, there is no 'honest broker' to monitor the implementation of the policy, with the result that there are no pressures on the state governments to make gender issues a priority.

The National Policy was promoted by the Hawke government as an important part of its National Agenda for Women — a long-term plan to improve the position of women in Australia by the year 2000 (Dept. of Prime Minister and Cabinet/Office of Status of Women, 1988). In contrast to previous policy documents on the education of girls, girls are not treated as a homogenous group, and it is argued that schools should ensure that what is being taught does justice to girls and women, 'taking account of their cultural, language and socio-economic diversity' (Schools Commission, 1987). There is an attempt to come to grips with the varying needs of girls from differing backgrounds, and the complex ways in which gender may intersect with class, ethnicity or disability. There is also some discussion of the problems of girls in rural areas, and a detailed appendix presenting the National Aboriginal Education Committee's (NAEC) perspective on the National Policy. It is significant that the NAEC report suggests that, for Aboriginal and Islander children, racial discrimination is a more pressing problem than gender discrimination, and the point is made that Aboriginal and Islander girls are doubly disadvantaged in the education system. The idea of the 'inclusive curriculum' that takes account of cultural differences, which is discussed in the policy document, was strongly supported in the NAEC report.

In a previous discussion (Henry and Taylor, 1989), we suggested that the significance of the National Policy seemed to be largely symbolic, with the first stage of implementation aimed at promoting awareness and understanding of the policy. We commented:

> Progress will depend to a large extent on commitment by individual state governments, and in the current economic climate progress it is likely to be slow — particularly in the non-Labor states. However, the National Policy does include a reporting and review process to document educational gains from the programs, to assess objectives and priorities in response to changing needs, and to allow regular examination of the principles underpinning the National Policy. This review process is to include an annual report to help in the dissemination of strategies, and the fact that all states have now agreed to this review is a positive step forward in keeping the education of girls on the agenda. (Henry and Taylor, 1989, p. 103)

We also indicated that some countervailing trends were apparent which needed to be understood within the broader context of macro-economic and labour market policy directions. The changes made to the National Policy between the Interim and Final report stages discussed above reflect the complexities of federal state relations. However, growing financial constraints also had a part to play, particularly at the federal level, heralding a change in policy directions with the appointment of John Dawkins as Commonwealth education minister in 1987 following the Hawke government's third electoral victory. Consequently, it is possible to conceptualize two distinct phases of policy under Hawke: an earlier more progressive phase under Susan Ryan as Minister, followed by a later phase under Dawkins where economic rationalism has prevailed. As it happened, this change in Ministers and in associated policy directions corresponded with the development and implementation phases of the National Policy.

Dawkins was an active participant in Labor's shift to accommodate the prevailing ascendancy of economic rationalism within the government and key sectors of the public service (Marginson, 1988; Pusey, 1988), and his appointment as Education Minister in 1987 in charge of the renamed Department of Employment, Education and Training (DEET) was significant. His task was to oversee the restructuring of the education system to bring it into closer alignment with the government's economic and social strategies, including an expansion of the tertiary education sector. He moved quickly to bring education more directly under government control: the statutory authorities, the Commonwealth Tertiary Education Commission and the Schools Commission, were disbanded and replaced by the more corporatist National Board of Employment, Education and Training (NBEET), and within the space of just one year he introduced the controversial *Higher Education: A Policy Statement* (generally known as the White Paper) on the restructuring of higher education (Dawkins, 1988a). The Dawkins' approach is also apparent in relation to schooling in publications such as *Skills for Australia* (Dawkins and Holding, 1987) and *Strengthening Australia's Schools* (Dawkins, 1988b). The clear emphasis in these documents is that education must be part of a skills-led economic recovery with social and cultural goals being given secondary attention. Where equity issues are mentioned it is in the context of the wastage of human resources for the economy. For example, in *Skills for Australia*, it is asserted that:

> This is not simply a matter of meeting social objectives related to equity. Rather, it is an economic argument about increasing the pool of human resources available . . . . A society which does not respond to the needs of its disadvantaged groups will incur the heavy socio-economic costs of under-developed and under-utilised human resources. (Dawkins and Holding, 1987, p. 16)

Australian Traditions of Reform

Many analysts have suggested that the economic rationalist orientation of the Hawke government, discussed above, conflicts with notions of equity and social justice. However, when we consider contemporary approaches to the welfare state in an historical context, we find a long tradition in Australia of providing for social justice through the market, a tradition which has also helped to shape public attitudes to the role of governments in the pursuit of social goals. A consideration of these Australian traditions of reform is valuable in clarifying contemporary debates around social justice issues (Beilharz, 1989). We will briefly discuss those aspects which are relevant to our consideration of policies relating to women and girls.

Three distinctive features characterize the Australian approaches to reform: an emphasis on wage justice rather than social justice, a concern about welfare *needs* rather than *rights*, and related to the emphasis on work, a gendered wage and welfare system which has enshrined women as dependants of men. The emphasis on wage justice can be traced back to conditions in nineteenth century Australia where, in contrast to Britain, there was no relief or poor law, and governments were slow to provide any insurance schemes for the poor. At the time, general social attitudes were hostile towards men who were dependent on the state or on charity, and the unemployed called on the government to provide work rather than relief (MacIntyre, 1985). Charities looked after women and children but men were expected to find work. In the nineteenth century the notion that poverty was a small scale personal problem rather than a problem of society as a whole was prevalent. This attitude, reflected in the practice of conducting interviews to weed out the deserving from the undeserving poor, continued through two Depressions. For example, in the 1930s Depression, state governments provided relief work or stringently means-tested allowances known as 'sustenance' for some of the unemployed (Watts, 1988). In 1945 the national system of unemployment benefits introduced in Australia was residual in nature; that is, welfare was provided as insurance, as a last resort or safety net to provide for those in real need (MacIntyre, 1985), in contrast to a universal approach as found, for example, in Sweden, where welfare policy is concerned with broader social goals (Davis, Wanna, Warhurst and Weller, 1988, p. 189).

Thus, there has been a tradition in Australia of targeted welfare on the basis of need, rather than universal basic provision as a right, together with a hostility to dependence on the state. This approach to social welfare, with social justice being provided through the market rather than being seen as in opposition to the market, has been characterized as a 'wage earner's welfare state' (Cass, 1989, p. 140). Such an approach underpinned the Harvester judgment in 1907 when the level of a fair and reasonable living wage for a man, his wife, and three children was set by Justice Higgins. According to Beilharz, 'Higgins argued, and Australian labour has long believed, that it is the market which is the ultimate and fundamental provider of welfare or social justice' (1989, p. 91).

However, the judgment, based on patriarchal ideologies, caused major problems for women by enshrining them as dependants of men, regardless of the fact that many women were in fact breadwinners. The judgment provided a basis for lower rates of pay for women until the Equal Pay Decision of 1972, with lasting effects on the position of women in the workforce. At the same time the basis of a dualized and gendered welfare system was laid down, with 'masculine' social insurance programs tied to the breadwinner role and 'feminine' programs directed to families without a male breadwinner (Fraser, 1989).

Recently, however, a major review of social security policies in Australia incorporating a new approach to welfare has been conducted by Bettina Cass as part of an attempt to address poverty and 'substantially reduce inequalities of income, wealth and life-chances' (Cass, 1989, pp. 135–6). According to Cass, the idea of the welfare state is 'to redress inequalities and enable people to participate fully in social and economic life' (Cass, 1989, p. 153). She argues that old dichotomies of universality or selectivity, insurance-based or social assistance support schemes, are outmoded and that an approach is now needed in the reform of the welfare state which integrates work, incomes policy and welfare. She cites Stretton's (1980) proposal for programmes which link the interests of the employed population with those outside the workforce and on welfare, citing his observation that 'when those two sets of interests were perceived as fundamentally in conflict . . . the conservatives, attempting to roll back the welfare state, would win' (Cass, 1989, p. 135).

Cass argues that comparisons between OECD countries indicate that in order to bring about more equitable outcomes in society, governments need to intervene in labour market processes, regulate wages, and become involved in job creation and in education and training programs to improve employability and lifetime earnings capacity. She claims that such programs are central to the economic welfare of disadvantaged groups, and to the attainment of adequate levels of income support, and concludes: 'This makes reform of labour market inequalities and reform of the social security system inseparable projects' (Cass, 1989, p. 139). It is significant that this integrated approach to reform, which has been adopted successfully in Sweden, is based on a government commitment to full employment (Cass, 1988/9, p. 23). The strategy has particular implications for women, because it cuts across the ideological separation between women's paid employment and their child rearing work, and takes account of new patterns of paid working life and family life in a changed labour market. This, Cass argues, is the reason why the dichotomy between work and welfare must be jettisoned (Cass, 1989) — at the same time pointing to the difficulties of achieving social reform in the current economic context:

> To be engaged in a process of social security reform in a period of fiscal restraint . . . , and to be concerned with social policies to combat poverty and reduce inequality, is to locate oneself in the interstices of contradictions, while remaining firmly convinced that the fundamental aim of the project is to assist principles of equity, redistribution and social justice to remain on the political agenda, and ultimately to prevail. (Cass, 1989, p. 135)

Thus, Cass's approach to social justice is consistent with Australian traditions of reform and is based on arguments that social goals can be attained through the market. Others disagree with this view, however, and argue that economic goals are quite separate from social goals, particularly if justice is defined, as it should be, in terms of non-exploitation or protection of the vulnerable (Goodin, 1988/9). Goodin argues that the main point of government intervention to bring about equity or social justice is to impose constraints on the market to ensure that 'the benefits and burdens incurred in the pursuit of some greater social good are shared in some defensible way among everybody involved' (Goodin, 1988/9, p. 7). He further argues that social justice principles based on 'moral desserts' or on 'unconstrained choices' are incapable of constraining the market because both actually embody market principles. Beilharz (1989), too, is critical of the dominant usages of social justice in Australian policy, claiming that, given the traditions of the labour movement, social justice will likely be rendered as ' "equity" circum-scribed by market relations' (ibid., p. 92). Furthermore, he contends that wage-based approaches to social justice tend to emphasize economic rights at the expense of broader notions of citizens rights.

Contradictions in Policy

The Hawke/Keating government claims, however, to have initiated a wide range of programs in which economic policy and social justice objectives are equal partners. It sets out its approach to social justice as follows:

> This government's fundamental objective is to develop a fairer, more prosperous and more just society; a society in which every Australian receives a share of the growing wealth. The four key elements of a just society are: equity in the distribution of economic resources; equality of civil, legal and industrial rights; fair and equal access to essential services such as housing, health and education; and the opportunity for participa-tion by all in personal development, community life and decision-making. (*Towards a Fairer Australia*, 1988, overview)

These elements are summarized in later government policy documents as: equity, equality, access and participation (Department of Finance and Department of Prime Minister and Cabinet, 1989, p. 3).

This recent approach to social justice builds on the Australian tradition of reform in which, as we have discussed in the previous section, elements of market needs and social reform are intertwined. Many of the critics of the Hawke gov-ernment strategy claimed, however, that contrary to the rhetoric, the two parts of the couplet, 'efficiency with equity', are by no means equally weighted. For example, Diane Bell comments that although economic goals and social justice are presented as 'interconnected strands' in the social justice strategy, economic management is the 'main game in town' (Bell, 1988/9, p. 3). Similarly, Gay Davidson (1989) refers to the brave words of *Towards a Fairer Australia*, which claimed that social justice was the centrepiece of the budget for 1989-90, but argues that there has been a 'narrow interpretation' of social justice by the Hawke government. MacIntyre (1988/9) is also critical of the reliance on the market and views the Hawke government policies as largely rhetorical. He writes that 'social justice denotes the social policies that Labor arrange around their economic policies.' He argues that social policies have been successful when they have been presented as conducive to efficiency, and least effective when they have run up against powerful economic interests, and cites as an example the successful lobbying of the mining industry against Aboriginal Land Rights in Western Australia with federal government compliance. MacIntyre concludes that social justice:

> serves as a conveniently imprecise surrogate for other, more precise but seemingly discredited projects of social change. Social justice is what was left when they crumbled. As such, it has taken into Labor rhetoric . . . . Efficiency and equity, one sanctioning the operation of the market and the other registering its social effects, are thus yoked into a couplet. It is all too clear which element is dominant. (MacIntyre, 1988/9, pp. 36-7)

Marian Sawer (1989) comments that the creation of social justice strategies
have been important for Labor governments in 'countering popular perceptions of
widening social and economic inequalities' (p. 150), but says that the current
notion that social justice may be equated with the tighter targeting of welfare
dollars has little to do with the traditions of social justice. As she aptly puts it:
'Giving responsibility for equity programs to those whose faith is in the market
has been compared to putting mice in charge of the cheese shop' (1989, p. 150).

Reflecting the twin influences of market needs and social reform, Labor's
social justice strategy gives education a central if ambivalent role: 'Adequate and
relevant education and training is the essential first step to giving the young,
particularly the underprivileged, the chance in life which they deserve' (*Towards
a Fairer Australia*, 1988, overview). Elsewhere in the paper the role of education
and training in 'improving life options, and through this enhancing the general
well-being of society', is emphasized, together with the current needs in Australia
for 'a highly skilled and adaptable labor force' (*ibid*, 1988, p. 4). While education
programs are linked with programs in higher education and training, with income
assistance schemes and labour market programs, it is argued that: A fundamental
principle of social justice is to provide all young people with equal opportunities
to maximise their levels of education and training and to ensure more equal
outcomes from schooling across population groups. (p. 4)

What, then, is the result of this contradictory policy context on the Commonwealth's policies on the education of girls?

Implementation of the National Policy

As we have already indicated, although the formulation of the policy occurred
during the early, more progressive phase of the Hawke government under Ryan
as Minister, implementation of the policy took place under Dawkins. Consequently,
we can see the constraining and narrowing influences of economic rationalism on
publications, materials and initiatives which have emerged within the framework
of the National Policy. For example, many of the initiatives which have been
taken have clear links with the 'new vocationalism' (Bates, Clarke, Cohen, Finn,
Moore and Willis, 1984; Watkins, 1988), and sit very comfortably with the Dawkins
emphasis on employment and training. Since Keating became Prime Minister
with Beazley as federal Minister for Employment, Education and Training in
1991, this policy emphasis has continued.

A number of publications have been produced by the federal government to
raise awareness about the National Policy; for example, the GEN newsletter,
produced monthly, provides information from all states about developments
relating to the education of girls. The other major publications have been *Girls
in Schools* (DEET,1988), and *Girls in Schools 2* (DEET, 1989) — the combined
reports from all governments on progress in implementing the National Policy.
Kenway (1990) suggests that the projects and various activities reported on in such
publications reveal how the curriculum objective of the National Policy has
narrowed from a broader orientation towards an approach which emphasizes
appropriate curriculum for girls as mathematics, science and technology. Further,
she notes, publications produced by the Curriculum Development Centre include
'a heavy proportion . . . which are concerned with girls, mathematics and science'
(Kenway, 1990, p. 72). Kenway continues, 'Clearly evident in the recent State and

Commonwealth policy literature on girls' schooling is an overwhelming emphasis on encouraging girls into 'non-traditional' subjects and vocations' (Kenway, 1990, p. 73).

Similar trends are evident in the research projects which have been funded in the area — most as part of the Projects of National Significance: Education of Girls element. An early project was the development of a national data base (NSW Ministry of Youth Affairs, 1988) to improve the statistical base for developing policies and programs and which is to be annually updated. Initially, a number of projects with a broad focus were funded, for example a series which focused on groups of girls with special needs; but once again more recently there has been a heavy emphasis on girls and maths and science (DEET, 1988). This reflects the narrowing of focus which is evident in the 1987 Guidelines for the Projects of National Significance programs: Projects should, where appropriate, highlight areas influencing the long term employment prospects of Australian students and their ultimate contribution to the economic welfare of Australia (Schools Commission, undated, p. 1).

In 1989 a Project of National Significance concerned with gender and retention rates was funded (Johnston, 1990), and the focus for 1990 is on 'Broadening girls' post-school options' — with the guidelines clearly defining 'post-school options' in terms of employment options. This focus is narrower than that in the Policy itself which gave more attention to girls' (and boys') future child-rearing roles, but one which is consistent with education for economic recovery. In relation to policy implementation, then, we would agree with Kenway's claims that the government has made a highly selective reading of the National Policy:

> What is in clear relief here is the way that the gender reform program is being tailored to the ALP's cloth. Gender justice is coming to mean an education designed to prepare girls for the sorts of vocations that the government believes will enhance the economy. (Kenway, 1990, p. 73)

Gender and the Politics of Change

The processes of policy 'refraction' (Freeland, 1981; Lingard, 1983) described here raise questions about the politics of gender reform and the nature of social change. As we have indicated, the contested agendas of federalism, feminist politics, economic and social reform have provided a heady mix in the Australian context within which gender equity strategies in general, and girls' schooling policies in particular, have been fought out. Not surprisingly then, the outcomes remain fragile. The precarious position of women and girls on the educational agenda was starkly illustrated, for example, in approaches adopted by the incoming Liberal government in NSW in 1988 following twelve years of Labor rule. In the name of effecting public sector efficiencies and returning to the educational basics, the Greiner government dismantled many Labor education reforms (Editorial, *Education Links*, 34, 1988); equal opportunity units, programs and personnel within TAFE and the education department were particularly affected. (See Sawer, 1990, p. 162, who notes the education minister's determination to rid his department of 'hairy legged lesbians'.) Equally notable in Queensland, after the bitter 'states' rights' battles between the commonwealth and the former ultra-conservative Queensland

National Party government (Lingard, *et al.*, 1987), were the rapid moves by the newly elected state Labor government in 1989 to begin the task of seriously addressing girls' educational disadvantages (Lingard and Collins, 1991).

But feminist politics, while to some extent echoing party-political divisions, also cut across the federal-state divide and traditional party loyalties. The Liberal Greiner government in NSW, for example, while downgrading the status of the Women's Coordination Unit, retained the Women's Advisory Council, albeit with new appointees of the Liberal hue. (See Sawer, 1990 for a detailed account of the underlying politics.) Predictably enough, many of the issues taken up by the Council reflect liberal feminist, somewhat individualist, equal opportunity priorities. At the same time, reports in its newsletter, *Hersay*, also reflect the Council's role in initiating and supporting more broadbased reforms for disadvantaged women's groups in areas such as health, housing, child-care and domestic violence. (See also Sawer, 1990, pp. 185–7.)

However, the most potent backdrop to the politics of gender reform remains, in our view, the imperatives of economic rationalism and the deeper fiscal and legitimation crises of the capitalist state within which such an ideology is embedded (Habermas, 1976; Offe, 1984, 1985; Bates, 1990; Codd, 1990). As we have already seen, Labor's response in recent years to juggling competing market-driven demands on the one hand and traditional political demands on the other has been to set about initiating a program of 'efficient reform'. Hence, set sharply against the 'progressive mistakes' (Stretton, 1987, p. 9) of the Whitlam era, contemporary Labor's overriding concern at both state and federal levels with demonstrating 'sound economic management' and public sector efficiency has resulted in policy orientations resonating strongly with those of their Liberal counterparts but in ways which tend to cut across gender reform. Commenting on 'the triumph of "technocratic Laborism"' (*The Australian*, 6/9/1990), columnist P.P. McGuinness noted approvingly the alignment of (Labor) Tasmania's and (Liberal) NSW'S budgetary strategies, further observing 'that both the Tasmanian and Victorian governments have accepted that it is necessary in cutting spending to make an attack on the bloated education bureaucracies; nearly 600 teaching positions will be made redundant in Tasmania' (*The Australian*, 5/9/1990). In this, Tasmania echoes moves in both NSW and, most recently Victoria following its fiscal collapse, to cut back on teachers. Which sex, one wonders, bears the brunt of these 'efficiency' measures? As we noted earlier, in NSW efficiency measures included cutbacks to equal opportunity programs and personnel.

Nevertheless, while it is tempting to see 'an apparent settlement between the New Right and technocratic Labor' (Junor 1988, p. 133; see also Kenway, 1987; Knight, Smith and Chant, 1989), in our view New Labor rightism should not be conflated with the Thatcher/Major or Reagan/Bush style new right conservatism (Yates, 1986; Henry, 1987) increasingly being promoted by Liberal free marketeers in Australia. So, importantly in terms of gender reform, while Liberals threaten to jettison many of Labor's equity initiatives, Labor's strategy attempts to harness equity and efficiency in complementary, rather than contradictory, agendas. This approach, dovetailing also with liberal feminist concerns, appears to have gained a measure of popular support. The attention now given in the corporate press to the 'wasted resources' of women's talents bears testimony to the direction in which the symbiosis of equity and efficiency is heading. The *Australian Financial Review*, for example, features a regular 'corporate woman' column with up to-date information on trends and statistics relating to women's labour market participation, *Portfolio*, a liberal feminist magazine for career-oriented women, co-sponsors with the Affirmative Action Agency annual prizes for outstanding Affirmative Action initiatives. *The Australian*'s weekly 'Investment in People' section emphasizes women's contributions to workforce productivity under such headlines as: 'Women executives: use them or lose them' (5/5/1990, p. 34). The concerns are also shared by the trade union movement: '[t]he pursuit of a more skilled labour force should combine both equity and efficiency. To deny equal employment and training opportunities to all reduces the productive efficiency of the workforce' (Australian Council of Trade Unions/Trade Development Corporation, 1987). Current initiatives in award restructuring aimed at providing, amongst other things, proper career paths for women, must be seen against this backdrop.

The convergence of economic rationalism and liberal feminism, then, has helped to place gender equity more firmly on the political agenda. However, this process has been accompanied by a philosophical reconceptualization of the notion of equality, away from its traditional connotation of empowering disadvantaged groups to more economistic concerns with individual rights. Marginson alludes to older versions of equality of opportunity underpinning policies which,

> connected on one hand with economic arguments about the need to broaden and deepen the skill base, and on the other with popular desires to share knowledges and cultural resources once monopolised by the upper middle class . . . . For social reformers equality of educational opportunity was the route to the abolition of class and inequality; for ambitious parents it was their children's route to the professions (1989, p. 3).

By contrast, he suggests, contemporary usages of equity are more ambiguous, used still in the old sense by education reformers, but increasingly by market economists in the 'opposing meaning of the right to invest in the education market — equal rights to participate in a market in which social inequalities are natural, are sanctioned and legitimated'. Thus, he claims, the 'substitution of "equity" for "equality" has blunted the sharp end of equality of opportunity policies and facilitated the switch from the progressivist education reformers' idea to the market economists' idea' (p. 5).

Kenway's (1990, p. 63) suggestive list of Commonwealth education policy key words reflects the shifts in discourse which connect with this philosophical realignment and changing policy orientation. In the 1973–5 period, she notes, 'equality of opportunity, access and provision' took their place alongside words such as 'cultural and educational pluralism', 'community involvement', 'democratization' and 'disadvantaged schools'. In the 1988–89 period, 'equity of outcomes' and 'social justice' sit alongside concepts such as 'efficiency', 'effectiveness', 'accountability', 'rationalization', 'performance indicators', 'corporate management', 'education markets and 'productivity'. In similar vein and commenting more generally on Labor's need to win public support for its market-driven educational 'reforms', Ryan (1990, p. 7) suggests that Labor has engaged in a process of 'ideological reconstruction' 'in terms that incorporate the most powerful themes of the old progressive alliance whilst also stripping them, of course, of any real association with the radical visions and hopes that originally animated them'. The same could be said, perhaps, for the incorporation of 'equality' (for girls) into 'equity'.

The malleability of the concept of equity in the hands of the economic rationalists is well illustrated in a NSW government White Paper, *Excellence and Equity: NSW Curriculum Reform* (NSW Ministry of Education and Youth Affairs, 1989). While proclaiming a commitment to 'two overriding principles: the vigorous promotion of excellence and the vigilant protection and promotion of equity', thereafter in the preamble, alongside such specific objectives as the 'increased efficiency in education in the use of taxpayers' money', the only reference to equity is the goal of achieving 'fair, publicly credible systems of assessment, examination, certification and credentialling which promote equity and excellence'!

Within the body of the Report, the references to equity are equally meagre, confined to two small statements about the need for girls to become more involved in maths and sciences (NSW Ministry of Education and Youth Affairs, 1989 p. 11) and for less gender stereotyped curriculum offerings in the technologies (p. 57). Given the overall context and flavour of the Report, equity considerations have been marginalized. For all that, and indicative of the philosophical connections between liberal feminism and economic rationalism, the White Paper was commendably reviewed by the chairperson of the NSW Women's Advisory Committee:

> The changes recommended . . . reflect the need to more fully prepare our children to meet the challenges of the 21st century. They are intended to ensure that all students, but particularly girls, have an opportunity to develop technological and vocational skills in the context of a much broader education than has been offered in the past. Presently, women and girls are denied a whole range of opportunities because of the inadequacies of their early education experiences and because of pre-conceived ideas about their capabilities. The reforms outlined in the White Paper represent a systematic attempt to overcome this. (*Hersay*, March 1990, p. 4)

Of course, the concerns expressed here are also shared in the National Policy. Indeed, there could be no national policy without the existence of 'common-denominator' concerns across the political spectrum of the various states. Whether this rather tenuously-based agreement represents a plus or a minus for gender equity reform remains, at this stage in our view, a moot question.

Corporate Managerialism, Devolution and Gender Reform

Inseparable in terms of the policy process from the forces driving policy formation, are the means by which policy goals are implemented or frustrated. The dual emphases on equity and efficiency, together with women's experiences of attempting to convert the rhetoric of gender equity into effective strategies, have converged to create within contemporary Labor a particular concern with demonstrating its ability to 'deliver'. Corporate managerialism, with its emphasis on outputs and results, has been the favoured tool (Lingard and Collins, 1991) for negotiating the tightrope of 'efficient reform'. This has entailed grafting onto Labor's older commitment to equality of outcomes new concerns with measurable outputs. On the surface, this seems reasonable, and indeed much of the work in gender equity reform has been predicated upon such strategies. Implementation of the Affirmative Action Act, for example, requires organizations to identify specific objectives, set forward estimates and develop strategies to achieve the objectives. (See also Harvey and Hergert, 1986.) But there is a significant slide in the shift from an *outcomes* to an *outputs* focus which requires closer examination.

Corporate management represents a modern technique for making complex organizations able to respond more 'efficiently' (more cheaply) and more sensitively to the multiplicity of tasks they characteristically face — a process described by Yeatman (1990, p. 16, citing a Senior Executive Management Program manual) as 'doing more with less; focussing on outcomes and results; managing change better'. The phenomenon of corporate managerialism and associated debates have been much discussed in recent years and need not take space here (see, Yeatman, 1987, 1990; Considine, 1988). Of significance to this chapter is the underlying assumption that purposive and task-oriented administration, harnessed to politically reformative goals, can deliver discernible results over and above rhetoric and, as we have indicated, many feminists working within institutions have supported this approach as a means of trying to enforce organizational commitment to equity goals. Perhaps not surprisingly, however, it is at this strategic level of implementation that the contradictions within the unequally weighted equity-efficiency couplet become most apparent; the broader political and economic context in which corporate managerialism typically operates, in conjunction with its technicist logic, serve to potentially deflect or subvert the reform agenda.

Specifically in relation to gender equity, a number of writers have shown how equity goals can be distorted by the very administrative practices that are meant to achieve them. (See, for example, Blackmore, 1988; Yeatman, 1987.) Sawer's (1989, 1990) detailed accounts of the bureaucracy at work show the multitude of administrative and budgetary mechanisms which may be used to subvert equity goals, no matter how programmatically spelled out. Henry and Ross (1991) have also shown how, in the higher education sphere, the corporate managerialist approach has resulted in a plethora of equity plans and documents, but little change for women who remain at the bottom of the higher education pyramid. Corporate managerialism, Blackmore (1989, p. 14) has suggested, co-opts the language and ideas of equity (and social justice) into techniques — sets of variables to be managed, either on the margins of organizational life, or swallowed into the organizational mainstreams — while discarding the underlying principles and values. In this process of equity management, women become policy targets, *objects* of policy rather than *empowered* by policy (Yeatman, 1990, p. 134). Outputs there certainly are: more refined equity plans and policy documents and more sophisticated administrative infrastructures to deal with the burgeoning demands for equity accountability. However, in terms of effecting changed organizational profiles or culture, the social justice outcomes remain elusive; equal opportunity becomes 'reframed in terms of what it can do to improve management, not of what it can do to develop the conditions of social justice and democratic citizenship in Australian society' (Yeatman, 1990, p. 16).

Discernible results, and social reform are not synonymous; outputs-oriented administration does not necessarily deal successfully with the powerful vested interests that the reform agenda invariably challenges. This is not mere administrative malfeasance, of course, but symptomatic of the deep contradictions between the competing demands of capital and social justice referred to earlier which are masked, rather than resolved, by the uneasy alliance between equity and efficiency.

Closely aligned with the corporate managerialist strategy are moves towards organizational devolution which have occurred within education systems Australia-wide and elsewhere (McCollow, 1989). The devolution strategy has a complex history and has been variously promoted as a means of enhancing community participation (Kirner, cited in Burke, 1990), effecting administrative efficiencies (Kidston, 1989), as a back-door mechanism for asserting central political, as distinct from administrative control (Lingard and Collins, 1991). Of significance to the implementation of gender equity policies, devolution has also been described as a mechanism for shedding central responsibility for difficult funding and awkward policy decisions — literally passing the buck (McCollow, 1989; Blackmore, 1989; Middleton, Codd and Jones, 1990). Bates (1990, p. 45) suggests that the devolution strategy has contributed to systemic fragmentation and the creation of a commodity market, with,

> schools competing to deliver 'most wanted' services and products to individual students and parents who will presumably shop around for the best buys. The supermarket concept of education [has] replaced any notion of collective responsibility for provision and standards.

In relation to controversial areas of reform such as overcoming girls' schooling disadvantages, the development of an education supermarket in place of a strong central policy and funding infrastructure is likely to prove critically damaging. Which brings us back to the National Policy.

The National Policy: More than Merely Symbolic?

> At worst, the endorsement of the *National Policy for the Education of Girls* could become an impressive substitute for specific action to improve the education of girls. At best, it could provide a more principled and explicit basis for the development of school reforms than is customary in Australian education. The outcome in practice will be dependent upon the political process and the way in which the education profession incorporates the Policy into both its epistemology and its practice. (Connors and McMorrow, 1988, p. 261)

The political, ideological and administrative complexities and contradictions surrounding gender reform sketched out above must raise serious doubts about the material, as distinct from the symbolic, efficacy of the National Policy, given its relatively weak voluntarist framework. The emphasis now on the efficient management of schools and education bureaucracies, together with current devolution approaches mean that the achievement of the National Policy goals are likely to rest to a very large extent on the degree to which gender equity is recognized as a local concern and then managed at the local (regional or school) level. It is perhaps ironic that the emergence of a well-coordinated and carefully structured national policy has coincided with, and is likely to be undermined by, the administrative fragmentation of state education systems. Further, the dovetailing of liberal feminist readings of the policy (Kenway, 1989; 1990) with the imperatives of economic rationalism is likely to shape an agenda which channels local concerns, if they do emerge, in highly selective and relatively narrowly focused directions — workforce skills and assertiveness training for girls, for example, rather than child-rearing skills and nurturance development for boys.

This is not to deny the value of the National Policy as a signifier of social priorities, as a source of limited funding and as a legitimating force for those attempting to implement progressive strategies. As we indicated in a previous article (Lingard, *et al.*, 1987), policy frameworks provide an invaluable weapon in the armoury of progressive teachers and administrators. Nor would we want to underestimate the extensive pool of knowledge and experience which has gone into the making of the National Policy. Taken at face value, the policy does have the potential to address specifically identified and differentiated needs of girls; it does allow a focus on tangible, measurable outcomes; and it is taking account of prevailing economic pressures. It builds on the considerable progress already made through the previous Participation and Equity Program in making the school curriculum more inclusive of girls' experiences and interests and in broadening subject options for girls. As Weiner (1989), for example, has pointed out in relation to the United Kingdom, even the narrow focus on vocationalism can be exploited — 'broadening girls' post school options', for instance, can be defined in other than employment terms. Certainly and despite earlier-expressed reservations, we would also point to programs generated by the National Policy and its predecessors, documented in the *Girls and Schools Reports* (DEET, 1988; 1989), which push beyond narrow vocationalism, particularly in those states where girls' schooling disadvantages have been taken seriously over an extended period of time. For example, a South Australian Project of National Significance investigated the learning needs of girls in low socio-economic situations (DEET, 1989, p. 52). South Australia has also established three state single-sex girls' high schools which function as 'lighthouse schools' in relation to curriculum for the education of girls (DEET,1989, p. 54). Also in South Australia, a Girls and Multicultural Education project has seen the establishment of a statewide network addressing the needs of girls of non-English speaking background and the production of Culturally Sensitive Affirmative Action Guidelines (DEET, 1989, p. 53). In Western Australia, a program aimed at supporting pregnant girls and teenage mothers was introduced to provide opportunities for completing studies through correspondence and tutor courses. Creche facilities and personal development workshops were also made available to assist these young women (DEET, 1989, p. 85).

In reviewing progress under the National Policy, as reported in *Girls in Schools* (DEET, 1988) and *Girls in Schools 2* (DEET, 1989) we are struck by the continuing uneven developments across the states. Beneath the rhetoric, the states which seem to have made the most progress are those where there has been a strong policy commitment at the state level for a number of years. In particular, South Australia stands out among the states in the development of a number of policies at state level relating to gender issues, as well as in the establishment of appropriate structures, support staff and networks to ensure that action is statewide. In addition, South Australia is the only state which seems to be coming to grips with meeting the needs of particular groups of girls, for example, Aboriginal girls, and girls with disabilities, in the research projects and strategies outlined (DEET, 1989, pp. 51–7).

A recent national research project has found marked differences between the states in awareness of gender issues in education and in initiatives which have been taken to broaden girls' post-school options (Johnston, Taylor and Watson, 1990).

This also supports research by Geraldine Lazarus (1989) which examined the perceptions of and attitudes towards gender equity among teachers and school principals in Melbourne, Brisbane and Toowoomba. Comparisons between the two states showed that:

> While there is a powerful push in Victoria from many committed teachers to pursue gender-inclusive curriculum, in Queensland much more needs to be done. Those who oppose gender equity (in either State) refer to those who espouse it as 'feminist' (said with a viperous hiss). Depressing numbers of women teachers believe deep in their hearts (and are quite happy to tell you) that a woman's place is really in the home. (Lazarus, 1989, p. 19)

The study highlighted the differences in the way in which gender equity has been approached in the two states — with more up-front strategies found in Victoria in contrast to the cautious approaches in Queensland. It is suggested that the more direct approach has been possible in Victoria 'because there are many more teachers prepared to reach out and embrace the idea of a gender inclusive curriculum' (Lazarus, 1989, p. 19). It is clear that the differences in the general level of awareness among teachers reflect the different levels of commitment and associated policy developments in the two states over the last decade or so. In Victoria, there has been a strong policy commitment over a number of years, while in Queensland there was a refusal to address the issues during the Bjelke-Petersen era.

We would argue, then, that in terms of what is happening 'on the ground' in schools, up to this point it is state policies rather than the National Policy which have been crucial in improving the education of girls. Indeed, it could perhaps be argued that the National Policy has helped progressive states to make further headway, thereby exacerbating existing differences. The extent to which a national policy, operating at a largely symbolic level, can, in the long term, transcend state patterns remains to be seen. As the 1990 round of new federalism talks revealed, the states still jealously guard their schooling territory in face of the threat of central control. More significantly perhaps, what also remains to be seen is the extent to which the National Policy can transcend the forces of economic rationalism. This returns us to broader questions of social policy and feminist strategy.

Although the National Policy attempts to disaggregate girls' needs and experiences and to go beyond liberal feminist equal opportunity concerns, by and large schooling policies for girls and the broader EEO/AA legislative framework in Australia, within which much gender equity reform has occurred, deal essentially with labour market concerns and the needs of women in the paid workforce. While the progress achieved through such means has been notable, attracting worldwide attention (Sawer, 1990), the restricted frame of reference of these policy approaches means that profoundly significant questions remain unaddressed: for example, they do not attempt to, indeed cannot, challenge the deep-seated inequities of modern patriarchal capitalism which globally and differentially impact on all aspects of women's and men's lives. Indeed, the very achievements of equal opportunity programs may be, precisely, a measure of their lack of threat to deeper structural inequalities. (See also Yates, 1986.) This is certainly not to suggest that any particular schooling policy can or ought to remedy the problems of the world. But it is to take up socialist feminists' concerns that schooling reforms for girls ought to encompass a wider set of questions than, simply, their ability to enter a socially unreconstructed and inegalitarian world. Thus, strategies aimed at giving girls entry into new areas of the labour market must also be set against the realization that modern capitalism is radically rewriting the meaning of work as old life-time jobs give way to a labour market increasingly dominated by part-time and casual work. What progress, then, is to be found in the new exploitation of women in an expanded secondary labour market, as computer rather than textile outworkers (Junor, 1990, p. 63)? And strategies aimed at providing women with expanded opportunities for work and economic independence, whilst absolutely valuable, must be set against contradictory tendencies in social policy. As we have seen, on the one hand, women's wasted talents are represented as a missed market opportunity; on the other hand women's traditional contributions to the unpaid or underpaid domestic economy are even more in demand as, in the name of sound economic management, state functions such as care of the elderly or the ill are returned to families and the community — meaning women. In such a context, the line between expanding opportunities for women, and merely doubling their responsibilities, may be indeed thin (Wicks, 1990).

Such issues might seem remote from the concerns of the National Policy, and indeed it might seem fanciful to hang so much on what is after all a relatively small cog in the wheel of social reform. However, we indicated at the outset our belief that an adequate exploration of the National Policy would cover complex terrain, and indeed, it is because gender reform is now so firmly established on the political agenda, that the imperative to extend the parameters of the debate takes on some urgency. For now, more than ever, politicians, bureaucrats, captains of industry and others are likely to see the debate as closed. 'But it's not like that any more,' our students tell us. Abortion reform is 'not on the agenda — we have more important priorities,' asserts Queensland's newly-elected Labor premier. 'The war's already been won,' claims ex-Labor politician Barry Cohen (*The Australian*, 28/9/90) in strident opposition to a Labor Women's document, *Half By 2000* (Queensland Labor Women's Organisation, 1990), setting out some targets for increased women's participation in politics. Responding to a recent initiative to achieve pay increases for women workers, the Australian Confederation of Industry maintained that: 'Wages and wage increases must be kept in line with movements in productivity if we are to keep our inflation rate down . . . we have policies which support equal opportunity and . . . affirmative action programs for women' (*The Sunday-Mail*, 5/8/1990). Responses such as these both reflect and shape the ongoing debates about gender equity. If this tricky area of social reform is allowed to be channelled into the relatively narrow dictates of labour market demand and constrained by what Bates (1990: 43) refers to as 'the dismal science of economics', things could indeed be like that again — the National Policy notwithstanding. Emphatically, the debate has to be about more than vocational skills and entry into non-traditional areas for girls, important as these things may be. As Jean Blackburn (1984) argued so persuasively a number of years ago, the debate also has to be about the kind of society we want to live in. Unless the National Policy is used to pursue a broader social agenda, it is likely to remain as an eloquent but largely symbolic testament to an era when we tried to do some-thing about girls' schooling but couldn't quite get beyond the rhetoric.

References

AUSTRALIAN COUNCIL OF TRADE UNIONS/TRADE DEVELOPMENT CORPORATION (1987) *Australia Reconstructed: A Report by Mission Members to the ACTV and the TDC*, Canberra, Australia: AGPS.

BATES, R. (1990) 'Educational policy and the new cult of efficiency', in MIDDLETON, S., CODD, J. and JONES, A. (Eds) *New Zealand Education Policy Today: Critical Perspectives*. Wellington, NZ: Allen and Unwin, pp. 40–52.

BATES, I., CLARKE, J., COHEN, D., FINN, D., MOORE, R. and WILLIS, P. (1984) *Schooling for the Dole?*, Basingstoke, UK: Macmillan.

BEILHARZ, P. (1989) 'Social democracy and social justice', *Australia and New Zealand Journal of Sociology*, **25**,1, pp. 85–99.

BELL, D. (1988/9) 'Still in search of justice', in *Social Justice in Australia*, supplement to *Australian Society*, December 1989/January 1990, pp. 3–4.

BLACKBURN, J. (1984) 'Schooling and injustice for girls', in BROOM, D. (Ed.), *Unfinished Business: Social Justice for Women in Australia*, Sydney, Australia: Allen and Unwin, pp. 3–18.

BLACKMORE, J. (1988) 'The historical construction of "masculinist" administrative cultures: Exclusionary theory and discriminatory practice', paper presented to the Conference on Theory and Policy, Griffith University, Brisbane, Australia December.

BLACKMORE, J. (1989) 'Working the system', *Education Links, **36**, Winter, pp. 13–15.

BURKE, C. (1989) 'Devolution of responsibility to Queensland Schools: Clarifying the rhetoric, critiquing the reality', paper presented to the Queensland Institute for Senior Education Officers Conference, Brisbane, Australia June.

BURTON, C. (1985) *Subordination: Feminism and Social Theory*, Sydney, Australia: Allen and Unwin.

CASS, B. (1988/9) 'New directions for work and welfare', in *Social Justice in Australia*, supplement to *Australian Society*, December 1989/January 1990, pp. 20–3.

CASS, B. (1989) 'Defending and reforming the Australian welfare state: Some ideas for the next decade', in ORCHARD, L. and DARE, R. (Eds) *Markets, Morals and Public Policy*, Sydney, Australia: The Federation Press, pp. 134–56.

CODD, J. (1990) 'Educational policy and the crisis of the New Zealand State', in MIDDLETON, S., CODD, J. and JONES, A. (Eds) *New Zealand Education Policy Today: Critical Perspectives*, Wellington, NZ: Allen and Unwin, pp. 191–205.

CONNORS, L. and McMORROW, J. (1988) 'National policy development: The significance of the National Policy for the Education of Girls', *Unicorn*, **14**, 4, pp. 256–65.

CONSIDINE, M. (1988) 'The corporate management framework as administrative science: A critique', *Australian Journal of Public Administration* **47**, 1, pp. 4–18.

DAVIDSON, G. (1989) 'Brave Words', *Australian Society*, October, p. 39.

DAVIS, G., WANNA, J., WARHURST, J. and WELLER, P. (1988) 'Public Policy in Australia', Australia, Sydney, Australia: Allen and Unwin.

DAWKINS, J. (1988a) *Higher Education: A Policy Statement*, Canberra, Australia: Australian Government Publishing Service [AGPS].

DAWKINS, J. (1988b) *Strengthening Australia's Schools*, Canberra, Australia: AGPS.

DAWKINS, J. and HOLDING, C. (1987) *Skills for Australia*, Canberra, Australia: AGPS.

DEPARTMENT OF EMPLOYMENT, EDUCATION AND TRAINING (1988) *Girls in Schools*, report on the National Policy for the Education of Girls in Australian Schools, Canberra: AGPS.

DEPARTMENT OF EMPLOYMENT, EDUCATION AND TRAINING (1989) *Girls in Schools 2*, report on the National Policy for the Education of Girls in Australian Schools, Canberra, Australia: AGPS.

DEPARTMENT OF FINANCE AND DEPARTMENT OF PRIME MINISTER AND CABINET (1989) *Towards a Fairer Australia: Social Justice and Program Management: A Guide*, Canberra, Australia: AGPS.

DEPARTMENT OF PRIME MINISTER AND CABINET/OFFICE OF STATUS OF WOMEN (1988) *A Say, a Choice, a Fair go, The Government's National Agenda for Women*, Canberra, Australia: AGPS.

EDITORIAL. *Education Links* 34 (1988)

EISENSTEIN, H. (1984) *Contemporary Feminist Thought*, London, UK: Unwin.

EISENSTEIN, H. (1985) 'The gender of bureaucracy: Reflections on feminism and the state', in GOODNOW, J. and PATEMEN, C. (Eds) *Women, Social Science and Public Policy*. Sydney, Australia: Allen and Unwin, pp. 104–15.

FRANZWAY, S. COURT, D. and CONNELL, R.W. (1989) *Staking a Claim: Feminism, Bureaucracy and the State*, Sydney, Australia: Allen and Unwin.

FRASER, N. (1989) *Unruly Practices: Power, Discourse and Gender in Contemporary Social Theory*, Cambridge, UK: Polity Press.

FREELAND, J. (1981) 'Where do they go after school?: A critical analysis of one education program for unemployed youth', *The Australian Quarterly*, Spring, pp. 351–73.

GOODIN, B. (1988/9) 'Markets: Their morals and ours', in *Social Justice in Australia*, supplement to *Australian Society*, December 1989/January 1990, pp. 7–9.

GRAYCAR, A. (Ed.) (1978) *Perspectives in Australian Social Policy*, Melbourne, Australia: Macmillan.

HABERMAS, J. (1976) *Legitimation Crisis*, London, UK: Heineman.

HARVEY, G. and HERGERT, L. (1986) 'Strategies for achieving sex equity in education', *Theory into Practice*, **25**, 4, pp. 290–99, and reproduced in KENWAY, J. (1990) *Gender and Education Policy. A Call for New Directions*, Geelong, Australia: Deakin University Press.

HENRY, M. (1987) 'Life on the coalface: The aftermath of amalgamation', *British Journal of Sociology of Education*, **8**, 4, pp. 357–77.

HENRY, M., ROSS, R. (1991) 'Managing academia: To what ends?', *Discourse*, **11**, 2.

HENRY, M. and TAYLOR, S. (1989) 'On the agenda at last? Recent developments in educational policy relating to women and girls', in TAYLOR, S. and HENRY, M. (Eds) *Battlers and Bluestockings: Women's Place in Australian Education*, Canberra, Australia: Australian College of Education, pp. 101–9.

HERSAY (1990) News Bulletin of the NSW Women's Advisory Council.

JOHNSTON, S. (1990) *Retention Rates: There is More to it Than Counting Heads*, Brisbane, Australia: Queensland Education Department.

JOHNSTON, S., TAYLOR, S. and WATSON, G. (1990) *Let's Talk Business*, unpublished research report, Brisbane, Australia: Queensland University of Technology.

JUNOR, A. (1988) 'Australian education reconstructed', *Arena* **84**, pp. 133–40.

JUNOR, A. (1990) *Employment Estimates and Projections Relevant to Commerce and Business Studies. Australia and New Zealand*, unpublished report prepared for 'Projects of National Significance: Broadening Girls' Post-School Options', Sydney, Australia: Macquarie University.

KENWAY, J. (1987) 'Left right out: Australian education and the politics of signification', *Journal of Education Policy*, **2**, 3, pp. 189–203.

KENWAY, J. (1989) 'After the Applause', *Education Links*, **36**, pp. 24–6.

KENWAY, J. (1990) *Gender and Education Policy: A Call for New Directions*, Geelong, Australia: Deakin University Press.

KIDSTON, R. (1989) *Managing Change: A Case Study of the Department of Education, Queensland*, Brisbane, Australia: Centre for Australian Public Sector Management, Griffith University.

KNIGHT, J., SMITH, R. and CHANT, D. (1989) 'Reconceptualising the dominant ideology debate: An Australian case study', *Australian and New Zealand Journal of Sociology*, **25**, 3, pp. 383–409.

LAZARUS, G. (1989) 'Gender equity: Teachers have the power to make it happen', *Ms Muffett*, **41**, pp. 16–9.

LINGARD, R. (1983) 'Multicultural education in Queensland: The assimilation of an ideal', *Discourse*, **4**, 1, pp. 13–31.

LINGARD, R. (1991) 'Policy making for Australian schooling: The new corporate federalism', *Journal of Education Policy*, **6**, 1, pp. 85–90.

LINGARD, R. and COLLINS, C. (1991) 'Radical reform or rationalisation? Education under Goss Labor in Queensland', *Discourse*, **11**, 2, pp. 98–114.

LINGARD, R., HENRY, M. and TAYLOR, S. (1987) ' "A girl in a militant pose": A chronology of struggle in girls' education in Queensland', *British Journal of Sociology of Education*, **8**, 2, pp. 135–52.

McCOLLOW, J. (1989) 'Devolution: Education and economics on a collision course', *Queensland Teachers Union Professional Magazine*, September, pp. 9–12.

MACINTYRE, S. (1985) *Winners and Losers*, Sydney, Australia: Allen and Unwin.

MACINTYRE, S. (1988/9) 'Less winners, more losers', in *Social Justice in Australia*, supplement to *Australian Society*, December 1989/January 1990, pp. 35–7.

MARGINSON, S. (1988) 'The economically rational individual', *Arena*, 84, pp. 105–14.

MARGINSON, S. (1989) 'The decline and fall of equality of opportunity', paper presented to the Australian and New Zealand Comparative and International Education Society Conference, Melbourne, December.

MIDDLETON, S., CODD, J. and JONES, A. (Eds) (1990) *New Zealand Education Policy Today: Critical Perspectives*, Wellington, New Zealand: Allen and Unwin.

NSW MINISTRY OF EDUCATION AND YOUTH AFFAIRS (1988) *National Data Base on the Education of Girls in Australian Schools*, Sydney, Australia: NSW Ministry of Education and Youth Affairs.

NSW MINISTRY OF EDUCATION AND YOUTH AFFAIRS (1989) *Excellence and Equity: New South Wales Curriculum Reform. A White Paper on Curriculum Reform in New South Wales Schools*, Sydney, Australia: NSW Ministry of Education and Youth Affairs.

OFFE, C. (1984) *Contradictions of the Welfare State*, London, UK: Hutchinson.

OFFE, C. (1985) *Disorganized Capitalism*, Oxford, UK: Polity Press.

PASCAL, G. (1986) *Social Policy: A Feminist Analysis*, London, UK: Tavistock.

POLK, K. and TAIT, D. (1990) 'Changing youth labour markets and youth life styles', *Youth Studies*, **9**, 1, pp. 17–32.

PRESS REPORT (1990) *The Australian*, 5 May.

PRESS REPORT (1990) *The Australian*, 5 September.

PRESS REPORT (1990) *The Australian*, 6 September.

PRESS REPORT (1990) *The Australian*, 28 September.

PRESS REPORT (1990) *The Australian*, 5 August.

PUSEY, M. (1988) 'From Canberra the outlook is dry', *Australian Society*, July, pp. 20–6.

QUEENSLAND DEPARTMENT OF EDUCATION (1981) 'Department Policy Statement', *Education Office Gazette*, January, 1981, p. 15.

QUEENSLAND LABOR WOMEN'S ORGANISATION (1990) *Half by 2000*, Brisbane, Australia.

RYAN, B. (1990) 'The Speedy agenda: Whose interests are being served?', paper presented to the ATEA Conference, Adelaide, Australia.

SAWER, M. (1989) 'Efficiency, effectiveness and equity?', in DAVIS, G., WELLER, P. and LEWIS, C. (Eds), *Corporate Management in Australia*, Melbourne, Australia: Macmillan, pp. 138–53.

SAWER, M. (1990) *'Sisters in Suits': Women and Public Policy in Australia*, Sydney, Australia: Allen and Unwin.

SCHOOLS COMMISSION (1975) *Girls, School and Society*, Canberra, Australia: AGPS.

SCHOOLS COMMISSION (1984a) *Girls and Tomorrow*. Canberra, Australia: AGPS.

SCHOOLS COMMISSION (1984b) *Participation and Equity in Australian Schools*, Canberra, Australia: AGPS.

SCHOOLS COMMISSION (1986) *A National Policy for the Education of Girls in Australian Schools*, interim report, Canberra, Australia: AGPS.

SCHOOLS COMMISSION (1987) *The National Policy for the Education of Girls in Australian Schools*, Final Report, Canberra, Australia: AGPS.

SCHOOLS COMMISSION (undated) Projects of National Significance Program 1987. 'Guidelines for proposals to undertake Commonwealth Schools Commission nominated projects', mimeo, Canberra, Australia: Commonwealth Schools Commission.

SHARP, R. and BROOMHILL, R. (1988) *'Short-changed': Women and Economic Policies*, Sydney, Australia: Allen and Unwin.

STRETTON, H. (1987) *Political Essays*, Melbourne, Australia: Georgian House.

STRETTON, H. (1980) 'Social policy: Has the welfare state all been a terrible mistake?', in EVANS, G. and REEVES, J. (Eds) *Labor Essays 1980*, Melbourne, Australia: Drummond.

TITMUSS, R. (1974) *Social Policy: An Introduction*, London, UK: Allen and Unwin. *Towards a Fairer Australia: Social Justice Under Labor* (1988) Canberra, Australia: AGPS.

WATKINS, P. (1988) 'Reassessing the work-experience bandwagon: Confronting students with employers' hopes and the reality of the workplace', *Discourse*, **9**, 1, pp. 81–97.

WATTS, R. (1988) 'As cold as charity,' in BURGMANN, V. and LEES, J. (Eds), *Making a Life*, Ringwood: Penguin, pp. 85–100.

WICKS, M. (1990) 'The battle for the family', *Marxism Today*, August, pp. 28–33.

WEINER, G. (1989) 'Feminism, equal opportunities and the new vocationalism: The changing context', in BURCHILL, H. and MILLMAN, V. (Eds) *Changing Perspectives on Gender: New Initiatives in Secondary Education*, Milton Keynes, UK: Open University Press, pp. 107–21.

YATES, L. (1986) 'Theorising inequality today', *British Journal of Sociology of Education*, **7**, 2, pp. 119–34.

YEATMAN, A. (1987) 'The concept of public management and the Australian state in the 1980s', *Australian Journal of Public Administration*, **47**, 4, pp. 339–53.

YEATMAN, A. (1990) *Bureaucrats, Technocrats, Femocrats: Essays on the Contemporary Australian State*, Sydney, Australia: Allen and Unwin.

Chapter 11

Corporate Restructuring of the Australian Disability Field

Cheryl Carpenter

Introduction

The Hawke Government's (1983–91) restructuring of the Australian disability field began in 1983. The Government used corporate initiatives such as a tripartite system of Government, service providers and clientele (people with disabilities) working through a national inquiry (Handicapped Programs Review) and a national advisory council (Disability Advisory Council of Australia) to ensure greater representation of people with disabilities on disability issues. The Government also appropriated a central concept, 'the least restrictive alternative', from the internationally acclaimed theory of normalization, to address past inequities and provide the *New Directions* (Handicapped Programs Review, 1985) for the disability field. Both normalization and the Hawke Government's restructurings were closely associated with human rights.

However, human rights are generally considered within a retrospective framework, in relation to the injustices of a past medical/institutional regime. The subsequent approach has been to take a mostly uncritical, pragmatic approach to implementing the 'New Directions' and establishing the new regime. Frequently overlooked are the changes which have occurred within the discourses of normalization and the Government's 'New Directions'. Issues of human rights have been marginalized by an economic rationalism which is creating new inequities within the disability field.

Also mediating the initiatives of the Hawke Government were the peculiarities of the Australian Constitution which defines Federal/State realms of authority. The disability field is predominantly a Federal responsibility. However, special education, as part of education in general, is predominantly a State responsibility. These peculiarities of the Australian constitution have created some ambiguities regarding special education and its relationship to the Hawke Government's restructurings of the disability field.

The Disability Field

Historically, the disability field has been ruled by a powerful medical/institutional regime. This regime was characterized by mass, segregated institutions run by the state and private organizations. Provision tended to be custodial with little intervention. Gross deprivations, the eugenics movement and violation of human rights were all realities within this discourse. (See Judge, 1987.)

It was not until the 1960s civil rights movements that people with disabilities, parents and advocates mounted a substantial challenge to the *status quo* of the disability field. Then in 1969, Nirje developed the theory of normalisation and coined the phrase 'the right to as normal a life as possible', which has since become the cliche of the disability field. The theory encapsulated the civil rights issues, as outlined in the United Nations Declaration of Rights, pertaining to the rights of the disabled individual to specialized treatment, to the rights of the normal citizen and the rights of parents to participation in decision-making (cited by Doherty, 1982).

Then in 1972, Wolfensberger presented another theory of normalization which he claimed was an 'operationalization' of the earlier theory. Both theories argued for disbanding the institutional model. The normalization model was to be characterized by intervention programs, the placement of people with disabilities and services within the mainstream of society (integration) and the least restrictive alternative.

The least restrictive alternative was a guiding principle for intervention and integration. The principle recognized that not all people with disabilities were capable of functioning independently within society. Intervention programs were to provide a continuum of support from full assistance/dependence (most restrictive alternative) to no assistance/independence (least restrictive alternative). Similarly, integration programs were to provide a continuum of services, such as accommodation and education. These services were to range from specialized, segregated services (most restrictive alternative) to generic, mainstream services (least restrictive alternative). Those options which provided the highest degree of independence and the most access to mainstream society were to be favoured when deciding on the programs and placements for an individual (Nirje, 1985; Wolfensberger, 1980b).

Normalization has become the dominant discourse, the international password, within the disability field to such an extent that we are now witnessing the 'Normalization Era' (Judge, 1987, pp. 1–2). However, normalization has become 'synomynous with the name, Wolf Wolfensberger' (Judge, 1987). Some developments, such as the Hawke Government's initiatives, did not officially recognize normalization and others arose prior to Wolfensberger's (1972) publication of 'The Principle of Normalization'. However, such developments still belong to the 'Normalization Era' with its provision of the normal for the disabled individual. We can, following Foucault (Rabinow, 1986: 101–20), say that Wolfensberger is not the name of the author, but the name of the discourse. However, there have been two major shifts in direction during the normalization era; they took place in the 1970s and the early 1980s.

The 1970s: From Nirje to Wolfensberger

The first shift occurred when Nirje's (1969) theory was superseded by Wolfensberger's (1972) theory. Writing much later on this shift, Nirje argues that Wolfensberger's theory 'deviates in many significant ways from the original concept', and that 'its focus on using normative means and on establishing normative behaviour, is built upon a fundamentally different value base and conception of people, with quite different implications for how we view and treat people' (Perrin and Nirje, 1985, p. 71). Perrin and Nirje provide an outline of the differences between the two theories:

> Normalisation as originally defined is based upon a humanistic, egalitarian value base, emphasising freedom of choice and the right to self determination. It emphasises clearly respect for the individual and his or her right to be different . . . Wolfensberger (1972, 1980a), on the contrary, interprets normalisation as specifying various standards of behaviour to which a mentally handicapped person must conform. He speaks openly of 'normalising' people through 'eliciting, shaping, and maintaining normative skills and habits' (Wolfensberger, 1972, p. 32; 1980a, p. 17) or even through the use of force: 'Normalising measures can be *offered* in some circumstances, and *imposed* in others.' (Wolfensberger, 1982, p. 28, italics in original)

The shift from Nirje to Wolfensberger was a shift from issues of human rights to issues of human management: management of individuals' behaviours and appearances through behaviourist means-end and reinforcement technologies and management of services through the objective-outcome and feedback processes of systems theory (Wolfensberger, 1972, 1973). The onus was now on individuals, and technocratic, behaviourist forms of intervention to achieve normality. The emphasis changed from providing normal experiences, environments and relationships as a right to imposing normality to gain social acceptance and access to the societal mainstream. The emphasis also changed from provision as a human right to economic concerns regarding the accountability, coordination, efficiency and effectiveness of intervention programs.

The supremacy of Wolfensberger's normalization can be attributed to its support by two quite contradictory interest groups. First, the disability movement was increasingly dissatisfied with the existing medical/institutional system. The efficiency and accountability rhetoric of normalization was used to challenge the existing system and to support an integrated system. Consequently, the economism within normalization was considered to be closely associated with human rights and little consideration was given to its other possible implications.

Second, the capitalist world was entering a period of economic restraint during the 1970s. The economism within normalization served the interests of those wishing to rationalise public sector spending. Two justifications for normalization and integration were that they were more efficient and more cost-effective than the large institutions. Consequently, integration and normalization policies were instigated because they fulfilled a higher priority within a time of economic constraint, that is, they were cheap. Soder (1984, p. 33) elaborates this point:

> Making the needs of the severely disabled invisible fills an economic function. The present economic crisis has created strong political pressures for cuts in public sector expenditure. Cuts in a sector that is primarily constructed to meet the needs of groups of less fortunate individuals will naturally affect these groups the most. There is therefore

every . . . reason to look closely at the ideological reasons for cuts.
That . . . motives are clothed in progressive words concerning integration and normalisation possibly makes critical inspection more difficult,
but no less necessary.

However, it was not until the 1980s that these practices of economic rationalism
become fully evident to people within the disability field.

The 1980s: From Normalization to Social Role Valorization

In the early 1980s, discourses such as normalization, that had reacted to the 1970s
economic constraints with a subtle but integral economism were now being redefined by an explicit economism. Consequently, Wolfensberger's intervention
technologies became explicitly concerned with the price one was willing to pay
for social acceptance.

[I]t will . . . come down . . . to the question of whether or not a person
wants to be accepted, whether or not a service worker wants a
person . . . to gain acceptance, and what *price* one is willing to pay in the
pursuit of that goal. (Wolfensberger, 1980a, emphasis added)

The price is an insistence of separation from other 'deviants' and striving to reduce
deviancy and enhance normality (Wolfensberger, 1972, 1980a,b, 1983, 1984).

In the general literature, however, the most explicit economic expression
came in 1983 when normalization was renamed as social role valorization.
Wolfensberger (1983, p. 236) provides the dictionary definition of valorization as
'attempting to give a market value to a commodity'. He refutes this meaning
because 'it implies the attachment of a value to objects instead of people' (p. 236).
Yet in the same article, Wolfensberger (p. 238) states: 'One of the first steps in
getting people to be less devaluing is to get them to approach the negatively
charged . . . stimulus *object*, i.e., a person with devalued characteristics' (emphasis
added).

Wolfensberger (1983, p. 237) also claims that the dictionary definition of
valorization is 'an unrelated technical concept . . . inapplicable to the context to
which it is being applied'. Yet the technical approach of normalization, its emphasis on behaviourist means-end/stimulus-response and systems theory process-
outcome technologies, has been one of its major justifications (See Beckey, 1982;
McCord, 1982; Wolfensberger, 1980a, b). McCord (1982) outlines the 'what' and
'how' of normalization's technology as the development of an individual's skills
and enhancement of an individual's image, respectively. This technology which
Wolfensberger refers to as both 'objectification' (1973, p. 26) and 'sequential
incremental normalisation' (1980b, p. 107) is also the commodification of an
individual's skills and image, subject to contracts and payment:

Business is now coming with educational programmes and will say to a
school system 'We will work with these children and guarantee results on
a contract basis, and if the children don't learn, you pay us nothing.'
(Wolfensberger, 1973, p. 26)

The dictionary definition of giving a market value to a commodity is applicable to normalization. The market value given to the commodity (skills and images of normality) can be in monetary terms as in the above example. However, the market value given to the commodity is often in societal terms such as a 'valued social role' and its associated rights, privileges and wealth. (See Wolfensberger, 1983.)

The ideology directing the economism in normalization is possessive individualism (MacPherson, 1962; cited by Moore, 1987). In normalization's case, the ideology begins with the skills and images highly valued by society (market demand). Those who do not meet the criteria are considered deviant. They require intervention to negate their deviancy and develop their normalcy. The skills and image produced through intervention are given a market value which is then exchanged for a social role. The attainment of a specific social role then leads naturally to a status, rights and friendships. Skills become a market commodity (market supply) and the image of normality, the market packaging, to enable a market exchange (See Wolfensberger, 1983, 1984). Human rights are deferred until after the acquisition of specific skills and images valued by society (cf. Briton, 1979).

The basis to provision is now to ensure that the individual acquires the skills and images that are in demand by society. Intervention is now espoused because it is the means to ensuring that disabled people are of worth, and will contribute, to society. The Advisory Council for Special Education in Queensland (Wanstall, 1983, p. 12) states:

[C]umulative effects threading through to adult life and the world of work can often be discerned. The tragedy . . . is the failure to achieve one's potential as a human being and the consequent loss to society of the complete contribution of one of its members.

Paradoxically, by the early 1980s, the economism that was assumed to ensure rights began to challenge special education, the disability field and many of their achievements. A state of crisis arose. Sapon-Shevin (1987, p. 305) describes the USA crisis for special education:

The Heritage Foundation's report (1984) states explicitly that special education services are being provided at the expense of other members of society. When discussions on educational policy are linked to economics, the underlying assumption is that the amount expended on education for any given individual is somehow linked to what the person is 'worth' to society (either in terms of projected income or other societal contributions). This has serious implications for those individuals considered to be 'surplus population'.

The Australian Context

Special education was one of the first disability services in Australia to advocate normalization. However, special education, in the 1970s, was provided by both State/Territory Governments and Federally funded, private organizations. Then, in 1979, the former Australian Schools Commission released its National Survey into Special Education (Andrews, Berry, Elkins and Burge, 1979). The Survey addressed issues across the disability field and gave the first official legitimation to normalization.

Consequently, the National Survey gave an official voice to the increasing criticisms of the existing structure, policies and programs of the field. Under the earlier 1974 Act, only government and service providers were involved in negotiating the directions of the field. Furthermore, the capital/resource based funding of the 1974 Act resulted in service providers having a high degree of autonomy with minimal accountability. Services and State/Territory organizations acted independently of each other, often with very specific and exclusionary criteria regarding clientele and with many overlaps and gaps in provision. Substantial numbers of people, especially those with severe disabilities, received either no provision or were placed in custodial health institutions run by the state. Even where organizations did exist for 'categories of handicap', the quality and availability of provision and programs was often questioned. Charges such as vested interests, the misappropriation of funds away from clients' needs/programs towards furthering the interests and capital of organizations, lack of and inadequate provision, and the denial of human rights were levelled at the 'human services' field in general and the monopoly of service providers in particular (Andrews, Berry, Elkins, Burge, 1979).

Both the existing institutional regime and the new normalization regime expanded through the funding arrangements of the 1974 Act. Some services, professionals, parents and people with disabilities, ideologically aligned with normalization, operated within the context of a medical/institutional power regime. The situation was volatile and the disparity between and within the various disability services was great.

Then in the early 1980s, economic rationalists began to challenge both the normalization and medical regimes for control of the disability field. In 1982 the initial rejection of the Doherty Report, by the New South Wales Labor Government, heralded the new era of economic challenge. Rod Cavalier (*Media Monitor*, 1985, p. 8) Minister for Education, argued that:

> [I]f there is going to be reports with massive resource implications that among the authors will be hard headed economists . . . who will be able to go through and say . . . 'Let's look at this in the world of reality, what real prospect is there of this having any real success in . . . parliament?'

The Hawke Labor Party, when elected to Government in 1983, inherited responsibility for an increasingly volatile disability field and so began its restructuring within the first year of Federal Government.

Labor Party Initiatives

The Hawke Government's restructuring of the disability field incorporated two stages. The first stage, from 1983 to 1985, involved a general inquiry and was characterized by concerns for representation and consultation. The second stage, from 1985 to 1988, was concerned with implementing the recommendations of the inquiry.

The first stage saw the establishment of the Disability Advisory Council of Australia and the instigation of a general inquiry (Handicapped Programs Review) into the disability services. The Disability Advisory Council of Australia (DACA) replaced the National Advisory Council for the Handicapped which had only represented the interests of service providers. The Disability Advisory Council, which directly advised the Minister for Social Security on disability issues, was revolutionary. It was the first national advisory body to have amongst its members people with disabilities. These people also represented some of the associated gender, age and State issues of disability (Warn, 1984, p. 2).

The Handicapped Programs Review was instigated in September 1983 and called for submissions. Consultations were conducted during 1984 and the final report was released in 1985. The Review consisted of a Review Steering Committee (Ministerial and Federal public servant representatives), a Review Secretariat (Federal, Department of Social Security staff) and numerous interest groups involved through submissions and consultations. Representation remained a primary issue. The participation of people with disabilities was stressed and special conditions were created to ensure access to the Review process. The representation of interest groups was comprehensive and included specific disability, age, gender, State, Aboriginal and Islander, race/ethnic, remote area and children's groups and issues. Service providers and official State/Territory departments were also included (Handicapped Programs Review, 1985).

The Review was all encompassing. While the terms of reference for the Review stated that it was primarily concerned with services administered by the Federal Department of Social Security, the majority of organizations received Federal funding under the 1974 Act. The Review also addressed State issues and advocated 'a unified service delivery structure where partnership arrangements can be developed' between State and Federal Governments (Handicapped Programs Review, 1985, pp. 104, 121). Furthermore, the Review admits that the scope of its terms of reference enabled it to extend well beyond 'Commonwealth Programs of Relevance' (Handicapped Programs Review, 1985, p. 1). Full details of the Terms of Reference are presented below:

> The review of the Commonwealth Government's programs of special services for disabled people, particularly those administered by the Department of Social Security, is to give particular emphasis on the principle of *the least restrictive alternative* in examining:
>
> a) the effectiveness of current programs, their coverage and the broad directions they should take in order to correct any identified deficiencies in existing arrangements;
>
> b) the needs of disabled people which are or could be appropriately catered for by these programs;
>
> c) the suitability of the existing range of program and service objectives;
>
> d) the adequacy of financial and human resource available to continue existing and desirable additional levels of service provision;
>
> e) the efficacy of the measures currently employed to facilitate consumer participation in the planning and management of services and those measures aimed at improving the accessibility of services;

f) the specific nature and effectiveness of the measures by which organizations in receipt of assistance are accountable for their operations, both to the funding source and to clients.

In the course of the review, specific recommendations or decisions considered appropriate in regard to both legislation and administrative changes will be made and those issues which are identified as requiring resolution in the context of other programs will be referred to the responsible author. (Handicapped Programs Review, 1985, p. 136)

The criteria (terms of reference) by which the deficiencies, effectiveness, suitability, objectives, adequacy, efficacy and accountability of special services were to be assessed by the Handicapped Programs Review was the 'principle of the least restrictive alternative'.

The second stage of restructurings was concerned with implementing the 'New Directions' of the 'least restrictive alternative'. There were three initiatives to this second stage. These were the publication of the Handicapped Programs Review's recommendations (1985), the enactment of the 1986 Disability Services Act, and the publication of a resource kit outlining the Commonwealth's principles and objectives for service provision (Office of Disability, 1988).

The Review's recommendations were concerned with operationalizing the Government's 'least restrictive alternative' strategy. The strategy meant mainstream or generic service provision with special purpose programs existing only as an interim measure during the transition period from the old to new structure (Handicapped Programs Review, 1985, p. 120). Consequently, the majority of recommendations referred to Commonwealth, and often State Ministers and their respective public service departments, assuming responsibility for disability services. However, the Federal Departments of Community Services, Social Security, and the Office of Disability, were to assume the major responsibility. Now under Government control are services providing for functional areas of disability, such as accommodation; specific disability groups, such as people with physical disabilities; and, particular groups, such as people with disabilities who also belong to minority/disadvantaged groups (Handicapped Programs Review, 1985, pp. 123–34).

New legislation was also recommended to ensure the implementation of the Government's new directions. In 1986, the Disability Services Act replaced the 1974 Handicapped Persons Assistance Act. The new Act was based on the principles of individual consumer outcomes, community-based service provision, the progression away from special purpose to general purpose service providers, individual needs, and the provision of a range of service options (Handicapped Programs Review, 1985, p. 121).

Finally, in 1988, the Office of Disability released a resource kit, *Disability, Society and Change*, outlining Government objectives and principles for services wishing to receive Government funding. The Kit outlined objectives such as image enhancement, consumer outcomes, adaptive behaviours and functional levels, consumer participation, individual needs, and issues of accountability, integration and consumer rights as the directions and requirements for services and programs wishing to receive government funding. These events have effected social and economic changes. The social effects will be discussed first.

Social Effects

The actual structure and location of the disability field has changed. Disability services have been moved out of segregated settings and integrated into mainstream Australian settings, especially mainstream Australian Government bureaucracies. The old structure, which relied on autonomous organizations providing for isolated areas of disability, has been rationalized so that specialized services have either been replaced or incorporated into a more integrated, corporate structure of co-ordination and consultation between Government, service providers and client representatives.

However, there are two conflicting forces, or two types of corporatism, operating within these restructurings. On the one hand, attempts to address earlier injustices saw the creation of representative structures and people with disabilities included in management decisions (HPR, 1985; Office of Disability, 1988). The authority of these people has risen and an increased accessibility to life opportunities has been gained. In the main, the injustices of a custodial institutional service have been reformed.

On the other hand, Triado (1984, p. 40) identifies an aspect of corporatism that is evident within the disability field, namely that:

> In return for participation in public policy formation, capital surrenders an untrammelled sovereignty of the market in the interests of 'capital in general' and unions, having become an 'estate of the realm', not only gain a share in decision-making but must control their constituencies and deliver compliance to a nationally adjudicated consensus.

Corporatism is also concerned with the realignment of regimes of power. Service providers, who once enjoyed minimal regulation under the 1974 Act, have, under the 1986 Act, surrendered their 'untrammelled sovereignty' in exchange for Government funding.

Control over the field's direction has moved to the Government with its 'review and accountability mechanisms to monitor and evaluate' the efficiency and effectiveness of services (Handicapped Programs Review, 1985, pp. 121–3). Services must now have consumer involvement and participation, coordinate with other services, direct efforts towards integration, and adhere to Government criteria to receive public funding. They must also provide a rationale, behavioural objectives and evaluation directed towards consumer outcomes. The increased control has also led to closer scrutiny of people with disabilities. Clients are repositioned within a behaviourist, technocratic discourse which assesses their functional levels, efficiency and effectiveness against abstract norms. (See Handicapped Programs Review, 1985; Office of Disability, 1988.)

The Hawke Government's restructurings, like normalization internationally, took a systems theory approach which equates with vulgar pragmatism. It privileged efficiency over thought and action over theory in the pursuit of improvements (Cherryholmes, 1988, pp. 230–1).

This pragmatic approach has seen consultation and research reshaped within a bureaucratic mechanistic framework. Consultation still forms part of the Government's strategy. However, it has been significantly modified in three ways. First, consultation has become a matter of Government bureaucratic, 'inter-departmental and inter-governmental liaison and consultation', mechanisms (Handicapped Programs Review, 1985, p. 123). Second, consultation with disabled people has become a matter of 'consumer participation' and 'consumer involvement' in the review structures of 'Commonwealth funded bodies' (private organizations) and Commonwealth/State programs at the 'State, regional and local levels' (Handicapped Programs Review, 1985, pp. 121, 132). Comment is limited to review of existing programs and to those people incorporated within the corporate structures of co-ordination and consultation. Third, consultation with consumer and self help groups is limited to action oriented advice on issues predetermined by the Government (Handicapped Programs Review, 1985, p. 123). Issues are bypassed for a focus on how to operationalize Government decisions.

The Government's approach of prioritizing the participation of people with disabilities was more than a corporate process of ensuring fair representation. It was a political alignment with the new regime of normalization. Normalization presents as a universal theory and solution for the disability field. The remaining issue is how to efficiently and effectively implement its directions. The theoretical traditions, standards and criteria are predefined and beyond question. The concern is to ensure that the *status quo* of the new corporate structure is implemented.

Prior to the Review, advocate groups were demanding improved services from the State. The Disability Advisory Council and the consultation of the Handicapped Programs Review provided a significant forum for these demands. However, they also provided a legitimation for Government directives and the means by which this social movement could be contained to the New Directions (HPR, 1985) through efforts to achieve consensus.

The emerging power is Government/bureaucratic control and intervention. The initial promises of greater representation and democratic governance have waned in the latter stages of reconstruction. However, the reconstruction of the disability field also includes an economic reorganization.

Economic Effects

An economic discourse is now directing the field. The Handicapped Programs Review (1985) frequently raised issues of efficiency, effectiveness and accountability. Services are no longer regarded as a civic or human right but as a commodity for consumers. People become consumers, services focus on consumer outcomes and human rights are narrowly redefined as consumer rights (HPR, 1985; Office of Disability, 1988).

The rationale for service provision has changed from human rights to economic grounds. The provision of services has become a matter of 'user pays' provision. The Office of Disability states:

> To be integrated means that the general community should be given
> assistance to provide specialist support themselves . . . . Some disability
> agencies could provide the specific workers/staff to support a few indi-
> viduals in their own rented house — or they could assist people to get a

loan to buy a house — and then provide the workers. Local industry could employ a person with a disability with some 'expert' advice and help (1988, p. 29).

Fully funded Government provision is being replaced by partial funding and moving towards 'user pays' provision, where service is conditional on purchasing power. There is another economic consideration. The United Nations Department of Economic and Social Affairs (1977; cited by ASTEC, 1984, p. 62) outlines this second condition:

> [D]isability will create a cost to society regardless of whether or not rehabilitation services exist . . . [T]he more a society recognises these costs, and the more it attempts to ameliorate them through . . . adequate disability prevention and rehabilitation services, the greater is the overall economic return.

Cost analysis must prove services cost effective. The justification for provision is that it is cheaper and more profitable than no provision.

The economic rationale for service provision has effected a rationalization and privatization of services. Rationalization means that where mainstream services exists such as State education systems, community housing or families, then special services have had to relinquish that domain (DACA, 1983; Disability Services Act, 1986; HPR, 1985; Office of Disability, 1988). Privatization has meant that families, especially the caregiver, now bear the costs being offset by Government. They provide otherwise expensive care without payment and also pay for that care through loss of employment (Holt, 1987). It is a Government cost reduction being paid for mostly by women.

It is also a cost reduction being paid for by people with disabilities who have extra costs associated with their disabilities and need for specialized technologies (ASTEC, 1984). The official report into technology for disabled people, places people into market relationships. Supply is dependent upon demand, that is, disabled people being part of a sizeable market, the product (disability technologies) being profitable and the disabled consumer being able to pay (ASTEC, 1984, p. 67). There are serious problems with this economic rationalism which privileges market profitability, while emphasizing individual purchasing power.

People with disabilities are a small group which incorporates a diverse range of disabilities. Their technological needs are also diverse and often unique. Consequently, disabled people hold no collective power as consumers. The effect of rationalizing services, by placing disabled people in economic relations of supply and demand, is poverty. However, this poverty is hidden by the isolation (integration) of people with disabilities from each other and, through this, the loss of any collective social/political power.

The disability field has been repositioned in the mainstream. However, mainstreaming (integration) does not necessarily give people with disabilities access to life opportunities. Mainstreaming also repositions people within dominant discourses of economism and normality where their civic rights are narrowly redefined and marginalized. While special education has been a part of these restructurings, it exists in a paradoxical relationship to the Federal Government's initiatives.

Special Education: Federal-State Relations

Special educators had long argued for the least restrictive alternative, integration, service coordination and cost efficiency (Andrews, Berry, Elkins, Burge, 1979). The directions were evident in the Australian Schools Commission (Karmel, 1973) reports, during the periods of the Whitlam Labor Government and Fraser Liberal Government (Commonwealth Schools Commission, 1981). Following the National Survey into Special Education (Andrews, *et al.*, 1979) and the 1981 International Year of the Disabled, a number of Australian States initiated legislative, policy and structural reforms (Beazley, 1984; Collins, 1984; Doherty, 1982; Wanstall, 1983). The directive of the Hawke Government through the 1985 Commonwealth Schools Commission Report and the Handicapped Programs Review (1985) followed the restructurings of special education.

Special education was recognized by the Federal Government as already operating within a corporatist framework, and so its authority rose during the initial restructurings. It was included in the Handicapped Programs Review (1985), and early guidelines cited special educators as legitimate consultants to services wishing to restructure (Department of Social Security, 1983, pp. 3, 5).

However, debate exists over whether special education and educational rights of disabled children are ensured entitlements within the 1986 Disability Services Act. (See Bain, 1991.) The situation arises from the Australian Constitution which was framed to protect States' rights (Crowley, 1974). The Federal Government was able to restructure the disability services because they operated privately. However, the Federal Government is constitutionally limited in its control of education which remains primarily the domain of the States. (See Bain, 1991.)

Some Federal influence was effected through the former Australian Schools Commission. The limited nature of this control was criticized by Ashby and Taylor (1984) and the Commonwealth School Commission (1985) which called for negotiation and shared objectives between the Commonwealth and States. Conversely, Federal control over Tasmanian education policy and legislation, which excluded some children with disabilities from educational provision, was achieved through a Commonwealth/State, general review of 'disability'. Tasmania then moved towards integration, away from its exclusionary practices (Fulcher, 1986).

The actual nature of reforms has varied according to the socio-economic contexts of each of the States. Some State systems have remained within strong professional (New South Wales and Tasmania), bureaucratic (Western Australia and Tasmania), or even medical (New South Wales) discourses (Doherty, 1982; Beazley, 1984; Fulcher, 1986). However, the common directions have been integration, individualized instruction, parental participation and service coordination. Even Victoria, which attempted to overcome the dominant regimes operating within special education, used a corporatist restructuring of devolution and integration (Collins, 1984; Fulcher, 1986).

Special education is now operating within a decentralized/devolved model of integration. Concerns are increasingly being raised regarding the market relationships of this model and the implications it has for a group of students who are considered surplus, who as a minority within a school community have a limited voice and power (Bain, 1991). Traditionally, special education defined this problem in terms of external trends. It has only been within recent years that the economism challenging the disability field, and especially special education, has been recognized as integral to its own discursive policies and practices. Harris (1986, p. 7) claims that there was an extraordinary acceptance of dramatic cuts to special education by the Federal Government and continues to explain this acceptance as the result of an economic view of education:

> [E]ducational thinking and development in recent years has been completely dominated by an economic view of education, to the point where a Government can cut special education funds . . . and receive less than ten letters of complaint . . . [B]ecause we have grown accustomed to thinking, writing about, and discussing education in terms of economy, efficiency, effectiveness, equity and priority, we are now, generally, accepting of cuts.

Ferguson (1989, p. 2) made the same point:

> It is an interesting phenomenon of our times that the compelling ideology which pervades the western democracies is not socialism, nor is it liberalism but rather economism which is driven by the product/output model evaluated in terms of profit generated. Clear evidence of the degree to which this ideology now permeates educational planning and administration is found in the current vocabulary of educators. We now talk about services to clients. We arrange our services in programs which are subject to annual performance auditing. We set quality control measures and look for performance outcomes.

Special education in many States has been subsumed (integrated) into regular education and in some cases has been left with little representation at administrative levels. Meanwhile, support services for students in regular schools is inadequate and some children requiring assistance are no longer recognized or acknowledged as special needs students.

Conclusion

During the 1980s the disability field on an international and national level has become increasingly alarmed by the challenge from the discourse of economic rationalism. What remains unrecognized is that the discourses of economic rationalism and corporatism are integral, not external, to the discourses of the disability field. These discourses require urgent addressing if the disability field is to challenge, rather than support, its own rationalization and maybe demise.

However, the Disability Services Legislation was recommended with a ten-year sunset clause (Statutory limits) (Handicapped Programs Review, 1985). A great potential and great danger exists in the possible readdressing of the disability field in 1996. The potential is to address the inequities, such as lack of support services, extra costs to caregivers and extra costs of disability which have arisen. However, within the current economic climate, the danger exists for a further rationalization of the disability field and challenges to the achievements of the Hawke/Keating Government. It is, therefore, crucial to acknowledge and support these achievements.

The restructurings of the disability field by both the Hawke Government and normalization in general have made substantial gains in providing equality of access to societal services and facilities and everyday opportunities and lifestyles. Many of the injustices and inhumanities of the previous medical/institutional regime have been addressed.

The Hawke Government's restructuring of the disability field through the Disability Services Act provides some assurance of the continuation of service provision at a time of economic rationalization. The situation for special education, however, is far more ambiguous. The establishment of representative bodies, such as the Disability Advisory Council of Australia, and the representation of people with disabilities on the governing boards of private organizations, are major achievements in terms of human rights and liberal democracy. However, these representative structures and consultation processes need to remain open to critical analysis, reflection and the addressing of issues rather than simply pragmatic concerns of operationalisation.

References

ANDREWS, R., BERRY, P., ELKINS, J., BURGE, J.A. (1979) *A Survey of Special Education in Australia. Provisions, Needs and Priorities in the Education of Children with Handicaps and Learning Difficulties*, St. Lucia, Australia: Schonell Educational Research Centre. Department of Education, University of Queensland.

ASHBY, G. and TAYLOR, J. (1984) *Responses to Policies: Review of Commonwealth Schools Commission Special Education Program*, Canberra, Australia: Report to the Commonwealth Schools Commission.

AUSTRALIAN SCIENCE AND TECHNOLOGY COUNCIL (ASTEC) (1984) *Technology and Handicapped People*, prepared by Technological Change Committee, Canberra, Australia: Australian Government Publishing Service.

BAIN, A. (1992) *Issues in the Integration of Regular and Special Education: An Australian Perspective*, Australian Journal of Education 36, 1, pp. 84–99.

BEAZLEY, K.E. (1984) *Education in Western Australia*, Perth, Australia: Report of the Committee of Inquiry into Education in Western Australia.

BECKEY, D. (1982) 'Normalisation's theoretical status and future residential models', *Australia and New Zealand Journal of Developmental Disabilities*, 8, 2, pp. 97–104.

BRITON, J. (1979) 'Normalisation: What of and what for?', Parts 1 and 11, *Australian Journal of Mental Retardation*, 5, 6, pp. 224–9.

CHERRYHOMES, C. (1988) 'Education and critical pragmatism', in CHERRYHOLMES, C. *Power and Criticism*, unpublished ms.

COLLINS (1984) *Integration in Victorian Education*. Report of the Ministerial Review of Educational Services for the Disabled, Melbourne, Australia: Government Printer.

COMMONWEALTH SCHOOLS COMMISSION (1981) *Report for the Triennium 1982–1984*, Canberra, Australia: Commonwealth Schools Commission.

COMMONWEALTH SCHOOLS COMMISSION (1985) *Report of the Working Party on Commonwealth Policy and Directions in Special Education*, Canberra, Australia: Commonwealth Schools Commission.

CROWLEY, F. (1974) *A New History of Australia*, Melbourne, Australia: William Heinemann.

DEPARTMENT OF SOCIAL SECURITY (1983) *Handicapped Persons Assistance Act, Guidelines for the Guidance of Applicants*, Canberra, Australia: Handicapped Persons Welfare Program.

DISABILITY ADVISORY COUNCIL OF AUSTRALIA (DACA) (1983) 'Wide-ranging look at programs for disabled people,' *Breakthrough: The National Bulletin for Disabled People*, Canberra, Australia: AGPS, 26,1.

Disability Services Act (1986) Commonwealth of Australia, No. 129 of 1986. Division of Special Education.

DOHERTY, P.J. (1982) *Strategies and Initiatives for Special Education In New South Wales.* Report of the working party on a plan for special education in New South Wales.

FERGUSON, R. (1989) *Towards New Rationales For School-Based Special Education Services*, Paper presented to Principals Conference, Queensland Education Department, November.

FULCHER, G. (1986) 'Australian policies on special education: Towards a sociological account', *Disability, Handicap and Society*, **1**, 1, pp. 19–51.

Handicapped Persons Assistance Act 1974, Commonwealth of Australia, Canberra, Australia: Government Printer, No. 134 of 1974.

HANDICAPPED PROGRAMS REVIEW (HPR) (1985) *New Directions*, Canberra, Australia: AGPS.

HARRIS, R. (1986) 'Recognition of special education needs: Co-operation at the political level', *The Australian Journal of Special Education*, **10**, 1, pp. 6–11.

HOLT, C. (1987) *Costs of Disability*, Paper presented to a parent's seminar of the Spina Bifida Association, Queensland, Australia, March.

JUDGE, C. (1987) *Civilization and Mental Retardation*, Mulgrave, Australia: Magenta Press.

KARMEL REPORT (1973) *Schools in Australia: Report of the Interim Committee for the Australian Schools Commission*, Canberra, Australia: AGPS.

McCORD, W. (1982) 'From theory to reality: Obstacles to the implementation of the normalisation principle in human Services', *Mental Retardation*, **20**, 6, pp. 247–53.

MACPHERSON, C.B. (1962) *The Political Theory of Possessive Individualism*, New York, NY: Oxford University Press.

MEDIA MONITOR (1985) 'Rod Cavalier, NSW Minister for Education, Interviewed on Special Education Program for the Handicapped', Radio 2BL Broadcast conducted by Jane Singleton, 29/3/85.

MOORE, R. (1987) 'Education and the ideology of production', *British Journal of Sociology of Education*, **8**, 2, pp. 227–42.

NIRJE, B. (1969) 'The normalisation principle and its human management implications', in KUGEL, R. and WOLFENSBERGER, W. (Eds), *Changing Patterns in Residential Services for the Mentally Retarded*, Washington, DC: President's Committee on Mental Retardation.

NIRJE, B. (1985) 'The basis and logic of the normalisation principle', *Australia and New Zealand Journal of Developmental Disabilities*, **11**, 2.

OFFICE OF DISABILITY (1988) *Disability, Society and Change: A Resource Kit Explaining the Commonwealth Government Statement of Principles and Objectives*, Sydney, Australia: Beaver Press.

PERRIN, B. and NIRJE, B. (1985) 'Setting the record straight: A critique of some frequent misconceptions of the normalisation principle', *Australia and New Zealand Journal of Developmental Disabilities*, **11**, 2.

RABINOW, P. (Ed.) (1986) *The Foucault Reader*, Harmondsworth, UK: Penguin.

SAPON-SHEVIN, M. (1987) 'The National Education Reports and special education: Implications for students', *Exceptional Children*, **53**, 4, pp. 300–6.

SODER, M. (1984) 'The mentally retarded: Ideologies of care and surplus population', in BARTON, L. and TOMLINSON, L. (Eds) *Special Education and Social Interests*, Beckenham, UK: Croom Helm.

TRIADO, J. (1984) 'Corporatism, democracy and modernity', *Thesis Eleven*, **9**, pp. 33–51.

WANSTALL, C.G. (1983) *Some Issues in Special Education*, Advisory Council for Special Education. A third report to the Minister for Education, Brisbane, Australia.

WARN, P. (1984) 'Opening address — Representing the minister for social security, the

Honourable Don Grimes', in *Proceedings from the WHAT Forum, Where and How of Accommodation for Today*, ACROD (Queensland Division), Convened at Yeronga College of TAFE, Brisbane, Australia, 23rd March.

WOLFENSBERGER, W. (1972) *The Principle of Normalisation in Human Services*, Toronto, Canada: National Institute on Mental Retardation.

WOLFENSBERGER, W. (1973) *A Look into the Future for Systems of Human Services*, Ontario, Canada: National Institute on Mental Retardation.

WOLFENSBERGER, W. (1980a) 'A brief overview of the principle of normalization', in FLYNN, R. and NITSCH, K. (Eds) *Normalization, Social Integration, and Community Services*, TX: Pro-ed, pp. 7–30.

WOLFENSBERGER, W. (1980b) 'The definition of normalization: Update, problems, disagreements, and misunderstandings', in FLYNN, R. and NITSCH, K. (Eds) *Normalization, Social Integration, and Community Services*, TX: Pro-ed, pp. 71–115.

WOLFENSBERGER, W. (1983) 'Social role valorisation: A proposed new term for the principle of normalisation', *Mental Retardation*, **21**, 6, pp. 234–39.

WOLFENSBERGER, W. (1984) 'A reconceptualization of normalisation as social role valorisation', *Mental Retardation*, **34**, 2, pp. 22–6.

Part IV: *Restructuring Policy and Administration: Four Case Studies*

Chapter 12

The Development of Representative Committees in Victorian Schools: New Structures in the Democratization of Educational Administration?[1]

Peter Watkins and Jill Blackmore

Introduction

In Victorian state schools, a recent organizational phenomenon since the early 1970s has been the development of representative committee systems in schools. Whilst these have been generally unique to Victoria, what is more significant is that these representative committees, more specifically the Local Administrative Committee (LAC) and the Curriculum Committee, have been formalized and legitimated through industrial agreements negotiated between the teacher unions and the government. Given the Labor government's rhetoric of participatory decision-making which has accompanied educational restructuring in Victoria during the 1980s, the central question of the research project which gave rise to the data presented was what part do representative committees play in furthering democratic and participative decision-making in the administration of education? In this chapter, we focus upon particular issues which have emerged from the current trend in Australian education towards the devolution of management to schools as the key units of decision-making. Whilst corporate management has become the dominant mode of educational management, this process of devolution has also been clothed in a rhetoric of participatory and democratic decision-making. Therefore, the chapter initially examines the historical background to the formation of these new structures while also addressing the theoretical issues, particularly that of corporate management. This section also places the Victorian initiatives within the wider Australian context. Second, the chapter presents the data from our case study of a post-primary school. Last, we offer some tentative conclusions and directions for future research.

Historical and Current Context

The Victorian Context

The past two decades have been a period of radical administrative reform in Victorian education. Historically, the Victorian state education system has, as with the other Australian states, been highly centralized. The Department of Education (then Public Instruction as established in 1872) placed the Director-General of Education, the permanent administrative head, directly responsible to the Minister of Education. Until the 1970s all decisions, professional and managerial, were made by senior officers in the department, and schools and teachers were evaluated on a regular basis by a Board of Inspectors. By the early 1970s the increasing complexity of administering over 2000 schools by a highly centralized bureaucracy meant the system was unable to respond effectively to local school-based needs. Demands for reform led to the then Liberal (conservative) government's decision, with the full support of the Director-General of Education, to decentralize administration to regions and schools in 1975. Regional Offices were established and teacher and student representation on what had previously been the largely advisory parent School Councils was initiated by 1976. At the same time, a more qualified, younger teaching force was making increasingly militant demands through their unions for greater involvement in school-based administrative and curriculum decision-making, improved working conditions and the salaries warranted by their profession. A major feature of this activity was the outright rejection by teachers of the top-down control of the Education Department perpetrated primarily through the inspectorial system, but also through prescriptive curricula and examinations. Although the more radical secondary union policy of elected school executives to replace principals was never fully accepted and only implemented in a few schools, many schools had developed some type of committee structure by the late 1970s. Most schools had formed a curriculum committee and some even an administrative committee elected from the school staff to liaise with the principal and School Council. School-based committees became increasingly important as curriculum and assessment became more school-based with the demise of all but the Higher School Certificate, and as the allocation of administrative responsibilities and eligibility for teacher promotion came to be determined by school-based committees.

By 1979, the Liberal Party Education Ministers, Alan Hunt and Norman Lacey, undertook a more radical administrative restructuring and devolution of responsibility. The process was outlined first in the Green Paper and then the White Paper on the *Strategies and Structures of Education in Victorian Government Schools* (1980). As economic management became a government priority after 1979 and because education constituted over a third of the state's annual expenditure, the Ministers of Education sought to assume greater direct control over all aspects of education from administration through to policy. The underlying agenda was first, to gain greater control over the teacher unions and second, to shift the control of policy from the Director-General to the Ministers. Furthermore, the review of Strategies and Structures carried out in 1980 suggested that Regional Boards and School Councils should take on greater responsibility in developing educational policy and curriculum, with the principal as the liaison between the schools, regions and the centre. The *PA Report* (PA Australia, 1981) written by an external consultant in 1981 also proposed increased devolution of responsibility to the local level (principal and parents) although its major thrust was accountability and efficiency. The outcome of this second phase of devolution until 1981 was therefore more towards administrative decentralization despite the rhetoric of participation.

But the massive structural changes initiated by the *PA Report* were halted midway with the election of the Labor Government in 1982, an electoral victory largely due to the support of teacher unions. The outcome of yet another Ministerial Review by the Labor government, the *Ministerial Papers 1–6* (Minister of Education, Victoria, 1983–5), took the notion of administrative devolution and participation to its logical conclusion. Central to the administration of education as outlined in these documents was a system of local and regional committees. This form of local, democratic governance professed to encourage local participation of the school community (encompassing parents, students and teachers), to develop collaborative decision-making processes, to create a responsive bureaucracy capable of serving school needs, and to promote equity for the disadvantaged. Schools were now to become the unit of decision-making, and Regions were to supply the resource infrastructure. The school principal was to play a central role, not only as the administrative link to the centre, but as the facilitator of a consultancy process between the school community as represented by the School Council, the teachers and their unions, the students as clients, and the central bureaucracy. School principals were also to be appointed by local committees appointed by School Councils, a practice already begun in technical schools. The State Board of Education was established as an advisory body to the Minister and a program of school self-evaluation through the School Improvement Program was instituted to replace the top-down model of evaluation of schools.

At that time, there was an apparent convergence between the Labor Party's position on educational (and industrial) democracy, teacher unions' moves for greater professional autonomy and control over the workplace at the school level, and the increased demands by parent organizations for participation in their children's schooling. Manifestations of this trend were the development of teacher support centres and the School Improvement Program. Furthermore, the push towards more collaborative school-based decision-making was supported by research in organizational and administrative theory, which suggested that the implementation of educational change was most successful when decisions were made by those most affected. At the same time, school-based decision-making, premised upon participation of teachers, parents and students, was the preferred direction taken in various Commonwealth programs initiated by the Schools Commission since 1972. Such programs as the Disadvantaged Schools Program, Transition Education Advisory Committee (TEAC) and the Participation and Equity Program (PEP) further engendered a strong sense of community involvement in public education.

Since 1983, the Labor government in Victoria and teacher unions have also negotiated unprecedented Industrial Agreements which determine that a local administrative committee and curriculum committee be set up in each school. These committees were to be consulted by the principal on all matters of policy and administration, and are generally linked to the School Council through Education Subcommittees, although the actual configuration is left to each school's discretion. In effect, the Industrial Agreement (now based on a single Log of

Claims rather than being fought out as single issues) was as much the legitimation of the *ad hoc* committee systems which had evolved in many schools, particularly the secondary high and technical schools, since the mid 1970s. The period from 1983–6 therefore witnessed a unique phase in the preferred style of school management, one couched in terms of collaborative and community-based decision-making and participation. It also encouraged the expectation amongst parents and teachers to be involved in policy and curriculum decisions.

The period was also one in which there was a rapid decline in school enrolments, leading to school reorganization amongst clusters of schools which took the form of multi-campus schools, amalgamations or even closure of many schools. At the same time that the system was undergoing recurrent restructures at the centre and locally, post-compulsory education was under review due to the low retention rate to Year 12 and the high rate of youth unemployment since the mid-1970s. The *Blackburn Report* (Ministerial Review of Post-Compulsory Schooling, 1985) had connected curriculum reform to the need for the reorganization of the provision of post-compulsory schooling (Years 11 and 12), contending that the content, assessment and organization of the curriculum and the structures of post-compulsory schooling had historically discouraged retention amongst particular social groups. In order to provide a general, more comprehensive education to all students in Years 7–12, and more specifically, to cater for the needs of all students and not merely the limited number continuing to higher education, school reorganisation was critical. A review of Years 11 and 12 curriculum, initially begun by the Victorian Institute of Secondary Education (VISE), was taken over by the new Victorian Curriculum and Assessment Board (VCAB), established in 1987.

Again, the process of review of post-compulsory curriculum and school organization has been largely a consultative one. Field of Study Committees in newly defined curriculum areas were established comprising representatives of universities, private schools, teacher unions, parent organizations and business interests. Teacher unions, parent organizations and parents have therefore increasingly expected to be represented on local school-based committees, regional boards and central negotiating bodies on school reorganization, curriculum and Industrial Agreement Implementation committees. In that sense, the model of policy-making has been a neo-corporatist one, where the state and 'peak' councils of educational interest groups have negotiated a consensus about what constitutes the public educational good (Blackmore, 1991).

With a succession of Labor ministers, and as the economic situation of the state and nation has become more uncertain, a contradictory trend has emerged with the introduction in particular of corporate management. Smith (1989) talks about how, under Labor in Victoria, the 'language and agendas of public administration' have altered with 'changes in approaches to strategy, structures and systems, values and ideas in currency, styles of program and policy analysis, preferences for staff and skills' which are drawn from approaches applied from governments of different political persuasions, for example, Thatcher and the 'New Right' (Smith, 1989, p. 78). It is now seen to be in the 'national interest' to restructure education and make it more productive in the economic sense. This has been linked with the view that education will be more efficient if it serves market forces, and that this requires schools to be able to respond more immediately to local 'client' demands. In 1986, a Ministry Structures Projects Team was established to again consider the administrative structures of the Ministry and the resulting Blue Paper, *Taking Schools into the 1990s* (Ministry Structure Project Team, 1986), was circulated to all schools for comment. Whilst the claimed purpose was 'making devolution into a reality', the essential proposal was to create self-governing schools in which School Councils had full responsibility for both curriculum and allocation of resources (including staffing). The argument was based upon the idea that devolution had been in name alone, and unless there was a devolution of allocation of all resources (including staffing) at school level where decisions on policy and curriculum were being made, real change would not occur. In *Taking Schools into the 1990s*, a single grant would allow schools to determine resource allocation and staffing according to local needs within broad state guidelines on curriculum, personnel, finance and facilities. Regions would still act as support centres to schools. But union and parent organization opposition led to the demise of the Blue Paper. Teacher unions foresaw that it undercut the centralized negotiating system and weakened the traditional union power base by making the school the unit of union activity, thus potentially dissipating union strength. Parent organizations opposed it on the grounds they were volunteers expected to take on significant administrative tasks for the Ministry without pay or expertise. The notion of the 'self-managing school', responding directly to client needs and market forces without the direct mediation of the state bureaucracy, was seen by many to be the thin edge of the wedge towards 'privatization'.

But the desire for a 'lean and mean' administration has continued unabated. Three consequent restructurings have occurred at the centre. The amalgamation, closure or clustering of schools, particularly in the inner suburbs of Melbourne, has facilitated the reduction of Regions from twelve to eight in 1987, thereby reducing support infrastructures. School-based decision-making has been significantly undermined as more recent reforms have implemented many of the *Taking Schools into the 1990s* proposals which had previously been rejected. These reforms include the introduction of corporate management structures and processes. As at the Federal level, corporate management has been introduced with the desire to reduce staff and increase productivity in an economistic drive. New management and accounting practices (program budgeting) have been introduced to make the system appear more accountable for expenditure. In so doing, by making schools the unit of decision-making in a period in which there is reduced resource allocation, the centre 'defuses' criticism about its failure to resource schools adequately by arguing that schools made the decisions about the distribution of resources according to needs. In this way, schools are forced to prioritize amongst competing equity claims. The prioritizing of managerialist over educational imperatives is further symbolized by recent career structure proposals in which the line management role of principals is emphasized and pedagogy and 'good teacher practices' are being redefined in a technical manner through the creation of Advanced Skills Teacher (AST) career paths.

A second thrust for the recent phase of restructuring has been the closer linking of curriculum and school reorganization. The development of the Victorian Certificate of Education (VCE) by VCAB has given the impetus for a further stage of school amalgamations, clusters or multi-campuses to be established under the notion of the District Provision of Comprehensive Curriculum. It is argued that schools must review their curriculum in order to meet the criteria of providing a comprehensive curriculum as laid down by the Victorian Certificate of Education thus offering opportunity for both access to and success in post-compulsory education to all students in that district. If not, school reorganizations within self-determined Districts must occur in order that such a curriculum offering is provided for their clientele. As in previous reorganization statements, any reorganization is seen to be done voluntarily after a process of consultation between School Councils. The determination of what constitutes a district, it is argued, depends upon the specific relationship between groups of schools and how they can collectively provide the required breadth of curriculum. Ironically, therefore, whilst the structures of school-based decision-making (School Councils, LACs and Curriculum Committees) are still relatively intact, and the rhetoric of devolution focusing upon consultation, participation and community involvement is a feature of such documents as *Comprehensive Curriculum Provision within a District: School Reorganisation* (Ministry of Education, Victoria, October 1989), in practice there is a different situation.

The combined effect of comprehensive curriculum reform and the corporate management structures, which have become the dominant mode of administration within the Ministry, has been to claw back control to the centre and more specifically to the Minister, through more subtle mechanisms of control. A tension therefore exists in which schools, asked to determine their own educational future within board policy guidelines through local community and school-based decision-making, are also expected to produce decisions which meet the requirements of the Ministry in terms of efficiency and effectiveness, as well as broad educational objectives (social justice, curriculum guidelines, and accountability for financial management). This is the unique situation in which Victorian educational reform must be framed. It raises questions regarding the nature and extent of the democratization of decision-making and about what particular modes of democratic process have been legitimated and why. Previous research on Regional Boards and the moves in education towards participative decision-making indicate how notions of representative and participatory democracy have been confused in policy documents and decision-making structures in ways which make committee systems and democratic processes problematic (Watkins, 1988; Blackmore, 1987). Within the scope of this project are questions regarding how democratic the school-based decision-making structures and processes which have evolved since the mid 1970s are, how they are being reconciled to recent administrative developments, especially within the corporate management context, and whose interests are being best served.

Corporate Management: The New Cult of Efficiency

In the 1970s and 1980s there arose a new efficiency movement or new cult of efficiency (Beare, 1982). This movement has been associated with the increasing economic crisis that most capitalist countries find themselves in. To counter the effects of the crisis, the state and the educational system under its control have increasingly turned to corporate models of management as a means of solving the problem. As Apple puts it:

> The current solution is to couple the tightening of control and accountability, reductions in spending, and closer ties between schools and industry on the one hand with the rhetoric of local control, parental choice and a 'free market' individualism on the other. (Apple, 1981, p. 383)

More recently Beare (1987) has pointed to the increasing perception of education as being within an economic, corporatist paradigm. In such a context the administration of education is a means through which national, economic priorities might be achieved. Indeed he asserts that 'it seems certain that education will become even more firmly an instrument of national, economic policy' (Beare, 1987, p. 7). Educational administration in these terms takes on the mantle of a business enterprise where 'education will be redefined as a financial corporation' (Beare, 1987, p. 8). Beare suggests that a firm indication of the rise of corporate management in the administration of education is provided through the recent changes in names. The shift from the old military model to the new corporate one can be illustrated through the change in name of the top administrator from Coordinator-General to Chief Executive Officer. Similarly, the Director-General of Education has become the Chief General-Manager (Office of Schools Administration), while Regional Directors have become General Managers (Regions) coordinating in the Region a Resources and Administration Facilities Manager, a Finance Manager, an Operations Manager and a Personnel Manager. With this trend in mind he surmises that:

> Frankly, if this is the mind-set which is being brought to the reconstruction of public education now going on in every State and Territory in Australia, then it seems likely that educational objectives will become subsidiary to corporatist ones. There might just be some people around who would be happy to replace heads of schools with business executives too. (Beare, 1987, p. 10)

The rhetoric of business management has indeed received substance through the publication of a number of documents by the Victorian Ministry of Education. In particular two publications, *Schools Division* (Ministry of Education, Victoria, 1986), and *The Structure and Organisation of the Schools Division* (Ministry of Education, Victoria, 1987), clearly illustrate the move towards functional management derived from the principles of scientific management. At the top of the organizational pyramid is a corporate management group which consists of 'fourteen people, the Chief General Manager, the five branch general managers, and the eight regional managers' (Ministry of Education, Victoria, 1987, p. 80). The intent was that such a group formulate policy guidelines which would be implemented at school level with support of the Regions. Whilst this initial corporate management group has since been abandoned, largely because of its incapacity to make the policy/administration dichotomy work in practice, the rhetoric and hierarchy remain. Indeed, there has been a debate as to whether the corporate management group has been substituted by other groups which operate in ambiguous and more subtle relationships with the Minister.

Lorange (1980), in a standard text on corporate planning and management, points out that such management structures have a strict division of labour within the organizational hierarchy with each manager in the line performing specific functional tasks. The subordinate receives orders from the superior and is then accountable to the superior person in the line. In this process 'corporate management interacts downwards in the organisational pyramid' (Lorange, 1980, p. 20). This downward line of decision-making with the determination of policies, planning and action originating in the elite corporate management group is necessary,

Lorange argues, to prevent 'potentially serious motivational' effects, for by involving people lower down in the hierarchy in contributing views on objectives, goals and strategies, 'but then having to disregard or modify these contributions in order to satisfy a general management viewpoint . . . there might be a loss of morale' (Lorange, 1980, p. 145).

Such corporate management techniques are clearly espoused in *The Structure and Organisation of the Schools Division* (Ministry of Education, Victoria, 1987). Here there is none of the commitment to democratic grass-roots decision-making alluded to in the earlier Ministerial Papers, but rather a reversion to the hard, strict discipline of real world business management rationalized in the ideology of efficiency and effectiveness. In these new structures, 'The Chief General Manager has the task, subject to the Chief Executive and the Minister, of determining Schools Division priorities and policies and coordinating the implementation of policy across the state' (Ministry of Education, Victoria, 1987, p. 6).

Further it is proclaimed that:

> The new administration has the following characteristics. First, it places the administration of the Schools Division as close as possible to schools, thus making for more efficient and effective use of resources. Second, it provides a clear policy focus for the Schools Division, enabling the identification of objectives and the establishment of strategic plans to achieve them. Third, it engages the general managers of regions, all of whom have operational responsibilities, directly in the making of Schools Division to act as a single body, which has the capacity to identify and analyse the educational needs of the community, to develop policies and priorities, to respond to them, to implement those policies effectively and efficiently, and to evaluate and review the outcomes as a basis for the future. (*ibid*)

The placement of management closer to schools enables the carrying out of priorities and policies to be subject to closer scrutiny. Moreover these priorities and policies are determined at the highest level in the hierarchy, not at the grass-roots level. Instead of being responsive to the needs of school communities, the corporate management group identifies those needs and responds rationally in an efficient and effective manner thus limiting the extent of any debate.

The setting up of a strict managerial hierarchy not only enhances control and coordination but also integration of the system. The activities of the managers in the line are fragmented or broken down into limited areas of responsibility but are integrated and recomposed through a rigid system of accountability. Thus 'principals and head teachers of schools are directly accountable to the general manager for the region who in turn reports to the Chief General Manager' (Ministry of Education, Victoria, 1987, p. 46). Moreover in the document the dual role of the principal, as set out earlier in the *Role of the Principal*, is attacked with the prospect of the earlier statement being revised and the role of the principal being redefined in terms of the new corporate management structures (Ministry of Education, Victoria, 1987, p. 12). Indeed a new statement on the *Role of the Principal* was released in July 1988. As a consequence of the argument in those documents, the principal in managerial rhetoric is merely a lower member in the corporate hierarchy who has specific functional duties to perform and a superior to report back on the accomplishment of those set tasks. So in corporate management terms, the principal has become 'a line manager who is accountable to the general manager of the region' (Ministry of Education, Victoria, 1987, p. 11).

But corporate management techniques have not only made inroads into the administration of education, they have indeed been co-opted from their widespread application in public administration. Two recent studies by Yeatman (1987) and Considine (1988), which have critically examined the current pervasive hold that corporate management has in the public sector, have particular relevance for education.

Yeatman (1987, p. 340) argues that the corporate management techniques adopted by the Canberra Public Service Board incorporate an essential scientific management approach. Such a form of administration is underpinned by a rational, technical approach to public administration. In particular the stress on 'management by objectives' and the implementation of operational goals within narrowly defined resource parameters means that:

> With these emphases on results-orientated management the purposes of public administration and public service tend to be reduced to the effective, efficient and economic management of human and financial resources. This is a technical approach to public administration and public service couched within a broader policy framework dominated by economic considerations. (Yeatman 1987, p. 340)

Yeatman concludes that scientific management, through the current techniques of corporate management, has become the dominant form governing the way the public sector is administered. Scientific management has become dominant because there is a mistaken belief by many politicians and the public at large 'that the precepts of good management hold true in public and private sectors and that therefore, the wisdom and experience of one (usually the private sector) can be transferred to the other' (Yeatman, 1987, p. 351). Considine (1988) reinforces this view by arguing that the proponents of corporate management collapse any distinction that might have been made between the private and public sectors. In this process, 'corporate management . . . elevates economic rationality to primary status in the organisation of the work of the public sector, and in so doing attempts to replace the legal and procedural framework of the classical model' (Considine, 1988, p. 10).

Other features of corporate management, as outlined by Considine as part of the new orthodoxy, are the creation of relatively autonomous units of decision-making (such as administrative units within the Ministry or schools within the system) which are coordinated through policy and budgetary guidelines (corporate planning and program budgets), which in turn are seen to facilitate flexible use of resources to meet client needs. The system is maintained and made accountable to both the centre and the client by the ongoing cycle of information collection, monitoring, evaluation and feedback processes. Another element is the emphasis on human resources as the valued added component. Multiskilling, professional development, and consultative and consensus style decision-making are also factors seen to lead to greater worker productivity. Yeatman makes the point that complex organizations cannot be insulated from the environment or other organizations and societal pressures. Executive modes of decision-making require and presuppose some form of administrative and personal collaboration by their employees and the capacity to be sensitive to the environment, (for example, clients). Therefore, many management theorists see that 'democratic cultures of decision-making are more likely to be functional in such contexts than what they view as old-fashioned top-down directive organisational cultures' (Yeatman, 1990, p. 45). She concludes that 'organisational effectiveness does not appear incongruent but congruent with the principles of democratisation that emphasise information sharing, participation and dialogue' (Yeatman, 1990, p. 46). Thus embedded in the corporate management structure and process is at least notionally, some element of participation. She goes on to argue that such complex systems require reciprocal power relations dependent upon two-way information exchange. The consequences are that 'procedural norms rather than substantive decisions become the reference points for organisational predictability and stability; and, rather than being highly precise statements of organisational objectives, decisions or laws take on enabling features which allow operating goals to be reinterpreted in relation to changing contexts,' particularly at the point of contact, for example, schools (Yeatman, 1990, p. 47).

At a broader level, Yeatman suggests that there have been three claims which have given legitimacy to the current administrative reforms towards corporate management: to make administration more efficient, more democratic and more equitable. (See Wilenski, 1986.) Yeatman points out that these three claims are in tension. On the one hand, the demands for a more democratic and equitable administration have grown out of the 'emergence of a plurality of social movements, pressure groups and single issue groups which are no longer containable in the old established party system and its reach into types of representation within the bureaucratic nodes of decision-making' (Yeatman, 1990, p. 4). Certainly in Victoria, many of the participants of these movements and groups such as teacher unionists have entered public administration to redevelop their citizenship and representative claims within the state (Radin and Cooper, 1989). In effect they have 'become architects of the new types of policies which fostered the democratisation of public administration' (Yeatman, 1990, p. 50). Hence the inclusion of equity and social justice objectives in corporate and institutional plans. On the other side is the question regarding the level of legitimate state activity and the size of the public sector set against the hegemony of the private, market-oriented principle of liberal individualism. The arguments regarding parental choice of schools and the notion of schools serving a particular type of local community (students and parents of students only) are bound up in this particular rhetoric.

Finally, Yeatman argues that the lack of perception of difference between public and private sector outcomes in terms of public service as in education has meant that the managerialist approach inflates the technical requirements of bureaucratic performance and rejects the social and substantive requirements for a more equitable and democratic administration on the grounds of budgetary constraints. Considine concurs that this trend towards corporate managerialism in public sector policy in general does present a number of problems. In summary, these problems are that the fervent optimism placed on technical rationality may be misguided; the results from corporative management may be neither democratic nor effective; and lastly the engineering techniques of corporate management do not seem to be generating change. Indeed, change seems to be derived from alternative, loosely structured networks (Considine, 1988, p. 16). Nevertheless such technical rationality still dominates public documents, not only in Victoria, but in the other Australian states, to which we will now briefly turn.

The Australian Context

Whilst Victoria had a relatively unique history in terms of the devolution of decision-making to schools, the other Australian states have tended to retain their centralized administration until more recent years. Since 1984, most state education systems have undergone similar reviews of curriculum and structures as the *Blackburn Report*, and, given the same imperatives, moved towards the introduction of corporate management. Each state report links curriculum to administrative reform as a means to increase national economic productivity and encourage student retention in a period of decline (Davis, Weller and Lewis, 1989). Education is expected to serve the economy in a time of economic rationalism. A major feature of these state reports is the devolution of decision-making to the school. The rhetoric associated with this shift argues that issues of resource allocation and disadvantage are best met by those most affected by the decisions, provided that there are system-level mechanisms of accountability, both in terms of curriculum provision and finance. And, as reflects the claims of corporate management in general, this move towards schools as more autonomous units of decision-making is seen to be both more democratic and more equitable in terms of serving the client more directly and being able to prioritise according to local community needs. In other ways, the trend towards school-based decision-making and community participation has taken on the language of the market by acceding to demands for economic and management accountability. Whilst the form and structure of school-based decision-making shows considerable variation between states, the way in which the centralist/decentralist tension is played out has remarkable similarity in terms of its political repercussions, for example, distribution of equity.

South Australia, perhaps the closest to Victoria in terms of schools structures and level of union involvement, and the Australian Capital Territory, also have traditions of school-based curriculum development and decision-making. School Boards or Councils have been relatively active in policy-making, particularly in curriculum. The trend in the 1970s towards school-based decision-making was encouraged by the federal Schools Commission. But with the cutback of federal funding, the demise, revival and ultimate abolition of the Schools Commission, and the creation of the Department of Employment, Education and Training in the late 1980s, this trend has largely been reversed. In South Australia, the Three Year Development Plan for the triennium 1989–1991 has pulled back much of the power to the Director and Minister. Whilst there is a rhetoric of community and participation in the form of Parent Participation Policy and the decentralization of administrative power to Areas and District clusters, there is a strong centralizing tendency with increased state-wide monitoring of student achievement and teacher evaluation, and policy guidelines. Much of the localised power lies with the principal rather than teachers and parents, and tends to be resource rather than policy focused. Recent negotiations between teacher unions (South Australian Institute of Teachers) and the Director, in the form of a Curriculum Guarantee package, focus on staffing formulae, career structures and contract teachers and country incentives, with no mention of staff involvement in committee systems. Still under discussion are the issues of devolution of responsibility to schools. Likewise in the ACT, there is a trend towards increasing control over teachers through development and evaluation programs, whilst the rhetoric of participation and devolution of the previous decade remains intact.

Queensland also has a history of community involvement in school-based decision-making with the Radford and ROSBA systems of assessment and school-based curriculum development since 1974. During this time, some Regions voluntarily formed educational advisory boards involving educational professionals, parents and interested community members. Whilst there has been genuine participation and learning in the processes which evolved, it is now argued that the structures which enable involvement must be institutionalized and clarified through administrative reorganization. Hence a pilot scheme for devolution to the community was instituted in 1989 (Kidston, 1989; Lingard and Collins, 1991). The principal, as in other states, is the key element in this restructuring, which is premised upon the assumption that community participation in collaborative decision-making will exemplify the concept of education as a shared responsibility (Department of Education, Queensland, 1989, p. 4).

Whilst in certain areas (e.g., assessment) Queensland, Victoria and South Australia have had a history of school-based decision-making, Western Australia, New South Wales, Tasmania and the Northern Territory have remained highly centralized systems. To some extent, this can be attributed to the size of the system. But each has seen this alter with the change of government. In Western Australia in 1987, the Labor Government, after a Functional Review Committee report, produced the outline for reorganization titled *Better Schools in Western Australia. A Program for Improvement* and reconstituted the Education Department into a Ministry. (See Porter, Knight and Lingard, Chapter 13, this volume.) Once again, the stimulus for such a change was, as stated in *Better Schools*, 'the emergence of new technologies, the desire for students to stay on longer at school and the call for education to be more in touch with the needs of the future'. At the same time, administrative styles had to become more responsive and adaptable to local needs and government priorities, flexible in the use of resources and accountable to the Government and community (Ministry of Education, Western Australia, *Better Schools*, 1987, p. 5). The reorganization was based on the principles of self-determining schools, because, it was argued, efficiency and effectiveness can only occur if the professionalism of teachers is exercised, decisions about educational needs of students are addressed, and programs reflect wishes of local school committees. The characteristics of this new direction in WA, to be phased in over three years, were the provision of a block grant to schools and a base school staffing entitlement determined by the Ministry, but devolution to schools with regard to staff management, responsibility for teacher selection and school program administration, the undertaking of school development plans, the establishment of school-based decision-making groups (e.g., Councils), and provision through regions' administrative support. In order to maintain staffing stability, new promotional and transfer procedures for teachers were to be instituted. Critical to this system, although not emphasized in *Better Schools*, is the qualification that to maintain standards and equity, there needs to be a system of monitoring, reporting and auditing of resource usage. More specifically, that schools are accountable for performance 'against centrally established standards and goals'

(p. 11). Western Australia, therefore, has in theory moved towards local decision-making and a more extreme form of self-managing schools which will have control over appointment of principals and staff. Currently, whilst financial devolution in the form of program budgeting has been considerable, largely in the hands of the principal, the formal structures facilitating greater participation of parents and teachers has not evolved. Decision-making is still largely in non-curriculum areas and parents still feel relatively powerless, although the parent organizations continue to demand greater involvement. Teacher unions likewise have argued for democratic decision-making in policy since 1982, but only on the condition it is resourced adequately, and that teachers receive additional payment for extra duties.

The Northern Territory Government has taken this trend one step further in its report of 1987, *Towards the 90s: Excellence, Accountability and Devolution in Education*. A Government Education Plan proposed the need for devolution of greater decision-making to local groups. At the same time, *Towards the 1990s* clearly states that certain responsibilities would remain with the centre: broad educational aims, objectives and policy guidelines, curriculum, accreditation and assessment, allocation of staffing and conditions of service and the size and allocation of direct grants. Staff and career restructure and appraisal, notions of teacher excellence awards are also dominant themes as in other states. These emphasize the development of a skills hierarchy similar to the notion of the AST in Victoria where productivity in the classroom is rewarded. As with the other states, principals and regional consultants are appraised for their management through performance indicators. There is an absence, as in WA, of committee systems in schools.

In New South Wales, the *Management Review of the Department of Education and Youth Affairs* (1989), chaired by Brian Scott, argued that the principle of equity was not guaranteed through a centralized system because decisions regarding resource allocation were not situated at the place of teaching and learning. Thus the system was highly unresponsive to local and individual needs. As with other reports, the central premise of the document, *School Renewal, The Strategy to Revitalise Schools within the New South Wales State Education System*, is that the school, not the system, is the key organizational unit of educational provision, because each school is different and its special needs are best determined by the school's teachers and the community. Furthermore, schools should be self-managing in order to maximize use of resources. The leadership of principals and support mechanisms is critical. Furthermore, there are increasingly connections between curriculum and assessment procedures and administrative structures, as indicated in the Carrick Report, *Curriculum in NSW Schools* (Ministry of Education, November, 1988).

Central to the discourse of school-based decision-making, therefore, is the claim familiar to Victorians: that school based decision-making is more efficient and effective because the participative process/partnership involving parents, community and teachers produces better decisions by those who are most affected in schools, since they can better determine local and individual needs and address disadvantage. The actual structural relationship between schools and parent bodies (therefore the community) varies considerably. In New South Wales, for example, there has been no history of School Councils and there is only a suggestion that they be mandatory. In other states, community refers more frequently to relatively non-representative advisory parent bodies comprised largely of those parents of professional background. What is common to these states is that the principal is seen to be the key in the determination of needs and negotiation between such interests. Whilst the language of corporate management is that of consultation and consensus, it is less clear what this means in practice. Another claim is that a block grant to schools is seen to encourage schools to maximize the use of limited funds. In other words, increase productivity. In effect, the shift towards school-based decision-making works as an economy measure in that conflict over limited resources occurs *in* schools and not *between* schools and the centre, which in turn is not held accountable for local decisions. Accordingly, the state is seen through the apparently consultative mechanisms of corporate management and system level accountability measures (performance indicators, teacher appraisal, etc) acting in the best interests of public education and community, and in so doing, seeking to raise public confidence in education through participation.

At the same time, there is an implicit emphasis on a system of accountability through the development of planning mechanisms and processes such as corporate budgeting and school development plans. What differs is the degree of participation, the role of the teacher unions and parent organizations and other community interests. Very few of the states have the highly institutionalized committee systems which are present in Victoria, and the presence of union representatives is not as marked or legitimate. Curriculum is perceived to be a legitimate activity for teacher decision-making, although moves to standardize assessment at the system level and prescribe curriculum even in terms of broad guidelines are limiting teacher discretion. Administration is, in most states, the prerogative of the principals. The principal largely determines the allocation of duties in schools, and the reviews suggest even greater power be transferred to the principal in appointing staff, particularly in the self-managing schools. Thus, in many states (for example, Western Australia, Northern Territory), professional development is focusing narrowly upon improving the leadership skills of principals, whilst the emphasis for teachers is on new career structures, additional qualifications and teacher appraisal. Victorian teachers, on the other hand, see their career paths as being inextricably linked to the committee system, in terms of providing professional and administrative experience and peer appraisal for promotion. The consequence of devolution in other states tends to be the reformulation of basically hierarchical rather than democratic relationships. In general, the assumption of educational reform and the trend towards school-based decision-making is that education will be more efficient and effective, that certification and curriculum reform will produce excellence and raise educational standards; that diversity and choice will be met at the school level; that schools will link more closely with industry; and that equity and disadvantage will be better recognized and addressed at the school site.

The move towards schools as the unit of decision-making, or self-managing, is premised on the view that the use of limited resources is maximized by making those responsible for implementation capable of determining priorities at the point of implementation. In this sense it would appear to give teachers and parents greater control over schools. At the same time, mechanisms of review and audit, that is, program budgeting, etc, increase centralized control through the budgetary process, whilst accountability is met through curriculum guidelines and standardized testing of student achievement. Thus school-based decision-making increasingly serves managerialist ends whilst maintaining a rhetoric of democracy and professional development. With the national context in mind we will now turn to the focus of this project and outline some of the patterns which emerged from our research.

Case Study of Representative Committees

Setting the Scene

The site of this research project is a secondary high school which has a long and established tradition in its middle socio-economic area. The school was established, as were many others, in the mid-1950s when there was an expansion in the numbers of children of school age following the post-war baby boom. Like the majority of schools built in this era the school consists of the typical 1950s chicken-coop structures clad in dull grey pseudo-brick painted green. These schools were claimed by the government of the day to be only temporary structures which would be replaced in a short time by more permanent buildings. However, over thirty years later, when public expenditure is being continually pulled back, the wholesale scrapping of these temporary structures for new, more costly, buildings looks extremely unlikely. Rather, such a scenario inherited from previous miscalculations gives rise to continual problems of cyclical maintenance.

Nevertheless, over the period of its existence, the school has established a strong sense of tradition and continuity. This sense can be amply illustrated by the fact that there have only been five principals at the school over a period of time when there was great stress and change on the role the principal plays in the administration of the school. Not only have the principals been long serving, but many staff choose to forgo promotion opportunities to remain. The stability and tradition engendered by these actions has led the school to be compared with many of private schools which are nearby. Indeed, a common saying in the area is that the school is the poorer person's private college.

Perceptions on the Importance and Operation of the Committee System

The foreshadowed problem of the research project relates to the devolution of administration within the Victorian Ministry of Education. In particular, the project seeks to study the part committees, especially the LAC and the Curriculum Committee established by the Industrial Agreement, play in this process.

The data were gathered through interviewing nineteen members of committees and the school's staff as well as by sitting in on a number of the committee meetings. The interviews were held not only with staff, but also with parents on the committees. In addition staff who were not on committees were also interviewed. From the analysis of the transcripts, several broad patterns have emerged which will be briefly addressed in this chapter.

The first pattern relates to the reasons why people have chosen to participate or not to participate on the committees. Linked to this issue is the concept of representation. Do some people represent the interests of a particular union, association, or subject group when they are involved in the various committees' decision-making processes? The second pattern is concerned with the dynamics of the committee meetings. Do any groups dominate? What is the role of the principal? How are agendas set? The third pattern, which seems to be of the most immediate importance, is the manifest tensions which have arisen through locally arrived at decision-making processes and the Ministry guidelines relating to reorganization, distinct provision and the provision of a comprehensive curriculum in line with the newly developed VCE program.

a) Participation and Representation on the Committees

When starting to research the school committees, the task seemed quite large. However, we soon found that there was a high degree of overlap in the membership of the committees. The members were generally staff who had been at the school for some time. One committee member thought that,

> It's because some of the more junior people who are not involved see their interests lying somewhere else, perhaps outside the school, and they don't want to increase their time involvement here.

However, a member of staff who was not on a committee felt that at the school,

> It became fairly evident that you have to put in your time generally before you sort of become treated as a senior member and your opinions, or whatever, therefore become accepted.

Because there were many in the staff who had been in the school for long periods of time, it was felt that you needed at least five years to prove your worth to your more experienced colleagues:

> So you really do have to sort of prove yourself. It's quite like an apprenticeship, and I'm sure it's far more so in this school than most other schools.

The lure of administration, however, did not interest all staff, many of them junior staff. Some were content to devote their efforts to the classroom. As a consequence, as one staff member commented, 'I've got no desire to be on any of the committees here at the present.' Not all members of committees were volunteers. One senior staff member was appointed to the curriculum committee by the Principal, 'because all the Senior Teachers have to be doing some kind of work and I guess I was not actually seeking to become a member'. Even the concession that career opportunities were related to being in administration were of little concern because, 'I'm far more interested in classroom teaching.' However, it was acknowledged that the committees had an important role to play in the school administration. But with regard to participating:

The bottom line is are you prepared to go on yourself. To me a lot of people complain about them but they are not prepared to go on it. So that is why I don't complain.

Another staff member suggested that more junior members of staff did not participate because:

You've now got . . . quite a large body of single people and I suppose they are interested more in a social life, perhaps finding their way in the world finding out more about themselves.

Moreover, participation in committees could also mean an added burden to married women on the staff who had shopping and household duties to complete as well as their classroom preparation. Until there is some sharing of home tasks women are not going to say, ' "Oh yes, I'm going to take on more work", and go home and then do a double shift.'

For those who did participate on the committees, the general reason given was that it offered them a greater say and involvement in the running of the school. As one person remarked, 'I like to be involved in decision-making rather than being told that this decision is being made and I've had no idea why.' This sentiment was endorsed by another participant who saw involvement on the committees as a way of achieving that extra degree of self-satisfaction on the job. Moreover, it was felt that:

It's very important to give more staff input into decision-making and also to be aware of all the policy that comes into the school from the Ministry and how that has to be acted on.

A senior administrator not only endorsed this point of view but also pointed to the relationship between school-based decision-making and the local community. As he put it:

I really am in favour of it, because it means the school is then accountable downwards to its community and I'm a great believer that by involving people in decision-making you are widening the exposure towards creativity. You are getting other people's ideas and they're just not your ideas. So it becomes more a partnership.

However, for some, staff involvement on committees meant representing a specific interest group thereby maintaining a particular agenda. In particular, union (Victorian Secondary Teachers' Association (VSTA)) representation is important when decision-making is conducted on the Local Administrative Committee, given the associated history of the development of committee systems and teacher unionism in Victoria. As one member remarked:

I'm very conscious of the fact that's a representative position. With other members, we have three union representatives on that committee. Through our branch meeting we have directions or guidance and we certainly try and see that union policy is brought to the forefront.

Another member of the Local Administrative Committee endorsed this view of representation, commenting that:

> I would say that VSTA members on the LAC have an obvious job and that is to implement the Agreement. Over the last, I suppose, two years, I've pursued several policies, one was to eliminate all classes over twenty-five, we had some in year eleven, [and] another program of eliminating oversize maths classes in year nine and ten, which were up to thirty, to allow for streaming . . . . Basically I'm saying we try to implement the Agreement and that is what the members would expect us to do.

What was evident about the representativeness of these committees was that whilst there was recognition that certain interests were legitimately present (e.g., union) and others were inherent in the school organization (e.g., subjects), other interests (e.g., Equal Opportunity) lacked that same legitimacy, either historically or morally. Women had failed to make significant inroads into the domination of both the *ex-officio* and elected positions on the more important curriculum and administrative committees, largely because all the Positions of Responsibilities were held by men as were the positions of principal and deputy principal. It was argued by many, primarily male interviewees, that gender was not an issue at the school and that Equal Opportunity (EO) was addressed through a policy of maintaining a gender balance which effectively meant guaranteeing the presence of one female on each committee when the election process did not meet this minimal condition. Furthermore, this apparent indifference to gender issues at the staff level was seen to be illustrated by the short life of an Equal Opportunity Committee which existed only for the time taken to write an Equal Opportunity School Policy as required by the Ministry and then 'self-destructed', supposedly through lack of need and interest. Other evidence suggested that those closely allied with representing the interests of women were seen to be less legitimate than being an advocate of equal opportunity for girls. They saw their association with EO, particularly in a formal position, as detrimental to their career opportunities, and, significantly as more energy-draining than other positions. Hence the lack of appointment in the advertized EO position. Whether the gender issue will gain greater legitimacy in this school, given that the latest industrial agreement states that committee representation and the carrying out of committee responsibilities must take into account due consideration of the Action Plan for Women in Education, is yet to be seen. In addition, the EO position is now a designated Special Duties Allowance position in all schools and may therefore be seen to provide a career path, whereas it had not in the past.

In general, what was evident was that representation on particular committees was seen as advantageous in terms of career mobility, personal satisfaction and gaining professional knowledge regarding overall school and system level change, but that it was more accessible to and amenable towards some individuals than others (Anwyl, 1987). At the same time, there existed a level of ignorance amongst many staff, generally the more junior, as to the functions of the committee system, thus signifying how particular decision-making processes had not only become embedded in the psyche of the school, but also how relative newcomers to the profession took for granted what in fact were historically hard-won gains by their older colleagues.

b) The Dynamics of the Committee Meetings

The current principal of the school has fostered the development of proper meeting procedures with the writing up of constitutions, agendas and minutes. As he remarked, 'I suppose my input has been to make the internal workings of the committees more productive, to make the process more time efficient.' For instance:

> The LAC has the industrial role, and it's an advisory body on conditions, it also allows me to continually share information with them. I believe that in getting these constitutions off the ground and having them well and truly spelt out, that it's made their boundaries very very clear.

This formalization has had the obvious advantages of allowing people to see the issued to be debated prior to the meeting and later to check what actual decisions were made. In this regard, it was noted that:

> The principal's requested that all meetings have agendas . . . [and] . . . have minutes, yes . . . . It's formal right down the line. I find that a tremendous advantage, actually, because I find if you have to sit down and write an agenda you are far better prepared, and before the current principal we didn't really . . . have to have agendas . . . but, now that we do run with agendas it's a lot better.

The importance of the agenda was manifest in the workings of the LAC which dealt with crucial matters such as staffing, allotments and class sizes. Accordingly, with the LAC,

> we get an agenda in advance. The secretary collects the agenda items from the members of the committee or those who approach her or from the principal. So that when you come before the meeting you've got an agenda and you can see what's up for discussion.

The role and importance of the LAC secretary was explained in the following way:

> I am responsible for making sure the agendas are ready for the meetings, and the input comes from a number of sources . . . . It's normally prepared only a few days in draft form after the previous meeting, and then I leave it with the principal . . . . But things can be added before it's finally printed ready for distribution. The LAC members who are union representatives may individually or jointly indicate they want to have motions put forward. We've got a general staff member representative who may also do the same. The principal and the deputy principal can give reports and suggest agenda items. There are opportunities for things to be formally put on the agenda and also in general business.

The decision-making process in the school committees is hopefully achieved through consensus. However, if consensus is not achievable then a two-thirds majority is required for a motion to be passed in the Curriculum Committee. In some instances it would appear that the achievement of a two-thirds majority acts as a barrier to more controversial motions being accepted, thereby preserving the status quo. As one committee member commented:

> Built into some of our committees, say for instance in the curriculum committee, is the concept of the two-thirds majority . . . . It has made it very difficult for any changes to occur. A lot of practices in the school which were established for all sorts of reasons . . . are now protected by the requirement that there shall be a two-thirds majority. It's virtually impossible in a lot of cases to get more than two-thirds of the people to agree to change.

Another member of the curriculum committee outlined the transition from consensus to two-thirds majority decision-making. While there is a search for consensus,

> if you run out of time or you're never going to get there, then you leave it lie, and hopefully various people, pressure groups or whatever will go around trying to get people to change their vote. Then it gets put to an actual vote and you need two-thirds majority.

Of course, one of the central people in the resolving of controversial issues is the principal. The role of the principal in nurturing school-based administration is crucial. It was observed that, in terms of decision-making under former principals, 'Power was more centralized.' However, at the present time it was recognized that the principal had power in the form of knowledge. As one member acknowledged, 'He has the knowledge so therefore he has far more power than anyone else on those committees.' In this respect, another member observed, 'He has both a strong position and strong knowledge.'

But in the present era of school administration, most principals have had some union background and have developed a concern for more democratic procedures. As one VSTA member remarked:

> [The principal] was an active [union] member in his teaching days and he understands it. He doesn't prevent us from expressing our views, and he is understanding of the union views.

Thus the principal was happy to let the committees work towards solving administrative problems as set out in the Agreement, for, as one person observed, 'Present day principals have really grown up with it. I think that's a big difference that I can notice looking back through the years.' Another member of the committees suggested that the principal's generally supportive role in the functioning of the committees, and the similar position he tends to hold to the majority of the staff, could reflect the fact that, 'The local selection, chose him from the candidates because he happens to have those sort of views.' Nevertheless, a common feeling was that the principal was supportive of the committees, with no one recounting a time when any form of veto had been applied. The principal substantiated this perception pointing out that, 'I've got the right of veto, but I haven't used it. I see my role there really as working with a group of people.'

Yet in the current context of corporate managerialism the principal could play the role of authoritarian manager and in this context it was noted that, 'We're told and it's been written that we owe allegiance to line management. But I don't see my role in that [way] at all, my role *is* towards the community of which this school is part . . . .' In this way not only has the committee system meant a greater staff input into decision-making, but it has also removed much of the old adversarial relationship between the principal and the staff. In this regard, committees:

> cut out a lot of criticism of the principal, because in the early years people would grumble about the principal all the time in the staffrooms. But it's cut out a lot of that, because committees are now making the decisions . . . . People can't say, 'Oh the principal did that or he did this, or he didn't do this, and he should have.' I think it has cut out a lot of that.

Through this process on a number of issues, it was obvious that a sense of unity existed between the staff, and senior administration. In that sense, it could be seen that the process of local selection of school principals was based upon a cultural hegemony which did not question the taken-for-grantedness of its position in relation to the broader community, or when it had, to opt for a conservative educational response. Indeed such cohesion between staff, administration and school council was felt to be necessary in order that any opposition to the Ministry might be successful. What was equally significant is that the emphasis on a particular version of democratic process (two-thirds majority) within the school system of decision-making to the neglect of outcome (in terms of whether it was a preferred policy or one in accordance with Ministry guidelines) frequently acted in favour of maintaining the *status quo*, particularly in terms of change which acted against the well established interests within the schools (male hegemony). Such was the case when an initiative which came from the staff for the introduction of human relations was rejected in that it caused mutual closing of ranks amongst well established interests. In other instances, the streaming of maths classes was rejected by the curriculum committee through an alliance of non-science/maths staff. The rejection of streaming was seen by many as challenging a perceived maths/science hegemony rather than bringing the school in line with Ministerial policy.

However, it was this overall sense of unity between staff, Council and administration on the 'stand alone' issues which combined in this instance to work against externally imposed change, and this was particularly significant when dealing with issues of school and district reorganisation.

c) Tensions between Local and Central Decision-making

The major issue which was evident during the period of the research into the school committees was the reorganization of schools, most immediately into districts, so that a comprehensive curriculum could be provided in the VCE years of schooling. The comprehensive curriculum is to be based on a State Board of Education report, *Programs for the VCE*. The report is founded on research at seven schools, four state and three Catholic, which explored the subject preferences of 700 Year 10 students. The selections of these students were sorted into nine programs. These programs were Arts, Business Studies, Humanities, Maths/Science, Technology, Health Science, Community and Personal Services, Maths/Electronics and Applied Science. The report went on to suggest that such a comprehensive curriculum could be provided on a district basis, but it was felt that most schools operating separately would not be able to provide the full range of programs which the report deems to be comprehensive. However, the agreed draft, *School Reorganization — A Curriculum-Centred Approach* (February, 1989), states that, while access to a comprehensive curriculum should be on a district basis, it can be done where government schools offer, through appropriate schooling structures and either collectively or individually, a comprehensive range of studies. Moreover, the document stresses that any school reorganization should not be externally imposed on schools. Rather it should stem from co-operative school-based reviews of curriculum provision at a district level. In July the draft statement was confirmed as Ministry policy (*VSTA News*, August 1989) with the basis of school reorganization being determined as to whether students can get access to five broad curriculum areas of: Arts, Business, Humanities, Mathematics/Science and Technology. However, the VSTA also stressed in a later News that any reorganization with the formation of districts should be at the instigation of schools and not at the initiation of the regional office or school support centres.

The school, with its tradition of stability and academic achievement, feels threatened by these moves toward reorganization. The school community fears that, if it is forced into some amalgamation with neighbouring schools, then its identity will be lost. Accordingly, the school is taking up any openings available through the devolution of administrative decision-making to put forward a case that it should stand alone. As a member of the curriculum committee observed, 'We're sort of fighting for our survival . . . . A lot of people would like to see the school made a "stand alone" school and so we're going ahead planning for VCE according to that.'

But any attempts to stand alone were tinged with the uncertainty that the Ministry would, when the final crunch came, order that some amalgamation must take place. So it was felt that:

> We can't go with very much confidence, because we don't know what's going to be imposed upon us. One minute we're told, 'No, no, nothing will happen unless you want it to.' The next minute we're told, 'Oh, there's the Tech up the road, with only a small number of people, you've got to take them into consideration.' We don't know where we'll be this time next year and that makes people feel, perhaps not insecure but very . . . it's frustrating because you can't plan too far down the track.

Even with such a degree of uncertainty, there was a high degree of unanimity that the school should continue as it had done in the past. Accordingly, 'The majority of staff wants to see [the school] continue to exist and improve and provide services that I believe we are providing and continue to improve it. The idea of access and success, I think we are trying very hard to fulfil that.' Indeed, it was felt that any new arrangement or structure devised by the Ministry would 'not necessarily improve access for success'. Moreover, the staff believed that they were '. . . getting into the comprehensiveness thing at the moment . . . . But [at] VCE we can offer that successfully, we've got a big enough group, I think the staff are getting more and more behind it.' Similarly, as a senior administrator in the school observed, 'Power itself still rests at the school level, there is precious little they (the Ministry) can do to *make* you do things.' So, in regard to the district provisioning for a comprehensive curriculum:

> There is still a lot of water to flow under the bridge about Districts, and I can assure you that there will be strong resistance to any centralist moves to sort of say a school will do this or a school will do that. And I think that that side of District provisioning has got a long way to go.

However, the offering of a more comprehensive curriculum was perceived as not only an educational concern but also an economic concern. As a senior administrator observed:

> Governments don't see great value at the moment in educational dollars, there is not a great deal of sympathy out there to spend more and more money. And so we're getting this sort of . . . prescriptive corporate management model, just thrust onto schools.

In the committee meetings as well, the opinion was put forward that a major impetus towards reorganization came from the present corporate management ideology of the Ministry which reflected the dominance of economic rationalism. As one prominent committee member put it:

> I can see why the Ministry wants to do it this way, but this is not necessarily the way individual schools feel about it. I suppose it depends on whether you're a teacher or a member of the Ministry. I can see reasons for many things that they're doing and if they can improve efficiency, that's really good. But schools aren't just about efficiency, are they?

Another consideration coming into the new comprehensive provisioning of VCE was the need to increase the retention rate, although some people might also link this to the economic rationalist position of keeping the youth unemployment figures down. Nevertheless it was stressed that 'Here at [the school] we haven't a problem of retention . . . . For the majority I don't foresee much change when VCE is introduced, they'll still do the same subjects, they'll still go on to the same courses.' Indeed it was pointed out that for some students 'the new VCE may not suit them.' Yet for the sake of a change, that was not deemed to be appropriate for the present situation. 'This school might be torn apart, broken into two pieces, my two subject areas could be telescoped and totally altered to meet needs which may not be a problem in this school.'

Parents on committees also were strongly opposed to any centrally imposed change. As one member commented,

> I think they have a plan which is somewhat contrary to devolution, because our community doesn't want change, or being forced to change. It's alright if the community want what they want, and it's terrific to

have community involvement and input, but not if they don't get the results they want.

Another parent supported this position with the belief, 'that there's a return or seeming return to centralist policy decision-making'. Indeed, the present thrust to impose the Ministry's will in face of the opposition from the local community reflected the fact that 'within the Victorian Educational scene decentralization or, whatever various names it's been given over the years, has never been a terribly sort of successful picture as such.' This was due to the fact, it was felt, that the historical legacy 'of the Education Department was so very tightly hierarchical'.

While the situation was clear to parents, for some teachers there were dual concerns which complicated the situation. As one committee member summed up the problem:

> I think there is a degree of frustration about the whole business really, because you are, in fact, wearing two hats every time you serve on a committee, aren't you? You're trying to put into effect the wishes of the local community, whether it's uniform or it's something to do with the standards of the course you're offering or whatever. And yet at the same time . . . you could have this responsibility as part of the line management within the corporate structure.

Such dual considerations will be further complicated when the new career re-structure for the Advanced Skills Teacher is in place and various allowances are judged to be payable or not by Ministry officials outside the school community.

What was evident about this particular process of decision-making was that change often had to be provoked from outside the insularity of the committees, usually by an external demand either from the Principal or the Ministry. The introduction of the Victorian Certificate of Education and Curriculum Frame-works was such a force for change in that it provided the principal with a legiti-mate agenda to require a review of all curriculum. Such a review was also seen to be necessary in terms of justifying the 'stand alone' status of the school. It was necessary for the principal to be able to argue that his school had gone through the correct consultancy and review procedures in order to support the school stance on reorganization. Implicit in the principal's position as both line manager and responsible to the school council is an ambiguity in ways which meant they could reject democratic processes at school level by claiming their responsibility lay primarily with line management (Lloyd, 1990).

Conclusion

This case study is the first in what is hoped to be a series of case studies which will explore the workings, dynamics and concerns of school committees within the broader context of educational restructuring and reform. The present school was chosen because it was recognised as a stable, traditional school with a strong academic background. In this respect it was considered that the data obtained from research into school committees at this place would provide a useful bench-mark to which subsequent studies might be compared.

While the school's stability was recognized, the research revealed an added depth with the discovery of, for instance, many positions of responsibility, a position which would have long disappeared from most state schools. The exist-ence of a long-serving staff assured a high degree of homogeneity in the positions of many of the people on the committees and the ultimate decisions arrived at. Also, the seniority of the staff serving on the committees tended to direct the more junior staff into classroom concerns, into a greater devotion of time and energy and into classroom preparation and teaching. The committee system there-fore exacerbated both the age and gender division 'of labour within the school, with women and younger (and newer) members of staff concentrated in the classroom and the well-established senior staff, largely males, in administration. Because of this particular construction certain issues remained marginalized or off the agenda. The apathy (seen to be indicated by the failure of many staff to stand for committee representation) of the younger staff (particularly female) was attrib-uted by those who participated to lack of interest, rather than understanding that the entrenched patterns of decision-making and the culture of the school may have excluded the less powerful in more subtle ways.

The tension between the democratizing tendencies of devolution and the centralist tendencies of corporate management are highlighted in the case study. One issue which emerged when considering the impact of apparently democratic administrative structures at school level in a framework of corporate managerialism was that of accountability. To whom was the school accountable and in what way? To the 'local school community', which could be variously defined as a geographical area, as a cluster of schools in an area, as the parents of the student body, or to the Ministry and public education at large? Given that student intake is no longer defined by geographical boundaries and catchment areas, this school defines its school community as its clients (the parent and student body) which in this instance is drawn from outside its immediate geographical area. In fact, the school, largely due to its academic reputation, attracts students away from other local schools, amongst them the Technical School with which it is expected to consider amalgamation under the District provision of a comprehensive curriculum. In that sense the school exploits market forces in arguing first, that it has a suf-ficiently large student population to provide a comprehensive curriculum without amalgamation, and second, that it meets the educational requirements of the student population it does attract. In so doing, the school perceives it is accountable only to a narrowly defined school community, and not to the provision of a public education in the district nor to the Ministry. This position is validated at the school level by the argument that all efforts toward an harmonious solution on amalgamation had been explored by following through the required consultative procedures. Given the full support of the parent body, the school feels justified in its concern to maintain the integrity of the school as paramount in the dispute with the Ministry over the provision of a more comprehensive curriculum.

This unity against the Ministry was not only fostered by the convergence of parental and staff opinion about the nature of educational provision for their students and staffing stability of the school, but also by the fact that a number of the staff, including the principal, had themselves been students at the school. Indeed, in the fight for a stand-alone position, the school community called upon the earlier rhetoric of school-based decision-making and participation in the Min-isterial Papers and turned it against tendencies toward a corporate management approach founded on economic rationalism. In so doing, it resisted externally imposed guidelines which may produce a more equitable provision of education in the district. So whilst this appeal to the democratic process has been made available historically, it was also evident that the school was able to decide what aspects of the social justice agenda it was prepared to adhere to in the provision of curriculum and school organization. For example, in its adherence to a largely academic definition of 'access and success', it was able to ignore local student demands for a less academic program, thereby implicitly suggesting that such students would be best served elsewhere.

Another issue which arises is the unpredictability of outcomes which can result from apparently democratic processes. This has two implications for the democratization of education. First, this case-study indicates that democratic processes do not necessarily guarantee progressive outcomes. Yeatman's comment about corporate management's emphasis on procedural norms as the mechanism for system maintenance and stability is relevant here, because emphasis on process shifts attention away from more substantive ethical and educational issues. Second, it does raise questions regarding the receptiveness of schools to statewide and federal policy initiatives (for example, social justice) in schools and the extent to which such policies can be either circumvented or implemented through due democratic process. Certainly, school-based decision-making has the potential to subvert the steering capacity of the state through top-down policy initiatives, by choosing which state agendas will become legitimate issues at school level (for example, Equal Opportunity) (See also Watkins, 1988, 1991.) At the same time, it is clearly evident that school-based decision-making and more particularly the committee system does empower teachers, students and parents in determining the type of education they value.

While this particular school presented a picture of much uniformity of thought and action, future research may offer different perspectives. Such views may emerge where future schools studied have different socio-economic, ethnic, cultural and gender mixes. Thus, a wider research perspective is needed to understanding the complexity of the process of democratization at the school level. There needs, for example, to be more research on issues of the socio-psychological dimensions of the collective and cultural aspects of schools which act as disincentives to certain individuals or groups to become involved more actively. In the school in this study, there was a significant group of non-participants who did not engage with the democratic processes but were happy for others to make the decisions for them. In that sense, they were accepting of a more representative, rather than participatory, style of democracy. That they were mainly female adds a further dimension, given the predominant hegemonic masculinity embodied in this particular school's administration and the notion of administration in general. The emphasis in the study so far, on the participants of the committee system in this school, did not unpick the more complex social relationships which the latter question would require. Further research in all-female schools and mixed technical/high schools may offer an understanding of the more complex gender dynamics at work.

At a wider level this study indicates that the current corporate managerialist imperative, which has stimulated moves towards school-based decision-making in other states and systems, may have unexpected consequences by instilling new sets of expectations which may not be fulfilled by the managerialist/corporatist

framework if the consultative processes which it establishes are more actively
engaged at the school level. This could be achieved, perhaps, by shifting emphasis
away from procedural norms towards more substantive issues and debate about
what constitutes equity, community and citizenship.

Note

1 This chapter is a result of research conducted by two members of the Social and
Administrative Studies group at Deakin University, and part of ongoing research
by the SAS Research Group on the Restructuring of Victorian Education. This case
study, as a pilot study, was funded by a Deakin University Internal Research
Grant.

References

ANWYL, J. (1987) 'Women's participation in school committees', BLACKMORE, J. and
KENWAY, J. (Eds) *Gender Issues in the Theory and Practice of Educational Administra-
tion and Policy*, Geelong, Australia: Social and Administrative Studies, School of
Education, Deakin, pp. 113–21.
APPLE, M. (1981) 'State bureaucracy and curriculum control', *Curriculum Inquiry*, **11**,
4, pp. 379–88.
BEARE, H. (1982) 'Education's corporate image', *Unicorn*, **8**, 1, pp. 12–28.
BEARE, H. (1987) *Shared Meanings about Education: the Economic Paradigm Considered*,
Carlton, Australia: The Australian College of Education.
BLACKMORE, J. (1987) 'Tensions to be resolved in participation and school-based
decision-making', *Educational Administration Review*, **4**, 1, pp. 29–47.
BLACKMORE, J. (1991) 'Corporatism, democracy and teacher unionism', in DAWKINS,
D. (Ed.) *Power and Politics in Australian Education*, London, UK: Falmer Press.
CONSIDINE, M. (1988) 'The corporate management framework as administrative
science: A critique', *Australian Journal of Public Administration*, **47**, pp. 4–18.
DAVIS, G., WELLER, P. and LEWIS, C. (Eds) (1989) *Corporate Management in Australian
Government*, Melbourne, Australia: Macmillan.
DEPARTMENT OF EDUCATION, QUEENSLAND (1989) *Community Participation in School
Decision-making*, Information Statement No. 124, 17 Feb.
KIDSTON, R. (1989) 'Implementing corporate management: The Queensland Education
Department', in DAVIS, G., WELLER, P. and LEWIS, C. (Eds) *Corporate Management
in Australian Government*, Melbourne Australia: Macmillan, pp. 64–77.
LINGARD, B. and COLLINS, C. (1991) 'Radical reform or rationalisation? Education
under Goss Labor in Queensland', *Discourse*, **11**, 2, pp. 98–114.
LLOYD, G. (1990) 'Decision-making processes at "Eastvale" Primary School', Master
of Educational Administration research paper, Geelong, Australia: Deakin Uni-
versity.
LORANGE, P. (1980) *Corporate Planning*, Englewood Cliffs, NJ: Prentice Hall.
MINISTER OF EDUCATION, NEW SOUTH WALES (1989) *Curriculum in New South Wales
Schools* (Carrick Report), Sydney, Australia.
MINISTER OF EDUCATION AND YOUTH AFFAIRS, NEW SOUTH WALES, (1989) *School
Renewal, The Strategy to Revitalise Schools within the New South Wales Education
System*, Sydney, Australia.
MINISTER OF EDUCATION, VICTORIA (1980) *Strategies and Structures for Education in Vic-
torian Government Schools*, Melbourne, Australia: Government Printer.

MINISTER OF EDUCATION, VICTORIA (1985) *Ministerial Papers 1–6*, Melbourne, Australia: Victorian Government Printer.

MINISTERIAL REVIEW OF POST-COMPULSORY SCHOOLING (1985) *Report: Vol. 1* (Blackburn Report), Melbourne, Australia: Ministerial Review of Post-compulsory Schooling.

MINISTRY OF EDUCATION, VICTORIA (1989) *Comprehensive Curriculum Provision Within a District: School Reorganisation*, Melbourne, Australia: Victorian Government Printer.

MINISTRY OF EDUCATION, VICTORIA (1986) *Schools Division*, Melbourne, Australia: Ministry of Education.

MINISTRY OF EDUCATION, VICTORIA (1987) *The Structure and Organisation of the Schools Division*, Melbourne, Australia: Ministry of Education.

MINISTRY OF EDUCATION, WESTERN AUSTRALIA (1987) *Better Schools in Western Australia: A Program for Improvement*, Perth, Australia: WA Government Printer.

MINISTRY STRUCTURES PROTECT TEAM (1986) *Taking Schools in the 1990s*, Melbourne, Australia: Government Printer.

NORTHERN TERRITORY, DEPARTMENT OF EDUCATION (1987) *Towards the 90s: Excellence, Accountability and Devolution in Education*, Darwin, Australia: Government Printer.

PA AUSTRALIA (1981) *The Rationale and Definition of the Proposed Organisation Structure*, Melbourne, Australia.

RADIN, B. and COOPER, T.L. (1989) 'From public action to public administration: Where does it lead?', *Public Administration Review*, **49**, (2), pp. 167–70.

REPORT (1989) Victorian Secondary Teachers' *Association News*, August.

SCOTT, B. (1989) *Schools Renewal: A Strategy to Revitalize Schools within the New South Wales Education System,* Sydney, Australia: Management Review, NSW Education Portfolio.

SMITH, R.F. (1989) 'Cabinet government and public sector performance: Recent experience in Victoria', in DAVIS, G., WELLER, P. and LEWIS, C. (Eds) *Corporate Management in Australian Government*, Melbourne, Australia: Macmillan.

WATKINS, P. (1988) 'Representative democracy in a Regional Board of Education', *International Journal of Educational Management*, **2**, 1, pp. 18–25.

WATKINS, P. (1991) 'Corporate management, school size and alienation', *Principal Matters*, **3**, (1):

WILENSKI, P. (1986) *Public Power, Public Administration*, Sydney, Australia: Hale and Iremonger.

YEATMAN, A. (1987) 'The concept of public management and the Australian state in the 1980s', *Australian Journal of Public Administration*, **46**, 4, pp. 339–53.

YEATMAN, A. (1990) *Bureaucrats, Technocrats, Femocrats*, Sydney, Australia: Allen and Unwin.

Chapter 13

The Efficient Corporate State: Labor Restructuring for Better Schools in Western Australia

Paige Porter, John Knight, Bob Lingard

Introduction

The study begins with an examination of theories of the state, particularly those which include the internal operation of the state as a factor, for contemporary educational reforms can only be understood against a backdrop of public sector reform. The economic and demographic context is then considered as a backdrop for the issues facing the Western Australian government (1983–1990) and its general response discussed. There is an overview of the timeline for the educational reforms under consideration, and analysis of the key reports. This is followed by a look at the official version of events as reported to Parliament. Finally, there is a discussion of the perceptions of a number of key players involved in the introduction of the reforms in terms of their understandings of the needs for the changes, and their reactions to the early stages of implementation. However, this is not a study of policy implementation, rather a study of policy-making. We reject, though, any simplistic policy/administration dichotomy (Wilenski, 1986) and instead acknowledge that policy becomes the policy in practice. In so doing, we agree with McLaughlin (1987) that policy implementation reflects an interactive policy system, stretching from policy-making to implementation. The last section discusses the reforms in Western Australia in the context of new national and international pressures.

The State and Educational Policy-Making

An understanding of the state (or organized political power) is central to an understanding of policy and policy formation in capitalist, quasi-market, liberal-democratic societies such as Australia (Lindberg, Alford, Crouch and Offe, 1975; Wolfe, 1977; Ham and Hill, 1984; Offe, 1975; 1984; 1985). Most theories of the state (marxist, neomarxist, pluralist, elitist) have tended to emphasize the society/state relationship and have played down the importance of the *internal* operation of the state itself. In this way, they have theorized a unitary and instrumental state, implying that the state is a coherent, unified instrument which simply responds to external pressures. The case study in question here very quickly disaffects us of such a view and does so in two directions, firstly, the internal organization of the state apparatus has an effect in a non-instrumental way and, secondly, the state apparatus is complex and diversified and, as such, different aspects respond to different pressures. Thus an adequate theory of the state and policy formation must reject instrumentalist and unitary metaphors, while still paying sufficient attention to the impact of social factors, particularly the economy and class, gender and racial politics.

Some neomarxist, or what Pierson (1986) calls postmarxist accounts, have begun to take some cognizance of the salience and impact of internal state arrangements on policy formation and delivery, while still accepting the importance of economic factors in policy formation. Feminist theories of the state (Franzway, Court and Connell, 1989; Connell, 1990) also stress the significance of the internal arrangement of the state to policy processes and outcomes. Such theorization is necessary given the importance of public sector management reform in the contemporary Australian political and policy context (Considine, 1988; Yeatman, 1990; Pusey, 1991). Here the work of Offe (1975; 1984, 1985) is very important. (Also see Clegg, Boreham and Dow, 1986.)

Offe, in a wide range of his work (1975; 1984; 1985), argues that the internal administrative and policy arrangements of the state are responses to pressures other than class ones, rather they operate through 'the rules of democratic and representative government' (1984, p. 121), which moves his analysis well beyond instrumental marxist theories. Clegg, Boreham and Dow (1986, p. 274) likewise give some emphasis to the 'politics of administration' and go on to argue that no interest representation made to the state is ever acted upon in an unmediated fashion. This is reminiscent of Offe's (1975, p. 135) insightful comment that, '. . . it is not only true that the emergence of a social problem puts into motion the procedural dynamics of policy formation, program design, and implementation, but also, conversely, the institutionalized formal mode of operation of political institutions determines what potential issues are, how they are defined, what solutions are proposed, and so on.' In the Australian education policy context, the federal arrangement is one important component of the internal state arrangement having such an agenda-setting effect (Lingard, 1991), as is the mode of policy formation and delivery; with respect to the latter, witness the impact of the new managerialism upon policy content as well as process.

The content of policy within Offe's account is framed by the tensions which the state in a capitalist society (not a capitalist state) has to manage, notably between ensuring simultaneously the continuity of capital accumulation, a balance of sufficient mass loyalty and legitimacy. Castles (1988, p. 4) has nicely encapsulated this tension when he notes that: 'The state is at one and the same time the guardian angel of the capitalist economic process and the chosen instrument for protecting society from the corrosive impact of that process.' Social policy, as such, is a temporary solution to this 'internal problem of the state apparatus' (Offe, 1984, p. 104). There are no permanent solutions to the problems faced by the state, only temporary settlements. A class instrumentalist account of the state in operation is rejected and replaced by a more empirically valid assertion that state policy 'seeks to implement and guarantee the collective interests of all members of a class society dominated by capital' (Offe, 1984, p. 120). Here, as with Cawson and Saunders' (1983) 'dual state' theory, allowance is made for political pressures which come from sources other than class-based ones, for instance those based in gender questions and ethnic politics and those emanating from the new social movements such as the green parties. Thus for example, Cawson and Saunders (1983, pp. 25–26) make a most useful distinction between 'politics of production' (broadly economic policies) and 'politics of consumption' (broadly services associated with the welfare state), with the former being framed by class politics and the latter subject to a broad range of other pressures in the manner of pluralist theories. The politics of production are akin to Offe's accumulation pressures upon the state, while the politics of consumption parallel democratic and legitimation pressures for the delivery of services and broadening of citizenship rights. Thus, this account allows us to cojoin the insights of neomarxist, neopluralist and feminist accounts (for example, Franzway, Court and Connell, 1989; Connell, 1990; Eisenstein, 1991) of the contemporary state in operation.

The main weakness of Offe's account of the dual accumulation and legitimation pressures upon the state is its failure to acknowledge the increasing impact of the world economy on the economy within a given nation state (Pusey, 1991, p. 210). This is even more particularly so when one moves to apply Offe's theory to the concrete case of the contemporary Australian federal state. Here we see the political desire, particularly at the national level, to integrate the Australian economy into the international economy in a non-tariff protected manner. Such integration mediates the state's capacity to meet democratic and legitimation pressures upon it. As Pusey (1991, pp. 210–11) so eloquently puts it: 'Integration with the world economy clearly presupposes a closer functional incorporation of the "political administrative system" (the state, and with it the obligatory conditions of elected governments) into an augmented economic system.' It is in that context then that Cerny (1990) speaks of a move from the welfare state to a competitive state. Here we have the international economic context of the efficient, corporate state strategy pursued by Labor governments across the 1980s into the 1990s and indeed the context of the reconstruction of Australian federalism (Lingard, 1991; Knight, Lingard, Porter, 1991).

Finally, in this brief exegesis of relevant state theories, we need an approach which rejects simplistic unitary accounts of state policy. Clearly, the extent of state intervention is such that different policy areas respond to different sorts of pressures and to different pressures at different historical moments. Thus, *education policy is clearly framed by both the politics of production (basically class and economic politics) and those of consumption (basically as constructed by neopluralist politics and taking account of parental involvement, and the politics of equity)*. Furthermore, since the collapse of the postwar economic boom in the mid 1970s, attempts have been made to reframe education policy primarily as a component of microeconomic policy. This has been most obviously manifest in recent years in the policy directions of John Dawkins as federal education minister. It can also been seen in the Western Australian case-study in education policy under consideration in the *Better Schools in Western Australia: A Programme for Improvement* (Pearce, 1987) (hereafter referred to as *Better Schools*) restructuring plan of 1987, and foreshadowed earlier in the 1984 *Education in Western Australia, Report of the Committee of Inquiry appointed by the Minister for Education in Western Australia*, chaired by Mr K.E. Beazley (hereafter referred to as the Beazley Report). These reports will be discussed in more detail in subsequent sections.

Another aspect of understanding the effects of the internal operation of the state itself is to consider the mode of policy formation and delivery. There is little doubt that changes in the administration and organization of education in Western Australia across the Labor years (1983-present), particularly the model of devolution envisaged by *Better Schools* (Pearce, 1987), must be seen as one manifestation of *Labor's reconstruction of public sector management in the direction of corporate managerialism.* This was a policy direction first put in place by the Wran Labor government in New South Wales following a 1977 review of administration in that state (Considine, 1990) and subsequently taken up by other Labor governments at both federal and state levels, the newest of which — the Goss Government in Queensland — has recently begun to implement a similar model (Lingard and Collins, 1991). The Wran New South Wales reform saw three basic developments, namely, a rationalization and streamlining of cabinet procedures; an increased involvement of the central agencies (Premier's and Treasury) in the policy and budget concerns of the other line departments; the introduction of program budgeting, corporate planning frameworks and performance monitoring of both staff and programs (Considine, 1990, p. 174). In the late sixties/early seventies, such public sector management reforms developed in the United States basically as internal, technical (rather than overtly political) mechanisms, a witness to Offe's arguments about the responsiveness of state administrative machinery to discourses other than class/political ones. In the Wran context there was such a basis, combined with the significant political lessons learnt from the Whitlam experiment regarding lack of cabinet solidarity and perceived intransigence of the bureaucracy itself. A significant result of these reforms is the strengthening of the executive over the legislative branches of government.

This framework has been pursued most assiduously by Labor in power at the federal level since 1983 (Considine, 1988) and particularly since the 1987 public service restructuring (Pusey, 1991). Yeatman (1990) would also see the creation of the Senior Executive Service and the concomitant reassertion of the politicians' ascendancy over the bureaucrat as another important component of what she calls a Labor revolution in public sector management. Moves to a leaner bureaucratic arrangement are part of this development, including attempts to devolve as many functions as possible to the site of service delivery (most often in the name of responsive and equitable policy delivery). Wilenski (1986), in many ways the intellectual architect of these developments, has written of equity, efficiency and effectiveness, along with democracy, as the motivating features of Labor's new model of public sector management. Yeatman (1990) would argue that Labor's managerial revolution may inhibit the achievement of Labor's broader equity goals. Indeed, she would suggest that managerialism has been the Trojan horse by which the state in straitened economic times has managed the political demands emanating from the new social movements such as the women's movement, ethnic groups and others.

It should be observed that such a revolution in public sector management has occurred in the non-Labor states (Greiner's New South Wales and National Party Queensland in 1987) without the same focus on equity. The latter developments indicate that what we are seeing is a general response to the fiscal crisis of the state experienced by state and federal governments in Australia since the mid 1970s, as well as a response to ideological pressures against big government. The Australian tradition of statism is also probably an important contributing factor in this specific policy response (Rosecrance, 1964; Pusey, 1988). *Labor's particular contribution to these developments is to construct equity, in both internal personnel policies and in service delivery, as a central component of this new efficiency.* This, in many ways, is a re-construction of the old 'pool of talent' argument. It can be observed particularly in the embracing of equal employment opportunity policies in the public sector, and in the pursuit of social justice strategies in many areas including education.

In Western Australia, the pursuit of equity in education policy is strongest in the Beazley Report (1984) in its traditional Labor concern for disadvantaged groups, but it is still a feature of *Better Schools* (Pearce, 1987), though transformed by the new Labor definition involving devolution and a joint definition of equity by the centre and the local school community.

Disillusionment with big government combined with corporate trends in the business world towards flatter management structures (the coat-hanger rather than the pyramid) have contributed to another characteristic of the new public sector reforms: *some aspect of devolution is a consistent feature.* This may be anything from administrative decentralization to new participatory modes of democracy. In Western Australia the Beazley Report (1984) supports devolution, but it is *Better Schools* (Pearce, 1987) which proposed significant restructuring around the model. The devolution move in education policy can be seen to be driven by two dis-courses, namely the newer corporate managerialist one and the older democratic participatory education one. Within the corporate managerialist framework, devolution is seen to be more responsive in recognizing needs and coordinating responses by bringing decision-making closer to those affected. It is believed that there are efficiency gains due to greater flexibility in resource allocation and the potentially greater integration of service delivery mechanisms, with cost-cutting seen to be a result. Within the democratic participatory education framework, the emphasis is on community, parental, teacher, and student participation in school decision-making as a means of ensuring more equitable and effective outcomes from schooling. Costs are not typically part of this discourse. In the Western Australian case, the latter discourse is more predominant in the Beazley Report (1984) and the former in *Better Schools* (1987). Whatever the rationale the reform is not neutral. This is yet another manifestation of Offe's (1984, p. 104) observa-tion that 'there is no such thing as an administrative reform that is nothing but an administrative reform; it always entails changes in the quality of the available social services, their accessibility to clients, the composition of the clientele, and so on.'

Many Left analyses of education policy developments in Australia since the mid-1970s, including those instigated by Labor governments, have simply applied a New Right argument as in Thatcher's Britain to such policy developments. We would eschew such a simplistic extrapolation and instead see the economic (and ideological) pressures upon the state in Australia being mediated to some extent by traditional Labor concerns for equity and the significance of statism within Australian political culture. Equity has remained on the agenda, but has been reframed more in economic rationalist terms (Henry and Taylor, 1989). We be-lieve that Yeatman is correct when she argues that Labor has responded to these pressures by moving to create a more efficient and effective state (and one committed to equity), rather than respond with a straightforward privatization model in a Thatcherite manner. Corporate managerialism has resulted, and given our position regarding the state outlined above, such a management mode has its own impact upon policy delivery.

As part of his theory of the state, Offe (1985) makes a useful distinction between what he calls structural and conjunctural policy rationales. The former operate in times of economic constraint, while the latter operate in better economic times. With conjunctural policies the state responds to policy demands by an incremental extension of policy coverage. With structural policies, by contrast and in recognition of the ceiling on funds, there is an attempt to manage demand. This attempt to frame demand so that it can be met within given funding parameters sees a full restructuring of public sector management according to Offe (1985). This is what we are seeing occurring right across Australia with corporate managerialist administrative reforms and their stress on 'tighter control, reduced lateral participation, narrower definitions of legitimate action and the expectation of greater levels of output on the part of less ambitious public programs' (Considine, 1988, p. 16). In a sense then, the Western Australian Beazley Report (1984) sits at a point of transition between the earlier conjunctural framework and the newer structural framework as outlined by Offe (1985), while *Better Schools* (Pearce, 1987) fits firmly within the constraints of structural policies. Devolution of a range of functions, including budgeting, to the school level, can be seen as possibly one way of managing demand (Watkins, 1988). (An unexpected result may also be the politicizing of otherwise unpoliticized sections of the population.) However, as Offe (1985) also notes, one rationale does not simply supercede the other, rather one dominates over the other at a given time. Thus, in Western Australia with *Better Schools* there are still residues of the older social democratic Labor construction of schooling despite its framing by the new managerialism.

Western Australia: The Context

Education policy must always be understood in context. In this case study we are trying to analyze particular government reactions to economic downturn. In doing this it must be accepted that education policy is only part of a total State government policy. A comment on significant features of Western Australia and the Labor (1983-present) government's approach is thus in order. Between 1983–1990, Western Australia was a state with the following general characteristics (Evatt Research Centre, 1989):

- a falling birthrate combined with the highest population growth rate of any state, exceeding the national growth rate, reflecting the high rate of net overseas and interstate in migration (pp. 311–12);
- a strong growth in the State Gross Domestic Product which is, nevertheless, more volatile than that of Australia as a whole due to the importance of primary product industries and hence an economic vulnerability to shifting world trade patterns (pp. 312–13);
- the most export-intensive trade performance of any of the Australian states (pp. 316–19);
- a sharp rise in unemployment combined with strong growth in employment reflecting a more rapid rate of population increase, a younger labour force and a higher rate of labour force participation (p. 319);
- a diversification of the economy as differential employment growth shifts from primary product industries — manufacturing, construction and public utilities — to the finance, property and business services sector (p. 320).

Paige Porter, John Knight, Bob Lingard

Table 1   W.A. State and Commonwealth Funds Real Growth Rates ($m)

	State CR/F	State Other	State Total	Real per cent Change	Commonwealth Total	Real per cent Change
79/80	787.74	268.97	1056.71	—	1199.10	
80/81	906.01	290.76	1196.77	4.11	1368.19	4.89
81/82	1023.20	352.94	1376.14	3.43	1490.28	−2.03
82/83	1183.12	821.56	2004.68	32.21	1674.42	1.97
83/84	1393.68	1041.03	2434.71	13.59	1936.90	8.19
84/85	1502.09	909.96	2412.05	−4.68	2090.39	3.84
85/86	1673.71	935.17	2608.88	0.11	2289.24	1.36
86/87	1692.69	1040.85	2733.54	−4.73	2469.39	−1.92
87/88	2052.83	854.30	2907.13	−0.74	2574.69	−2.68
88/89	2465.12	1139.72	3604.84	17.00	—	—

Source: Western Australian Budget Papers 79/89–88/89
(Adapted from Evatt Research Centre, 1989, p. 332)

The progressive reductions in Western Australia's share of Federal tax and the financial stringency applied by the Commonwealth in its budgeting in general, led the Western Australian government during this period to make greater revenue raising efforts, to seek new forms of taxation, and to look for a variety of ways to improve public sector efficiency and economy. The following tables and graphs illustrate this situation. Table 1 shows all State and Commonwealth funds and their growth rates.

Graph A shows the comparative growth of revenue of the Consolidated Revenue Fund (CRF) between State and Commonwealth sources. Graph B shows the relative shares of the total revenue (CRF plus other sources).

The Burke Labor Government, elected in 1983, clearly saw these revenue-raising and efficiency tasks as central to its mission. Its 1986 policy platform argued the need for:

direct government involvement in commercial activities to stimulate economic growth and to return financial benefits to the whole community through the capacity to reduce taxation and extend public services. (ALP, WA Branch, 1986, p. 70, quoted in Evatt Research Centre, 1989)

In this party platform can clearly be seen the harbinger of what became known as 'W.A. Inc.' or extensive government involvement in industry and investment. W.A. Inc. can be characterized as corporatism in the public sector, which in part failed to distinguish between legitimate active industry development policies which reflect a long-term commitment by government to economic growth, and the desire by government to raise revenue in general. The result was a longstanding inquiry into government-business relations given subsequent substantial public and private financial losses. Evatt Research Centre (1989, p. 343) makes the point that:

For State Governments whose tax base is invariably regressive, alternative sources of revenue are important both politically and economically,

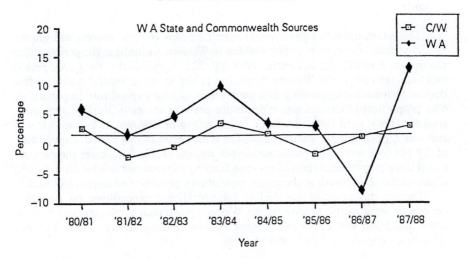

Graph A

Growth of Revenue on the CRF

Source: Weatern Australian Budget Papers 79/80 – 88/89.

(Adapted from Evatt Research Centre, 1989, p. 331)

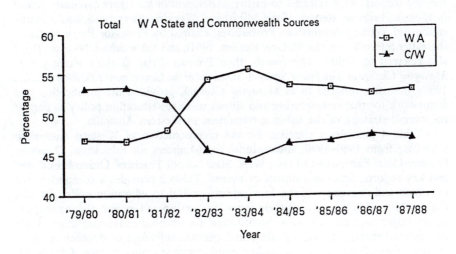

Graph B

Relative Shares of Total Revenue

Source: Weatern Australian Budget Papers 79/80 – 88/89.

(Adapted from Evatt Research Centre, 1989, p. 333)

but without full accountability for these sources to parliament, they may enhance executive power at the expense of the legislature, thereby dissembling the balance of powers deemed essential in democratic governance.

This environment of government search for new revenue sources and greater efficiency frames education policy-making in Western Australia in the period under discussion. Evatt Research Centre (1989, pp. 322–3) argues that the Labor period sees fiscal restraint in the Western Australian public sector in general, and a relative decline for education spending as a proportion of total expenditure in particular. The proportion of educational expenditure grew in the early Burke Labor government (1983) until 1984/85 when it began falling in 1985/86. Its average growth rate was 2.1 per cent per annum compared with a growth rate of total expenditure of 2.9 per cent across the public sector per annum. Table 2 indicates the proportional share of total consolidated revenue funding expenditure in education. Graph C shows the real growth in the major expenditure groups of education and health.

Despite this proportional decline for educational expenditure (as part of a general slowing of the growth of the Western Australian public service) there is some indication that education funding is now holding steady. Table 3 shows schooling expenditure from 1986 to 1990.

Educational Restructuring in Western Australia and the Key Reports: An Overview of Beazley, McGaw, Better Schools and Managing Change in the Public Sector (1983–1990)

The recent restructuring of education in Western Australia can be traced through four crucial policy documents. Three of these deal explicitly with education: The Beazley Report, 1984 referred to earlier; *Assessment in the Upper Secondary School in Western Australia*, Report of the Ministerial Working Party on School Certification and Tertiary Admissions Procedures, chaired by Professor Barry McGaw, (hereafter referred to as the McGaw Report, 1984); and *Better Schools* (Pearce, 1987) also referred to earlier. The fourth, then Premier Brian Burke's white paper, *Managing Change in The Public Sector A Statement of the Government's Position* (Burke, 1986) (hereafter referred to as *Managing Change*), provided the justification and framework for that restructuring and allows us to see education policy as part of the overall strategy of the Labor government in Western Australia.

Table 4 provides a timeline for the reconstruction of Western Australian schooling from 1980–1990, and includes the Ministers for Education; Directors General-Chief Executive Officers; W.A. State School Teachers' Union Presidents; and key reports, acts, committees or events. Table 5 provides a comprehensive overview and summary of the four reports central to education policy in WA during this period in terms of their focus; authorship and extent of consultation; goals; major recommendations; justification for recommendations; implied organizational form; type of organizational control; reference to devolution; conception of social equality and inequality; emphasis upon equity, nature of discourse; expenditure recommended; major tasks of implementation; and funding provided. These tables may be used as a reference point for the more detailed discussion which follows.

Table 2   W.A. Total CRF Expenditure All Major CRF Expenditure Groups Relative Share of Total (per cent)

	79/80	80/81	81/82	82/83	83/84	84/85	85/86	86/87	87/88
Education	28.1	28.0	28.9	29.2	27.5	28.4	28.1	27.9	26.8
Recreation and Culture	1.7	1.5	1.4	1.4	1.4	1.6	1.7	1.9	1.9
Health	19.8	20.1	18.9	17.0	16.9	17.7	18.0	19.5	19.9
Welfare	3.4	3.5	2.5	4.1	5.0	5.3	5.1	5.6	5.6
Public Order	6.0	6.1	6.4	7.3	6.7	7.0	7.4	7.4	7.5
Housing	1.4	1.3	1.2	5.2	5.0	5.1	3.6	3.3	3.2
Transportation and Commerce	3.6	4.6	4.9	15.0	14.9	14.5	13.1	11.1	10.2

Source: Western Australian Budget Paper 79/89–88/89
(Adapted from Evatt Research Centre, 1989, p. 323)

Graph C

Real Growth in Major Expenditure Groups (Education and Health) W A

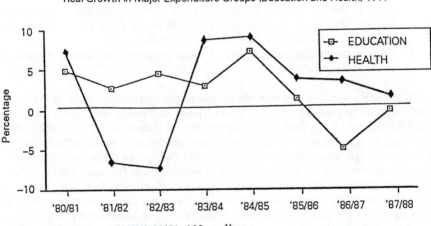

Real Growth Calculated CPI WA 80/81=100   Year

Source: Western Australian Budget Papers 79/80 – 88/89.

(Adapted from Evatt Research Centre, 1989, p. 328)

In the case-study of education policy in a period of economic constraint under discussion here, there are five inter-related questions which we seek, in particular, to address in relation to these Central Reports:

- In what frame do these Reports primarily conceptualize education — as the class-based politics of production (economic policies) or the pluralistic politics of consumption (social services)?

Table 3   Western Australian Schools Expenditure 1986–1990 ($)

	1986–1987	1987–1988	1988–1990
Total Expenditure	787,886,109	719,014,489	796,012,285
Minus			
– Assistance to Private Schools	40,634,241	44,878,290	50,954,790
– Subsidies and Grants	4,266,900	3,868,541	4,704,419
– Office of TAFE	103,311,627	—	—
Expenditure			
Government Schools	639,673,341	670,267,658	740,353,076

Source: Compiled from WA CRF Estimates of Revenue and Expenditure presented to Parliament by Treasurer. The increase in expenditure from 1987–1988 to 1988–1989 is essentially due to increased salaries [4 per cent Second Tier National Wage Agreement] i.e., $60m.

- What solution, if any, do the Reports offer to the problem of economic constraints upon the provision of educational services — corporate managerialism or forms of privatization?
- What is the justification for devolution where recommended, corporate managerialism for the more effective delivery of prescribed services, or participation for a more democratic education?
- What is the mediation of equity or social justice in the education policies in these Reports?

There are a number of points that relate to the earlier discussion of the state which need to be emphasized here. First, reports and policy documents are produced for the state by groups commissioned by the state to address specific issues which are of concern to it. In that way, they can be seen as the articulation of themes and issues into a perceived problem and the role of the state in its consequent resolution (Burton and Carlen, 1977; Schon, 1979; Beilharz, 1987). Policy documents are as much about constructing a policy problem in a given way, as about anything else. Second, an adequate analysis must take account not only of the texts but of the conditions of their production. Put another way, these texts must be apprehended in their social-historical context (cf. Thompson, 1984: 134–7; Hodge and Kress, 1988). Third, these conditions of production include the internal environment of the state itself as described earlier. Following Offe (1984, 1985) and others (Clegg, Boreham and Dow, 1986; Cawson, 1982; Cawson and Saunders, 1983; Franzway, Court and Connell, 1989; Connell, 1990), we would emphasize the importance of the internal organizational arrangements and administrative ideology of the state upon the creation of a perceived need for policy in a particular area, and upon the processes of policy formulation and implementation. Finally, given the sociohistorical and institutional framing of successive reports and policy documents, we may expect a pre-figuring in earlier documents of themes and issues and solutions which become central to later documents. In thus noting 'intertextuality', we recognize that meanings and emphases are in no way fixed or given, but are open to change according to the context to which they are transposed.

In considering the analysis of the Reports in Table 5, what of the four questions

Table 4 Western Australian Schooling Reconstructed: Key Officials and Features 1980–1990

Date	Minister for Education	DG/CEO for Education	STUWA President	Key Report/ Act/Committee/Event
1980	W.L. Grayden (L.P.)	D. Mossenson	J. Negus	• Vickery Report 11/80 (Teacher Education)
1981	J.G. Clarko (L.P.)	D. Mossenson	J. Negus	• Priest Report 6/81 (Education Standards in Lower Secondary Schools)
1982	J.G. Clarko (L.P.)	R.L. Vickery	J. Negus	
1983 (ALP elected 25/2/83, Premier B. Burke)	R.J. Pearce (A.L.P.)	R.L. Vickery	J. Negus	• Dormer Report 1/83 (Technical Education) • Loudon Report 7/83 (Early Childhood Education) • Kelly Report 12/83 (Intellectually Talented Students)
1984	R.J. Pearce (A.L.P.)	R.L. Vickery	J. Negus	• Beazley Report 3/84 (Education in WA) • McGaw Report 4/84 (Assessment in Upper Secondary School) • WA Government Functional Review Committee (commenced review of Education Department)
1985	R.J. Pearce (A.L.P.)	R.L. Vickery	J. Negus	• Board of Secondary Education replaced by Secondary Education Authority 1/85 (as recommended by McGaw Report)
1986 (ALP re-elected 25/2/86, Premier B. Burke)	R.J. Pearce (A.L.P.)	R.L. Vickery (retired 9/86) L.W. Louden (from 9/86)	J. Bateman	• Managing Change in the Public Sector 6/86 (WA Government White Paper)
1987	R.J. Pearce (A.L.P.)	L.W. Louden	J. Bateman	• Better Schools Report 1/87 (Report following conclusion of WA Government Functional Review of Education Department) • Education Department restructured into Ministry of Education as set out in Better Schools • Unit Curriculum piloted (following recommendations of Beazley Report)
1988	C. Lawrence (A.L.P.)	L.W. Louden	J. Bateman	• Office of TAFE established 3/88 • Industrial Relations Discussion Paper published by Ministry of Education 9/88
1989 (ALP re-elected 2/89, Premier P. Dowding)	C. Lawrence (A.L.P.)	L.W. Louden (retired 11/89) J. Taplin (acting from 11/89 – DG of Transport)	J. Bateman	• Andrich Report 3/89 (Upper Secondary Certification and Tertiary Entrance) • Higher Education in WA (Review Committee report chaired by Minister) • Primary and Secondary Schools Conditions of Work Agreement 1/89 (between Minister and SSTUWA)
1990 (C. Lawrence appointed as Premier)	G. Gallop	M. Nadebaum (from 3/90, first woman)	E. Harken	• Memorandum of Agreement between Ministry and SSTUWA 4/90 (Structural Efficiency Principle — 2nd Instalment)

Table 5 *The Framing of Education Policy and Management: Key Reports in Western Australia 1984–1988*

REPORT	Beazley 1984	McGaw 1984	Managing Change in Public Sector 1986	Better Schools 1987
THE CONTEXT OF THE REPORT				
Focus	Comprehensive review of schools in 1980s; major curriculum development, unitization, reflects changed upper school participation; terms of reference did not include structure of department.	Terms of reference focus only on secondary assessment and tertiary selection.	Restructuring the public sector in period of economic constraint, taking as given traditional Labor goals.	Structure and management of schooling in 1990s; no focus on curriculum.
Authorship and Consultation	Broadly representative committee with wide consultation.	Small and specialized; state department and tertiary education composition; all males.	New Labor government Parliamentary White Paper; narrow consultation.	Small membership, Public Service Commission and Education Department; a functional review established by Labor government as part of public sector restructuring.
CONCEPTUALIZATION OF EDUCATION				
Goals	Reduce social inequality for groups and individuals; equal opportunity in education; human development in the national interest; more relevant curriculum; better teachers; community participation. Education conceptualized as politics of consumption.	Broaden upper secondary curriculum for tertiary bound students; open up options for others; fairness through technical efficiency. Education conceptualized as politics of consumption.	Public sector reform; outputs and outcomes rather than inputs; better delivery of services; more efficient and effective provision of equity; greater participation; humane treatment of public sector staff. Education conceptualized as both politics of consumption and production but production prioritized.	More effective and efficient schooling; increased community participation; more efficient provision of equity and greater participation; school-based selection of principals and staff; one-line budgeting. Education conceptualized as both politics of consumption and production but production prioritized.

Major Recommendations	Changes in curriculum; unitized curriculum; better literacy and numeracy; changes in certification and tertiary selection; replacement of Achievement Certificate; improved teacher quality; community participation in school-based decision-making; needs of special groups met (Aborigines, ethnic minorities, girls, NESB . . .); better treatment of disruptive children; incremental change.	Broader curriculum and modularized units in upper school; changes in assessment and certification including tertiary entrance; establishment of Secondary Education Authority; incremental change.	Restructured public sector on corporate model; Cabinet and ministers set broad policy goals; use external consultants; SES advise and oversee implementation; policy delivery by decentralized decision-making; accountability through performance agreements, functional reviews and human resource management; improved management of change; major restructuring necessary.	Self-determining schools with community participation: control over own budgets, local staffing, school development plans; restructured head office on corporate model; replace regions with districts; major restructuring necessary.
Justification for recommendations	Education a public good; changing economic climate and school population; education as part of opportunity structure; devolution ensures democratic participation.	'Fairness' in assessment and selection; can be facilitated through technical adjustment.	Tighter economic scene and increased demand for government services; Labor goals can be met through effectiveness and efficiency.	Better management; better articulation of educational goals between centre and schools; devolution ensures efficiency/effectiveness and democratic participation.
Organizational form implied	Department of Education; bureaucratic frame; organizational form taken for granted, but different forms of devolution from involvement to participation discussed.	Department of Education; Secondary Education Authority; bureaucratic frame; centralized model of school exit and tertiary entrance; assessment with 50% school-based and 50% external component.	Public sector management model; restructured, corporate managerial and devolved; established functional reviews of all government departments; no public sector redundancy; retraining.	Department of Education restructured as Ministry of Education; leaner head office; new districts part of centre and less autonomy; schools more responsible; centralized, corporate managerial and devolved.
Type of control	Bureaucratic assumed but managerialist perspective on teacher performance appraisal.	Bureaucratic and technical.	Corporate managerialist.	Corporate managerialist and devolved to appropriate level.

Table 5 The Framing of Education Policy and Management: Key Reports in Western Australia 1984–1988

REPORT	Beazley 1984	McGaw 1984	Managing Change in Public Sector 1986	Better Schools 1987
Devolution	Not major thrust though a range of community devolution options raised; educational and democratic participation rationale.	Rejection of complete devolution; equal sharing of assessment between moderated school and centre processes; rationale 'fairness'.	Devolution of administration and delivery of services, but not political devolution; political and economic rationale.	Devolution of administration and service, delivery; economic and educational rationale; funding, broad policy goals and political power kept at centre; means of implementation devolved to schools; opens door to political devolution.
Conception of social equality/ inequality	Broad; traditional Labor; equality of opportunity; disadvantage attributed to group factors but individual mobility the solution — cultural deprivation model.	Technical notion of 'fairness' as ensuring equality of opportunity; meritocratic.	Equity for those within public sector; participatory democracy assumed; little reference to specific social groups.	New Labor definition; equity rather than equality; jointly defined by centre and local community.
Emphasis on equity and social justice	Strong; traditional Labor perspective.	Recognition of test bias re social group characteristics (e.g., gender).	Some emphasis, on Labor equity goals to be met by efficient and effective service delivery in times of economic stringency.	Equity relates to provision; threshold of provision achieved through prior uniformity; now need diversity for greater equity and for quality.
Discourses	Primarily Liberal progressive; traces of economic rationalism and managerialism.	Technocratic.	Corporate managerial; economic rationalism; human capital (in public sector); neo-corporatist (with respect to Union involvement).	Corporate managerial; economic rationalism; participatory democratic.
Expenditure recommended	Recommendations not framed by funding concerns but no extra expenditure recommended unless provided by Commonwealth; emphasis on better use of existing resources to improve quality.	Funding needed in implement proposals implied.	Better outcomes essential though no increase in expenditure expected; extra funds for equity etc. to come from government sponsored entrepreneurial actions.	Better outcomes essential though no increase in expenditure expected.

INITIAL IMPLEMENTATION

Major aspects	Curriculum to be developed, piloted and implemented (Unit Curriculum); department to be reorganized to cater for special groups.	Secondary Education Authority to be established for post-compulsory education and tertiary selection.	Public service to be restructured including Senior Executive Service; functional reviews of all departments to occur; regular economic and social auditing to be initiated.	Department restructured into Ministry; staff to be reduced at centre and moved to periphery; regions to be closed and districts created; school development plans to be formulated for self-determining schools; school-based decision making groups to be formed; school staffing and budgeting to be implemented; substantial staffing changes throughout Ministry.
Funding	Increased funding during implementation.	Increased funding during implementation.	No increased funding.	Decreased proportional funding of education.

which we raised initially? In terms of its overall emphasis, the Beazley Report (1984) conceptualizes education primarily as the politics of consumption (services) rather than production (economics). What response there is to economic restraints is to be found chiefly in the notion that the federal government should provide additional funding for education. There is little evidence of corporate managerialism and a clear rejection of privatization. By and large, though some elements of managerialism can be inferred (e.g., presses for school and teacher accountability), the general justification for devolution is participative democracy and a concern for more effective schooling. With respect to the mediation of equity and social justice, we would make the following points. First, equity issues feature extensively and prominently in the Report. Second, their treatment is very much in the liberal-progressive and Labor tradition of action by the state to redress the situation of disadvantaged groups, and to ensure not only adequate access to educational provisions, but better treatment within the education system and fairer outcomes. Third, the notion of equity as a provision of the state is modified and open to redefinition by the state's move to involve parents and local communities in their schools.

In short, in content and recommendations the Beazley Report (1984) is essentially a liberal-progressive document which is clearly shaped by Labor concerns, including equity issues. Its conception of education is primarily within the framework of the politics of consumption thus reflecting its view of education as servicing a pluralistic community. At the same time, there are signifiers or traces of later economic rationalism and corporate managerialism which occur at crucial locations in the text. There is also a prefiguring of aspects of the later restructuring, in particular its press to devolution and for accountability. Put another way, the Beazley Report (1984) can be seen as opening a small space on the field of possibilities for the later development of the *Better Schools* (Pearce, 1987) document.

In contrast to the Beazley Report (1984), there is little evidence that the McGaw Report is a Labor document. Given the overlap of membership and concerns between the Beazley and McGaw Reports, there are significant differences in tone and values between them. Thus, whereas the former is largely predicated in the discourse of liberal-progressive education, the latter is much more technocratic in its expression. In our view, however, such differences are related to the contrast in focus of the two committees, in particular the extremely broad brief of the former and the limited brief of the latter upon an area much more open to technocratic fixes. (However, the subsequent [1990] Queensland Goss Labor government's efforts at tertiary selection reform were much more based in traditional Labor equity concerns.)

Nevertheless, to return to our questions, so far as the McGaw Report is concerned, education is largely conceptualized in terms of the politics of consumption (services). Its formulation is more in the old bureaucratic mode than the new managerial mode; notions of privatization are unexplored. Its treatment of devolution is constrained. There is a limited (rather than central) concern for equity; the discourse of meritocracy appears to be ascendant, and notions of social justice are not strongly evident.

On the other hand, *Managing Change in the Public Sector*, the white paper by Premier Brian Burke, is concerned with the *management* of *both* the politics of consumption (social services) *and* the politics of production (economic policies), but it is framed by a *prioritization* of the economic policies. It sees the need to create the efficient corporate state *as a result of* the perceived limited economic policy options open to the state, most particularly the constraint on revenue raising. It is clearly a document which reflects a government trying to respond to multiple demands, and trying to simultaneously facilitate the capital accumulation process and ensure the continuity of legitimation and loyalty in the provision of sufficient social services. The solution to the problem of economic constraints upon the provision of government services is corporate managerialism, although forms of privatization are hinted at and some were, in fact, later developed, including some in education such as the School Assistants vs. volunteers issue. (See Evatt Research Centre, 1989.) The nature of the proposed devolution involves the devolution of administration and delivery of services, but not political devolution. Its rationale is part of the corporate managerialist concept of providing for the more effective and efficient delivery of largely prescribed services. Equity for employees within the public service is espoused, and there is a moderate but not strong emphasis on how social inequities can be better met through more efficient and effective public service.

Finally, *Better Schools* is a report which conceptualizes education within a framework which also includes both the politics of production (economic policies) and the politics of consumption (services), but it, like *Managing Change*, prioritizes economic policies through its corporate managerialist thrust and through its partial assumption of the prior achievement of some crucial social welfare objectives, for example, equity. Its discussion of devolution, though primarily within the administrative devolution frame (more effective delivery of prescribed services), is sufficiently extensive particularly in terms of parental and community involvement and recognition of their legitimate concerns to foreshadow more significant political devolution. It is in this area — devolution rather than equity — that more traditional Labor rhetoric can be seen. Any other meaning of equity than that of the claimed already achieved provision, is left to be jointly defined by the local school community and the Centre, thus reflecting a new Labor approach: equity is to be mediated through devolution. Hence the discourse about devolution is driven at one and the same time in *Better Schools* by both corporate managerialist and participatory education themes. It is also clear that its solution to the problems of economic constraints is corporate managerialist and there is no discussion of privatization as an option. These features make this education restructuring document significantly different from aspects of New Zealand's Picot Report (see Chapter 14) or Thatcherite schooling policies in the United Kingdom (Dale and Ozga, 1992).

In summary, then, we can see both the Labor liberal-progressive and efficient corporate state agendas in operation through these policy documents over time. However, different agendas are much more dominant at different times. The discourse of the Beazley Report is primarily liberal/progressive with traces of economic rationalism and managerialism. McGaw is basically a technocratic footnote to Beazley albeit an extremely important one. *Managing Change* advocates an economic rationalist and corporate managerialist approach in response to economic hard times. This approach is seen as creating the kind of efficient corporate state needed to balance the demand for social services and the capital accumulation process. In *Better Schools* the efficient corporate state approach is also dominant, yet the liberal/progressive agenda is not entirely omitted and the traces which remain open spaces for those who wish to pursue these goals.

The Official View of Educational Change and Restructuring: The Annual Western Australian Education Department/Ministry Reports to Parliament 1980–1989

A contrasting analysis of Labor education policy during this period can be found in the Education Department/Ministries Reports to Parliament. An examination of the annual Western Australia Education Department Annual Reports to Parliament from 1980 to 1989 suggests much more continuity in Labor education policy than the analysis of the Reports just discussed reveals. It also suggests a considerable difference in focus and processes between the previous Coalition government and the current Labor government. Thus while reports from 1980–82 show concern for and action on rural and isolated children, intellectually gifted students, Aboriginal education, special education, and equal opportunity for girls, each issue is constructed independently. There is no evident concept of equity, nor any overarching report or program to give form and coherence to the education process. The discourse which frames them is essentially technocratic, enabling a neutral presentation of facts and actions.

In contrast, despite the apparent discontinuity between the Beazley and McGaw Reports and the *Better Schools* document as described in the earlier analysis, there was, in fact, substantial continuity in the development of education during the period of Labor administration from 1983 to 1989 as seen in The Departmental Annual Reports. The initial period was marked by the establishment of six committees, reflecting Labor's intent to review and reshape the whole field of education. These committees included not only those chaired by Beazley and McGaw but also reviews of early childhood, TAFE, the intellectually talented and special education.

Twelve objectives were listed in 1983 as priority areas for action in 1984. They included curriculum review; devolution of decision-making; school improvement/self evaluation; community involvement; standards and accountability and corporate strategic planning. To these issues, the 1984 report added special groups (e.g., Aborigines, girls, ethnic minorities and those disadvantaged by home backgrounds). These objectives continued throughout the period under review.

Thus from the beginning of the Labor era we find an agenda and a framework for the curriculum reform, the restructuring of education and the associated transition from a Department to a Ministry. In that setting, the White Paper on *Managing Change in the Public Sector* (Chadbourne, 1986) and the completion of the Functional Review Committee's work in the same year, can be seen as logical steps in the ongoing restructuring of public education in Western Australia. This is not, of course, to deny that the actual structural changes required by *Better Schools* are a watershed in the history of schooling in Western Australia. However, to follow the Education Department Reports year by year is to see a growing elaboration of action towards a corporate managerial and devolved model of schooling, within which concerns for equity remain prominent if defined differently. Given also that changes in the content and processes of schooling, including a unitized curriculum for the junior secondary schooling, and new programs and assessment and certification procedures in the upper secondary school, were being progressively implemented throughout this period, there is added justification for inferring a linear progression in development from 1983–89. This view is supported by the principles enunciated in 1983 for the process:

Implementation should be evolutionary rather than revolutionary . . .
school administrators and teachers should be prepared adequately for the
introduction of changes . . . allocation of responsibility for implementation of sets of recommendations to various institutions . . . involvement
of a cross-section of the educational community in the development of
implementation strategies . . . implementation to be undertaken within
the financial parameters reflected in annual budgets. (1983: pp. 22–3)

The implied degree of consonance between the State and Federal Labor governments is also significant. Thus the report links the establishment of the federal
Department of Employment, Education and Training with the changes in Western
Australia. Indeed, local developments are seen as complementing the Commonwealth's approach. Significantly in the 1988–89 report, the changes are also linked
with the federal drive for industry and award restructuring. The impact of business, industry and other community groups on the new post-compulsory education
program is also acknowledged.

Issues in Educational Reform: Perceptions of Players — Views from the Top

While the history of educational reform in Australia over the last decade has not
been smooth at any level, it is fair to say that the period under discussion in
Western Australia (WA) has been particularly rocky. An understanding of theories
of the state, knowledge of the context, an analysis of crucial reports, and an
awareness of the official view, allow us to view these reforms from certain perspectives. Other insights may be gained by considering the key issues as they have
appeared to significant players and observers within the WA system at the time.
The following section is based on in-depth interviews carried out in WA late in
1989 and 1990 with key players in the WA scene. These include primarily political
leaders, key central office Education Ministry officials, and teacher union officers.
Thus the focus in this discussion is on the reasons for the changes proposed and
reaction to early implementation issues as they were seen from the top.

The Beazley and McGaw Reports

The Beazley Report (1984) was clearly the culmination of Australian Labor Party
(ALP) education policy while in opposition. Bob Pearce, the first Minister for
Education, had been a school teacher, Vice President of the Teachers' Union and
member of the Progressive Education Association, and on the Council of the
Fremantle Education Centre set up under the Schools Commission (to facilitate
teacher control of in-service education). Entering Parliament in 1977, he and Bob
Hetherington, with whom he alternated as Shadow Minister for Education and
Chair of the ALP Education Policy Committee, virtually wrote Labor policy in
this area. During this time the only substantial controversy over education policy
within the WA Labor Party was in the tertiary area, particularly in relation to the

creation of the Curtin University of Technology from the Western Australian Institute of Technology. The ALP in opposition had foreshadowed a major enquiry into schooling and the main thrust of what later became the Beazley Report — reforming lower secondary education by doing away with the achievement certificate and academic streaming — was Labor education platform policy (Pearce, 1/11/89).

Senior central office Education Ministry officials also point out that the problems of lower secondary education in relation to upper secondary education had been a Department concern, particularly of high school principals for some time. The growing number of students staying on for Year 11 and 12, many of whom were not university-bound, meant that curriculum, achievement levels, organizational and discipline issues right across the secondary school were high on the internal bureaucratic agenda as well (Western Australian Education Ministry officials, interviews 1–16/11/89). The previous Coalition government actually initiated the examination of tertiary selection procedures, a process taken over by the ALP upon election in what became the McGaw Report. The Coalition had also examined education standards in the lower secondary school in the Priest Report in 1981.

In a sense then, both the Beazley and McGaw Reports were partially joint responses by education professionals and Labor politicians (one and the same in the person of Education Minister Pearce) to issues arising essentially from the rapidly increasing school retention rates discussed earlier. The Beazley Report was a somewhat more party political exercise, and McGaw a more bureaucratic/professional one, but the impetus to consider the problems they both identified was the same.

It is well to keep in mind that the development of the modern comprehensive high school in Australia was only a post-World War II development. The Wyndham Scheme in New South Wales in 1958 is typically cited as the first major move into secondary schooling for all. In this area Australia was considerably behind most of Europe and North America. Even until the seventies, secondary schooling was conceptualized as providing a broad general education only until the end of Year 10 for the vast majority of students. Those who attended Years 11 and 12 were the students who went on to tertiary study; they were a clear minority. As the combination of youth unemployment and changing social attitudes about the need for further education coincided in the eighties — and, in WA, a population growth due to immigration — secondary schools began to have to cope with a very different clientele. Resulting pressures on children, their parents, teachers and schools were quite dramatic and, indeed, are still being worked through in WA and in most Australian states. Witness the recent Finn Report on post-compulsory schooling which has advocated yet more growth and change (*Young People's Participation in Post-compulsory Education and Training*, Finn, 1991).

The other set of pressures which culminated in the Beazley Report, in particular, were the pressures for greater equality of educational opportunity for a number of groups. While a main thrust of federal education policy during the Whitlam years, and receiving some attention in WA by previous State Coalition governments, there is little doubt that equity received a major impetus under Labor in 1984 (led again, of course, by the former federal Education Minister under Whitlam, Kim Beazley sen.).

Much of the discussion about getting rid of streaming and changing the

Achievement Certificate was couched in the context of various disadvantaged social groups, including the working class, and the ways in which schooling confirmed their social position. An impetus was also provided for gender equity which resulted in an Equal Opportunity Branch being established with its first Head, Sandra Brown, at Superintendent level. Aboriginal education also underwent serious examination (and Aboriginalization) by the Education Department during this period. Bob Vickery, Director-General from 1982–86, observed that 'Bob Pearce was the first minister that I'd worked with who had any genuine sympathy that these students needed a form of education that required resources above and beyond the rest of the population and that the situation as it existed was indecent to say the least . . .' (Vickery, 6/11/89). There was somewhat less of a push for multicultural education which did not seem to capture the attention of the WA State government in the same way and which relied primarily upon federal government funds for support.

The most far reaching result of the Beazley Report has been the introduction of the Unit Curriculum, which has been seen as a solution to the need to eliminate the adverse social effects of academic streaming, while still catering for the multiplicity of student interests, talents and abilities. Basically, Unit Curriculum modularizes the curricula in each subject area vertically and horizontally. It breaks subject curriculum into separate units of work which are designated at different levels of difficulty yet which provide for all students a pathway appropriate to their abilities to the same bodies of knowledge. It is intended to integrate curricula within a broad framework while breaking the content into bite-sized pieces. Some units, however, are seen as essential and others as optional. A student must, with advice, choose her/his own courses and may theoretically progress at her/his own pace and level. A school must also decide what choice it is able to provide within the constraints of staffing, state of curriculum development, student interests and timetabling possibilities.

The Unit Curriculum itself was not specifically recommended as such by Beazley, but rather it became the major mode of implementation of the thrust of the curricular concerns that were actively expressed in Beazley. It actually resulted from a departmental committee set up to consider Beazley implementation. That committee pulled in a large number of school-based personnel, teachers, Deputy Principals, etc. to put together the overall plan. One significant decision made was to let as much curriculum development as possible occur at the school level. This was done with the professionalism of teachers in mind and under the influence of the widespread school-based curriculum development movement. In the ensuing years, particularly with economic belt tightening and the resultant public sector restructuring, Unit Curriculum ran into major implementation difficulties. The more teachers worked to introduce this reform and deal with its problems the more burdened many of them felt when later restructuring seemed to mean primarily just more change with even less system support.

The major problems perceived to be associated with the implementation of Unit Curriculum include the following: teacher overload; curriculum quality; timetabling; advisory services to students and parents; competition between subjects; the lowest ability/most poorly motivated students as a group; and lack of resources. In terms of actually getting the scheme into operation the greatest difficulty seems to have been encountered in timetabling or trying to provide a comprehensive range of units, in different subject areas, for different ability level students, making term-by-term decisions in small schools, within existing resources (Vickery, 6/11/89). The negative way in which teacher overload interacted with economic constraint was emphasized by then Minister Bob Pearce:

> In the implementation . . . probably we made a mistake in letting too much of the curriculum development be done at the individual school level. There was a huge amount of reinventing the wheel from school to school. But it had a concomitant advantage in that it did give schools much more ownership of their own curriculum and that was part of the general proposition. But my view is we could have given them more help and still got there. The down side of it turned out to be a lot of the industrial problems that we had because it put a huge load onto teachers and the funding of schools and teachers really did feel that they were being asked to do more and more and that schools were being given less and less and both of those things were true. After a year the very shortsighted attitude that we'd taken in terms of funding cuts at schools was reversed but a lot of damage had been done in that time. (Pearce, 1/11/89)

Carmen Lawrence, Minister for Education from 1988–1990 (and Premier from 1990) came into her portfolio a few months into the system-wide implementation of Unit Curriculum — a process she feels was somewhat premature, particularly given the fact that implementation was proceeding in the context of the more recent *Better Schools* restructuring (Lawrence, 16/11/89). At the time she felt there was 'not to put too fine a point on it, something close to chaos reigning in the system'. Parental perceptions were 'ill-informed and confused', students were 'uncertain', teachers were 'overwhelmed':

> Now in some cases it really was simply a matter of reorganising material they (teachers) already had, but this was to be accompanied by a newer significant restructuring of the Ministry . . . which had seen the effective demise of permanent curriculum writers and subject consultants. There was a great sense of . . . we're out on our own. (Lawrence, 16/11/89)

Lawrence believes that the Unit Curriculum has improved, if not solved, the major problem Beazley was primarily addressing, that of the negative social and educational effects of academic streaming. As students are not classed entirely as advanced, intermediate or basic students, but rather do a selection of subjects which may be at a mixture of levels, there is less labelling at least for the two upper groups. Basic students, however, remain a problem. She suggests that:

> On balance Unit Curriculum has achieved some of its original objectives, but to work really effectively it probably needed to have something like an additional 20 per cent of resources, a longer time frame for implementation, better curriculum preparation in terms of materials available particularly for the lower ability student, and certainly clearer guidelines for all concerned. (Lawrence, 16/11/89)

There is no doubt that the major thrust of the Beazley Report involved attempting to grapple with a significant educational issue that had substantial equity and traditional Labor concerns embedded in it. Former Director-General Vickery referred to it as a problem 'that's proven insoluble in secondary education the world over . . . whether to stream students or not'. On the one hand, 'good students' are entitled to the challenges of abstract symbolic subjects, but on the other students who cannot handle or who are not interested in such theoretical knowledge:

> are streamed into a self fulfilling prophecy in that children in the lower stream no matter what you call them are of lower esteem in the eyes of their peers, their teachers, their parents and future employers. They get further and further apart as the more able students accelerate and they spiral downwards leading almost to a cycle of despair among those children. (Vickery 6/11/89)

Its fate, however, was to be inevitably tied up with the later Better Schools restructuring and the cumulative effects of change.

Public Sector Reform and the Better Schools Report

As has been discussed earlier, the Functional Reviews of government departments were one of the key elements of the Burke Labor government's public sector reform. Burke's white paper on *Managing Change in the Public Sector* (Burke, 1986) set out the corporate managerialist approach to achieving efficiency and effectiveness. While the WA situation did not involve the very public flagging of this significant new approach to the public service (unlike for example the publicity associated with the later Queensland Goss Labor government's introduction of its Public Sector Management Commission), it was nevertheless an extremely important contextual feature for the nature of the educational restructuring introduced. The articulation of central authorities' desired ends, a reduction in size of Central Office, a devolution of administrative services and resources, an empowerment of various local authorities, a focus on accountability for outputs rather than inputs, and on performance rather than provision, were the theoretical features of all the departmental reforms. A complementary element of the WA changes was the introduction of the Financial Administration and Audit Act (Western Australian Government, 1987) which considerably broadened the previously narrow conception of governmental internal auditing to focus on service outputs and not just budgetary inputs and processes.

Another feature of the WA political context paralleled in other Australian States has been the gradual shift of power and influence from the permanent heads of public service departments towards the relevant ministers. This growth in the power of the executive and cabinet over both the legislative arm and the bureaucracy has been a feature of Australian political life over the past decade accelerated with the advent of the first Hawke federal government. In WA this shift began before Labor, during the previous Court Liberal Party/National Party government and has been documented in the education portfolio by Smart and Alderson (1980).

In education, this can also be seen in the way in which the Australian Education Council (AEC), composed of all state ministers for education together with the federal minister for education, has increasingly become a powerful force in

Australian education. There is little doubt that the existence of Labor governments in the majority of states and at federal level has also helped to support the
ministers' power and fuel joint or national initiatives that have resulted in the
recent political, rather than bureaucratic, leadership in education. This trend has
been even more accelerated with the Special Premiers' Conferences organized by
Hawke in 1990 and 1991. The changing nature of the AEC meetings was described
by one former Director General:

> There was a very big difference in the flavour of AEC meetings across
> the same time. In the early meetings it was very much a group of people
> from a state — the Minister and his senior advisers — who between items
> would caucus and say now how in WA are we going to address this
> question. By the time I left it had changed to a group of ministers from
> Labor caucussing and saying now how are we going to stitch this up,
> with the senior officers almost becoming an embarrassing impediment
> from time to time in the relationship. (Vickery, 6/11/89)

A related feature of the Burke Labor government in WA appears to have
been a distrust of senior officers. The Functional Reviews themselves were typically
carried out secretly with no or little involvement by the Head of the department
under review. Vickery noted that it was reported to him that the briefing provided by the Premier prior to the Review stressed that the Review was to be
independent because 'the interests of senior officers in individual departments
were almost bound to be self-serving so you really shouldn't ask them' (Vickery,
6/11/89). It is interesting to observe this same perception being made by others
during the subsequent inquiry into WA Inc. Liz Harman, former adviser to the
Premier on economic development, commented during the WA Inc. inquiry 'that
Mr Burke had a distrust for heads of departments in the public service and had
employed advisers like herself to discuss matters of a confidential nature' (The
Australian, 9/5/91, p. 4). This latter aspect was another major feature of the Burke
government — the heavy use of non-public service advisers — and in a sense was
part of the reform of the public sector in WA (again in contrast to the more recent
Queensland Goss Labor government where advisers are less apparent and change
within the public service ranks predominates).

The result of the Functional Review of the Education Department, never
publicly released as such, did produce the blueprint for restructuring that came
out as *Better Schools in Western Australia: A Programme for Improvement* (Pearce, 1987).
The Review was conducted primarily by a small group comprising senior officers
from the Public Service Commission and the Education Department. Minister
Pearce attempted to keep control of the Review rather than letting the Public
Service Commission dominate the process (as they had in previous reviews):

> I would not let the Functional Review get away from the Ministry or
> myself and so although we had the same process of having a small work-
> ing group of experts and a committee dominated by the PSC who in-
> teracted with each other, in fact, the working group met constantly with
> myself and Warren Louden, then Director General, particularly, and with
> other Education Department officers. (Pearce, 1/11/89)

Having come up with a general framework for reform and considered overseas experience, visits were then paid to Victoria and New South Wales. The Victorian education reform experience was particularly influential. The proposal that emerged was seen by Pearce to involve both economic devolution and educational decentralization. It was not seen by him as a plan formulated to cut funds but rather to redirect and better use the existing scarce resources. It was also seen as directly related to the educational philosophy of Beazley:

> The basic break-up of the Ministry was suggested by me . . . breaking it up with an over-arching coordinative group . . . . They (the working party) came up with a proposal which cut down on the size of head office dramatically and its whole aim was to devolve resources to the schools and that was a concomitant of the Beazley Report's aim. In fact a lot of the decentralisation itself was actually supported in Beazley . . . the idea was that the education budget was growing dramatically year by year but resources were going just into growing numbers and most of them into head office . . . schools were getting more and more squeezed.

> What we proposed to do was to devolve more decision-making power to the schools, but if we were going to devolve decision-making, you have to devolve the resources with which to make the decisions. That was the clear philosophy of it. It was replicated in other functionary reviews of other departments . . . . It became very controversial because the Teachers' Union opposed it. They didn't initially but in the end they did. They worked out that it was just a device to get schools on the cheap which simply wasn't true. (Pearce 1/11/89)

Another member of the working party also stressed that cost cutting was not the primary motivation behind the *Better Schools* restructuring. While the most effective use of funds was seen as important, a belief in devolution and equity was paramount:

> If we are getting short of cash . . . it seems to me that it's a much better system to have a school making its own decisions instead of the Central Office making decisions for the whole of the system because it can't be as sensitive to the individual concerns of the school. I think that less money will go further if the decision-making is closer to where the action is . . . . I also see it as a much better way to go from an equity point of view. In fact on the task force that put together the *Better Schools* Report that was the key argument, it wasn't a money argument. (Functional Review Committee member, 4/11/89)

Committee members were also convinced that this was the Minister's motivation as well. On one occasion when the concept of the workings of the restructuring was being explained to another Minister, Peter Dowding (later Premier), turned to Pearce and said:

> 'Why would you go through all that mess just to save $9m?' And Pearce said 'You're not going to save a cent out of this, it's going to cost you

money but the reason we should do it is because it's a better bloody system'. (Functional Review Committee member, 4/11/89)

A Committee member also pointed out that under the operation of the old Department the primary internal mechanism of control was staffing, and the people who had power had direct staffing responsibilities, such as the Subject Superintendents. By and large other areas, like equity, did not have staffing control and hence little power. Even money coming in from the federal government for equity areas was not particularly helpful since 'money doesn't make any difference because all you can buy with money is people doing things, but you can't actually buy them doing the right things, or consistent things, or continuing things' (Functional Review Committee member, 4/11/89).

A major concept behind the new Ministry was the establishment of a different system of control and one that could be more sensitive to equity areas as well as to local needs. It was to involve the Central Office having a policy-setting mandate with targets and some sort of audit and resource agreements between the Centre and a school. The targets were to be very broad system targets and it would be up to the schools to determine how they handled and achieved their own targets within the context of the system targets. A shift in responsibility was envisioned from the Centre to the school. For example, where there was a Unit Curriculum target on gender and participation rates in science, 'in the past schools would ring central office and say you've got a problem because our girls aren't doing science. Now they ring up and say we've got a problem at this school, can you come and help us' (Functional Review Committee member, 4/11/89).

Both the Minister and Review Committee members also stressed the logical connection with the philosophy of the Beazley Report and with dominant educational thinking. Thus, while the public sector reform movement was extremely important, it also coincided in education with both earlier Teachers' Union policy on democratic decision-making and the current preferred educational paradigms, especially school-based decision-making. Pearce noted that while he had been active in the union, the old philosophical approach had been 'very Principal-based and very supportive of hierarchy', but had changed to the 'proposition that more things should be happening at the school level and teachers should have a more direct say in educational decisions at the school level' and that 'all of the union's own policies then ran that way' (Pearce, 1/11/89). Another Review Committee member commented that while they relied heavily on the education literature, 'the prevailing paradigm in education was emerging at the same time as the related prevailing paradigm was emerging in the public sector, and it's not strange that they were connected . . . . I'm a bit of a believer in paradigms floating through the atmosphere and you pick them up somehow' (Functional Review Committee member, 4/11/89.)

A Review Committee member described the process that the task force went through as one in which the primary search was for a valid educational critique and solution, with the public administration literature influential only in the background. The OECD and North American literature on effective schooling, which supports a whole school approach to educational change with clear targets and accountability built in, was influential. A review paper (Angus, Brown, McGaw, Robson, 1983) prepared for Peter Tannock as Chair of the Schools Commission in 1983, which summarized all the international research and literature available on what resources schools needed to do their work properly, was important, as was the Australian literature on Commonwealth programs such as the Disadvantaged Schools Program, the Innovations Program, the Choice and Diversity Program:

> In fact they were all saying exactly the same thing, which is you've got to have a whole school approach, you've got to have clear targets, so we just built in those understandings. That's where we got the ideas from, the critique in the systems that came out of those equity oriented programs. (Functional Review Committee member, 4/11/89)

Despite the fact that the *Better Schools* Report should have presented no surprises for anyone in terms of the current educational thinking, the Beazley Report, Labor Party policy, public sector reform ideas, or what was going on in other states and overseas, the reality is that its release caused considerable concern in many quarters. As Chadbourne (1990) argues (in a study of District Superintendents — crucial figures — in the post *Better Schools* system):

> . . . when *Better Schools* was released, many people in the education system felt ambushed and violated. They accused the management of hatching the Report in secrecy, failing to consult with the rank and file, and deliberately releasing the Report while teachers were away on Christmas holidays. [A particular incident] was widely condemned as an entirely inappropriate way to treat officers who had served the Department loyally for many years . . . . School staff were incensed by what they saw as the politicalisation and corporatisation of their system, the hypocrisy of introducing bottom-up reforms by top-down edicts, and the imposition of new duties without the provision of adequate resources. In short, the manner in which the radical restructuring took place in 1987 seriously injured relations between the schools and Central Office. (Chadbourne, 1990, p. 59)

According to Minister Pearce, the Teachers Unions' reaction in particular 'stunned' him. The Report was produced early in January, 1987 and an advance copy was discussed with senior Union officials (but not the President who was away) who were 'enthusiastic'. However, when the President of the Union (Jeff Bateman) returned from holidays he made it publicly clear that the Union was not going to support *Better Schools* (Pearce, 1/11/89).

Pearce's view as to how to explain much of early reaction includes the following points (1/11/89):

1 Because the Report was short it was criticized for not containing enough detail. Yet the trick lay in being a governmental functional review that was acceptable to the government, yet did not dictate to education professionals (as other reviews had done to other departments), and still provided sufficient guidance for a further reform process which could use the Report as its base.

2 There was little consultation, which is true in the nature of functional reviews. Yet the intention was that with only a brief framework the

consultation and the detail could be worked out subsequently. 'In fact, fleshing out the *Better Schools* Report was going to be the beginning of the devolution of responsibility and so it was quite deliberately put in those short terms so there was a set of principles on which we worked rather than the detailed blueprint which everyone would follow.'

3   Many teachers (but not all) felt it was just all too much, coming close on the heels of the Beazley implementation which was changing everything inside the school; this would now change everything outside the school 'and they don't have a feeling of a secure point anywhere. It's something I didn't appreciate enough at the time . . . . I felt that unless we could maintain the impetus of change you hit a point where it will drag out and become too hard and the whole thing would just fritter away, so I tried to keep the pressure on to keep things rolling. On the other hand a lot of teachers were very pleased that they could see themselves getting greater control of their educational destiny.'

4   The strengthened role of Principals was one of particular controversy in the proposals. Many Principals were opposed because of their concern about increased parent involvement in schools. Parent groups on the other hand were very supportive. Other Principals saw the opportunities for greater autonomy. However, some school staffs in primary schools 'didn't see any great hope of *them* getting much say because a lot of primary schools tend to be very authoritarian in their structures and any devolution meant the devolution of authority to Principals'.

5   With regard to the reaction of the Teachers' Union, it is likely that they were concerned that devolution might erode their centralised power base. 'Insofar as you have devolved policymaking or educational standards or even staffing you possibly remove the power base for a centralised Teachers' Union.' (Indeed this has happened in New Zealand.) This would involve quite different organizing strategies and could work against the union movement (Pearce, 1/11/89). (Note: this might be the case but then how does one explain the current federal Labor government support together with the ACTU for some enterprize bargaining?)

In Pearce's view, a major purpose of the exercise was to get the Ministry out of doing so much day-to-day administration on quite small school matters that typically involved hours of principals' time in making requests to Central Office which were usually decided much later by a junior clerk. 'The Ministry was to be given the job of being the educational leaders in a policy sense and not so much the administrators' (Pearce, 1/11/89).

There is certainly little doubt that the State School Teachers Union of Western Australia (SSTUWA) interpreted the release of *Better Schools* in a very much less favourable light. Cheaper Schools or Bitter Schools is what it was more commonly referred to by then President of the Teachers Union, Jeff Bateman. Bateman confirms that there was little consultation: 'I was actually on leave. I found out when I read the *West Australian* and what I found out was that the education system had been turned on its head' (Bateman, 7/11/89).

Bateman's views of the Report and what he saw as its industrial implications were extremely negative. In his Presidential Address to the 1989 Conference he said:

As I see it, part of the broader government/employer agenda is devolution of power. The *Better Schools* proposals fit within this context. Delegates would be well aware that there are presently people in positions of power and influence, they don't all belong to the New Right who are very keen to promote decentralisation of decision-making on wages and working conditions, and to reduce industrial relations to the enterprise level so that negotiations are limited to specific employers and specific groups of employees. This then limits the capacity for arbitration groups or unions to intervene . . . .

The Government/Ministry restructuring proposals confirm this. They too are about deregulation. You don't have to be Einstein to realise that decentralisation of labour relations will strengthen the hand of the employer over employee. Unions will become increasingly irrelevant. Sweeping decentralisation of educational decision-making will have similar reactionary implications for schools and teachers. And in this context the establishment of school-based community decision-making groups are the linchpin to the revolution (although I prefer to call it abrogation of responsibility) of power and influence by the government to these groups. (Bateman, Presidential Address, 1989)

Aside from the industrial issues Bateman was also concerned that the educational/political atmosphere created around *Better Schools* was unsettling to teachers and creating unnecessary insecurity:

I don't know what [some senior Education Ministry officers] do except go around and stir up a lot of trouble. It is disturbing, [they] get out there and float ideas with teachers . . . and say, 'What do you think about this idea of opening up your positions so people from the public service and private industry can apply as well?' I suppose teachers are like most people, suddenly they get this sense of insecurity and phones start ringing here and we get letters coming in . . . . It's all of this 'off the top' thinking and people feel pretty insecure particularly with all the change going on around them, to have all these other fairly radical proposals. (Bateman, 7/11/89)

Max Angus, a senior Education Ministry official, makes the point that in terms of devolution in education, the *Better Schools* reforms were a case of 'the second time around' in that school-based devolution had been previously pushed through the Schools Commission from 1973 on. At that time the arguments were educational and democratic, based on the belief that responsibility for teaching and learning lay best with those carrying out the work. Angus points out that the newer imperative of governments is to find ways to get better value from increasingly scarce revenue.

Angus argues that:

In the Western Australian case the origins [of devolution] are found in the drive to reform the public sector management with its focus on efficiency and the better use of existing resources. The language used to describe the devolution machinery and the restructuring has the ring of corporate managerialism (audit, performance appraisal, corporate plan, performance indicators and so on). However, it would be inaccurate to describe *Better Schools* as a straightforward example of economic rationalism. Incorporated in the *Better Schools* ideology is the belief that quality of education will improve when the responsibility for problem solving is shifted from the central bureaucracy to the school or individual. The assumption that school improvement can be better achieved through local control is the under-exposed side of the *Better Schools* reforms. (Angus, 1990, p. 7)

In the process of devolution, one of the groups which particularly lost out and about which there was much controversy, were the middle managers who inhabited regional offices, and in the secondary area subject offices, the superintendents. They comprised a third tier in the organization of the WA Education Department, but after 1987 regions were disbanded in favour of districts, the number of officers was reduced, the subject superintendents were eliminated, and all superintendents' roles were changed so as to clearly attach them to the central office, leaving all other personnel in both schools and district offices to belong to the schools. Devolution meant that there should be a small central office and schools, with as little organizational structure between them as possible.

For many teachers in the old system, the Superintendent *was* the Education Department. He (as they nearly all were) was the contact that connected farflung schools to Perth. Former Director-General Vickery is of the view that 'almost all innovation in government schools . . . in the last thirty years has come from the superintendency' in terms of new curriculum, facilities, staffing patterns. However, he also points out that while that means the superintendents were worthwhile, it 'also says that the capacity and expectation that [innovation] should be done at the school level has been overridden by the expectation that the superintendents will do it' (Vickery, 1/11/89). A Functional Review Committee member also pointed out that, previously, 'the superintendency actually ran the department and they ran it very well, particularly the subject superintendents, they were the backbone of the department. Unfortunately because they were the backbone they're the thing that you had to break if you wanted a new system to be brought in. If you want self-determining schools, you've got to take away the thing that's stopping them from being self-determining' (Functional Review Committee Member, 4/11/89).

In his study of the WA superintendency, Chadbourne points out that the old regional offices and superintendents 'limited the scope of the schools to respond to the needs of their communities and they restricted the capacity of Central Office to respond to the needs of schools. Their removal was intended to rectify this situation and increase the power of the schools and the centre' (Chadbourne, 1990, p. 8). Because it was superintendents and not principals who did things like assessing teachers and evaluating school programs, whole school needs could not be considered by the people most concerned with them at the level where it mattered.

Chadbourne argues that the new superintendency still has a very important role to play, albeit different from its pre-1987 one. He suggests that the superintendency is not needed for planning, for organizing or even for leading, but rather it is needed in the restructured system for quality control. He sees the prime importance of the role of superintendents as being 'agents of excellence' as well as 'agents of equity'. Without some form of central regulation, self-determining schools could pursue self interest to the detriment of the public education system as a whole. In other words the way to limit inappropriate deregulation is to build into the system a strong central control function that monitors both equity and quality:

> It might seem that assigning superintendents predominately to the area of control devalues their role, given the negative stereotypes surrounding the notion of 'control'. The reality is quite different. The type of control which superintendents exercise is an integral part of a broader challenge, namely; to bring into balance the conditions for excellence, enterprise and economic growth on the one hand, with the conditions for equality of opportunity, participation and social worth on the other. It is difficult to think of a role more demanding, or more important. (Chadbourne, 1990, p. 85)

Implementation of the restructuring is continuing in WA, a reminder of the length of time that change takes. By 1990, the major features of implementation included the following: a significant restructuring of central and district offices although not as great a reduction as intended; the passage of legislation enabling school-based decision-making groups to operate; the issuance of school development plan guidelines and work by many schools on theirs; the consolidation of school funding into a single grant with phasing in; the slow development of the superintendents' role as an auditing agent due to the fact that the means of accounting for schools' performance have not yet been developed; the withdrawal by the government of the notion of local staff selection due to strong Teachers Union opposition (there was a major teachers' strike in 1989 which focused on *Better Schools* reforms and especially local hiring) (Angus, 1990, p. 10).

Increasingly, schooling reform has been caught up in the award restructuring process that is presently pervasive in Australia. This process has the possible advantage of being able to negotiate features of educational reform which might previously be thought of as *outside* the industrial arena *into* the industrial arena through the tripartite involvement of employers, unions and the federal government (c.f. Angus, 1991). For example, this was done in WA in the agreement between the Ministry of Education and the SSTUWA on the 'Structural Efficiency Principle — Second Instalment for Government School Teachers' (Western Australian Ministry of Education, 1990). This agreement increased salaries, reflecting changed responsibilities flowing from devolution of central office functions to the school level, and created Advanced Skills Teachers. In the agreement both parties also committed themselves to the following objectives for award restructuring:

- quality education for students which will be enhanced by retaining and attracting high quality teachers who have opportunities to develop their skills;
- increased flexibility in the use of resources both within the system as a whole and within the school;
- the promotion of high quality working life for teachers by providing access to more varied, fulfilling and better paid jobs;

- increased accountability to the community through improved planning and decision-making processes at the school level (Memorandum of Agreement, 1990, pp. 1–2).

Some of the problems in hitching educational restructuring and reform to award restructuring have been discussed by the authors elsewhere (Knight, Lingard, Porter, 1991).

Discussion and Conclusion

Thus by 1991 the major outcome of the Beazley Report (1984), the development of Unit Curriculum, is well down the track in its implementation, albeit in a significantly altered form given the distance of the idea — well supported at its inception — from the realities of schools. One is reminded of McLaughlin's nuanced and descriptive concept of 'mutual adaptation' to illustrate the process of the implementation of educational innovations (McLaughlin, 1987). Elsewhere, she has made the related point that policy is never simply 'installed', rather implementation always involves contestation (McLaughlin, 1985, p. 100).

The *Better Schools* reforms (1987), despite the hostility originally shown, are also still on the agenda, although again with some very significant changes and adjustments. A change in the leadership of the Teachers' Union, several changes in education Ministers, the redeployment of many of the original senior Education Ministry officials, including a new Chief Executive Officer (the first woman), the early retirement of many middle management level education officers (superintendents and principals), and the adaptation of many of the first versions of proposals have all contributed to movement towards the central objectives of the *Better Schools* reforms. In this case, however, given the manner of its introduction and the misunderstanding engendered, considerable bitterness is still prevalent.

In the meantime, other nationally driven changes have also been ascendant, some of which are actually in direct contradiction to many of the reforms that have been introduced and implemented in Western Australia and in most other Australian states. These have to do with the role of the federal government and its push to use education and training as a microeconomic tool to gear up the Australian economy so as to have a competitive edge in the international arena. These changes have as their theme a national focus: national curriculum frameworks, national assessment, national registration of teachers, portability of qualifications, preferred models of teacher education, national competency based standards and so on. They form part of the broader attempt to restructure Australian Federalism (Lingard, 1991) and to create a national economic infrastructure which, it is claimed, will enable Australia to compete in a non-tariff protected fashion in the global economy.

The centre-periphery dilemma emerging for schooling policy was well stated by Carmen Lawrence then Education Minister and now Premier of WA:

My view is that if we're serious in saying to schools at State level, 'Look we really want you to respond to your particular and unique community', we can't also say, 'and this is how you'll do it'. (Lawrence, 16/11/89)

In our view there appears to be some sense in the development of broad national curriculum frameworks, provided they allow for a significant degree of experimentation and diversity rather than bland uniformity. There is also sense in the portability of teacher qualifications and national registration, provided it is based on maximums rather than minimums and the lowest common denominator does not dominate. However, there seems to be little good sense in the move towards national assessment primarily because of the possibility of delimiting schooling goals to a narrow and minimal set of competencies. Nor is there any justification in the imposition of one model of teacher education without any evidence whatsoever that one model would suit all learners, all teachers, and all contexts (Knight, Lingard, Bartlett, 1991).

Following on from Lawrence, there are a number of points we would wish to make in relation to devolution in school systems. If one believes in devolution in education for participatory and democratic reasons, that is one argument, even if it is one subsumed at the moment by Labor governments' 'efficient state' response to economic hard times. The democratic rationale has usually been accompanied by an argument that more local control and recognition of teacher professionalism will ensure better learning outcomes for students. But even if one accepts the corporatist approach and believes in responsive bureaucracies that attend to their clients through administrative devolution, then national goals, except in the very broadest form, are not likely to be achievable. How is it possible for decision-making power in any meaningful sense to be pushed down to the schools while being geared up to the national economy at the same time? While theoretically one could propose national objectives to be pursued by schools across Australia, that vision, in our view, is unrealizable. It ignores local needs, community concerns, teacher abilities and interest, student abilities and interest. In a word, it ignores people, whether they are constructed as citizens or consumers. In a sense, whatever the *raison d'etre* for devolution, once teachers and school communities have gained some autonomy, they will not readily relinquish it. It is likely to prove difficult to put the devolution tiger back in the bag.

Aside from democratic imperatives, one of the educational and managerial reasons why devolution in schooling has been promoted has to do with the well known results of the studies of the implementation of social programs in the sixties and seventies, which showed so clearly how top-down reforms were always resisted, sabotaged, coopted, adapted, adjusted, pursued maniacally, played with, made fun of, or in general significantly altered at every level in their implementation. People at all levels of the system are able to modify centrally determined policies. This is particularly the case where policies are implemented by professionals. Similarly, parents and other community members will adapt policies to their own needs. As Elmore (1985, p. 37) puts it, the success or failure of policy depends on the relationship between players at all levels in the implementation process. It is blatantly not possible to create a teacher-proof, curriculum-proof, assessment-proof, student-proof and community-proof education system, though governments never seem to give up trying. Everything we know and keep discovering and rediscovering about the process of change makes this obvious. (See Chadbourne, 1991, for a discussion of the barriers to implementation of *Better Schools* at the school level.) Nevertheless, such national developments are presently being overlaid upon a decade of prior educational reform in Western

Australia. In this context it is not difficult to identify with teacher disaffection with the plethora of policy changes with which they have had to cope.

However, given this recognition of the power of teachers in policy implementation, there is still the difficult policy consideration of how one achieves desirable common equity goals within such an arrangement. In Australia, traditionally, equity has been defined as uniformity of provision as dictated by the centre. This is no longer appropriate. A major policy dilemma at present concerns the desirable balance between centrally determined uniformity and peripherally created difference. Indeed, in relation to equity the current core problem of educational administration appears to be allowing for diversity at the school level, while simultaneously ensuring the achievement of social justice goals. There are a number of mechanisms for achieving this, such as: the New Zealand approach of legally requiring equity goals to be built into school charters; the requirement of a demonstrable commitment to equity for the purposes of promotion; the building in of such objectives in school development plans; and the assignment of specific roles in monitoring equity to specific people such as superintendents.

Aside from all of these policy considerations, there is also the reality that more not less is being expected of the education system, schools and teachers at the same moment as available resources are shrinking. Optimal implementation of the WA educational restructuring would also require more, not fewer resources, including the adequate provision of inservice education for principals, teachers, parents, departmental officials and teacher educators, as well as adequate infrastructural support. The shrinking resources stem, in this case, from the poor economic management of WA and the more parlous economic circumstances facing Australia. It is these economic realities, of course, which have seen the development of Labor's efficient state strategy which is the context of the educational policy developments outlined in this research. The internationalization of the economy is the other contributing factor to this efficient state strategy.

In terms of our original questions for consideration in this case-study of educational reform in WA, where are we now? When the relevant educational reports are analysed, it is apparent that they appear to be pulled in somewhat different directions by different dominant Labor perspectives at the time, for example, the conception of education within Beazley is more characteristic of the pluralistic politics of consumption, while the conception of education within *Better Schools* is more closely in line with the politics of production. Nevertheless, it is apparent from the mixed perceptions of people involved, that the Reports can be understood at one and the same time from different frameworks. It is not only the eye, but the position of the beholder which is relevant. What is the solution offered to the prevalent economic constraints? Beazley looks to Canberra as has been traditional. *Better Schools* bites the bullet and proposes moving the efficient state into the public education sphere. While some perceive the move as pushing towards complete deregulation and privatization, there is little doubt that in comparison with Thatcherite, and now Major policies in the UK or similar policies in New Zealand, *Better Schools* has a long way to go, to be fully characterized in that fashion. In the Australian context, deregulation has its strongest hold in the central public school departments such as Treasury, while a social democratic residue remains in service departments such as Education (Pusey, 1991). What about the approach to devolution? Devolution is a theme in both Beazley and *Better Schools*. In Beazley it is tied more to traditional Labor notions of progressive democratic participation, although other agendas are foreshadowed. *Better Schools* is more clearly within the corporate managerialist mode of devolution conceived as a strategy for better achieving efficiency and effectiveness in education. Yet it is seen as building upon Beazley, and participants use the language of democracy as much as that of economic rationalism. What is the mediation of equity and social justice? Equity and social justice are up front as central features of Beazley, while rather vague assumptions in *Better Schools*. Nevertheless, they still feature as primary concerns for those significant policy players interviewed in this study of implementation. It is clear, though, that the managerialist revolution in the public sector aimed at achieving greater efficiency and effectiveness, has reframed the equity agenda in a narrowed fashion (Yeatman, 1990).

Overall, this case study of educational reform in WA over an eight-year period of Labor governments shows the development of Laborist perspectives and the interaction of both the liberal/progressive agenda and the efficient corporate state agenda. In a sense, while one dominates the other at different times, elements of both are always present. Of course, ongoing financial constraints will probably mean, for Labor, the continuing pursuit of the efficient corporate state strategy. Whether either will be able to live so compatibly with the newer national microeconomic and corporate federalist reform agendas, as well as international economic pressures, remains to be seen. However, the efficient corporate state approach appears more compatible with such pressures. With more conservative governments, there is the very real possibility of a further step down the deregulation/privatization track and a related weakening of the equity commitment.

A concluding point that must be made, however, is that teacher ideology appears to be bifurcated around either liberal/progressive perspectives on one hand or culturally conservative perspectives on the other, both of which sit in opposition to either the efficient state or privatization approaches. These teacher perspectives seem to be more congruent with the nature of teachers' work, their interaction in the teaching/learning process with students and their knowledge base. Put another way, there is an incommensurability between the realities of teachers and students in classrooms and the imperatives of policy makers. This is a point that has been made by one Western Australian teacher recently when she commented that in 1991, five years after the introduction of *Better Schools*, few teachers at the school level were aware of the existence of the restructuring proposals. Those that were aware, were those applying for promotion (Western Australian Ministry of Education, 1991). Policy implementation always involves an interaction process between policymaking through to implementation (McLaughlin, 1987). National or international educational policymakers will need to be as aware of that reality as policymakers in WA are becoming. The next stage on research on WA educational reforms clearly needs to focus on implementation, particularly at the school and classroom level.

References

ANGUS, M.J. (1990) 'Making better schools: Devolution the second time around', paper presented to the Annual Meeting of the American Education Research Association, Boston, MA, April, pp. 1–25.

ANGUS, M.M. (1991) 'Award restructuring: The new paradigm for school reform', *Unicorn*, **17**, 2, May, pp. 78–84.

ANGUS, M.J., BROWN, S.K., McGAW, B. and ROBSON, G. (1983) *Setting Standards for School Resources: The Contribution of Research*, Target Recurrent Resource Standards Study, Discussion Paper No. 2. Canberra, Australia: Commonwealth Schools Commission. pp. 1–107.

BATEMAN, J. (1989) President, State School Teachers Union of Western Australia (SSTUWA), 1986–89, Interview, Nov. 7. Perth, Australia.

BATEMAN, J. (1989) 'Presidential address', address to the 1989 SSTUWA Annual Conference, Perth, August, 1989.

BEAZLEY, K.E. (1984) *Education in Western Australia*, report of the Committee of Inquiry, K.E. BEAZLEY (Chairperson), Perth, Australia: W.A. Government Printer. pp. 1–415.

BEILHARZ, P. (1987) 'Reading politics: Social theory and social policy', *The Australian and New Zealand Journal of Sociology*, **23**, 3. pp. 388–406.

BURKE, B. (1986) *Managing Change in the Public Sector, A Statement of the Government's Position*, a Parliamentary White Paper Presented by the Hon. Brian Burke, MLA, Premier of Western Australia, Perth, Australia: W.A. Government Printer. pp. 1–23.

BURTON, P. and CARLEN, F. (1977) 'Official discourse', *Economy and Society* **6**, 4, pp. 377–407.

CASTLES, F. (1988) *Australian Public Policy and Economic Vulnerability*, Sydney, Australia: Allen and Unwin.

CAWSON, A. (1982) *Corporatism and Welfare: Social Policy and State Intervention in Britain*, London, UK: Heinemann.

CAWSON, A. and SAUNDERS, P. (1983) 'Corporatism, competitive politics and class struggle', in KING, R. (Ed.), *Capital and Politics*, London, UK: Routledge and Kegan Paul, pp. 8–28.

CENRY, P. (1990) *The Changing Architecture of Politics: Structure, Agency and the Future of the State* London, UK: Sage.

CHADBOURNE, R. (1990) *Issues Facing and Shaping the Role of District Superintendents during a Period of Radical Change*, International Institute for Policy and Administrative Studies, Perth, Australia: W.A.C.A.E. (now Edith Cowan University), pp. 1–107.

CHABOURNE, R. (1991) *Managing Change in Schools: A Review of the Western Australian Project*, International Institute for Policy and Administrative Studies, Perth, Australia: Edith Cowan University, pp. 1–71.

CLEGG, S., BOREHAM, P. and DOW, G. (1986) *Class, Politics and the Economy*, London, UK: Routledge and Kegan Paul.

CONNELL, R.W. (1990) 'The state, gender and sexual politics', in *Theory and Society*, **19**, pp. 507–44.

CONSIDINE, M. (1988) 'The corporate management framework as administrative science: A critique', *Australian Journal of Public Administration*, **47**, pp. 4–19.

CONSIDINE, M. (1990) 'Administrative reform "Down-under": Recent public sector change in Australia and New Zealand,' *International Review of Administrative Science*, **56**, pp. 171–84.

DALE, R. and OZGA, J. (1992) '1980s education reform in New Zealand and England and Wales: Two hemispheres, both "New Right"?' in LINGARD, R., KNIGHT, J. and PORTER, P. (Eds) *Schooling Reform in Hard Times*, London, UK: Falmer Press.

EDUCATION DEPARTMENT WESTERN AUSTRALIA (1981) *Annual Report 1980*.

EDUCATION DEPARTMENT WESTERN AUSTRALIA (1982) *Annual Report 1981*.

EDUCATION DEPARTMENT WESTERN AUSTRALIA (1983) *Annual Report 1982*.

EDUCATION DEPARTMENT WESTERN AUSTRALIA (1984) *Annual Report 1983*.

EDUCATION DEPARTMENT WESTERN AUSTRALIA (1985) *Annual Report 1984*.

EDUCATION DEPARTMENT WESTERN AUSTRALIA (1986) *Annual Report 1985*.

EDUCATION DEPARTMENT WESTERN AUSTRALIA (1987) *Annual Report 1986.*

EDUCATION DEPARTMENT WESTERN AUSTRALIA (1987) *Annual Report 1986–87.*

EDUCATION DEPARTMENT WESTERN AUSTRALIA (1989) *Annual Report 1988–89.*

EDUCATION DEPARTMENT WESTERN AUSTRALIA (1988) *Annual Report 1987–88.*

EISENSTEIN, H. (1991) *Gender Shock: Practising Feminism on Two Continents,* Sydney, Australia: Allen and Unwin.

ELMORE, R.F. (1985) 'Forward and backward mapping: Reversible logic in the analysis of public policy', in HANF, K. and TOONEN, T.A.J. (Eds) *Policy Implementation in Federal and Unitary Systems,* Dordrecht, Netherlands: Martinus Nijhoff.

EVATT RESEARCH CENTRE (1989) 'Western Australia', in *State of Siege: Renewal or Privatisation for Australian State Public Services?,* Sydney, Australia: Evatt Foundation/ Pluto Press, pp. 311–68.

FINN, B. (1991) *Young People's Participation in Post-compulsory Education and Training,* Report of the Australian Education Council Review Committee, Brian Finn (Chairperson), Canberra, Australia: AGPS, pp. 1–188.

FRANZWAY, S., COURT, D. and CONNELL, R.W. (1989) *Staking a Claim: Feminism, Bureaucracy and the State,* Sydney, Australia: Allen and Unwin.

FUNCTIONAL REVIEW OF WESTERN AUSTRALIAN EDUCATION DEPARTMENT (1989) Interviews with Committee Members. Nov. 1–16, Perth, Australia.

HAM, C. and HILL, M. (1984) *The Policy Process in the Modern Capitalist State,* Brighton, UK: Wheatsheaf.

HARMAN, L. (1991) Report, *The Australian,* 9 May.

HENRY, M. and TAYLOR, S. (1989) 'On the agenda at last? Recent developments in educational policy relating to women and girls', in TAYLOR, S. and HENRY, M. (Eds) *Battlers and Bluestockings, Australia: Women's Places in Australian Education,* Canberra, Australia: ACE, pp. 101–9.

HODGE, R. and KRESS, G. (1988) *Social Semiotics,* Cambridge, UK: Polity Press.

KNIGHT, J., LINGARD, R. and BARTLETT, L. (1991) 'Re-forming teacher education: The shape of current developments', Unpublished paper, University of Queensland, Australia.

KNIGHT, J., LINGARD, R. and PORTER, P. (1991) 'Re-forming the Education Industry through award restructuring and the New Federalism?', *Unicorn,* **17,** 3, pp. 133–38.

LAWRENCE, C., THE HON., MLA, PREMIER, WESTERN AUSTRALIA (1989) Interview, Perth, Australia.

LINDBERG, L.N., ALFORD, R., CROUCH, C. and OFFE, C. (Eds) (1975) *Stress and Contradiction in Modern Capitalism,* Lexington, MA: D.C. Heath.

LINGARD, R. (1991) 'Policy-making for Australian schooling: The new corporate federalism', *Journal of Education Policy,* **6,** 1, pp. 85–90.

LINGARD, R. and COLLINS, C. (1991) 'Radical reform or rationalisation? Education under Goss Labor in Queensland', *Discourse,* **11,** 2, pp. 98–114.

McGAW, B. (1984) *Assessment in the Upper Secondary School in Western Australia,* report of the ministerial working party on school certification and tertiary admissions procedures, Barry McGaw (Chairperson).

McLAUGHLIN, M.W. (1987) 'Learning from Experience: Lessons from Policy Implementation', *Educational Evaluation and Policy Analysis,* **9,** pp. 171–78.

McLAUGHLIN, M.W. (1985) 'Implementation realities and evaluation design', in SHOTLAND, R.L. and MARK, M.M. (Eds), *Social Science and Social Policy,* London, UK: Sage.

MEMORANDUM OF AGREEMENT BETWEEN MINISTRY OF EDUCATION AND STATE SCHOOL TEACHERS' UNION OF WESTERN AUSTRALIA (1990) (Structural Efficiency Principle— Second Instalment Government School Teachers), Perth, Australia, 4 April.

OFFE, C. (1975) 'The theory of the capitalist state and the problem of policy formation', in LINDBERG, N., ALFORD, R., CROUCH, C. and OFFE, C. (Eds) *Stress and Contradiction in Modern Capitalism*, Lexington, MA: D.C. Heath, pp. 125–44.

OFFE, C. (1984) *Contradictions of the Welfare State*, London, UK: Hutchinson.

OFFE, C. (1985) *Disorganised Capitalism: Contemporary Transformations of Work and Politics*, Cambridge, UK: Polity Press.

PEARCE, R.J. (1987) *Better Schools in Western Australia: A Programme for Improvement*, presented by the Hon. R.J. Pearce, MLA, Minister for Education. Perth, Australia: Ministry of Education, pp. 1–25.

PEARCE, R.J. THE HON., MLA (1989) Interview, Nov. 1. Perth, Australia.

PIERSON, C. (1986) *Marxist Theory and Democratic Politics*, Cambridge, UK: Polity Press.

PUSEY, M. (1988) 'State and polity', in NAJMAN, J. and WESTERN, J. (Eds), *A Sociology of Australian Society: Introductory Readings*, Melbourne, Australia: Macmillan, pp. 22–49.

PUSEY, M. (1991) *Economic Rationalism in Canberra: A Nation Building State Changes its Mind*, Cambridge, UK: Cambridge University Press.

ROSECRANCE, R. (1964) 'The radical culture of Australia', in HARTZ, L. (Ed.), *The Founding of New Societies*, New York, NY: Harcourt, Brace and World. pp. 275–318.

SCHON, D. (1979) 'Generative Metaplor: A perspective on problem setting in social policy', in A. ORTONY (Ed.) *Metaphor and Thought*, Cambridge, UK: Cambridge University Press, pp. 254–83.

SMART, D. and ALDERSON, A.C. (1980) *The Politics of Education in Western Australia: An Exploratory Study of State Education Department Policy-Making*, Centre for the Study of Higher Education, Parkville, Melbourne, Australia: University of Melbourne, pp. 1–123.

THOMPSON, J.B. (1984) *Studies in the Theory of Ideology*, Cambridge, UK: Polity Press.

VICKERY, R. DIRECTOR-GENERAL OF EDUCATION, 1982–1986 (1989) Interview, Nov. 6, Perth, Australia.

WATKINS, P. (1988) 'Regional boards of education: Mediating links between social investment and social consumption', *British Journal of Sociology of Education*, 9, 4. pp. 453–72.

WESTERN AUSTRALIAN MINISTRY OF EDUCATION (1991) Interview with teacher, October, Perth, Australia.

WESTERN AUSTRALIAN MINISTRY OF EDUCATION (1990) 'Structural efficiency principle — second instalment for government school teachers', April.

WESTERN AUSTRALIAN MINISTRY OF EDUCATION (1989) Interviews with Senior Ministry Officers, Nov. 1–16, Perth, Australia.

WESTERN AUSTRALIAN GOVERNMENT (1987) *Financial Administration and Audit Act of Western Australia*, Perth, Australia: WA Government Printer.

WILENSKI, P. (1986) *Public Power and Public Administration*, Sydney, Australia: Hale and Iremonger.

WOLFE, A. (1977) *The Limits of Legitimacy*, New York, NY: The Free Press.

YEATMAN, A. (1990) *Bureaucrats, Technocrats, Femocrats: Essays on the Contemporary Australian State*, Sydney, Australia: Allen and Unwin.

Chapter 14

Picot — Vision and Reality in New Zealand Schools: An Insider's View[1]

Peter D.K. Ramsay

Introduction

Why is it that one particular statement appears rather than another? Why is more importance attached to some discourses than to others? These questions, posed by Foucault (1980) have more than passing relevance for anyone interested in analyzing the world-wide restructuring of educational administration. They are of particular interest to an insider (i.e., a person involved on the committee established to recommend policy on restructuring) whose own discourses were often oppositional to those being put forward as representing the mainstream. The tale which I will unfold in this chapter is one of contestation, of negotiation, of competing powers, and finally, of compromise. It is a story which demonstrates the power of history and tradition, but also how that power can be challenged and how *the status quo* may be changed.

In describing the restructuring of education and administration in New Zealand (which is sometimes held to be the most radical of any of the changes in the western world) I will begin by recounting the historical background to, and the context of the change. Some time will then be spent on noting the role of two major non-educational agencies which have been heavily involved in educational policy-making in New Zealand: the State Services Commission and the New Zealand Treasury. The next section will contain a brief account of the main features of the report of the Task Force in Educational Administration, *Administering for Excellence* (NZ Department of Education, 1988), referred to hereafter as the Picot Report. Some indication of the fury of the aftermath is then given as I trace the implementation of some of the Picot ideas. A section, based mainly on two research projects, one complete and one still under way, of the major gains and losses, follows. (These projects are the Curriculum Research Review in Schools Project [CRRISP], which I directed, and the Monitoring Today's Schools Project [MTS], a piece of research being carried out cooperatively by fifteen researchers, coordinated by David Mitchell at the University of Waikato.) The chapter concludes with some suggestions as to what is needed at present if the dreams and aspirations of the Picot Committee are to be realized.

Part 1: The Process

Some History and Context

Deal (1990) has argued that we need to look to the past in order to frame the future. The members of the Picot Committee did just that. Several of the members of the committee were familiar with the many attempts that had been made to restructure the education administrative system since the Atmore Report (NZ Department of Education, 1930). The other members of the committee were rapidly brought up-to-date on those proposals via a series of papers and discussions led by the secretary to the committee, Maurice Gianotti. The committee as a whole were, therefore, very aware of the many attempts that had been made over a number of years to change some of the features of the educational administrative system.

Recently, Barrington (1990) has noted the extent of agreement between a number of the Picot recommendations and those of groups which preceded it, for example, the McCoombs Report (NZ Department of Education, 1976), the Nordmeyer Report (Nordmeyer, *et al.*, 1974), and the Curriculum Review Report (NZ Department of Education 1987). As Barrington (1990) noted, these reports recommended, *inter alia*, greater decentralization of decision-making, the bulk funding of grants to school, the opportunity for primary school committees to participate in the appointments of principals and other staffs, the abolition of the Education Boards which governed primary education, etc. It is important to make these points early in this chapter as much of the criticism that has arisen stems from a belief that the New Zealand educational system was being taken over by the New Right. I will shortly relate the efforts made by Treasury in particular to impose its will on educational matters. However, Barrington's argument is accurate, inasmuch that many of the changes recommended by Picot reflected a direction indicated by earlier reports in New Zealand education.

The Picot Report came at a time when schools were under considerable attack. Prior to the 1987 election, the opposition party had uncovered a high level of discontent with the provision of education in New Zealand. In particular the administrative structure was heavily and publicly criticized. It was claimed that teachers had obtained control of the school system through infiltration of the Department of Education and that they were the prime policy-makers within the system itself. Teachers controlled the curriculum (although within given, clearly understood parameters of 'safe knowledge'; see Ramsay, 1985). Moreover, the dominant elite of largely white, male and affluent New Zealanders were the most influential group in New Zealand schools. Challenges to the system came not only from the so-called New Right as represented by Treasury and the Business Roundtable, but the near hegemonic conditions were being contested by women and Maori groups.

This, then, was the context within which the Picot Committee began its considerations in July 1987. It is also worth noting that following Labour's success at the polls, the Prime Minister, the Right Honourable David Lange, surprised the nation by taking on the portfolio of education himself. This was a signal of the importance the Labour government was to attach to educational restructuring over the next few years.

The Role of Non-Educational Organizations

In New Zealand, as elsewhere (Western Australia provides a very interesting parallel study) the State Services commission had advised Government on the restructuring of Government departments. Their expressed view, which had considerable public support, was that the central government agencies were too large, were not providing appropriate policy advice to their Ministers and they were not implementing the policies of Government quickly or effectively enough. The drive, which came from the State Services Commission, was towards the development of smaller, more efficient central units and devolution of decision-making to regional agencies. The impact of the State Services Commission on education came through its desire to restructure the Education Department. They argued in their submissions to the Picot Committee that this agency had grown far too much in size and was not adequately responding to changes in other sectors of the Government. The educational reforms, therefore, became caught up in the overall public sector reform as enunciated in the *State Services Sector Act*. This enactment focused on outputs and outcomes rather than inputs. Its primary goals were for better delivery of services, more effective and efficient provision of equity, greater participation by the people concerned with the Government agencies' function and a devolution of some authority to local sources. The State Services Commission itself became enshrined as a key government agency, responsible for negotiations on a whole range of matters including salaries and conditions of service of teachers.

As in Western Australia, the restructuring of the public sector was on a corporate model with the cabinet and ministers setting broad policy goals but the State Departments advising and overseeing its implementation. The policy delivery was to be by decentralized agencies, and accountability was to be established through performance agreements, reviews and regular audits with, again, the State Services Commission playing a major role.

The State Services Commission position was similar to that of Treasury, although the officials within the latter department went further in advising Government on educational policy. In 1987 Treasury's produced a set of briefing papers for the incoming Labour Government. Fundamental to Treasury's argument was the issue of whether education is for the public good or whether individuals gain an economic advantage from receiving education. The notion that education was for the public good had long been held in New Zealand and was premised on a concept of community schooling and a belief that it is necessary for the well-being of a nation for everybody to be educated to the fullest extent of their abilities and capabilities. In the well-known words of an earlier Labour Prime Minister:

> The Government's objective, broadly expressed, is that every person, whatever his [sic] level of academic ability, whether he be rich or poor, whether he live in town or country, has a right, as a citizen, to a free education of the kind for which he is best fitted and to fullest extent of his powers. (Fraser, 1939, cited in the Currie Report, NZ Department of Education, 1962, p. 11)

The alternative view, which sees individuals gaining an economic advantage from education, is based on the assumption that education is a product consumed by individuals and that those individuals who consume the most will benefit the most. Education thus becomes a personal investment. It follows in this line of argument, that individuals should pay according to the amount of education received. The outgrowth of this is either a voucher system or, worse still, complete privatization of the school system with the user paying for the goods he or she receives.

There is no question that Treasury supported the user-pays, free market philosophy in education. It is somewhat ironic that they based many of their criticisms on research carried out by writers who ideologically were well to the left of the centre (e.g., Codd, Harker and Nash, 1985). All of these writers agreed that all was not well with New Zealand schooling, particularly in areas of equality of opportunity. The Treasury Officials, in citing the research and commentaries, came to the conclusion that Government was not receiving value for money. They then made a quantum leap and suggested that rather than the State paying more for the provision of education, those who consumed education should pay for it. They argued further that the school system should be made much more accountable, that results of outcomes of learning in individual schools should be published regularly, and that parents should be allowed free and unlimited choice as to which schools they sent their children. Under this model it was expected that good schools would flourish with large numbers of students and that bad schools would wither away and eventually die.

When the Picot Committee began its sittings, then, the positions of two powerful Government agencies were well known and were being discussed widely. Officials from both agencies sat with the Picot Committee throughout its sessions. Their papers were the first to be tabled, and the officials offered to write sections of the report for and on behalf of the committee. The scene was thus set for contestation.

Administering For Excellence: The Picot Report

The Picot Committee sat for approximately twelve months. It heard a large range of submissions and was guided by a number of professional consultancies. Background reading was provided with illustrations from a number of overseas states as well as theoretical literature and research. It became evident to the committee that many groups and individuals were dissatisfied with the present system. Submission after submission pointed out that the system was cumbersome, that decision-making was slow, that professional groups seemed to have achieved the high ground in terms of critical resource and curriculum decisions and that the system, to use the Treasury jargon, was 'non-transparent'. For newcomers, it was said, the system was so confusing that many gave up before they really got started. Moreover, it became apparent that it was a mistake to speak of the old system of administration as one system. Indeed, there were at least four systems each serving a different sector of education, with some overlap of function but, for the most part, highly confusing for those people who had tried to work their way through the labyrinths of educational decision-making. The systems, as we saw them in 1988, were the result of over one hundred years of minor meddling. All earlier attempts to substantially reform the system had failed, mainly as a result of the powerful lobby of the teacher unions and the Education Boards.

Faced with these comments, the Picot Committee suggested a very bold approach to educational administrative decision-making in New Zealand. From the outset, the committee rejected the notion of user-pays and/or vouchers. To quote:

> . . . we have worked on the assumption that the State will continue to be the principal funder of formal education, that education will remain compulsory for six to fifteen year olds and that the provisions of the Treaty of Waitangi will be observed . . . . Education should be fair and just for every learner regardless of their gender, and of their social, cultural or geographic circumstances. (NZ Department of Education, 1988, p. 3)

These underpinning assumptions are extremely important and give the lie, at least to some extent, of those who believe that the committee was driven solely by New Right ideas.

The Picot Committee was, in fact, dedicated to four major goals. First, they wished to create an administrative system that was more efficient and more responsive to those who used it. The committee borrowed computer terminology; they wanted an educational administrative structure that was 'user friendly'. To achieve this, they argued that the highly complex systems that existed needed to be simplified and that decision-making should be brought to a level as close as possible to those who were affected by the decisions. Second, part of the Picot Committee's brief was to consider devolution. In line with the point just made, the committee decided that they wanted to encourage greater local decision-making and argued a case for collaborative decision-making both within schools and between schools and community. This proposition was firmly entrenched in both New Zealand and overseas research.

Third, the Picot Committee, perhaps more so than any other group that has reported on educational matters in New Zealand, was committed to principles of equity and fairness. They considered points relating to discrimination in the school system on the basis of race, class and gender and argued that every school in New Zealand should be committed to fair approaches and to equitable distribution of resources. Fourth, and finally, the Picot committee, having considered the present structure, believed that efficiency savings could be made. This did not mean that educational expenditure should be cut. In fact, the Picot Committee pointed out that if savings could be made, then the money saved should be retained in the education system and placed where it would achieve the most benefit, that is, for children and students in classrooms and in lecture theatres. To quote once again from the report: 'Every learner should gain the maximum individual and social benefit from the money spent on education' (NZ Department of Education, 1988, p. 4).

These, then, were some of the goals and basic assumptions of the Picot Committee. The foundation of the report lay in educational partnership. It argued a case for a sharing of decision-making between teachers, parents, the community, and Government. The report writers saw the development of a school charter as the linchpin. While the charters were to be approved by the Minister of Education, there was, as Barrington (1990, p. 7) points out, a clear requirement that institutions should consult with their communities. In its original form (later to be changed by the Labour Government) the schools charter was to be a contract between, on the one hand, schools and the community, and on the other hand, schools and Government. The notion was that the teachers and the Board of Trustees, working together, should develop a charter collaboratively with their school community. Once worked through, the charter was to be agreed to by the Minister. Hence funding to fulfil the charter requirements would be the responsibility of the State. The significance of this point was not lost on a number of the commentators who saw it as being one of the most forward-looking provisions in the whole revision process. Unfortunately, the contractual arrangement, especially as it related to fiscal areas, was not lost on the Government of the day either! I comment further on this point below.

Grace (1990) has referred to the Picot Report and the various reports which followed as a 'complex compromise'. Grace is correct. The report, in fact, reflects the fierce, often acrimonious debate which occurred on the committee. Quite frequently the committee divided along the lines of the key interests of its members: the educationists, the business people and the Treasury and State Service Commission officials. These divisions are reflected in a number of tensions to be found within the report itself. I identify only a few here.

A prime example of the kinds of compromise reached by the committee is located in the area of inspection and accountability. All parties agreed that some kind of external monitoring of schools was both necessary any desirable. (The CRRISP research provides ample evidence of teachers' ability to be both myopic and self-delusory! It also demonstrates the value of external consultancies. See Ramsay, Harold, Hawk, Kaai, Marriott and Poskett, 1990.) It was agreed that complete devolution of responsibility in a small notion state like New Zealand was not appropriate. It was also agreed that in the area of negotiation of teachers' salaries, awards and conditions of service, the setting of national curriculum objectives, and the approval of school charters, central authorities had a major role to play. This also applied to the maintenance of national standards in schools. Traditionally, the inspectorate (who were employed by the central Department of Education but who were regionally based) had carried out this role.

Here, however, the Committee divided. The educationists on the Picot Committee, basing their assumptions on the research on effective schooling, argued that mere inspection was insufficient and that schools should be encouraged to systematically and regularly review their achievements and their failures. It was argued that this was an extremely complex task, given the differential nature of school populations and given the differing aspirations of some school communities. A simplistic output model, it was argued, was not sufficient. In order to encourage this kind of self review, it was suggested that a group of professionals, in co-operation with some of the client group, should, on a biennial basis, conduct school reviews. The prime intention for these reviews was educational. As the report states, 'The purpose of the review will be to help the institution assess its own progress towards achieving its objectives [as set out in its charter]' (NZ Department of Education, 1988, p. 60).

This view was not entirely shared by the officials who wanted clear and understandable accountability measures. There was a second part to the recommendations. The agency was to be known as the Review and *Audit* Agency. It was intended to provide, in addition to the purposes just stated, an independent audit of performance of schools in the public interest. Herein lies the tension: educational review on the one hand, audit in the interests of accountability on the other. A careful reading of pages 60 through 63 of the final report indicates in more detail the kind of tension arising from requiring an agency to perform both of these roles. On the one hand, it is clear that the reports produced by the review team, would be of considerable educational benefit. For example, the report states:

> The review team would . . . produce a report which identifies strengths and weaknesses in its administration and makes recommendations for improvements. The institution would have an opportunity to comment on the report and make changes in its teaching and management. (NZ Department of Education, 1988: 61)

It was envisaged that this report would result from a quite lengthy initial visit by a team of highly qualified professionals. One term later the team would return and a more detailed report on the basis of that review was to be published and made available to the public. In this way, less effective schools in which teachers and, indeed, the client group themselves, may be myopic about their performance, would be forced into a regular review situation. However, on the audit side, the report also suggests quite draconian measures for dealing with those schools who did not meet the required output levels. In fact, the committee recommended that trustees could be dismissed and a statutory manager be appointed it the review recommendations were not fulfilled. Thus, on the one hand, the report reflected the importance of an educational review conducted over substantial period of times but, on the other hand, also supported the rather more simple notion of an accountability audit, based on learning outcomes as measured by tests. The contradictions are obvious.

The tension within the Picot Committee and the kind of compromises reached are also reflected in the area of bulk funding. The treasury and State Services Commission were clear in their view that both teachers' salaries and operational grants should be bulk funded to schools. There was very little argument in the area of the operational grants, but the bulk funding of teachers' salaries aroused considerable debate between members of the committee. The business-people and officials in supporting bulk funding of salaries based their arguments on the fact that in excess of 70 per cent of all expenditure was in that area. If the newly formed Board of Trustees did not have authority over teachers' salaries as well as other areas of expenditure, then the possibilities of virement (transferring items from one financial account to another) would be severely limited. The supporters of bulk funding of teachers' salaries also argued that the Board of Trustees should have the right to establish the rate of teachers' pay and where teachers should start on a given salary scale. On the other hand, the educationists on the Picot Committee argued against the bulk funding of teachers' salaries on the grounds that there would be uneconomic and inefficient use of people's time if the physical payment of salaries was to be passed on to the local Board of Trustees. Secondly, they raised questions relating to the danger of Boards of Trustees getting into the act of setting teachers' salaries, especially in rural and small communities where, traditionally, close relationships existed between parent and teachers. In addition, it was argued that the Board of Trustees' potential involvement in the setting of teachers' salaries might act against equal partnership and the collaborative form of decision-making which underpinned much of the report.

The compromise arising from these arguments is one which still sits rather uncomfortably with the present writer. First, and perhaps most importantly, the Picot Committee agreed that teachers' salaries should be set nationally in the usual award and wage negotiation rounds. The committee did not see the Board of Trustees playing a role in these negotiations. Second, the Picot Committee suggested that the actual payment of teachers' salaries should be through a central pay unit. New Zealand is a small nation state with under 20,000 teachers. In a day and age of computers it seemed to make good sense that the payment of teachers' salaries should be centralized. So far so good, but the most problematic area for the committee related to the question of virement. The committee wanted to give Boards and staff of schools some flexibility in determining how their money should be spent. The compromise reached was a recommendation that schools could use one teacher's salary for purposes other than employing teachers. The committee was convinced that high quality teaching staff was the key to high quality educational provision and that to reduce the number of staff beyond plus or minus one of the national schedule would be dangerous.

Again the tensions can be seen here: on the one hand, a hands off approach to the bulk funding of teachers' salaries, but on the other hand, a desire to allow for some flexibility. The compromise reached was a very uneasy one indeed.

A further area of tension related to the amount of parental choice which should be allowed in the school system. The Treasury position has already been outlined and was based on the free market philosophy of consumers being permitted to select whichever school they so desired. This was a particularly fiercely debated area. The argument centred on the zoning of enrolments to particular school districts. Traditionally, New Zealand has had a system of enrolment at the nearest neighbourhood school. This particular condition was safeguarded by the Picot Committee. However, where places existed in schools outside of the neighbourhood school, the committee agreed that these could be filled to a maximum enrolment in line with that which prevailed prior to the restructuring. In order to ensure that some schools were not selected according to particular criteria, the Picot Committee recommended that where schools could take enrolments from outside their defined neighbourhood, a supervised ballot should be held to decide which students could be enrolled. Again the compromise between complete free choice and some limited amount of choice is obvious. What was rejected by the committee was the publication of the results of assessment tests and free choice by parents: a small but important victory for the educationists.

The most acrimonious debate occurred over the establishment of a national policy council. The proposed council had three goals:

> To provide overall policy advice to the Minister on all educational issues including the setting of national education objectives; to monitor the social environment to ensure the policy developers, administrators and providers of education are meeting the social, educational and economic requirements of the education system; to evaluate the impact of current policies and to develop new policies. (NZ Department of Education, 1988, p. 58)

The reason behind the recommendation of the formation of a council was that the policy offered to the Minister of Education from the previous Department of Education was often lacking in substance and had often been little more than a wish list. The Picot Committee's notion was that a high level group of people who were acknowledged leaders in their field, should, on a part-time basis, monitor the policy-making of the Ministry of Education and should act as a watch-dog for both the public and professionals alike. This suggestion was violently opposed by the officials from the State Services Commission in particular, and also Treasury. They argued that it would corrupt the accountability of the proposed Ministry of Education and might result in 'Sir Humphreyism'. It is also notable, although significantly not admitted by the officials, that some of the advice that would have been proffered by the proposed council fell within the rubric of the two departments most opposed to the council. Again the tension was between the educators, who were seeking to foster a system under which education would flourish, and the officials who had a vested interest to preserve the status quo and the powers of their own agencies. It is significant that the officials' report, Tomorrow's Schools, (Lange, 1988) which followed the Picot Report, dropped any mention of the policy council.

These, then, were the significant features of the Picot Report and an account of some, albeit not all, of the tensions which existed between the officials who served with the Picot Committee and members of the committee itself. The compromise was, indeed, complex but in many areas the educators won out. This was nowhere more apparent than in their determination to make sure that a properly funded system of state education remained in place. The spectre of privatization was ever present but was strongly resisted at the time of the publication of the Picot Report. This principle was endorsed by parliamentarians. In addition, some of the sillier ideas proposed by the Treasury officials, for example, schools paying interest and/or rent on the properties on which they were built, were also rejected.

The Aftermath

Following the publication of the Picot Report, the Minister established a committee of officials to write a policy document. It was their task to study the many submissions on the Picot Report (some 20,000 of them) and to produce a document reflective of both the Picot Committee and the tenor of comments on it. It was significant that the same officials who served the Picot Committee (with the exception of the Education Department official, Gianotti, who had subsequently resigned his position within the department to join another Government department) sat on the group which developed the policy document which was entitled 'Tomorrow's Schools' (Lange, 1988). Although the bulk of Picot's recommendations was embodied in 'Tomorrow's Schools', there were some quite significant changes not only in terms of the dropping of certain sections of the report but also in degrees of emphasis (Nash, 1989). The cult of efficiency, as noted by Codd (1990), became more prominent with major sections dealing with professional leadership, amongst other things, disappearing from the 'Tomorrow's Schools' document. In addition the distinction between governance and management, later to be enshrined in the Lough Report (Lough, *et al.*, 1990), was more sharply defined.

Government very quickly endorsed 'Tomorrow's Schools' despite a large amount of academic and media criticism and proceeded to put it into legislation. It is not within the scope of this chapter to summarize or comment on the academic debate. It is worth noting, though, that the academic community was split. Most especially, those from the left were vehemently opposed, which was unsurprising given the possible conservative tendencies of devolution and the lessening of centralist decision-making. The inbuilt suspicion of former teachers, now academics, of parents playing a greater role in decision-making in schools, was also noticeable.

An implementation unit was established within the Department of Education to drive the changes. A Director-General of Education, who had no background in education itself, was appointed to make sure that the change was implemented in a remarkably short period of time. I comment in more detail on the implementation process later. For now it is worth noting that evidence from the Curriculum Review Research and Schools Project (Ramsay *et al.*, 1990), indicated that the process was uneven, that it was too rapid and that the learning curve demanded of School Principals and Boards of Trustees was, in most instances, too steep. Moreover, the implementation was accompanied by an advertising campaign which was misleading. Many parents elected onto the Boards of Trustees subsequent to the legislative changes, were misled by the glossy and slick media compaign conducted by Government. A number of the problems which have arisen may be placed not only at the door of the transition itself, but also at the techniques used by the advertisers, who were undoubtedly politically motivated.

It should be noted also that the implementation process itself was far from smooth. Members of the new boards became increasingly frustrated by changes to instructions and further changes to those changes. Moreover, the education and training program which was promised to accompany the introduction of the new procedures, was far from being sufficient or even well organized. Many of the changes, such as the conditions of the contract between schools and government as outlined above, were significant. (See Codd and Gordon, 1991, for a full account.) Indeed, they were of such consequence that many boards refused to sign the charter agreement when it was completed.

Despite the shambles accompanying much of the change, the Boards of Trustees and Principals of most of the schools which were being monitored under the Monitoring Today's Schools project have survived and have slowly but surely worked their way into an understanding of the new system. There have been some significant gains as well as some losses. I turn now to an account of some gains and some problems.

Part 2: Some Outcomes

Throughout the restructuring process in New Zealand, the public has been fed a steady diet of negative media publicity. We should not be surprised that the media appears to be interested only in disasters. For eighteen months in connection with education, television, radio and the print media seem to have delighted in reporting on schools with financial difficulties, on trustees in conflict with teachers, on disenchanted Board of Trustees' members resigning, and on over-burdened principals leaving the teaching profession. While these kinds of reports are not surprising, what is surprising to the present commentator is that there have been so few cases reported. Indeed, while problems persist, and these will be covered later in the chapter, there is some evidence now emerging from both the MTS Project and CRRISP, that there are quite major gains. These may be summed up under the following headings: improved flexibility and responsiveness; financial independence, community and parental involvement; more emphasis on equity issues and the Treaty of Waitangi; the sharpening of goals, and in some instances full school reviews, under the charter provisions; and more staff and school development. Each of these areas is now briefly covered. The Gains section will conclude with an account of unfulfilled fears.

Gains

Increased Flexibility and Responsiveness

This was one of the major claims make by the proponents of the education reforms. A considerable amount of evidence is now emerging to demonstrate that there is faster delivery of day-to-day resources to schools and that decision-making, which was hitherto delayed and cumbersome, has now been sharpened up and is much more rapid. The expectation of more immediate and efficient action has been confirmed by a number of board members. As McConnell and Jeffries (1991) point out, Board of Trustee members and many staff and principals as well, have agreed with this particular principle. For example, the following statements by Board of Trustee members have been cited by McConnell and Jeffries (1991, p. 23) in their review of the first year of the reforms:

- We address problems quickly.
- I get the impression that teaching staff are starting to like it. They can go to the staff rep in charge of certain things like resource materials; it's faster and there is money available.
- Maintenance and purchasing can be quicker and more efficient. We can staff the school now to suit our needs.

There are many specific examples emerging from the evidence collected by both CRRISP and MTS which support the contention just stated. For example, at least one school in our study group has been able to undertake minor remodelling to fit the educational needs of the students. This same school had endeavoured to get the remodelling done for many years under Education Board control but had not been able to get a decision. There are also many instances of teachers being treated better under local control than they would have been under the old board control, especially in areas like overseas leave. This, then, appears to be one of the major gain resulting from the reforms.

Financial Independence

This, of course, relates to the points just made in terms of flexibility in the use of resources. According to an editorial in a recent issue of *The New Zealand Principal*, this gain has been 'universally acclaimed as the single most successful move' (Lovegrove, 1991, p. 5). According to the writer of this editorial, the Boards of Trustees and principals now have a feeling of input, priority-setting and decision-making that was not present before the reforms. The writer does go on to state that, as always, there are never enough dollars but that local needs and requirements are now much better served than was the case formerly.

There is also a very important related issue to financial independence. The authors of the reforms were determined to make the financial structures transparent. As Noonan (1990, p. 11) has recently stated, this goal has been achieved. In her words:

> . . . the new financial structures have made clear just what it does cost to run a school. The ability to make decisions within the school about priorities for expenditure has been welcomed.

The Picot Committee anticipated that once funds flowed to the school level, a high level of entrepreneurial skill, of both parents and teachers, would be realized when they knew that their efforts would have direct benefits for children in their own schools. The committee based this judgment on their knowledge of the ways that many school committees and teachers, prior to the change, had made creative use of the very limited funds available to them. Many examples of creativity are now emerging. Three examples are worth noting. In one school area, a group of schools has clustered together and has obtained a 42.5 per cent discount on school stationery. In another district a group of schools has negotiated the purchase of photocopying paper by the pallet at well below wholesale rates. Indeed, some businesses in that district have endeavoured to buy the photocopying paper from the schools! Perhaps the most interesting venture occurred in yet another district where a large number of schools formed a co-operative to supply basic materials to the schools. The co-operative has proved to be extremely successful with materials being bought at a cheaper rate than was previously possible. At the end of the first financial year the co-operative declared a quite substantial dividend for the schools involved. Financial independence then, has been appreciated by many schools and has resulted in considerable gains.

Community and Parent Involvement

One of the major claims made for the reforms was that there would be much greater parental interest in and involvement with teachers and schools. There is no question that during the initial stages of the changes, there was a substantial increase in both interest and involvement. The election of the Board of Trustees themselves demonstrated the widespread interest, although it would have to be reported that some of the advertising which accompanied the elections was grossly misleading and led to some problems which are discussed below. It was also significant that large numbers of parents and caregivers offered themselves for these elections. In some schools, where it had been impossible prior to the reforms to get sufficient numbers to form a school committee, up to thirty people offered themselves for the election. It is also significant that 25 per cent of the people elected were Maori, arguably the highest percentage of the indigenous population ever to serve on the governing bodies of schools in this country. (The census figure on the proportion of Maori in New Zealand in about 15 per cent, but some commentators argue that it is closer to 30 per cent.) The initial upsurge of interest though, has not continued at that high level. Evidence is now emerging that, while the gains have in some areas been significant, there is an uneven spread of interest. Noonan (1990) reports that there is a growing partnership between parents and teachers and that this 'has already had success in winning much needed additional resources at a time of severe economic recession.' She goes on to state that school communities successfully resisted the attempt of Treasury to pass on to parents and teachers the cost of the back-log of maintenance of schools. Again in her words, 'Teachers and parents in primary schools increasingly recognise and articulate their common interests, their common objectives; they are allies and not enemies.'

The CRRISP project has demonstrated with abundant clarity that if appropriate strategies are adopted a very high level of parental involvement can occur (Ramsay, Hawk, Harold, Kaai, Marriott and Poskett, 1989; Ramsay *et al.*, 1990). However, the report of the MTS researchers on the first year suggests that parental involvement is not as high as anticipated. The citations that they provide indicate a variety of opinions on this matter. For example, the following contrasting comments were given:

- 'I think there is (sic) a lot of changes. Parents are getting more involved within the schools.'
- 'Parents are getting more control and involvement in the operation of the school. Community involvement is far greater in the school.'
- 'In administration it is far better — more parent involvement has been advantageous.'
- 'It gives the parents more input. Parents are responsible for their children's education and although they are given guidelines they can adapt those guidelines to the children's needs.'
- 'People are more aware of what is going on in schools. More involved with having input into policy writing.'
- 'In our area, the people involved now are by and large the same ones that would have been involved anyway.'
- 'We have not been able to involve all parent groups. Ethnic groups have not come forward to participate in the decision making.'
- 'It is hard to get the community groups involved.' (McConnell and Jeffries, 1991, p. 42)

Sixty-nine per cent of those surveyed felt that parental support had either stayed the same or had decreased, while 28 per cent felt that parental involvement had increased significantly during the first year of the reforms. This is an area in which it is difficult to come to a firm conclusion. The MTS conclusions are not based on observations, but on the views of parents and teachers. The evidence from CRRISP, on the other hand, demonstrates a very strong desire on the part of parents to become involved, but not in the ways traditionally offered by schools. There was also a considerable body of opinion to suggest that as it becomes obvious that parents are empowered by the reforms, more people will become involved in the school in a range of ways, albeit not always in taking responsibility for school administration.

These mixed results cannot allow us to reach a firm conclusion as yet. We must await further surveys and better based research material before coming to any final decision on parent involvement in schools. It is indisputable though, that the period post-reform has created more interest amongst parents in the education of their children than probably at anytime of our earlier history.

Equity Issues and the Treaty of Waitangi

This is one of the areas which has received favourable comment by almost all of the commentators and researchers on the report. For example, Noonan (1990, p. 11) has stated, 'The equity and Treaty of Waitangi statements in the compulsory section of the [schools] charter focused attention on areas largely neglected until now.' One of the early reports of the Monitoring Today's Schools Project (Middleton and Oliver, 1990) ascertained that Board of Trustees members were largely sympathetic to Treaty of Waitangi and equity provisions in schools. They admitted though, that they had much to learn about these areas and that there was a gap between believing in equity principles and actually putting them into operation. Later reports (McConnell and Jeffries, 1991) have reached similar conclusions. (The Treaty of Waitangi was signed in 1840 by representatives of some Maori tribes and the Crown. The Treaty sets out the rights and responsibilities inherent in the partnership between the signatories.)

Despite the gap between rhetoric and reality, there is no question at all that equity has received more discussion than has ever been the case before. Many teachers and parents have become more aware of the need for equality of educational opportunity and the difficulties faced by people from disadvantaged groups than was the case earlier. In a most interesting analysis, Middleton (1990) has demonstrated the mediatory role of the Parliamentary Labour Party in emphasizing equity more than has been the case in similar reforms in Australia, Canada and the United Kingdom. She also points out the potential losses that will be made under the new National Government. Already the new Minister of Education, the Honourable Lockwood Smith, has indicated that the equity drive was 'a Labour Party attempt at social engineering'. He has introduced new legislation which gives schools the right to strike out the compulsory equity and Treaty of Waitangi provisions in the schools charter. Evidence on the reaction of Boards of Trustees and school staff to this suggestion has not yet come to hand. However, it is heartening to note that over half of the schools in the MTS project have already decided to retain the equity and Treaty clauses in their schools charter.

Sharpening of the Goals under the Charter

Again, most commentators and researchers are agreed that the process of developing the charter was both positive and educational. Noonan (1990, p. 4) puts it in this way: '. . . the Charter development process encouraged more extensive debate about both educational objectives and educational means than has occurred previously.' Hall and McGee (1991) have demonstrated that where the Charters were properly developed by schools and where they have been used subsequent to their development, there has been a set of conditions created for positive school review which has been reflected in improved classroom practice. However, both Hall and McGee (1991) and McConnell and Jeffries (1991) have noted the uneven treatment of Charter development by schools. The latter writers have concluded that for many schools this was a process which was mandatory, and therefore had to be done, but that since the development of the Charter and its signing, it has become a document which 'is gathering dust on the shelves of the principals' offices.' Again, while some gains were made by many schools, the results have been rather mixed.

Staff and School Development

Critics of the reform claimed that there would be very little school development or staff development undertaken because of the demands of the reform itself. Certainly it is true that principals in particular have been preoccupied with learning new managerial roles. However, recent evidence suggests that there have been more staff and parent developmental programs in education than probably at any other time of our history. Money has become available for these programmes at a local level and the importance of staff development has been recognized by almost all Boards of Trustees. Researchers have also noted the availability of developmental programmes spread across the spectrum of the school rather than being limited to a few individuals. It has been claimed by some researchers that this spread is fairer and more equitable (Hall and McGee, 1991). It has also been recognized that the cost of appropriate school developments programmes in rural areas may be three to four times greater than in urban areas (Shallcrass, Hopa, Bycroft, Newth and Haines, 1991). The answer, of course, lies in discriminatory funding and also in the development of summer school programmes for both teachers and parents.

Unfulfilled Fears

In concluding this section, it is worthwhile noting that a number of fears expressed by the critics of the system appear, at this time, to be virtually unfounded. There has been no capture of schools by fundamentalists of either the Right or Left wing (Middleton and Oliver, 1990). The fears of nepotism and unfair appointments have been largely without foundation. Indeed, the appointments procedures that the MTS Team have observed, in both primary and secondary schools, have been carried out scrupulously and with great fairness. Apart from some isolated reported instances, which probably would have occurred under the old conditions anyway, there appears to have been no witch-hunt against teachers who have adopted alternative or different styles of delivery. Finally, at the time of writing, there is no evidence to support the claim that the new system would favour male teachers over female teachers. No firm quantitative data has yet been published, but the indications are that most Board of Trustees are appointing the people whom they believe to be the best suited for the job regardless of race, gender or class. This is hardly surprising given that it is *their* children who will be taught by their appointees!

Some Problems

There has, of course, been a down-side to all this. There is no questioning the high work load placed on principals and Boards of Trustees. The gains that have been catalogued have been made at considerable personal cost to people who have been willing to take on the new jobs. I return to this point below. Other losses relate to the maintenance of schools, to confusion amongst the support agencies, to some re-centralization of power and to the changed role of the school principal. I deal with each of these in turn and then discuss the time-frame of the changes and what has been referred to by Wylie (1990) as the 'paper war'.

School Maintenance

The maintenance of school buildings in New Zealand has been a longstanding problem. Long before the reforms, it was well known that many New Zealand schools fell well below what had been determined by the Education Department and the teachers' unions in a shared agreement, of the optimal condition. The editor of the Principals' Federation Journal puts it succinctly in this way:

> Before 1984 [school buildings] were neglected, run down, poorly main-tained and work was deferred. Some lucky schools were remodelled. Since 1984 they have become shabby, unkempt and grossly underfunded. "Deferred" became extraordinary. And schools already old and leaking and unhygienic have become an embarrassment. The situation is dis-graceful. Government should be ashamed of what they have allowed to happen to school properties. (Lovegrove, 1991, p. 5)

The state of school buildings, therefore, was not an artefact of the change itself. However, the responsibility for the upkeep of buildings became the re-sponsibility of the new Board of Trustees, and the uneven quality of buildings became rapidly apparent. In order to overcome this, shortly before the 1990 elections, the then Labour government promised $224m (obtained from the sale of Telecom) for school maintenance and remodelling. This promise was not acceded to by the new National Government; however, they too have recognized the urgency of the situation and have recently decided to devote a substantial sum of money to remodelling schools. The whole question of maintenance and re-modelling of schools is one requiring urgent political decision-making. It is likely to become the political 'hot potato' of the year, given the now transparent funding of schools.

Support Agencies

The structural reforms created two new support agencies and left one in limbo. The Special Education Services Board (SES) has been established as a quasi-autonomous Government agency designed to provide special education advice to schools, eventually on a cost-recovery basis. Little evidence is yet available on the success or otherwise of their work. It is notable that in the survey conducted by McConnell and Jeffries (1991) that, of all the agencies, the SES was found to be the least understood by Boards of Trustees.

The Education Review Office (ERO) has also been hard hit by events sub-sequent to the initial reforms. I have already noted the tension which existed on the Picot Committee relating to the appropriate role of the Education Review Office. Scarcely before it started, the Education Review Office has been subjected to two external reviews. The first of these, conducted by the Lough Committee (Lough, *et al.*, 1990), indicated that the task which they viewed as being necessary was much narrower than that envisaged by the Picot Committee. Accordingly, the Lough Committee recommended that the establishment of ERO be cut by half. Subsequently, Government reduced the ERO establishment by one-third. This has left the professionals within the Education Review Office in an exceptionally difficult situation. They are now caught on the horns of a dilemma: they can either do the job as originally intended (that is, as part of a cyclic review of schools' achievements) in fewer schools or, alternatively, they can narrow their function to an audit basis whereby the review would be both superficial and non-professional.

The Advisory Services have also been very much in limbo since the publication of the *Tomorrow's Schools* document. They have been transferred into the colleges of education for administrative purposes and a variety of relationships between their host colleges and the Advisory Services have grown up. For the most part though, the relationships are federal with very little integration of the Advisory Services into the pre-service functioning of the colleges and very little involvement of college personnel in in-service education. Recently a review of the Advisory Services has been completed (Shallcrass, *et al.*, 1990). The thrust of the Shallcrass Report is that the Advisory Service should continue to remain in the colleges of education but that they should be integrated and refocused on to school development rather than the provision of individual in-service experiences for teachers. They would, therefore, help schools with the regular reviewing recommended by both the Picot Committee and the more recent research on the curriculum development at school level (Ramsay, *et al.*, 1990). At the time of writing, no decision has been made on the recommendations of the Shallcrass Report, which means the Advisory Service remains uncertain of their future.

Overall, the review process of support services has not been very helpful. Many of the schools in the MTS Project reported that they did not appear to be getting as good service from the groups concerned as had been the case in the past. In particular, principals noted that the demise of the liaison inspector had left a very large vacuum in the guidance and counselling area. The whole area of support services for schools needs to be dealt with very quickly indeed.

Recentralization of Power

As has already been stated, it was not the intention of the reforms to completely devolve responsibility for educational policy-making or delivery. Nonetheless, there was an intention to give local Boards of Trustees much more power than they had enjoyed in the past. There is some evidence emerging to suggest that there has been a recentralization of decision-making. Indeed, as Barrington (1990, p. 7) points out, many parents, trustees and principals had expected considerable autonomy over decision-making at local level, but were surprised when they discovered the large number of mandatory requirements issued by the new Ministry of Education for the schools charter. Another example of recentralizing process given by Barrington was the creation of a new central property division in the

Peter D.K. Ramsay

Ministry of Education. Moreover, recent evidence suggests that rather than reducing the amount of work done by the central agencies and the number of people
employed within the Ministry, it now appears that, in fact, the central operation
is more expensive and that more people have been employed than was formerly
the case. The Principals' Federation puts it thus: 'Our information suggests that
the Sir Humphreys of old have survived and have thrived under the new system'
(Lovegrove, 1991, p. 5).

The Role of the Principal

Perhaps the most pressing issue of all, and where perhaps the most serious loss has
been recorded, is in the area of the role of the principal. Research evidence
worldwide argues that the principal performs a pivotal role within each and every
school. In summarizing this literature, it is not too simplistic to state that a good
principal is necessary for quality educational provision. Moreover, research evidence is very clear in concluding that the best principals are professional leaders
who have developed collaborative decision-making techniques within their individual schools. The research evidence also shows that good principals have to be
good managers, but merely being a good manager is not in itself a sufficient
condition for being a good principal. The writers of the Picot Report were well
aware of the overwhelming thrust of this research; after all, I, later one of the
Picot Committee's members, had been responsible for the pioneer work on effective schooling in New Zealand (Ramsay, Sneddon, Grenfell and Ford, 1981; 1983).
The committee made their position clear by stating, 'whatever system is developed, the collaborative relationship between principal and staff must be protected
and enhanced' (NZ Department of Education, 1988, p. 51). The report went on
to state that the teachers and the principal should participate regularly in reviewing
the quality of the institution's educational performance. The process, the report
said, should be a collaborative one which almost invariably generates high levels
of enthusiasm and commitment and high levels of learner success. The committee
rejected hierarchical managerial structures.

It is a matter of concern that since the publication of the Picot Report,
subsequent reports (and in particular, the Lough Report) have endeavoured to
develop a managerial regime borrowed from other sectors in the public service
and generated mostly by Treasury and State Services Commission Officials. It is
significant, as Codd (1990) points out in his excellent analysis of managerialism,
that 'Tomorrow's Schools' (Lange, 1988) dropped most of the Picot account of
collaborative management and leadership from its policy statement (cf. Nash,
1989). The Lough Report went even further and the cult of efficient managerialism
became well and truly established. This committee argued for a strict division
between policy determination and the implementation of those policies. Put in
simple and crude terms, the report may be summed up by commenting that
boards should govern, principals should manage and teachers should operate (Codd,
1990, p. 22). As Codd has pointed out, what this defines is 'an organisational
culture that is hierarchical, competitive, individualistic and highly task oriented'.
He says that it is an instrumental culture in which ends are separated from means
and people are only valued for what they produce. He continues, 'If it is imposed
upon schools, it is a culture that tends to be undemocratic, uneducational and

wasteful for human initiative and capacity.' While I disagree with Codd's final conclusions (he argues that educators must take the high ground in policy-making, which is scarcely democratic or collaborative), there is no questioning the points that he raises in the main body of his commentary. The role confusion that is now apparent amongst principals is something requiring urgent attention. It was one of the predominant concerns uncovered by McConnell and Jeffries (1991) in their recent report. For example, they found principals saying, 'I've got to straighten out my role as principal by the end of the year,' and, 'I have to sort out the principal's role.'

The principals in the MTS study made it clear that the managerial role was distancing them from both professional staff guidance and curriculum concerns. Many had become extremely frustrated and believed that the excessive work-load was not only a result of the transition but of the new role. The Picot recommendations for a continuation of professional leadership and for the more managerial roles to be carried out by support services, have not come to fruition. This is yet another area that must be addressed with some urgency, particularly as Treasury and State Service Commission officials continue to argue a case for a clear-cut division between governance and management.

Excessive Workloads

Perhaps the major problem which arose was the very high work loads and the rapid learning curves required of principals and members of Boards of Trustees. The gains noted earlier in this chapter have been made at considerable personal cost to people who have been willing to take on new jobs. Some of the high work load may be laid at the door of the transition itself and the mistakes that were made by the implementation unit as they hastened to meet the politically motivated deadlines. McConnell and Jeffries (1991) have ascertained that principals are working on average between fifty and sixty hours per week.

Moreover, the rate of change was too fast for many people. Ramsay and his colleagues (1990) warned the implementors several times in the course of their indepth research in a number of New Zealand schools that many principals and teachers were becoming 'future shocked'. The pace was so fast that many had given up. Despite these warnings, the implementation unit pressed on. Unfortunately, as just noted, they made many mistakes and, indeed, information from the implementation unit which corrected previous corrections was met with some derision by principals and Boards of Trustees, many of whom lost faith in the change process. Additionally, the promised training programmes were not established, thus creating a fresh dimension to the problems. Some excellent material is now coming to hand (for example, the material produced by the Principal's Task Force) but as McConnell and Jeffries (1991) note, it was too little and too late. In addition, the transition has also been made more difficult by what Wylie (1990) refers to as the paper war. She cites a trustee as follows:

I filled three rubbish bags with all the paper I have had so far. How many trees do your think it took to make 'Tomorrow's Schools'?

Not all of the increased work-load, particularly on principals, is the result of the transition. Indeed, some of it has to do with the changed nature of responsibilities. The time has arrived to carefully investigate what is happening to principals as they try to carry out their professional, as well as their managerial, functions. The simple answer is to make sure the principals and boards do not get caught up in the minutiae of accounting and clerical issues. The Picot Committee anticipated that groups of schools would cluster together in order to buy appropriate secretarial and accountancy support. This has occurred in some areas, but it is disappointing to note that the majority of schools have failed to spontaneously develop cluster groupings. Of course, the development of clusters depends on schools wishing to establish a cooperative network. In this connection it is worth noting that the simplistic Treasury model of developing successful schooling through competition and free parental choice based on the results of standardized tests, will not encourage the kind of cooperative spirit which is necessary for local school management to succeed. Overseas experience, in Scotland for example, where parental choice has been in place for several years, indicates that the winners in parental choice are the children of parents who are already doing well in the school system; the losers come from working class and ethnic minority groups (Echols, McPherson and Willms, 1990). Given the New Zealand emphasis on equality of opportunity, such a system would hardly be acceptable to the bulk of New Zealanders.

Finally, in this section, we should note the critical nature of the change to the Schools Charter. In clause 8 of the original Charter, following directly from the Picot Committee's recommendation, the Minister promised to provide funding to meet the requirements of the Charter. This particular clause was deleted. Moreover, a change was made from 'agreement' to 'undertaking', and the partnership notion 'became reconstituted as one between the school and its community with no mention at all of the state' (Codd and Gordon, 1991, p. 17). Thus, in one action, the government distanced itself from its responsibilities in providing appropriate educational finance. Codd and Gordon conclude:

> Despite all the rhetoric about "partnership" and the blatant propaganda about the empowerment of communities, the new educational structures could never be permitted to provide the space wherein school committees, through their trustees, would be free to contest state action. (Codd and Gordon, 1991, p. 18)

Leaving aside Codd and Gordon's own excessive rhetoric, the point is a good one. The notion of making the state responsible for education in the public good, and being held accountable to the public for any shortfall in educational financing, was removed by the change of the wording of the Schools Charter and the subsequent legislation. The only good thing to come out of this particular debate was that, once again, parents become very aware of the short-comings of current educational provision.

Conclusions

Despite the shambles accompanying much of the change, the Boards of Trustees and principals of most of the schools in the MTS Project have survived and have slowly but surely worked their way into an understanding of the new system. There have been a number of gains and losses under the new system. It is interesting to note, though, that the majority of Boards of Trustees' members remain optimistic about the reforms and do not wish to go back to the old systems. Many principals are also in favour of the changes (particularly the original Picot recommendations), but have become very concerned about the excessively high work load. It is interesting to note that Robertson (1990) found that while the costs have been very high, particularly in the case of teaching principals in rural areas, well over 90 per cent of the principals in her survey stated that they were better off now than they had been before the reforms. Indeed, one principal went so far as to say that 'the reforms were the best things that had happened since sliced bread.' What is desperately needed in New Zealand now is a time of consolidation, a working through of the many problems which are being encountered and a continuation of the co-operation between boards, their communities and the professional staff in our schools. Consolidation is not easy in the face of seventeen reviews of education being conducted by the new government, reviews incidentally, in which the teacher unions and the Boards of Trustees' Association are playing no part.

This chapter of New Zealand educational history has been one of overt contestation as hegemonies associated with traditional power relationships have been disturbed. Many commentators (e.g., Althusser, 1971; Apple, 1982; and Giroux, 1981) have argued that schools are part of the ideological state apparatus serving the dominant elite. Some New Zealand commentators and researchers have demonstrated that this has been the case in this country (see e.g., Codd, 1985; Ramsay, 1985; Middleton, 1990; Lauder, 1990; Codd, Gordon and Harker, 1990). Given this widespread evidence, any change to the system at the very least gives an opportunity for a relocation of power. The increasing role played by parents, and even more significantly the curriculum and pedagogical changes in schools with predominantly Maori population, are indications that the contest has not always been won by those formerly holding the most curriculum authority, that is, teachers and Pakehas. There is much yet to be achieved. But it does appear that there is no going back, that the future holds many challenges but that significant gains are to be made by a well-balanced system of central and local decision-making, with as much autonomy being given as is possible to people at the local area.

Note

1   The author acknowledges the critical reading by Alan Hall of the first draft. Both CRRISP and the Monitoring Today's Schools Project were financed by the Ministry of Education, whose help is gratefully acknowledged.

References

ALTHUSSER, L. (1971) 'Ideology and ideological state apparatus', in ALTHUSSER, L. (Ed.) *Lenin and Philosophy and Other Essays*, London, UK: New Left Books.
APPLE, N.W. (Ed.) (1982) *Cultural and Economic Reproduction in Education: Essays on Class, Ideology and the State*, London, UK: Routledge and Kegan Paul.

BARRINGTON, J. (1990) 'The reality of the education reforms: Introduction and overview', *Public Sector*, **13**, 4, pp. 6–8.

CODD, J.A. (1985) 'Images of schooling and the discourse of the state', in CODD, J., HARKER, R. and NASH, R. (Eds) *Political Issues in New Zealand Education*, Palmerston North, NZ: Dunmore Press, pp. 23–41.

CODD, J.A. (1990) 'Managerialism: The problem with today's schools', *Delta*, **44**, pp. 17–25.

CODD, J. and GORDON, L. (1991) 'School charters: The contractualist state and education policy', *New Zealand Journal of Educational Studies*, **26**, 1, pp. 21–34.

CODD, J.A., GORDON, L. and HARKER, R. (1990) 'Education and the role of the state: Devolution and control post-Picot', in LAUDER, H. and WYLIE, C. (Eds) *Towards Successful Schooling*. London, UK: Falmer Press, pp. 15–32.

CODD, J., HARKER, R. and NASH, R. (Eds) (1985) *Political Issues in New Zealand Education*, Palmerston North, NZ: Dunmore Press.

DEAL, T.E. (1990) 'Reframing reform', *Educational Leadership*, **47**, 8, pp. 6–12.

ECHOLS, F., MCPHERSON, A. and WILLMS, J. (1990) 'Parental choice in Scotland', *Journal of Education Policy*, **5**, pp. 207–22.

FOUCAULT, M. (1980) *Power/Knowledge and Other Interviews*, London, UK: Pantheon Books.

GIROUX, H. (1981) *Ideology, Culture and the Process of Schooling*, London, UK: Falmer Press.

GRACE, G. (1990) 'Labour and Education: the Crisis and Settlements of Education Policy', in HOLLAND, M. and BOSTON, J. (Eds) *The Fourth Labour Government: Politics and Policy in New Zealand*, 2nd ed. Auckland, NZ: Oxford University Press, pp. 165–91.

HALL, A. and MCGEE, C. (1991) *Charter Development*, Report No. 3, Monitoring Today's Schools Project, Hamilton, NZ: The University of Waikato.

LANGE, D. (1988) *Tomorrow's Schools: The Reform of Education Administration in New Zealand*, Wellington, NZ: Government Printer.

LAUDER, H. (1990) 'Education democracy and the crisis of the welfare state', in LAUDER, H. and WYLIE, C. (Eds) *Towards Successful Schooling*, London, UK: Falmer Press, pp. 33–52.

LOVEGROVE, G. (Ed.) (1991) 'In tray out tray', *New Zealand Principal*, **5**, 4, p. 5.

LOUGH, N., COWIE, D., CARPINTER, P., GREIG, D. and O'ROURKE, M. (1990) *Today's Schools, A Review of the Education Reform Implementation Process*, prepared for the Minister of Education, Wellington, NZ: Government Printer.

MCCONNELL, R. and JEFFERIES, R. (1991) *The First Year*, Report No. 4, Monitoring Today's Schools Project, Hamilton, NZ: The University of Waikato.

MIDDLETON, S. (1990) 'Gender Equity and School Charters: Theoretical and Political Questions for the 1990s', in MIDDLETON, S. and JONES, A. (Eds) *Women in Education in Aotearoa*, **II**, Wellington, NZ: Bridget Williams Books, (in press). Revised version of keynote address to NZARE Conference, December, 1990.

MIDDLETON, S. and OLIVER, D. (1990) *Who Governs Our Schools? The Educational Perspectives of Members of Boards of Trustees*, Report No. 2, Monitoring Today's Schools Research Project, Hamilton, NZ: The University of Waikato.

NASH, R. (1989) 'Tomorrow's schools: State power and parent participation', *New Zealand Journal of Educational Studies*, **24**, 2, pp. 113–28.

NEW ZEALAND DEPARTMENT OF EDUCATION (1930) *Educational Reorganisation in New Zealand: (The Atmore Report)*, Report of the Parliamentary Recess Education Committee, Wellington, NZ: Government Printer.

NEW ZEALAND DEPARTMENT OF EDUCATION (1962) *Report of the Commission on Education in New Zealand (The Currie Report)*, Wellington, NZ: Government Printer.

NEW ZEALAND DEPARTMENT OF EDUCATION (1976) *Towards Partnership (McCombes Report)*, Wellington, NZ: Department of Education.

NEW ZEALAND DEPARTMENT OF EDUCATION (1987) *The Curriculum Review*, Wellington, NZ: Department of Education.

NEW ZEALAND DEPARTMENT OF EDUCATION (1988) *Administering for Excellence: Effective Administration in Education* (The Picot Report), Report of the Taskforce to Review Education Administration, Wellington, NZ: Government Printer.

NOONAN, R. (1990) 'The Primary Reforms', *Public Sector*, **13**, 4, p. 5.

NORDMEYER, A.H., ASKIN, F., BROOKES, R., GALLAGHER, C., HAYDEN, H., MANNING, L., PINDER, B. (1974) *Organisation and Administration of Education*, Report of the Working Party on Organisation and Administration, Educational Development Conference, Wellington.

RAMSAY, P. (1985) 'The domestication of teachers: A case of social control', in CODD, J. HARKER, R. and NASH, R. (Eds) *Political Issues in New Zealand Education*, Palmerston North, NZ: Dunmore Press, pp. 103–22.

RAMSAY, P., SNEDDON, D., GRENFELL, J. and FORD, I. (1981) *Tomorrow May Be Too Late*, Final Report of the SSN Project, Hamilton, NZ: The University of Waikato.

RAMSAY, P., SNEDDON, D., GRENFELL, J., FORD, I. (1983) 'Successful and unsuccessful schools: A study in Southern Auckland', *Australian and New Zealand Journal of Sociology*, **19**, 2, pp. 272–304.

RAMSAY, P., HAWK, K., HAROLD, B., KAAI, T., MARRIOTT, R., POSKETT, J. (1989) *Towards Success: Some Examples of Improved School-Community Relationships*, Occasional Paper No. 5, CRRISP, Hamilton, NZ: The University of Waikato.

RAMSAY, P., HAROLD, B., HAWK, K., KAAI, T., MARRIOTT, R., POSKETT, J. (1990.) *'There's No Going Back': Collaborative Decision Making in Education*, Final Report of the Curriculum Review Research in Schools Project (CRRISP), Hamilton, NZ: The University of Waikato.

ROBERTSON, J. (1990) *Developing Educational Leadership: An Action Research Study into the Professional Development of the New Zealand School Principal*, A Thesis Submitted in Partial Fulfilment of the Requirements for the Degree of Master of Education at the University of Waikato, Hamilton, NZ.

SHALLCRASS, J., HOPA, N., BYCROFT, D., NEWTH, A. and HAINES, L. (1990) *School Development: Review of Advisory Services*, Wellington, NZ: Ministry of Education.

WYLIE, C. (1990) 'Volunteers and conscripts in the paper war: Principal and trustee experiences of "tomorrow's schools"', *Public Sector*, **13**, 4, pp. 14–5.

Chapter 15

'Nothing But Facts, Sir': Curriculum Reform as a Function of Corporate Federalism

Leo Bartlett

> We hope to have, before long, a board of fact, composed of commissioners of fact, who will force the people to be people of fact, and of nothing but fact. You must discard the word Fancy altogether (the Gentleman, p. 16. *Hard Times*).

The author of *Hard Times*, Charles Dickens, was always interested in the serious human problems resulting from an increasing industrialized society and its government to which people of his time so meekly surrendered. The capitulation was to the gods of science and the technical rationality that accompanied it, and to the axioms of mediocrity and mechanical-like behaviours that crept into all aspects of life. The inhumanity that accompanied this capitulation invaded not only factories but the very institutions where humanity itself was educated — the schools or as he described them, the 'teacher factories'.

It is significant, as Charles Shapiro observes, that *Hard Times* opens and closes in the world of children in classrooms and the world of those who are assumed to be uniformed. In the book, the schoolroom is seen to dehumanize its scholars, but the circus, all fancy and love, gives humanity back. We are exposed to two worlds in which the possibility of dehumanization with its underlying hard, pragmatic values, a parody of utilitarianism, is transmitted undistilled to children.

According to Dickens, this was the way curriculum was represented nearly 140 years ago. One has to ask today whether the developments in national curriculum promote the possibilities for similar forms of utilitarianism and dehumanization; and whether the 'representation problem' (Lundgren, 1983) is as problematic in contemporary Australia as it was in mid-nineteenth century England, at a time when the classroom that persists to the present day had almost reached a moment of final evolution.

The representation problem provokes the question: How shall the curriculum be represented in schools to best reflect how society thinks of itself? Lundgren (1983, p. 11) speaks about the representation problem in the following way:

> The moment production processes [processes for the creation of the necessities for social life and the creation of knowledge from which production can develop] are separated from reproduction processes

[processes for the re-creation and reproduction of knowledge and skills for production but also the reproduction of the conditions for production], the representation problem arises; that is, the problem of how to represent production processes so that they can be reproduced.

If the learning of knowledge and skills takes place in the context where the same knowledge and skills are used, the relationships between production and reproduction processes are less problematic. Hence, when a young person in Aboriginal society learns hunting skills, the production of knowledge involving a knowledge-base underlying skill development, and indeed a learning community of tribal elders and young people, occurs where the knowledge and skills about hunting are exercised. Knowledge is produced and consumed in the same spatial and temporal contexts. But when learning takes place away from the place of production, there arises the problem of decontextualization of knowledge and skills from the context of production; that is, there is the problem of decontextualization and of deciding which knowledge and skills are appropriate, and the problem of recontextualization, that is, the problem of deciding how knowledge and skills are to be selected, arranged and delivered in a learning setting.

In Dickens' classrooms, the production of knowledge and skills occurred where they were reproduced. State governed centralized bureaucratic education systems had not developed at that time. Contemporary education systems including the six states and two territories in Australia have long-developed education bureaucracies where contexts of production and reproduction are separated. Hence, a representation problem exists and may give rise to potential problems in the curriculum. Who will be involved in the decontextualizing and recontextualizing processes becomes a critical question. Perhaps more significantly, it has to be asked whether there will be 'commissioners of fact' whose particular codes or sets of principles will be dominant in determining what curriculum will be represented.

This chapter reviews how the curriculum was represented and the changes that have occurred under Labor in the 1970s and 1980s. It provides an analysis of an emerging national curriculum for Australian schools and the effects and consequences of these changes. Finally, it assesses Labor mediations and the policy framework being promoted by the stakeholders or *commissioners of fact* who are largely responsible for the national curriculum.

Curriculum and the Social Movement of the 1970s

Prior to the 1970s, state education systems were highly centralized and monolithic administrative organisations exercised an unquestioned authority over the curriculum in schools. According to Kemmis (1989), the authority and legitimacy of state bureaucracies were threatened by the social movements of the late sixties, including the expanding professional status of teaching and teachers, civil rights movements, an expanding economy and a groundswell of democratic reconstruction.

These movements established the possibility and reality of an expansion and flux in the structures of control of schooling and in curriculum in schools. Aided by the Commonwealth and the Whitlam Labor government, there was a surge of enthusiasm in schools for changing the curriculum throughout the six States and two territories in Australia. This took the form of decentralization and a move to school-based curriculum development. The Commonwealth funded large projects in the Innovations Program and the Disadvantaged Schools Program arguably on the grounds that the states were not making adequate provision for education. Hence, the Commonwealth directly sought to change the curriculum in schools by diverting extra funds from state channels directly to the schools.

There were accompanying changes during the decade, most notably the almost universal move in schools in Australian states to forms of local assessment and curriculum responsibility. School improvement programs were embraced with a varying mix of understanding and control as guiding principles. Minimal (self) accountability (Kemmis and Stake, 1988) replaced or was added to systems accountability. Community (alternative) schools first appeared and were to increase rapidly in numbers to form a non-government non-systemic grouping. In brief, the school-based movement of the 1970s was accompanied by a participatory democratic spirit and an expanding economy.

A singularly important event during this period was the establishment of a central curriculum agency called the Curriculum Development Centre (CDC). It became a statutory body in 1975 and among its tasks was to liaise with the states, to undertake joint curriculum projects, and to promulgate school-based curriculum development. Its power was through resourcing, and it granted funding directly to schools and to states. It had a high profile in federal-state relations especially in areas where there was conflict and difference of opinion. Many aspects of the CDC's work reflected the Whitlam Labor Government's unstated (in curriculum terms) policy of idealism and reform. Despite some anomalous events and confusion in decision-taking, it could be claimed that the 1970s could be equated with a Dickens-like version of the *good times* of curriculum in Australia.

The Curriculum of the 1980s

At the beginning of the eighties, the CDC produced possibly its most significant statement on *Core Curriculum for Australian Schools* (1980). It advocated priority areas in knowledge and skills which were to be accessible to all. The debate was about core curriculum, not a national curriculum; it was driven by educational argument and reflected more the curriculum culture of the 1970s than what was to become the national curriculum of the 1980s.

A contracting economy early in the 1980s witnessed quite different curriculum events. There was a focus on young people 15–19 years-old who were the at-risk unemployed group in society. This gave rise to more explicit statements by the Commonwealth relating first to selective labour policies and second to education and training policies. The Organization for Economic Cooperation and Development (OECD, 1986) recommendations during a visit early in the decade focused on broadening the curriculum, on 'life skills', on flexible credentialling arrangements, on increased student participation (pupil-retention especially in the post-compulsory years), and on vocationalism. Kennedy (1989a) notes that all the curriculum events of the period were initiated in an economic context. He makes little distinction between economism and the economic rationalism which during the decade was dominant in curriculum policy formulation.

The first explicit sign of emerging hard times in curriculum policy was the abolition of CDC in 1981 and its subsumption into a Commonwealth Department.

This was effected by the 'razor gang' of the newly elected Liberal government. It was resurrected under the Hawke Labor government in 1984 as one of four departments in the Schools Commission. Its function was to advise the states and national government; it was entrusted to develop curriculum policy and to engage in materials production; it also became involved in the emerging emphasis on quality of teaching and learning. It formed an uneasy established relationship with the states, but its budget was low and its real strength and purpose diffuse. The significance of the second generation CDC was that it was to have a national perspective and a partnership climate with the states; second, it was to draw upon the expertise of the states. The concepts of 'national' and 'agreed' were soon to become important terms in the discourse of curriculum policy formulation. CDC was finally overcome by bigger events relating to the Hawke Labor government's agenda for schooling. In 1987 it was subsumed within a megadepartment of the newly formed Department of Employment, Education and Training (DEET).

In a context of stringency of resourcing, there was an increasing number of statements about schooling and curriculum from the mid-1980s onward. The *Quality of Education Review Committee* (QERC) (Karmel, 1985) recognizing the imperatives of economic constraints, adopted a systems-approach to curriculum and educational outcomes. Educational inputs in the curriculum were to be judged in terms of specified outputs related to principal policy areas of government concern. What was important perhaps in the context of curriculum events to come in the next five years was that QERC recommended that future expenditure on general recurrent funds to schools should be undertaken through negotiated resources agreements, and funds should be directed to a limited range of policy objectives. These two events, the reinstatement of CDC and the outcomes focus of QERC set the conditions for implementation of a national curriculum which was to have [assumedly] all the attributes of being agreed, compatible, streamlined and accountable.

As might be expected from historical precedence and the known effects of 'ideological discharge' (Habermas, 1979:34) in periods of economic downturn, from the mid-1980s the impetus to focus on the curriculum of schools was increasingly seized upon by policy-makers (politicians) who looked for ready and easy answers to complex issues. Thus in 1986, the Australian Education Council (AEC), composed of Federal and State Ministers of Education, took 'the tentative, first steps' (Kennedy, 1989a) towards 'a national collaborative effort in curriculum development' (AEC, 1986). The thrust of their concern was to maximise scant curriculum development resources and to minimize unnecessary differences in curriculums across the States; underlying this was an agreed rationalism of resources use. (These issues were to be picked up and amplified in April, 1989 by the AEC's agreement on 'national cooperation in curriculum development' (AEC, 1989a).)

In 1987, the document *Skills for Australia* was written and released by the Minister for Employment, Education and Training, John Dawkins and the Minister for Employment Services and Youth Affairs, Clyde Holding. Most of its statements dealt with post-school training opportunities, but it also alluded to both the quality and quantity of education and training. Its opening sentence in the Foreword left little doubt about the national government's view of the relationship between the economy and education, the replacement of the latter with the idea of training, and the technical approach to skills formation. In the document Dawkins and Holding (1987: iii) wrote:

The Government is determined that our education and training systems should play an active role in responding to the major economic challenges now facing Australia.

In relation to increased participation, *Skills for Australia* had this to say:

Achievement of this target (65 per cent retention rate to Year 12 by 1990) will require approaches to make the final years of secondary education more attractive and relevant. Curriculum reform will be an essential element in this process.

By the following year however, there was little real progress in curriculum reform. There were national statements, guidelines and reference groups in science, literacy, numeracy, and Languages other than English (LOTE), and English as a Second Language (ESL), but these appeared to have little focus in terms of the aspirations of the above document and AEC Statements.

The first and most significant policy document that translated *Skills for Australia* into desired curriculum and schooling directions was released in 1988. It was titled *Strengthening Australia's Schools* (*SAS*) (Dawkins, 1988). It was not a blueprint for action, but it provided the foundations and recommendations that would find their way onto the AEC agenda. The document was to be the basis also for the neocorporatist policy of the fourth Hawke Labor government.

SAS proposed that curriculum was central to an integrated education and training system. It proposed this through a common curriculum framework.

A common curriculum framework could, for example, emphasise a need for higher general levels of literacy, numeracy and analytical skills across the nation . . . . A major feature of a common curriculum framework would be criteria for determining content in major subject areas. Criteria for methods of assessing the achievement of curriculum objectives should be outlined (p. 4).

The invitation by the Commonwealth to 'develop a national effort for schools' was explicit:

[The government] is inviting the cooperation of the states to develop and implement a national effort to strengthen the capacity of our schools to meet the challenges they face. Consultation and negotiation will be central to this task (p. 4).

The 'national effort' was to be considered in six points:

1   A common curriculum framework.
2   A common approach to assessment.
3   Priorities for improving the training of teachers.
4   Increasing the number of young Australians completing school.
5   Improving equity in education.
6   Maximizing investment in education.

SAS was followed immediately in July, 1988 by a meeting of the AEC. It was agreed that five tasks arising from *SAS* would be implemented. Three of these were:

1 Curriculum mapping (under the direction of the Conference of Directors-General from each state).
2 National goals for schooling.
3 Basic skills testing and program evaluation.

The remaining tasks were related to a basis for future funding levels for schools and a review of CDC, the Australian Council of Educational Research (ACER) and the Australian Schools Cataloguing Information Service (ASCIS). *SAS* proposed a more radical view of self-styled collaboration, which is interpreted to mean in the next section, neocorporatism. Evidence for this collaboration between state and federal governments may be witnessed in the fact that within one year the AEC, at its. Hobart meeting, supported the so-called Hobart Declaration (Australian Education Council, 1989b) in the document *Common and Agreed National Goals for Schooling in Australia*. The contents of the document had a particular emphasis on the economy and culture in the development of a common curriculum framework. This was the real beginning of the formulation of what has been called 'national' in a national curriculum.

One further task of the AEC which was chaired by Federal Minister Dawkins was the setting up of a Working Party on Cooperative Structures (June, 1988). Its final report was tabled in April, 1989, and one of its five recommendations was to establish a private company, the Curriculum Corporation of Australia (CCA) subsequently incorporated as the Coordinated Curriculum Corporation. Its services were to be associated with those of the former CDC and ASCIS. Subsequently however, there have been ambiguities about the role of CCA. There appear to be vaguely defined and shifting expectations of its unexplicated role. Three issues are evident. First, the CCA has had no major role in the Mapping Phase One of the development of a national curriculum framework. Second, the CCA is to engage in commercial activity primarily through the sale of curriculum materials. Third, the CCA is aligned with and responsible to the authority of the AEC, which has a centralized control over the direction and development of a national curriculum.

The development of a national curriculum has proceeded in three phases. Phase One has involved the mapping of curriculum in each of the states and territories. Phase Two represents the production of guidelines or statements that represent a consensus about typical experiences of curriculum. Phase Three will result in the development of profiles and the delivery of mandated assessment statements.

The order of curriculum development for subjects approximates the following: Science, Mathematics, Technology, English, Studies of Society and Environment, Languages other than English (LOTE). Language is assumed to be mapped (through the Australian Language Learning — the ALL Project); the Arts are to be mapped (October, 1991 after a low-cost hastily contrived activity); and Health, which includes Physical Education is finally to be included in the exercise.

The first *National Statement on Mathematics* was intended to be released (June, 1991). It is being discussed (September, 1991) in a contractual arrangement through

DEET and the Australian Association of Mathematic Teachers. Enthusiasm for the current tasks of mapping and constructing guideline statements is evident in one author's statements (Boomer, 1990), that without Phase Three the task looks more like the *National Statement on Girls and Mathematics* (Australian Association of Mathematics Teachers, 1990). At the same time the chair of the national committee responsible for developing these statements, Boomer (1991) claimed that the guidelines were 'not an imposed curriculum' and the 'states would jealously guard their constitutional rights for control over education'. This logic was extended to the statement that there would be local or state differences in implementing the national guidelines. The argument was made that a broad understanding of mathematics was needed and that 'an education that excited and inspired confidence in many more students to continue with mathematics' was necessary. Finally, the President-elect of the Australian Association of Mathematic Teachers (Reeves, 1991) claimed that the statement was not really a document that locked states together but it had the effect of bringing them closer. The enthusiasm of the classroom practitioner is unknown; wider consultation with this group is not evident.

In the absence of wider implementation and a limited consultation with teacher practitioners, it is difficult to see how the above unwarranted assertions (which are in fact *non-sequitur*) can be justified. There are, however, several further criticisms that one can make about the national curriculum and these are summarized in the next section.

A National Australian Curriculum

There are a number of criticisms that can be levelled at the nature and progress of the national curriculum. The curriculum is referred to as an 'agreed curriculum', the result of national collaborative action. It is the result of what is seen by its authors, the relevant working parties under the direction of the AEC, as the product of wide consultation. There is some argument that in this sense the national curriculum will provide some direction for Australian curriculum in schools' in the national interest.

The first phase of mapping may offer, as Piper (1989: 5) notes, 'a useful contribution to the debate'. But in this sense it is reactionary and reflects a *status quo* view of curriculum formulation. It reflects *what is*, not what *should be*; where we *are*, not where we are *going*. It is hardly a liberating curriculum for the twenty-first century. Furthermore, in as much as it needs to be complemented by studies of practice, it is not a substitute for hard work and the thinking required to define needs beyond 1991.

While it may be claimed that the mapping exercises of Phase One represent a conservative approach, the statement of guidelines for each subject may be seen by some educators, such as Boomer (1990), to have a reforming aspect. However, given that a consultative and consensus approach has or will be used, it is still difficult to see that the statements do not have a standardizing aspect that may be detrimental to practice, that is, to practice in contexts where the curriculum is enacted. The purpose of these statements, as Francis (1991: 32) suggests, is not to modify the behaviour of teachers and students (although this may ultimately be the situation in Phase Three), but to:

provide a design structure within which a system authority locates its own negotiated system syllabus and/or framework . . . a national statement provides the structure within which development occurs — it is not an instrument of compliance.

As will be argued in the next section of this chapter, the national curriculum is an instrument of corporate compliance which, in effect, may be necessary at this time of the country's educational history.

There are at least three critiques of the mapping and statements phases of national curriculum development. First, mapping and formulating statements or guidelines represent a conservative approach which may result in a pathology of normalcy. That is, the curriculums in selected subjects in each of the states have been interrogated for their commonalities, their regularities and consequentially the least common factorial content elements. When each state looks at each other, it is possible that they will in effect be looking at the lowest curriculum denominator (this is an inevitable consequence perhaps and an innate attribute of the term national in a federal arrangement). Second, it is unreasonable to assume that in formulating an agreed curriculum that a national will-formation to enact it will logically or necessarily follow. This assumption represents history without hindsight and a recurrence of the meritocratic error in curriculum implementation. It is a fallacy that there will be an easy or consequent match between an agreed curriculum formulation and a national will-formation. Third, the reform aspect has, to date, been about uniformity and has been uniformly distant from the struggle to enact curriculum at the local level. This struggle will be further complicated with the likely event of the introduction of performance indicators and competency-based standards for the teaching workforce. Hence, these have the potential to regulate teachers' pedagogy, which will act as a conduit for national curriculum implementation and a resultant mediocrity. This kind of regulation will have added impetus in the context of an agreed national framework which by definition involves a search for the lowest curriculum denominator and possible forms of mediocrity.

The approach to developing a national curriculum follows closely the intent of *SAS*. The focus is on identification of curriculum content from documents, not from curriculum practice. Hence, the statement in *SAS*:

The goals are intended to assist schools and systems to develop specific objectives and strategies particularly in accessing curriculum and assessment (p. 87).

Goals are not linked to strategies, content to transmission, or the 'what' to the 'how'. There is a dichotomy between theory (goals) and practice (strategies). The *SAS* quote also indicates the national curriculum approach, in that it assumes that the derivation of objectives is directly and logically related to broadly defined state goals. The uselessness of national curriculum approaches to teachers and their willingness to distort prescribed overarching goal statements is well acknowledged in the history of curriculum.

Another uncertainty about the mapping of a national curriculum is a knowledge of what exactly is being mapped. *SAS* appears confused in this regard. It speaks about areas of knowledge and experience and subject areas. This kind of interchange of terms is seen in later documents relating to resourcing agreements such as the *Commonwealth Programs for Schools* (Department of Employment,

Education and Training, 1989). An emphasis on a subject-specific curriculum would appear necessary to meet the needs for economic restructuring, a principal policy agenda behind the drive for a national curriculum. An areas of knowledge and skills emphasis would appear more general and comprehensive to meet the needs of interstate mobility. The confusion remains unresolved although it is clear that a) a subject approach has been adopted; and b) there is a contradiction, in that the Commonwealth's concern for student mobility across states (together with uniformity in school-age entry, handwriting and assessment) is only one issue on the Commonwealth's agenda.

There are two further criticisms of the subject approach to national curriculum development. First, the ordering and inclusion of specific subjects (listed previously) for curriculum mapping and the formulation of statements reflect the Commonwealth's economic priorities. The priority of ordering allocated to the sciences technology and mathematics reflects the national government's policy (and state counterparts) that there is a need to educate young scientists, and then a clever, if not economic country may or will be created.

Second, the approach to developing maps and statements of the specific subjects listed above is undertheorized, in that there is no comprehensive view of curriculum, although the claim is made (Australian Education Council, 1991) that the CCA will *post facto* undertake this task. The Working Parties for each subject areas have well-defined territories reproducing all the dysfunctions of subject interests identified by Goodson (1987). Connors (1989: 13), the Chair of Schools Council at the time, notes '. . . the need to keep a comprehensive view of the curriculum in mind while individual subject-based curriculum mapping exercises are in progress'. Noting the need does not replace the visible lack of a comprehensive view. It also remains unclear how subjects are related conceptually.

The principal problems with the approach to the development of a national curriculum, however, relate to the dichotomization of learning (the statements of Phase Two), and assessment. Again, the AEC Working Party on national assessment is working independently of the Working Parties who are developing national statements for subjects. This dichotomy may reflect the fact that the purpose of assessment is not clear in *SAS*. What is certain is that in the history of curriculum reform, whoever controls assessment controls the curriculum. In the development of national curriculum, curriculum advice is separated temporally, and apparently conceptually, from assessment advice.

In the final analysis however, the effectiveness of a national curriculum will depend on the development of subject profiles and a national assessment framework. It is in this area that industry, business, and union groups with their more prescriptive and limited view of what actually constitutes curriculum show most interest.

The difficulties associated with subject profiling, which may be regarded as a form of national testing, are conceptual and technical, and only a select number are indicated here. Phase Three involves the establishment of six bands which are intended to act as a template against which levels of attainment may be judged and against which levels of attainment must be specified. How to specify these levels is not clear. In addition, it is possible that teachers will overspecify a level of attainment or achievement of their students. The latter may be balanced by moderation procedures, but the logistics of this kind of exercise demand a high level of resourcing; in addition, there is as yet little solid evidence available about the effectiveness of moderation. More importantly, there is the problem of assessment being derived and executed away from teacher practice. This position has been advocated by the Australian Council for Educational Research (ACER) (Masters, 1990) and signals the introduction of national reference testing. In a bid to avoid this situation, an attempt is being made to move to teacher-graded assessment which has a reforming aspect (Boomer, 1990). The aim is to identify exemplary practice-teacher practice that is recognized by peers for its excellence — and to use the six bands as templates. Hence, assessment judgements of teachers would be guided by exemplary assignments etc. Benchmarks would be promulgated forms of good practice, and implicit in good practice would be a pedagogy for the twenty-first century.

Teacher promulgation of attainment levels has a number of apparent advantages, if only because it restores at least partially, the importance of the teacher in the curriculum development process. Such a process may be used, for example, in teachers' professional development where they engage in critique of their own benchmarks. Promulgated benchmarks may also be used collaboratively between students and teachers. There is a social justice issue here and the injection of a productive tension in curriculum work through the public nature of the process. There is also a downside to this approach to assessment, in that it could have the potential of developing into a situation where teachers do more of the same especially in a context where no resources (for example, time to reflect) are made available for professional development. In addition, while bands and levels of attainment are being advanced, through the attempts of educators sympathetic to the intimate relationship between theory and practice and the role of the practitioner, it would take little to slip into the normative reference and national testing advocated by (and described elsewhere in this book as) the New Right populist (Reeves, 1991). Similarly, the work on national testing to date would provide a basis for teacher graded assessment and nationally imposed standard reference tests similar to those in the UK's national program. This view must be tempered of course by the fact that central national testing in the UK will probably only occur in English and Mathematics, and even then the system may collapse under its own weight (Springer, 1991). A change to conservative government in Australia could accelerate a shift to the second emphasis on external reference testing.

Two further considerations need to be included in any review of the development of national curriculum in Australia. First, the approach to curriculum development that is being witnessed at present is not new. It typifies curriculum that is caught, not taught. It is the preferred approach of bureaucratic systems (Bartlett, 1991) and inevitably and historically has resulted in higher teacher workloads and loss of morale. Because curriculum is produced and implemented at a central policy-making place, distant geographically and conceptually from its place of consumption and reproduction in the classroom, and because this is attempted without adequate resources, there are high educational and social costs to be paid by teachers, students and society generally. The morale of the majority of teachers in this situation declines in proportion to the magnitude of the task imposed on them. This situation is usually exaggerated by political pressures exerted by New Right populists from macro-contexts external to schooling; pressures which Habermas (1979) refers to as 'ideological discharge' that emerges in periods of economic stringency.

The second consideration relates to the emergence of this New Right populist

Leo Bartlett

group who have been influential in the directions of curriculum. It is significant that the private sector of schooling (elite and alternative) has not been included in the three phases of development of a national curriculum. With an increasing market share of the clients of secondary curriculum, it could be expected that they would be subjected also to the same rigour of implementation that the public sector schooling will have to endure. All this occurs at a time when market force spending is based on the community's apparently misconceived notion that best practice exists in private schools. This notion of best practice is aligned with the mythology that the private sector produces better academic results because it has better teachers, a form of thinking advocated by the New Right populist movement. However, the reality is that should bands be introduced in the Phase Three of national curriculum testing, there will be a levelling effect on the academic results of private schools. Where private sector schooling depends on the establishment of differences between themselves and public sector schooling, these differences may well disappear, resulting in comparative disadvantage for the former system. Alternately, nationally promulgated standards applied to the private sector may lead to the extension of inequitable selection and exclusion of students, a situation witnessed in many private elite schools; that is, there will be a greater press to exclude or dismiss students who attain lower standards of achievement. This kind of practice from the elite private schools has long raised equity and discrimination issues in Australian schooling. The additional irony is that promulgated standards may force private schools to change their practice. With respect to selection and exclusion practices, this could have a reverse effect and result in private schools having greater income through higher enrolment of increased numbers of failed students, who return to school to achieve the required standards in the upper bands.

These are a few of the more general and select criticisms of recent developments in constructing a national curriculum development in Australia. The question to be addressed next is: What aspects of Labor policy have led to these developments?

Metapolicy and National Curriculum Development

The developments in national curriculum described above represent Labor mediations of curriculum which is driven by a curriculum 'code' (Lundgren, 1983) that is described in this book as corporate federalism (Lingard, Knight and Bartlett, 1990; Lingard,1991; Bartlett, Lingard and Knight, 1991). The code has metapolicy status (Yeatman, 1990) and is an amalgam of neocorporatism, economic rationalism, modified human capital theory and corporate managerialism. Corporate federalism is analyzed in Chapter 1; however, a brief description is given here.

Neocorporatism occurs when the State, acting in the national interest, draws together all representative groups and establishes a working relationship among them. The interest here is that there is a focus on a national interest which is reflected in such entities as a national curriculum. With respect to schooling in Australia, it will be argued that neocorporatism has a more explicit status in the Commonwealth's intent to change curriculum at the national and corporate level.

An emphasis on economic rationalism assumes that there is an overarching stress on efficiency and economy, effectiveness and performance, and the outputs of the public sector — in this instance, schools and the product of their curriculum. Corporate managerialism focuses on the administrative arrangements of a system and its constituencies to achieve the goals of the state. Hence, by formulating the goals or inputs of an education system, and by targeting specific groups for more effective delivery of service (Considine, 1988), a greater efficiency and effectiveness is assumed. Finally, the discourse of human capital presumes that human knowledge and skill form a kind of capital which can be invested and for which returns for both the individual and the economy can be expected.

While corporate federalism with its attendant four policy attributes is central in the analysis of curriculum development in the past twenty years, it is proposed that the contemporary overarching policy attribute driving national curriculum development is neocorporatism; that while this does not result in a corporate curriculum, arguments for a curriculum based on a view of neocorporatism can be justified; that a neocorporatist agenda is supported by the apparent imperatives of economic rationalism and human capital; and that the apparent dysfunctional aspects of current national curriculum development are due to the management of curriculum implementation; that is, to implementation (Phases One to Three described above) guided by a dominant crew of corporate managerialism. It is the influence of corporate manageralism as an implementation strategy that raised significant issues in the development of a national curriculum.

A Neocorporate Curriculum?

Kennedy's (1990) claim that what is emerging is a corporate curriculum is probably inaccurate if one takes cognizance of the fragmentation of approach and dichotomization of learning and assessment in the current development of a national curriculum. However, this is not to say that the policy agenda underpinning Labor mediations is not neocorporatist; and that the management of national curriculum implementation is not corporatist. Both these issues are the focus of this section of the chapter.

To understand the neocorporatist basis for contemporary national curriculum, it is necessary to understand the origins of corporatism and the shifts in its meaning as it applied to Post World War II Labor policy. The significant emergence of corporatism dates to World War II and Commonwealth responsibility for the collection of all income tax in exchange for compensatory funding to states for their agreement not to collect taxes. The post-war Labor government also sought to extend its powers in banking, aviation and standardized railway gauges but with less success. The important issue however, is that Labor's agenda was driven by the possibility of purposeful social engineering in a private enterprise capitalist society.

Not least of the influential thinking behind Labor's policy was H.C. (Nuggett) Coombs who wrote (Coombs, 1981: 60) that he and his colleagues were 'stimulated to believe that human communities could by *corporate* action, shape the context in which the lives of their members were to be lived.'

The idea of corporatism in Curtin's World War II Labor Government was not that proposed by Schmitter (1974), an idealised vision of how state society relations can be ordered politically; however, it did conceive it as a specialized means of bargaining and in this sense was an idealized political form.

The question of the Commonwealth's accumulation of power at the expense of the state through financial leverages (Bolton, 1990) was raised again in the early 1970s at the time the first centralized national curriculum agency was established by the Commonwealth. The brand of corporatism of the Whitlam years, when the Commonwealth for the first time systematically intervened in the curricula of each state, emerged as a form of 'coercive federalism' (Mathews, 1977). Labor bypassed state funding channels and filtered extra funding directly to schools.

Labor's intervention in curriculum in Australian schools in the 1970s was motivated by the concern to create equality of opportunity for the education of all young people by topping up funds for the states. At the same time, Labor policy held firmly to the notion that teacher autonomy was not to be interfered with and would, in fact, lead to curriculum diversity, opportunity and better life chances for students. Explicit in the Whitlam approach was a respect for teacher professionalization along with community consultation. If there was a coherent policy in the Whitlam reforms of curriculum, it was motivated by human capital theory and the view that education was an essential investment in the youth of the nation.

In contrast with the Labor Government of the 1970s which espoused corporatism more as an idealized political form to achieve social ends, the Hawke Labor Government of the 1980s reinterpreted the concept as a policy process. This is not to say that prior to the 1980s corporatism viewed as a policy process did not exist, but after the 1980s corporatism together with other policy was elevated to meta-policy status and expressed as neocorporatism.

The Hawke Labor Governments' interventions in state's curricula in the 1980s was motivated by policy that framed education within an agenda of microeconomic reform that treated education as an industry like any other industry where the aim was to create greater efficiency and effectiveness. The proposed microrestructuring of curriculum in schools was one aspect of micro-reform that represented a deliberate attempt to change many aspects of Australian life and activities which contribute to a national economy.

Some contrasts may be drawn between Labor policy affecting curriculum of the 1970s and 1980s. In the 1970s the Whitlam government fairly reflected Labor policy. Reform of State curricula within a framework of increasing expenditure on schooling achieved an equality of educational opportunity. The increased funding for the Disadvantaged Schools Program in the mid-1970s was intended to lead to greater achievement of life chances for disadvantaged people through education. Corporatism was the means of achieving equality of outcomes on a national scale.

Across the 1980s the Hawke government increasingly viewed scholars and curricula as one means of creating a 'clever country — in the national interest'. Their neocorporatist policy was managed through the Australian Education Council, a corporate grouping of Federal States and Territories Education Ministers. Their aim is to create 'educational and economic advantages' (AEC, 1991) by sharing expertise and developing 'a more comprehensive product', by 'reducing unnecessary differences'; and by achieving 'considerable cost savings'. Hence, the emphasis is economic rationalist within a neocorporate strategy to create a national curriculum that is efficient and productive within a framework of decreasing expenditure.

The corporatist policy influencing curriculum nationally in the 1970s aimed at quality for better economic outcomes. The Labor government of this period channelled resources into curriculum for initiatives aimed particularly at disadvantaged schools. Hence, Commonwealth funds channelled directly to schools and not through the states sought to achieve a fairer distribution of resources according to needs and ultimately to attain better outcomes of schooling for all. In contrast, by 1990, the Hawke Labor Government appeared prepared to release all funding that might be distributed to disadvantaged schools to the states, but only in return for the rights of national testing (Dawkins, 1990). By means of national testing it is anticipated that the Federal government will give direction to the goals of schooling to create a more skilled workforce, while at the same time retaining at least a semblance of equity and social justice in developing a more efficient economy.

The narrowing effects of national testing upon school curriculum are well known (Fensham, 1980). While the specific nature of future developments in this area is not yet clear, what is evident is that national testing will be promoted through the development of competency-based schemes for students, teachers and the professions generally.

The political shift to a 'One Nation' policy (February, 1992) under the current Keating Labor government (1991–present) signifies greater federal intervention in education and the professions (Bartlett, 1992). The policy is designed to maximise the nation's strength on the basis that economic rationalism, in part, has failed. Keating's 'One Nation' strategy therefore requires greater collaborative effort by the nation to develop a more internationally competitive economy.

One means of achieving this is through the implementation of nationally imposed competency-based standards. Here, prescribed student competencies formulated from the Finn Report (1991) will be overlaid on national curriculum frameworks. At the same time, there will be a move to develop nationally agreed competency-based standards for teachers.

The approaches to a national curriculum in the 1980s and 1990s indicate well defined shifts in policy with the focus moving to curriculum outcomes and their assessment. This outputs/accountability focus will persist into the near future, regardless of the political persuasion of the government.

The Commissioners of Fact

The greatest potential for 'dehumanizing' and technologizing curriculum in Australian schools will be effected through the rationality or code of corporate managerialism. This approach is evident when the current national curriculum is analysed in a context of the four concepts that underly corporate managerialism: product format, instrumentalism, integration and purposive action (Considine, 1988).

1   *Product format* — The discourse of the text in the most recent statement from the AEC (AEC, 1991) locates curriculum as a product-like entity and locates or invests curriculum authority in different units (states) for defined outputs represented in subject statements and profiles. This product emphasis can be witnessed in the agreed national goals for schooling (Hall, 1989). However as Piper (1989) notes, we already have a nationally compatible curriculum. The current approach

to develop a national curriculum product represents a corporate managerialist approach to a *promulgated and assured curriculum*. The emphasis now is not on *quality* but *guaranteed quality*.

Corporate manageralism emphasises outputs from work units. In the collaborative national curriculum different states opt or are commissioned to take responsibility for Phases One and/or Two in a selected subject area. In Mathematics and English, for example, Phase Two, once complete, was succeeded by Phase Three, which was managed by a committee of the Australian Cooperative Assessment Programme (ACAP). The decision has been made to proceed with subject profiles in these two areas — to be completed by groups quite different from those who completed Phase Two. The Mathematics and English/literacy profiles are expected to be completed by the end of 1991. The Phase Three approach brings with it, as Piper (1991) observes, all the issues relating to national frameworks competing with state assessment frameworks. Hence, the work units (subjects) vary across outputs. Phases are separated and theory-practice relationships fragmented.

2   *Instrumentalism* — Instrumentalism in the national curriculum may be seen in the operational targets set for each work unit by the AEC, the autocratic nature of relationships across groups, and the controls on resourcing for curriculum within more narrowly circumscribed areas of expenditure.

Instrumentalism is most clearly evident in *SAS* where literacy and numeracy are seen as the essential outcomes of schooling. Curriculum is a means to an end, a context for ensuring an expanded skills base for Australian industry. The nature of relationships across groups involved in national curriculum development may be seen in the approach to consultation which is more autocratic than democratic. The agreed consensus (agreed by new curriculum practitioners) used to define guidelines reflects the corporate technique used in the Economic Planning and Advisory Committee (EPAC) which is dominated by employers and unions, and not curriculum practitioners or their educators, the higher education institutions. The nature of consultation is far removed from the democratic form proposed by the Australian Curriculum Studies Association (1990).

3   *Integration* — Integration within a corporate manageralist approach to curriculum implementation is best seen in the drive to uniformity and consistence across subjects, states and the *modus operandi* of procedures for curriculum development. The division of labour across units is orchestrated by corporate managers, the AEC, the Conference of Directors General (ACDG) and to a lesser extent the CCA.

The commitment to integration is probably best seen in the implementation of what is by now widely recognized (in the literature) as the failed research, development and dissemination approach to national curriculum development. Hence, there is a nationally, logically and abstractly conceived set of relationships among the AEC, ACDG, CCA (the experts in different states) and the practitioners in classrooms. In implementing profiles and assessment guidelines, it seems that those who enact the curriculum in classrooms are being subjected to coercive as well as corporate compliance by those at the apex of the hierarchy — the commissioners of fact.

4 *Purposive action* elevates economic rationality to a primary status and is a response to the policy expectation that public expenditure will be reduced. Purposive action seeks to steer rather than adjudicate (Considine, 1988: 10).

The emphasis on economic rationalism is evident in all documents from *SAS* to the Hobart Declaration (the agreed national goals), and more recently by the statements by the AEC. The economic emphasis and focus is evident in the order of tasks subjects mapped in the AEC's work program.

But perhaps purposive action is most evident in the private sector style relationships exemplified in the operations of the CCA. This organization is not powerless as some would claim (Boomer, 1990). It is only powerless in as much as the states within the AEC might wish to divert control from the Federal government, and there are clear examples of this. The CCA in effect has all the attributes of an organization established to create a commercial curriculum and privatized curriculum knowledge. Furthermore, the Board structure of the CCA and other groups in the national curriculum is based on a view of private sector relationships. The CCA is under direct control of the AEC and an instrument of neocorporatism and manageralism. It is not, as MacPherson (1991) claims, an expression of elitism or pluralism in a pluralist state.

The AEC's imprimatur of corporate managerialism as the primary means of developing a national curriculum represents a grasp at certainty in difficult economic times. Perhaps the best statement about managerialism in relation to processes has been made by Kemmis (1990: 22) when he says:

Regrettably the rhetoric of corporate management now widely adopted in public administration in Australia (including the administration of education) has come to be seen only as 'corporate' for managers — for others in departmental bureaucracies (and for people in schools), it is not seen as expressing authentic local commitment to corporate identity ... corporate management is seen by these groups as the muscular imposition of systemic objectives in local groups and agencies.

Conclusion

The Federal Labor government of the mid-1980s appears to have had few difficulties in solving the representation problem. The curriculum code or way of thinking was already at their disposal in the form of corporate federalism, the overarching agenda for reform and restructuring. How the curriculum would be represented was equally accessible through the application of neocorporate policy. In Phase One and Two (mapping and construction of national statements for individual subjects) such a policy allowed Labor's commissioners of fact to decontextualize the already decontextualized curriculum documents from each of the states.

The whole of this exercise was managed by the same neocorporate view. A similar approach is being adopted in Phase Three in the construction of national testing benchmarks and achievement levels. But at this point, the process of recontextualization must begin, that is, at the point when learning, reflected in the national statement guidelines, is linked with assessment. As might be expected in any corporate implementation, it is the decontextualized wish statements, instrumentalized and potentially dehumanized, that must be recontextualized by curriculum practitioners and teachers in contexts of curriculum enactment.

There are good economic reasons why anyone might want to invent a national curriculum for a more efficient organized schooling system in Australia. It may be argued that neocorporatism provides a sound basis for such an enterprise, though all relevant groups need to be represented, if neocorporatism is to operate in a democratic fashion. Here lies the real problem: national curriculum implementation is seen to be only a management exercise, one whose implementation is informed by corporate managerialist strategies.

References

AUSTRALIAN ASSOCIATION OF MATHEMATICS TEACHERS (1990) *National Statement on Girls and Mathematics*. Adelaide, Australia: Government Printer.

AUSTRALIAN CURRICULUM STUDIES ASSOCIATION (1990) 'ACSA principles for Australian curriculum reform', *Curriculum Perspectives Newsletter*, March 30–31.

AUSTRALIAN EDUCATION COUNCIL (1986) *Minutes of the 53rd AEC Meeting*, June.

AUSTRALIAN EDUCATION COUNCIL (1989a) Statement from the 60th AEC Meeting: *National Co-operation in Curriculum Development*, April.

AUSTRALIAN EDUCATION COUNCIL (1989b) Statement from the 60th AEC Meeting: *Common and Agreed National Goals for Schooling in Australia* (Hobart Declaration), April.

AUSTRALIAN EDUCATION COUNCIL (1991) Statement from the 64th AEC Meeting: *National Curriculum Colloboration*, April.

BARTLETT, V.L. (1991) 'Rationality and the management of curriculum change', *Educational Management and Administration*, **19**, 1, pp. 20–9.

BARTLETT, V.L. (1992) 'One Nation': The regulation of teacher quality and the deregulation of the teaching profession, inaugural lecture, University of Central Queensland, Rockhampton, Australia, April.

BARTLETT, V.L., KNIGHT, J. and LINGARD, R. (1991) 'Corporate federalism and the restructuring of teacher education in Australia', *Journal of Education Policy*, **6**, 1, pp. 91–5.

BARTLETT, V.L., LINGARD, R. and KNIGHT, J. (1992) 'Restructuring teacher education in Australia', *British Journal of Sociology of Education*, **13**, 1, pp. 19–36.

BOLTON, G. (1990) *The Middle Way: 1942–1988*, Oxford History of Australia, **5**, Melbourne, Australia: Oxford University Press.

BOOMER, G. (1990) *National Curriculum Seminar*, Coffs Harbour, Australia: National Board of Employment, Education and Training (NBEET), October.

BOOMER, G. (1991) Report, *The Australian*, June 8–9, p. 7.

COOMBS, H. (1981) *Trial Balance: Issues of My Working Life*, South Melbourne, Australia: Sun Paperbacks.

CONNORS, L. (1989) 'Commonwealth and agreed national goals: Implications for schooling in Australia', *Access*, **3**, 4, pp. 12–13.

CONSIDINE, M. (1988) 'The corporate management framework as administrative science: A critique', *Australian Journal of Public Administration*, **47**, 1, pp. 4–19.

CURRICULUM DEVELOPMENT CENTRE (1980) *Core Curriculum for Australian Schools*, Canberra, Australia: CDC.

DAWKINS, J. (1988) *Strengthening Australia's Schools*, Canberra, Australia: Australian Government Publishing Service (AGPS).

DAWKINS, J. (1990) *Ministerial Address*, NBEET Conference, Coffs Harbour, Australia: October.

DAWKINS, J. and HOLDING, A. (1987) *Skills for Australia*, Camberra: Australia: AGPS.

DEPARTMENT OF EMPLOYMENT, EDUCATION AND TRAINING. (1989) *Commonwealth Programs for Schools, 1989*, Canberra, Australia: AGPS.

DICKENS, C. (1961) *Hard Times*, New York, NY: Signet Classics.

ECONOMIC PLANNING and ADVISORY COUNCIL (1986) *Human Capital and Productivity*, Canberra, Australia: Office of EPAC.

FENSHAM, P. (1980) 'Setting priorities in educational research: National testing is counterproductive to the educational task', *Vestes*, **23**, 2, pp. 43–6.

FINN, B. (1991) *Young People's Participation in Post-Compulsory Education and Training*, Report of the AEC Review Committee, Canberra, Australia: AGPS.

FRANCIS, D. (1991) 'Making sense of a national curriculum', *Unicorn*, **17**, 1, pp. 30–33.

GOODSON, I. (1987) *School Subjects and Curriculum Change*, London, UK: Falmer Press.

HABERMAS, J. (1979) 'Conservation and capitalist crisis', *New Left Review*, **115**, pp. 73–86.

HALL, G. (1989) 'The national goals for schooling in Australia', *Curriculum Perspectives Newsletter*, September, pp. 8–9.

KARMEL, P. (1985) *Quality of Education in Australia: Report of the Quality of Education Review Committee*, Canberra, Australia: AGPS.

KEMMIS, S. (1989) *Curriculum Theory and the State in Australia*, paper presented at the American Educational Research Association Conference, San Francisco, CA, April.

KEMMIS, S. (1990) *The Curriculum Corporation: Observations and Implications*, Occasional Paper No. 1, Melbourne, Australia: Australian Curriculum Studies Association.

KEMMIS, S. and STAKE, R. (1988) *Evaluating Curriculum*, Geelong, Australia, Deakin University Press.

KENNEDY, K. (1989a) 'National initiatives in curriculum: The Australian context', *British Journal of Educational Studies*, **37**, 2, pp. 111–24.

KENNEDY, K. (1989b) 'Reconceptualising efforts at national curriculum development', *Journal of Education Policy*, **4**, 1, pp. 53–61.

KENNEDY, K. (1990) 'The politics of Australian education: A corporate curriculum?', paper presented to the Australian Association for Research in Education conference, University of Sydney, Sydney, Australia, November.

LINGARD, R. (1990) '*Corporate federalism: The emerging context of schooling policy-making in Australia*', paper presented to the Australian Sociological Association Conference, University of Queensland, Australia; 12–16 December.

LINGARD, R. (1991) 'Policy-making for Australian schooling: The new corporate federalism', *Journal of Educational Policy*, **6**, 1, pp. 85–90.

LINGARD, R., KNIGHT, J. and BARTLETT, V.L. (1990) 'Teacher education: Developments and context', *The Australian Teacher*, **26**, pp. 20–3.

LUNDGREN, U.P. (1983) *Between Hope and Happening: Text and Context in Curriculum*, Deakin University, Victoria.

MASTERS, G. (1990) *Profiles of Learning: The Basic Skills Testing Program in New South Wales, 1989*. Hawthorn, Australia: ACER.

MATHEWS, J. (1977) Foreward in Wiltshire, K. (Ed.) *Administrative Federalism: Documents in Australian Inter-governmental Relations*, St. Lucia, Australia: University of Queensland Press, pp. ix–x.

MACPHERSON, R.J.S. (1991) 'The politics of Australian curriculum: The third coming of a national curriculum agency in a neo-pluralist state', *Journal of Education Policy*, **5**, 5, pp. 203–18.

Leo Bartlett

ORGANIZATION FOR ECONOMIC COOPERATION AND DEVELOPMENT (1986) *Youth and Work in Australia Policy Agenda*, (Paris, France: OECD)

PIPER, K. (1989) 'National curriculum: prospects and possibilities', *Curriculum Perspectives Newsletter*, September, **9**, 3, pp. 3–7.

PIPER, K. (1991) 'National curriculum two years on: An undelivered paper', *Curriculum Perspectives* (Newsletter Edition), September, 2–6.

ACSA PRINCIPLES FOR AUSTRALIAN CURRICULUM REFORM (1990) *Curriculum Perspectives Newsletter*, March 30–31.

REEVES, H. (1991) Report, *The Australian*, June 8–9, p. 7.

SCHMITTER, P.C. (1974) 'Still the century of corporatism', *Review of Politics*, **36**, pp. 85–131.

SHAPIRO, C. (1961) 'Afterword', in DICKENS, C., *Hard Times*, New York, NY: Signet Classics, pp. 293–7.

SPRINGER, W. (1991) 'National curriculum: The UK experience', *Curriculum Perspectives*, (Newsletter Edition), September, pp. 6–13.

YEATMAN, A. (1990) *Bureaucrats, Technocrats, Femocrats: Essays on the Contemporary Australian State*, Sydney, Australia: Allen and Unwin.

Notes on Contributors

MICHAEL W. APPLE
Michael W. Apple is Professor of Curriculum and Instruction and Educational Policy Studies at the University of Wisconsin. He has written extensively on ideology, curriculum, technology, reproduction theory and the discourses of equality in education. His most recent book is *The Politics of the Textbook* (Boston, Routledge, 1991).

LEO BARTLETT
Leo Bartlett is Professor and Dean of Education at the University of Central Queensland. He is a Past President of the Australian Association for Research in Education. His research interests include qualitative methods in educational research, curriculum policy, competencies and changing federal/state relations in education policy.

JILL BLACKMORE
Jill Blackmore is a Senior Lecturer in Social and Administrative Studies in Education at Deakin University. Her current research interests include gender relations and reforms in education, teacher unions, school-based decision-making and administration, school-to-work transition and organisational evaluation.

CHERYL CARPENTER
Cheryl Carpenter is a Tutor and full-time PhD student in Education at James Cook University of North Queensland. Her research interests are Special Education and Aboriginal and Islander Education. Her theoretical interests include structuralist and post-structuralist theory, and Bernstein's theory of pedagogic discourse.

ROGER DALE
Roger Dale has been Professor of Education at the University of Auckland since 1989. Before that he was Senior Lecturer in Sociology of Education at The Open University in England. He is the author of *The State and Education Policy* (Milton Keynes, Open University Press, 1989) and *The TVEI Story: Policy, Practice and Preparation for Work* (Milton Keynes, Open University Press, 1990). In addition he has edited and co-edited several readers in the sociology of education, including *School and Society* (London, Routledge & Kegan Paul, 1971), *Schooling and Capitalism*

(London, Routledge & Kegan Paul, 1976) and *Education and the State* (London, Falmer Press, 1981). His main current interests are in education policy and school effectiveness.

LINDSAY FITZCLARENCE

Lindsay Fitzclarence is a Senior Lecturer in the Faculty of Education at Deakin University. He has a specialist interest in the connections between curriculum and culture and is currently involved in major research projects which explore the relationship between post-modernity and students' subjectivity.

MICHAEL GARBUTCHEON SINGH

Michael Garbutcheon Singh teaches cross-cultural and social education at James Cook University of North Queensland. His work on educational policy, multiculturalism and literacy has appeared in the *Journal of Education, Discourse, Australian Journal of Reading*, and other journals. He is author of *Performance Indicators in Education* (Seelong, Deakin University Press, 1990).

MIRIAM HENRY

Miriam Henry is a Senior Lecturer in the Faculty of Education at Queensland University of Technology. She is co-author of *Understanding Schooling* (London, Routledge, 1988) and co-editor of *Battlers and Bluestockings: Women's Place in Australian Education* (Canberra, ACE, 1989). Her research interests are in education policy, particularly in relation to gender issues and the restructuring of higher education.

KEN JOHNSTON

Ken Johnston is a Senior Lecturer in Sociology in the School of Behavioural Sciences at Macquarie University. He has been interested in social justice issues in education for some time and his recent research has focused upon poverty, education and the Disadvantaged Schools Program. Ken has also published research on ideological conflicts within and around schooling.

JANE KENWAY

Jane Kenway works as a Senior Lecturer in Social and Administrative Studies in the Faculty of Education at Deakin University. Her research and publications concentrate on the connections between education and social inequality. Her current research project focuses on gender reform in schools. It draws on poststructuralist theory to explore the feminist struggle for educational change.

JOHN KNIGHT

John Knight teaches the sociology of education at the University of Queensland. His research interests include teacher education policy, higher education policy, fundamentalism and the restructuring of schooling. He is co-author of *Understanding Schooling* (London, Routledge, 1988).

BOB LINGARD

Bob Lingard is a Sociologist of Education interested in changing federal/state relations and schooling, gender and multi-cultural policy reforms, teacher education and higher education policy. He is co-author of *Understanding Schooling*

(London, Routledge, 1988) and co-editor of *Institute of Modern Art: A Documentary History, 1975–1989* (Brisbane, IMA, 1990).

ALLAN LUKE

Allan Luke teaches language education, discourse analysis and sociology at James Cook University of North Queensland. His most recent book is *Towards a Critical Sociology of Reading Pedagogy* (with Carolyn D. Baker).

MARTIN NAKATA

Martin Nakata is a Research Associate in the Department of Social and Cultural Studies, James Cook University of North Queensland, also employed by the commonwealth Department of Employment, Education and Training. He is currently completing a discourse analysis of policy and research documents on Torres Strait Islanders.

JENNY OZGA

Jenny Ozga is Dean and Professor of Education at Bristol Polytechnic Bristol, England. She was previously Lecturer in Education at The Open University where she chaired the course teams that created the course 'Education Policy Making'. She has published widely in the area of teachers' work, including *Teachers, Professionalism and Class* (London, Falmer Press, 1981) (with Martin Lawn) and has co-edited (with Ian McNay) *Policy-Making in Education: The Breakdown of Consensus* (Oxford, Pergammon Press, 1985).

PAIGE PORTER

Professor Paige Porter works in the sociology and politics of education and has been Dean of the Faculty of Education at The University of Queensland since 1988. Her research and publications focus on innovation in education, federal/state relations in education, gender relations and feminist theory, and higher education policy.

PETER RAMSAY

Professor Peter Ramsay is a teacher and researcher at the University of Waikato, Hamilton, New Zealand. He is currently Associate Dean of the School of Education. He has published over ninety journal articles, books and research monographs. His *Family, School and Community* (Sydney, Allen & Unwin, 1984) has been the standard sociology of education text in New Zealand for a number of years. His research interests include schools with special needs, urban schools, race, class and gender in education, as well as both Teacher and Nurse Education. He was a member of the New Zealand government's review of Educational Administration, the precursor of current reforms.

FAZAL RIZVI

Fazal Rizvi is a philosopher of education interested in issues of structural responses to cultural diversity. His other research interests include theories of racism, democratic theory and problems of democratic reforms in educational governance. He is currently an Associate Professor at the University of Queensland.

RICHARD SMITH

Richard Smith is Professor and Head of the Department of Social and Cultural Studies at James Cook University of North Queensland. His work on sociology of education and policy has appeared in the *British Journal of Sociology of Education, Discourse, Sociology of Education*, and other journals.

SANDRA TAYLOR

Sandra Taylor is a Senior Lecturer in the School of Cultural and Policy Studies at Queensland University of Technology (Kelvin Grove Campus). She has a special interest in gender and schooling, and in policy issues relating to the education of girls. She is co-author of *Understanding Schooling* (London, Routledge, 1988) and co-editor of *Battlers and Bluestockings: Women's Place in Australian Education* (Canberra, ACE, 1989). Her most recent publication (with Pam Gilbert) is *Fashioning the Feminine* (Sydney, Allen & Unwin, 1991).

PETER WATKINS

Peter Watkins is a Senior Lecturer in Social and Administrative Studies in Education at Deakin University. He has published widely in areas of work, technology and education, devolution and educational administration, and the restructuring of the discourse of work.

Index